Old Testament Prophecy

Old Testament Prophecy
From Oracles to Canon

RONALD E. CLEMENTS

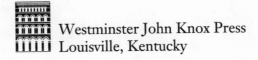

Westminster John Knox Press
Louisville, Kentucky

© 1996 Westminster John Knox Press

Scripture quotations from the New Revised Standard Version of the Bible are copyright © 1989 by the Division of Christian Education of the National Council of the Churches of Christ in the U.S.A. and are used by permission.

The following chapters by R. E. Clements are reprinted by permission of Sheffield Academic Press, Limited: "The Messianic Hope in the Old Testament," copyright © 1989, and "Beyond Tradition History: Deutero-Isaianic Development of First Isaiah's Themes," copyright © 1985, from *Journal for the Study of the Old Testament*, Issues 43 and 31; "Jeremiah 1–25 and the Deuteronomistic History," copyright © 1993, and "The Prophet and His Editors," copyright © 1990, from *Journal for the Study of the Old Testament Supplements*, Numbers 152 and 87.

Book design by Jennifer K. Cox
Cover design by Kevin Darst

First edition

Published by Westminster John Knox Press
Louisville, Kentucky

This book is printed on acid-free paper that meets the American National Standards Institute Z39.48 standard. ∞

PRINTED IN THE UNITED STATES OF AMERICA

96 97 98 99 00 01 02 03 04 05 — 10 9 8 7 6 5 4 3 2 1

Library of Congress Cataloging-in-Publication Data

Clements, R. E. (Ronald Ernest), 1929–
    Old Testament prophecy : from oracle to canon / Ronald E.
Clements. — 1st ed.
        p.   cm.
    Includes bibliographical references (p.   ) and indexes.
    ISBN 0-664-22082-7 (alk. paper)
    1. Bible. O.T. Prophets—Criticism, interpretation, etc.
2. Bible—Prophecies.   3. Bible—Canon.   4. Apocalyptic literature—
History and criticism.   I. Title.
BS1505.2.C56   1996
224'.06—dc20   95-46240

To Brevard Childs

Contents

Preface ix

Introduction: The Interpretation of Old Testament Prophecy,
    1965–1995 1

PART 1: PROPHET, KING, AND MESSIAH 21

  1   Amos and the Politics of Israel 23
  2   The Prophecies of Isaiah to Hezekiah
      concerning Sennacherib 35
  3   The Messianic Hope in the Old Testament 49

PART 2: ISAIAH 63

  4   The Immanuel Prophecy of Isaiah 7:10–17
      and Its Messianic Interpretation 65
  5   Beyond Tradition-History: Deutero-Isaianic
      Development of First Isaiah's Themes 78
  6   The Unity of the Book of Isaiah 93

PART 3: JEREMIAH 105

  7   Jeremiah 1—25 and the
      Deuteronomistic History 107
  8   Jeremiah: Prophet of Hope 123

PART 4: EZEKIEL 143

  9   The Ezekiel Tradition:
      Prophecy in a Time of Crisis 145
  10 The Chronology of Redaction
      in Ezekiel 1—24 159

PART 5: THE RISE OF APOCALYPTIC   171

  11   Apocalyptic, Literacy, and
        the Canonical Tradition   173
  12   The Interpretation of Prophecy and
        the Origin of Apocalyptic   182

PART 6: THE CANON OF THE PROPHETS   189

  13   Patterns in the Prophetic Canon   191
  14   Prophecy as Literature: A Reappraisal   203
  15   The Prophet and His Editors   217

Abbreviations   230

Notes   233

Selected Works by Ronald E. Clements   265

Acknowledgments   271

Index of Names   273

Scripture Index   275

Preface

It is a matter of particular pleasure for me to see a number of my essays on the subject of Old Testament prophecy republished at the present time in a collected form. Many of them appeared in volumes that were published in honor of particular scholars, and others appeared in journals with a specialized circulation, which meant that they are not readily available in libraries. I am therefore especially indebted to Dr. Jon Berquist and his colleagues of Westminster John Knox Press for their willingness to assist in making them more widely accessible. Apart from the introductory essay, all of them have appeared in print previously and, apart from minor corrections, the text remains unchanged. The decision to follow such a format, even in the case of essays written as much as two decades ago, has been dictated by the value of reading them in their context of research, notwithstanding the fact that many of them touch on subjects that have received much further attention since.

The study of the prophetic literature of ancient Israel is an ongoing quest, and there is no reason to suppose that it has currently reached a plateau from which long-researched issues can be regarded as closed. It has been an immense privilege to have shared in such a quest, and much of the pleasure in doing so lies not simply in the discoveries made, but in the friendships built up and enjoyed in such a pursuit. The sharing of a desire to know and the excitement of seeing familiar questions in a new light are rich rewards for the scholarly inquirer.

No one can engage in a prolonged period of study of any part of the biblical literature without becoming deeply conscious of the familiar adage "What do you have that you did not receive?" So much has been written on these great books, and so many fresh avenues explored over the centuries, that a sense of great indebtedness to a galaxy of past scholars and a veritable host of contemporary ones becomes strongly present. To so many such figures, both past and present, I can only express my gratitude, without singling out particular names. Nor can the recollection of many students be left aside, since so often it has been their questionings that have demanded a rethinking of familiar proposals and assumed conclusions.

My own interests began with a strongly theological sense of conviction, which may appear to stand rather at odds with a close study of the prophetic literature of the Bible. In this a number of fundamental issues of a historical and literary nature obtrude so strongly as to push the wider theological horizon into a hazy distance. Yet that horizon remains present, and has done so even when the historical and literary problems appear at times almost insurmountable. In many ways the simple belief that it is God who is causing certain events to take place has provided humankind with the simplest and most basic of reasons for a religious interpretation of the world. It is when such beliefs are pressed to question how and why such events have happened, and what their outcome will be, that the foundations of a prophetic theology are laid. We change the words and formulations, but essentially the same questions remain with us, even when we feel that they have no final answer.

To anyone who has spent much time with the prophetic writings of the Bible, it becomes apparent that their essential meaning and message is often of a highly complex character. Their language also is poetic and represents a highly distinctive rhetorical and literary application of human intellectual skills. A wealth of tersely formulated images of hope, and at times some deeply disturbing relapses into despair, are all to be found there.

I hope that the reader of this collection of essays will find in it sufficient stimulus and encouragement to turn again to consider the prophetic corpus of the biblical canon. To question old methods and to try to devise new ones is an ever-recurrent scholarly necessity. It is a special pleasure for me to dedicate this volume to a scholar whose friendship and encouragement have meant a great deal over a long period of years.

R. E. CLEMENTS
CAMBRIDGE

Introduction: The Interpretation of Old Testament Prophecy, 1965–1995

The subject of Old Testament prophecy has witnessed far-reaching changes and developments in methods and strategies of biblical scholarship since the beginning of the nineteenth century. The reader concerned with the general state of attention to earlier critical studies is well served by the survey and selection of key extracts edited by P.H.A. Neumann in 1979.[1] Although several useful surveys and critical reviews are available, there is no comparably detailed study of British works in the interpretation of prophecy during the period. This is regrettable since a number of distinctive features characterize such a particular development. However, by the late nineteenth century, in Britain too, the continental methods of criticism linked with the names of Heinrich Ewald and Bernard Duhm increasingly set the agenda.[2] In the thirty years since my first short book, *Prophecy and Covenant*, was published,[3] further distinctive changes have occurred in critical method and the broader principles of interpretation of prophecy.

The Rise of Form Criticism

What was new about the study of the Old Testament prophetic writings in the 1960s was the extensive and rigorous application of form criticism to the material. So far as the analysis of the methods and problems was concerned, the pioneering work in the field had been undertaken almost half a century earlier by Hermann Gunkel. Nevertheless, wider attention to the issues raised owes much to the work of Claus Westermann, whose study *Basic Forms of Prophetic Speech*[4] both introduced Gunkel's observations to a wider readership and pinpointed some of the major questions. Central to Westermann's analysis is that, once the narratives and superscriptions are set aside, the prophetic writings retain much of the prophet's original spoken forms of address, which consist essentially of two elements. These are pronouncements concerning God's intended future action, frequently couched in a first-person style in which the prophet becomes God's mouthpiece, and reasons that declare why this action will occur. In turn such spoken addresses can be divided between those that are threatening in what they

1

declare, and where the reason takes the form of invective, and those that are hopeful and reassuring. Here the reasons frequently make appeal to the nature of God and the divine promises that had earlier been made to Israel. Although fewer in number than the threatening addresses, these assurances contain some of the most distinctive theological elements of the prophetic literature.

Attention in the 1960s was being turned toward particular features of prophecy for another reason. This concerned the relationship between prophecy and psalmody. For me it provided a significant connection, since I had written a dissertation on the subject of the interpretation of the Jerusalem temple and its worship.[5] The debate over this relationship had its origins in a series of studies and hypotheses concerning the psalms that marked a difference of opinion between Hermann Gunkel and Sigmund Mowinckel. Both scholars had noted the close similarities between prophecy and some psalm passages that employed the distinctive divine first-person prophetic form of speech.[6] Gunkel had argued that this was a case where the psalmists were imitating the prophets, whereas Mowinckel had interpreted the development as taking place in the opposite direction. Psalmody was basic to the style and language of the cultus, and prophets must themselves at one time have been at home in the cult. It was natural therefore for psalm-writers, who may themselves have been cult-prophets, to employ distinctive prophetic forms in their compositions. In some cases the psalms reflected the responses enshrined in elaborate liturgical dialogue.

The issue remains an important one and has served to draw attention to the fact that psalm-forms also appear in prophecy, most especially in the prophecies of Isaiah 40—55. This had been explored before the Second World War in the work of Gunkel's pupil Joachim Begrich[7] and subsequently, with very good effect, in James Muilenburg's commentary on Isaiah 40—66.[8] Rather against Gunkel's earlier conclusion, that the psalmists were simply imitating the prophetic style, the weight of evidence pointed to the conclusion that the relationship between prophecy and psalmody had at one time been very close. Accordingly, where liturgical forms and modes of address appear in prophecy, this points back to a situation in which a central cultic origin and association of the prophets themselves has shaped the tradition.

During the 1960s a wide range of studies began to explore quite extensively the implications of these connections. Even the prophet Amos, whose whole ethos appears so sharply critical of the cultus and whose role scarcely fits within a tightly structured cultic setting, exhibits a number of significant connections with cultic forms of speech and psalmody. In any event, even if this appeared doubtful on other grounds, there was ample cause for close investigation into the structured speech forms used by the prophet and the many hymnic echoes and allusions that can readily be noted in the prophetic book that bears his name. Questions concerning the background and setting of each of the prophets began to appear as a major issue for understanding who the prophet really was and how he had learned his undoubtedly mature and highly skillful modes of address. Instead of being a strange intruder, with little by way of a recognizable background or clearly identifiable persona, the prophet now took on a new guise. He was himself the product of a long tradition, not simply of prophets like himself, but of a whole history of piety, worship, and political expectation with which he necessarily engaged in a kind of dialogue.

The most far-reaching and innovative expression of this significantly changed perception of the Old Testament prophets is to be found in the second volume of *Old Testament Theology*, by Gerhard von Rad.[9] By the time von Rad's work was published the methodologies of *Gattungsgeschichte* and *Formgeschichte* had broadened into a rather wider methodology of what can best be described as *Traditionsgeschichte*, or perhaps more properly *Motivgeschichte*. It was proving impossible to separate the speech-forms as embodied in the text from the *Sitz im Leben*—the life-situation—in which the form had originally been located. Moreover, this life-situation not only gave structure and lent a distinctive style to specific modes of address, as for instance the language used in the conduct of lawsuits, but inevitably reflected the themes, vocabulary, and cultural context of particular institutions such as the Jerusalem temple. So the distinctive idioms, divine titles, and historical traditions of the varied sanctuaries of Israel and Judah were inevitably reflected in the speeches of prophets who had been brought up within reach of them.

The differing voices of the prophets could then be regarded not only as a reflection of the fact that each was an individual human being, with personal insights, feelings, and a distinctive creativity, but also as a reflection of the varied locations from which the prophets emerged and the local political and religious training that each of them had received. A new measure of breadth and variety could then be discerned within their sayings. They were not merely individual critics and leaders, addressing themselves to a more or less uniform national community that we can loosely describe as "Israel." Rather they were themselves voices expressive of far older traditions, and their speeches and messages were closely related to the unique historical situations that they faced. Their prophecies inevitably displayed a regional coloring that their upbringing had given to them. Just as each must have spoken with a local accent and dialect, so in a sense the quest to understand the tradition that lay behind the prophet was a search to understand the distinctive religious and political accent the prophet employed.

Among the most significant conclusions drawn by von Rad from this

3

particular extension of what had begun as a branch of form criticism was a marked regionalizing of each prophet. Especially this marked a difference between those prophets who had been active in the Southern Kingdom, Judah, such as Isaiah and Micah, and those who had addressed themselves to audiences in the Northern Kingdom, such as Hosea and Jeremiah. No doubt the "regional effect" is rather heavily stressed in von Rad's work, and other factors also need to be taken into account. Among these is the question of whether the main collection of one prophet's sayings was preserved and had become accessible to another later prophet. So, for example, Amos's prophecies may have influenced those of the later Isaiah and, similarly, a written collection of the prophecies of Hosea may have been read and greatly pondered over by Jeremiah.

All of this amounts to a recognition that the individuality and creativity of each of the great prophets needs to be set in context. They were heirs and critics of a great tradition so that their confrontation with, and critique of, this older tradition contains many of the unspoken impulses toward what was striking and innovative about their work. This recognition may at first appear rather self-evident and unspectacular, since it had not so much been denied by earlier scholars as ignored by them. Nevertheless for scholarship it marked a significant new emphasis and was able to highlight the fact that the prophets needed to be interpreted against a wider background. To some extent the very conventions of research, which encouraged the treatment of the prophets as a separate section, or branch, of the ancient religion of Israel, had fostered an approach that contrasted them too dramatically with their religious forbears. The result had been a rather circular type of portrayal in which the prophetic background was largely drawn from what the prophets themselves said about their opponents.

It was with a view to redressing the balance in such a perspective that my book *Prophecy and Covenant* and also its sequel, *Prophecy and Tradition*,[10] were written. In the former I endeavored to bring into the study of the prophets an awareness of the very extensive and long-running debate that was current concerning the forms, origins, and theological implications of the concept of covenant in Old Testament studies.[11] For almost two decades the efforts to gain a fuller grasp of the forms and ideas of covenant in ancient Israel in the light of ancient Near Eastern treaty forms constituted a central field of enquiry. In the end the very momentum of the debate developed a kind of manic destructiveness of its own. It succumbed to the temptation to draw too many disparate areas and texts into its orbit and finished up explaining too much to be properly convincing. Echoes and supposed allusions to covenant-forms were found in every corner of the Old Testament, with the result that far too little attention was given to the actual vocabulary of covenants and covenant making and the clearly formulated descriptions of covenant-making ceremonies.[12]

At the time when this development of a traditio-historical approach to the prophets was attracting intense scholarly attention, a different approach that was ultimately as significant was emerging. From the very beginning of modern study of these figures it was evident that their messages had a strongly political content. They belonged to a particular time and addressed their words to specific situations that they expected to confirm, or refute, what they had to say. In the course of this engagement with a specific set of political judgments and policies they clearly intended to influence the policies adopted and thereby the outcome of events. To interpret them therefore required a much larger awareness of the political scene in the ancient Near East than was readily available. A volume that greatly influenced my own thinking in this direction was Norman Gottwald's *All the Kingdoms of the Earth*.[13] Undoubtedly the issues raised by this deepened awareness of an old perspective were in many cases different from those highlighted by the insights of tradition-history. It was something of a challenge therefore to endeavor to draw the different approaches closer together.

Seen in a larger retrospect it seems inevitable that both these interests, which appeared fresh and full of promise in the 1960s, should point toward further areas of investigation that have ultimately become a more dominant and persistent quest in biblical research.

The concern with the political relevance of the prophetic literature points inescapably to an awareness that, in the process of preserving and shaping the individual sayings into scrolls or books, a necessary "de-politicizing," or "de-historicizing" has taken place. Words and pronouncements addressed to one specific set of circumstances are not timeless or necessarily universally applicable. Threats may be in order at one time, only to require replacement by renewed hope and assurance once the time of danger has passed. Furthermore the reasons for an earlier threat may appear relevant, and even more intensely applicable, to a later situation. So a process of editing and elaboration has taken place to make a collection of individual sayings into a coherent whole. This process of redaction-history had mostly been viewed negatively in the first century of critical research, largely because it seemed to be a process that was without clear reason or meaningful intent. The aim of the great prophetic scholars of the late nineteenth century had chiefly been one of stripping away the secondary material, which was judged not to have been authentic to the prophet. Yet the work of shaping and elaborating the prophecies to form them into a book was a very prominent feature of the extant prophetic literature.[14] Editorial introductions and interpretative comments form a vital guide to both the process of preservation and the ways in which continued meaning was found within the prophecies. Only by understanding this process can the formation of the scroll in its surviving form be understood.

Many of the same issues arise as a consequence of the scholarly investigation into the particular "tradition" from which each prophet emerged. It has proved in reality very difficult to distinguish between whether the prophet was simply echoing the words of a cultic hymn or ritual catchphase, or whether this echo was introduced by a scribe who was bent on drawing out the significance, or marking the association, of what the prophet said so as to interpret it to a wider audience. The different approaches of scholarly research, which can all too often be regarded as independent of one another, quickly begin to overlap and interlock.

The Problem of the Book of Isaiah

It is no doubt a reflection of my own personal confessional background that the book of the prophet Isaiah should have presented itself a subject of particular interest. That the present book should be divided into three separated parts, only the first of which can properly be ascribed to the eighth-century prophet Isaiah had, by the beginning of this century, become a point of fundamental critical importance for scholarship. The division into at least two parts had been advocated by the great Jewish medieval scholar Ibn Ezra and had been important to the rise of modern study of the prophets since the end of the eighteenth century.[15]

Yet such a viewpoint appears to challenge the widely accepted assumption of evangelical scholarship that the biblical ascriptions of authorship reflect directly upon the understanding of its authority. As a result rather speculative, yet well-intended, efforts have frequently been made to reassert the unity and integrity of the book as a work of the eighth-century Isaiah. It has been a case of the tail wagging the dog, since the meaning of many crucial passages becomes heavily colored by the concern to defend its possible origin in eighth-century Judah. That this is not the most obvious, or likely, meaning is then discounted. The whole problem hinges on the question of whether the shaping and final compilation of the book of Isaiah, and by implication also of the other prophetic books, has primarily been determined by considerations of authorship or by other concerns. In the face of the evidence it seemed unlikely that authorship was a major issue, since ultimately the prophetic word was believed to be of divine origin. More central was the need to discover what the message revealed about the plans and purposes of God.

The issue became a significant one personally when the opportunity came to compose a commentary on the book of Isaiah. Having chosen to follow the critical convention of writing only on chapters 1—39,[16] I found it reasonable to leave the later chapters for another commentator to deal with. At the outset this appeared to be the proper course to follow, since even such older scholars as George Adam Smith,[17] O. C. Whitehouse,[18] and John Skinner,[19] who had written commentaries on the entire book, had effectively treated it as two separate compilations.

For reasons other than trying to understand the shape of a very long and complicated prophetic scroll, attention to Isaiah was a timely interest. Gerhard von Rad's traditio-historical treatment of the prophet in the second volume of his *Old Testament Theology* had brought to the fore a far greater awareness of what it meant to interpret his words as those of a "spokesman of Zion." That he had been heavily influenced by the cultic traditions of the Jerusalem temple, especially by the themes and expectations in such Zion psalms as Psalms 46 and 48, powerfully shaped von Rad's exegesis.[20] Both the place of the royal-messianic passages in the book, and more strikingly the attitude adopted by the prophet to Hezekiah at the time of the crisis posed in 701 B.C. by Sennacherib's assault on Judah, aroused strong interest. This was undoubtedly an area of research in which several long-held assumptions regarding what could, or could not, be regarded as authentic words of Isaiah were being substantially revised.[21]

Much of the new traditio-historical approach to the book was also reflected in the brilliant and careful work of H. Wildberger, whose magisterial commentary is the epitome of this scholar's life work.[22] Its progressive publication in German brought further awareness that new approaches to the prophetic literature were demanded. These could no longer set aside the supposedly "secondary" parts of the book as of little importance and regard them as of very obscure meaning. From other directions as well interesting new perspectives were opening up for a better understanding of this most intriguing composition.

Clearly one remarkable feature that pertains to all the prophetic literature of the Old Testament is its very uniqueness. Although we now have evidence of the recording of prophetic oracles from such ancient Near Eastern cities as Mari and Babylon, no comparative writings survive in which extensive compilations of large numbers of prophetic sayings have been preserved. Ample biblical narratives report briefly the gist of prophetic messages, but only in the prophetic writings are such lengthy collections preserved. The task of understanding them, therefore, can only be undertaken inductively, from within the evidence of the surviving scroll itself, since no comparable nonbiblical works from the ancient world are to be found. For too long the prophetic books had been regarded as little more than anthologies in which a whole variety of sayings had been preserved, brought together by only very loose and unclear connections and associations.

The quest to find a planned structure and coherent shape to a book such as Isaiah became a very challenging task. Besides the illuminating possibilities uncovered by tracing the influence upon the prophet of the Zion themes and motifs reflected in a number of psalms, the question remained of who had given the book its present shape and for what purposes. In this respect a yet further avenue of fresh enquiry was opening up, led most especially by O. H. Steck[23] and worked out in one important direction by his pupil Hermann Barth. When this scholar was kind enough to place in my hands a copy of his dissertation, subsequently published as *Die Jesaja-Worte in der Josiazeit*,[24] I gained further enthusiasm for a fresh look at the prophet Isaiah and his message.

Hermann Barth's study reflected a significant change in the lines of questioning regarding those passages and introductory comments in the prophetic books that were classified as later additions. Originally the interest had largely been preoccupied with the task of identifying them and setting them aside as extraneous to the original prophet's words. Increasingly, however, the concern arose to consider whether or not these comments and additions were not part of a much larger, and more coherent, attempt at editing and interpreting the prophet's words in relation to the events of a particular period. Barth's thesis was a result of the desire to identify the formative stages in the process of preserving, writing down, and interpreting what Isaiah had actually said. In pursuit of this aim the most likely explanation was that, since it was Isaiah's messages that had been primarily responsible for providing a religious interpretation of Judah's situation during the Assyrian assaults upon Judah and Israel in the years from 735 to 701 B.C., his sayings would also offer a key to when the time of Assyrian domination would end. Accordingly Barth's valuable thesis sought to trace both an anti-Assyrian redaction of Isaiah's prophecies during the reign of King Josiah, followed later by a further extensive revision and supplementation of the prophecies after the debacle in which the Jerusalem temple was destroyed by the Babylonians in 587 B.C.

The thesis of an extended work of collecting, supplementing, and editing Isaiah's prophecies during the reign of King Josiah (639–609 B.C.) appeared a very plausible one and greatly influenced my published commentary.[25] In several respects the new approaches opened up exciting new possibilities for further investigation in the interpretation of the book. In particular there was a primary need for rethinking the evidence concerning the narrative account of a miraculous deliverance wrought by God for Jerusalem in the year 701 B.C. when Sennacherib invaded Judah and threatened the great city of Jerusalem itself.

Several issues presented themselves, not the least of which was how closely the narrative of Jerusalem's deliverance presented in 2 Kings 18:16–19:37 (=Isa. 36:1–37:38) could be reconciled with the evidence of Sennacherib's Assyrian Annals and with the biblical record of Hezekieh's surrender (2 Kings 18:13–16). That there was a problem had been recognized for more than a century, but this was primarily treated as one of literary composition and of the reconstruction of the historical course of events. Increasingly, however, it appeared to me that the problem was also very directly a theological one. It hinged upon the evident concern on the part of the author of the biblical narrative to present a version of the events of 701 B.C. that demonstrated a very distinctive interpretation of how God shapes and controls events, at least so far as the history of the monarchy was concerned.

The subject remains an important one since it has a direct bearing, not simply on understanding how the book of Isaiah acquired its present form, but also regarding the purpose, structure, and theological outlook of the entire history now embraced within the Former Prophets (Joshua–2 Kings). That these biblical books have been widely understood, since the publication in 1943 of Martin Noth's seminal work on this major historical writing, to have been composed as a "Deuteronomistic History"[26] adds further interest to the subject. If God could send an angel to slaughter 185,000 Assyrians (2 Kings 19:35) in order to protect Jerusalem and the royal house of David, why had such victories not happened more often? It was very evident that the events reported as having occurred in 701 B.C. contrasted strangely with those that occurred in 587 B.C., when similar considerations might have been expected to prevail. Quite evidently the biblical historian had intended to find some meaning, or explanation, for the manner in which the two contrasting threats to Jerusalem and the Davidic royal dynasty had worked out. The first such threat was reported as leading to a miraculous success, while the second was presented as a terrible, and scarcely explicable, defeat.

Such a need for obtaining a better understanding of the story of Jerusalem's deliverance in 701 B.C. also provided a major clue for understanding several aspects of the structure of Isaiah's prophecies. Where Hermann Barth had drawn attention to the age of Josiah as providing a kind of counterpoint to Isaiah's prophecies warning of the threat from Assyria, it now appeared that a more direct contrasting balance was presented by the need to set the events of 587 B.C. over against those of 701 B.C. Throughout the entire sixty-six chapters of the book this contrast appears as the most vital clue to understanding the edited shape and complex structure of the prophecies of Isaiah 1—39.[27]

My first essay setting this basis for understanding Isaiah 1—39 was published in 1980,[28] and others have followed.[29] The very extensive investigation of the subject of how Isaiah's prophecies have been edited and related to events that for the most part undoubtedly occurred in a much later age than that of the prophet himself shows that a very long process took place.

Subsequent to my own early essays in exploring the subject very comprehensive reexaminations of the whole problem have now been presented, most notably by J. Vermeylen,[30] C. R. Seitz,[31] and H.G.M. Williamson.[32] Nor can we fail to notice that the major commentaries from H. Wildberger,[33] O. Kaiser,[34] and W.A.M. Beuken[35] have all recognized the need for tracing, so far as may be possible, the intricate stages of literary composition and editing that have given us the surviving book. It has seemed to me a rather reactionary and unadventurous step therefore for recent commentary work on this so majestic prophetic writing to cling forlornly to the threadbare claims of an eighth-century date for most of Isaiah 1—39, and even of the whole book, when the very assumptions upon which such claims rested relate so poorly to the very nature of the text itself.[36]

The Formation of the Prophetic Literature

It may be claimed that this process of prophetic book formation is part of the process of canon formation of the Old Testament. To an extent this is true, and it has become important to give full weight to the recognition that, alongside the literary currents that gave rise to the individual prophetic books, there took place a larger work of forming a prophetic corpus of writings that now constitute the *nebi'im*—the second (Hebrew) part of the Old Testament canon. Some overlapping of interest and activity becomes evident since the later elements of this large prophetic corpus show heavy use of allusions to, and citations of, earlier prophetic passages. This is quite markedly evident, for example, in Isaiah 24—27[37]—a section of the book of Isaiah that has, in my judgment quite erroneously, sometimes been treated as though it constitutes an independent apocalyptic writing.

Questions of intertextuality as well as of canon formation all begin to intrude heavily into the study of the prophetic writings,[38] and so the student of even one firmly defined section of the Old Testament finds it impossible to remain wholly within its confines. It spills over into a larger quest concerning an understanding of what took place between the prophet's own spoken messages and the written preservation and editing of his words.

In this respect it is necessary to note that a wide range of contemporary literary concerns and interests, loosely summed up as a core of literary theory, have also presented themselves as important to the study of the books of the prophets.[39] They have had a special relevance for the book of Isaiah, reminding us that ultimately it is the task of the interpreter to understand the text as it is, in its surviving form. To use criticism as itself a process of editing and rearrangement, setting aside large tracts of a text as of only secondary or minor importance, is undoubtedly a rather arbitrary proceeding.

During the latter half of the twentieth century there has taken place a major reawakening of attention to the Bible that we have actually received, and there has been a significant return to examining the biblical books in the form in which they now exist. It may rightly be claimed that this is, in any case, what we mean by the Bible. In part, however, it must also be admitted that many scholars have felt a growing disenchantment with the methods and assumptions of traditional literary criticism. The very lack of any consensus as to what were the supposed "original" words of the prophet and what words were added by later disciples and scribes has scarcely served as a strong recommendation for the methods of biblical criticism.

It comes as no surprise therefore to find scholars who have argued vigorously for a fundamental acceptance of the final form of the biblical text as the only significant form of it with which we need to be concerned. So, for instance, Rolf Rendtorff[40] and E. W. Conrad,[41] starting from rather different positions, have argued that it is this alone that matters when it comes to confronting a text that we can understand and interpret. All that lies behind this extant form is little more than a scholarly hypothesis, or collection of hypotheses.

To some extent this is a valid line of reasoning, but it can clearly be pressed too far. It depends on the nature of the text itself how it is to be read. We have only to look across to the biblical Pentateuch that exists now as a single work, rather arbitrarily divided for literary convenience into five books, to see that what is formally a single comprehensive work is in reality a whole series of writings and units skillfully joined together. Admittedly it is true that it is this final form that has been given to us, and which we are intended to read as a unity. Nevertheless, as soon as we display any concern with its origin, we are presented with the fact that it is not the work of one single mind, nor does it emanate from only one period of a complex national history.

Such considerations bring us back to the very fundamental recognition that religious writings, precisely because of their religious character and function, tend to be distinct from other kinds of writing. Their very retention and use in liturgical and instructional situations strongly suggests that these situations have had much to do with the shape and origin of the books themselves. Different types of literature fulfill different purposes and acquire different characteristics in the process. When we come to consider the prophetic writings of the Old Testament, therefore, we must first ask questions as to the type of literature that it is and the purposes that it was intended to fulfill. We may go on to ask whether it should be regarded as shaped to fulfill such intentions from the outset, or whether it has simply been adapted to do so.

Such at least have been my responses to the many interesting and exciting new approaches to the study of the prophetic writings that have appeared. Certainly much that is fresh and stimulating has come to light by setting aside the assumed divisions and barriers with which scholars have tended to break up the final form of the prophetic writings. All too frequently these have been too hastily concerned to consider only those parts that were thought to be oldest and to share a common time of origin and authorship.

The goal set by the great biblical scholars of the nineteenth century of endeavoring to "hear" the words of the prophet as they would have sounded to his original hearers is over-ambitious, and probably unhelpful. This is not to set aside the quite evident fact that prophets were primarily preachers and speakers and that the process of collecting and shaping their words into book form was a secondary process. Yet this literary process took place, and we are entitled to ask how it was done and with what ultimate aims.[42]

If this appears to be no less hazardous a task than that of reconstructing the original prophetic oracles and messages on the basis of what has been preserved of them, at least it is a proper literary proceeding. We have the text. The task is to find out how it came to be what it is. If indeed it was all written at one time by one scribe, then we should expect it to conform to certain structural and compositional patterns that still make sense to us. The fact is that so often this is not the case. There appear too many contradictions and too many inconsistencies of style, subject matter, and theological assumption for this to have been the case.

Once such a recognition of the unevennesses of the prophetic literature is made, then some explanation of how, and why, they appear is called for. Since my own background was strongly conservative and highly "biblicist," in the best sense of that word, I have reacted very negatively to the tendency on the part of some scholars to speculate and engage in highly implausible suppositions by defenders of the claims that the books all emanated from the same individual prophet. It is the interpreter's task to discover what the text actually says to us, rather than to engage in unsupported speculations that might allow the prophet's words to appear inconsistent and irrational, as they now sometimes do. The only effective response to such a puzzle is to search out diligently how the prophetic literature was actually compiled and what aims and intentions have contributed to give it its final form.

In part this may be viewed as an attempt to redress the balance of scholarly interest from that which prevailed in the nineteenth century, when all critical eyes were focused on getting back to the original prophet's words. The aim ought now to be to accept the text as it is, to wrestle with its complexities, and to try to discover from its form and shape, and from whatever comparative resources we can find, how it came to be. We may call this a redaction history, aiming to identify the various parts and units that make up the whole. In the best sense this must be concerned with the final form of the text, since we must explain the whole of it. Yet, having set aside as no more than an assumption the belief that the various parts were all written at the same time, we can identify the history of its composition.

Such might appear to be no more than a literary exercise were it not for the evident conviction that prophecy was the means God used for explaining through chosen messengers the nature, calling, and destiny of the people called Israel. The literary side of the quest is also therefore a very deeply and profoundly religious undertaking. If God is the one who is presented to us as the faithful, gracious, and sovereign Lord, then the actions in which Israel perceived this divine Lordship to be realized are nothing less than a disclosure of the nature and manner of what it is to be God. Not surprisingly therefore biblical prophecy, for all its conventions and complexities, is itself a very basic form of theology. Thus it is a kind of "theology in the making," in which images, ideas, and convictions about the relationship between Israel and God were tested in the fires of historical reality. That this was no simple triumphalist, or minimalist, process in which good experiences were signs of God's favor and bad ones indications of his wrath is what makes the quest such an interesting one. The task of understanding the processes by which the prophetic writings of the Old Testament were formed is consequently a profoundly theological one.[43]

From the perspective of my own combination of historical, literary, and theological interests those developments could be focused on the problem of understanding the structure and shape of the book of Isaiah. Once two traditional assumptions were set aside, a whole new range of issues called to be answered. These two inherited assumptions were first that Isaiah 1—39 had once formed a separate book, or prophetic collection, in its own independent form. It is surprising that it was ever thought to have done so in view of the substantial part of its contents that must certainly be of later origin than material in chapters 40—55. Secondly, the assumption that chapters 40—66 had little, and perhaps nothing at all, to do with the material in chapters 1—39, save for the use of certain established titles and images of God's action, appears wholly unconvincing in the light of the many evident literary connections.[44] I drafted a first look at these issues in the short essay "Second Isaiah's Development of First Isaiah's Themes."

Certainly it was clear that it was no longer possible to regard the shape of the book of Isaiah, with all its sixty-six chapters, as a kind of literary accident. Quite obviously a circle of scribes, with serious intent, produced such a work with some clear aims and intentions, and by the use of recognizable techniques and methods. At least one worthwhile task of scholarship would appear to be to understand what these aims and intentions were, and how such literary processes were employed. In view of the long period of approximately two hundred years since the writings of Robert Lowth, J. G. Herder, and J. G. Eichhorn had raised fundamental questions about the structure of the prophetic literature of the Old Testament, it was surprising that so little was actually known about the processes that led to the formation of it.

It must certainly be recognized that some possible explanations had been forthcoming that could serve to account for the collection of a large number of prophecies, eventually covering sixty-six chapters in a major scroll. This was based on the assumption that the prophet, who was on any reckoning an outstanding poet and leader and who delivered his messages orally, must have drawn to himself a band of disciples and faithful followers who would have listened, memorized, and eventually written down his words. They were assumed to have been largely responsible for creating the prophetic book, although they were not themselves the master figures who had created the awareness that God had spoken to his people in a new way. They were followers and not leaders.

So it had been argued there could have grown up a *traditio*—a corpus of memorized sayings and reports of actions concerning the prophet master— that would have been remembered and added to by later followers. The present prophetic books were taken to be the literary deposit of whole schools of prophets, initially brought into being by a great master, but outliving him by many centuries.

Two objections to such a speculative theory are of paramount importance. The first is quite simply that it is a theory aimed at saving the appearance of some kind of unity in a prophetic book like Isaiah, but in reality destroying its substance by telling us nothing at all about it. Apparently almost anyone could have become a "disciple" of the prophet, even centuries after he was dead! The assumption that because a saying was included in a major collection, it was written by a disciple, does little to answer the question, "Why is it included in the scroll?

My second objection to the theory of authorship by a school of disciples is concerned with the way in which such a theory obliterates the sense of uniqueness and unrepeatable divine inspiration that the great prophet possessed. If his words could simply be repeated, adapted, and imitated by later disciples, then the unique inspiration that was claimed for him was of no great importance. If anyone could speak or write prophecy, then the very uniqueness of the prophet was undermined. Yet it was this very sense of uniqueness that was inseparable from the claim to his inspiration, since this cannot have been simply a matter of the formulas and stylistic idioms that he employed. It must have been occasioned by issues of genuine substance. The singling out of particular prophets as the unique and distinctive revealers of God's will toward the people Israel was fundamental to the retention of their sayings. This does not, of course, rule out the possibility, strongly evident from many considerations, that there is much in each of the prophetic writings that cannot have originated either from the lips or the pen of the prophet whose name now heads the collection.

It is in this regard that my own development of the study of the prophetic writings was greatly helped, as it has been for many others, by the work of the remarkable German sociologist Max Weber. It is worth bearing in mind that Weber was not only very interested in, and attracted to, the work of the Old Testament prophets, but was especially concerned to understand how fundamental changes take place in the structure, ideological ethos, and direction of human communities.

Much of Weber's rethinking of the social structure of ancient Israel was published in a series of essays from the very close of his life that were translated into English and published as *Ancient Judaism*.[45] In spite of their strong attention to the role of prophecy in ancient Israelite-Jewish social development, they do not deal directly with the issue of how the prophetic literature arose. In fact Weber pays little attention to the questions that bear on the needs and processes that have served to create the biblical prophetic writings. In a forthcoming essay[46] I have sought to point out more closely those aspects of Weber's thinking that bear directly on this question.

Weber was well aware of the role played by individual human beings in bringing about fundamental changes in human society.[47] Their ability and "gift" for being empowered to do so he summed up broadly by the term "charisma." This was far more than a matter of a forceful personality and recognizable qualities of leadership. It concerned rather the ability to initiate change. In some cases such leaders may have appeared to their contemporaries as surprisingly "uncharismatic" personalities in the popular sense of the term. In a quite fundamental way it was only in retrospect that the efficacy of an individual's charisma could be recognized and evaluated. Yet often the very language, themes, and pronouncements of the "charismatic" leader proved strange and sometimes difficult for their contemporaries to grasp in their radical originality. In any case, they needed to be digested, thought through, and applied so that their innovative freshness could issue in a fundamental shift of direction for the communities they served. Weber termed this process one of "routinisation" by which the starkly original features of the leader were developed into an effective program for others to act upon and implement in their lives.

It has seemed to me that this, as much as any broad categorization is able to do, can best help us understand the processes that have led to the shaping of the prophetic books. It is, admittedly, only a partially relevant presentation of the overall picture, but it is a very helpful one. The sayings and words of the original prophet, precisely because of their originality, needed to be digested and elaborated in order to enable their full meaning to produce the reshaping of life that the preservation of a great writing was intended to achieve. It comes as no surprise therefore to find that the words of a remarkable and highly individual prophet like Jeremiah should have been preserved and edited for us in the broader context of the movement that we have loosely come to designate as "Deuteronomistic."[48] Although extensively debated since the pioneering studies by Duhm and Mowinckel, this has been a major contribution toward the better understanding of that prophet's book. So I have touched upon the issue in more than one attempt at relating prophecy to other aspects of the rise of the Israelite-Jewish religion.

So far as understanding how the prophetic writings came to exist, the analogy of a great poet and writer and his editors has seemed to me to be a helpful one.[49] Two of my attempts to understand the literary shape of the book of the prophet Ezekiel along these lines were published as "The Ezekiel Tradition: Prophecy in a Time of Crisis"[50] and "The Chronology of Redaction in Ezekiel 1—24."[51]

A partial background to these essays was a high regard for the magisterial commentary on Ezekiel by Walter Zimmerli.[52] In this work Zimmerli sought to trace to a "school" of the prophet much of the elaborative and developmental work that has given rise to the present form of the book. Admittedly the term "school" was used loosely, but it says too little about the need to appropriate and relate the words of the original prophet, often very enigmatic and unclear in their fuller meaning, to a situation that emerged later. In the case of Ezekiel this has seemed most plausibly to relate to the hoped-for ending of the time of exile. Accordingly the period for this activity that seems most probable was that toward the close of the sixth century, when expectations of rebuilding the Jerusalem temple and restoring some surviving heir of the Davidic family to the throne of Israel all reemerged with great vigor.

This could quite possibly be labeled a "school," but the issue is not a minor one. Instead of a rather protracted and indeterminate work of continuing the message and activity displayed by the original prophet, the work of editing has appeared rather to be one of applying and interpreting the deposit of his sayings to face a new situation.

As all of the major prophets had begun with words of warning and threat, it was understandable that a major concern should have arisen to glean from these warnings some hint concerning the time of their ending, when renewal and restoration would bring an end to the years of darkness. In this context, to consider the words of Isaiah 40—55 as forming a quite separate and independent work, as has frequently been assumed among scholars, would appear to be a major misdirection of critical acumen that can only have arisen as a consequence of indifference to the present shape of the book. These prophecies, together with those that follow them in chapters 56—66, belong inseparably to the structure of the book of Isaiah as a whole. In this regard, once the critically intelligible but over-presumptuous conclusions of an earlier generation of scholarship are set aside, the new perspectives open up a whole range of exciting paths of fresh interpretation.

To understand the factors that have given rise to each of the four major prophetic writings, it is important to see how greatly this process has been affected by the larger community needs of Judaism. While serious critical discussion was directed chiefly at recovering the original words voiced by the prophet, too little concern was given to those factors that have led to the production and preservation of the prophetic writings. To an extent this may be said to correspond to the broad fundamental shift in literary criticism, which has turned from seeking to reconstruct the original author's intention, interesting as this would be, to understanding who the original readers were and what light the surviving book sheds upon their needs and concerns. To a significant level it does matter greatly to us who the readers of the prophetic writings may have been and in what fashion their needs and hopes have shaped the literature that they have passed down to us.

The Interpretation of Prophecy

There can be no doubt that, beginning with the work of Herder and Eichhorn, a new level of interest in the religious significance of prophecy began to appear in Germany. It is of special interest that much of the seminal rethinking that influenced these scholars should have been begun in England by Lowth. Reciprocally, it was then the work of Eichhorn in particular that so strongly caught the attention of the English poet and writer S. T. Coleridge and formed such a basic stimulus to the English Romantic movement. Not until the middle of the nineteenth century, when the writings of Ewald began to appear in English translation, did the impact of this significant reappraisal of prophecy that had taken shape in Germany rekindle a flame of scholarly reexamination in Great Britain. In fact, it was only in the last part of the nineteenth century that the major writings on the prophets of William Robertson Smith and the lesser-known Alexander Kirkpatrick ushered in a whole new critical era of British scholarship on these great writings.[53]

It has been an interesting pursuit to explore more fully the background of these developments in the history of the interpretation of biblical prophecy and of the very distinctive role that it has played in British church life and theological thinking. Along the way the serious student finds out so many interesting truths and learns so much from the eager researchers of the present, as well as of the past. To all of them I have been immensely grateful.

To the casual reader the critical exposition of the meaning and message of the great biblical prophets has often appeared to be a truly historical, unbiased, and nonpartisan task. In reality this is not the case, and not only does every present-day reader bring a measure of predetermined expectation to the task of reading the prophetic literature but scholars of the past, however impartial their motivation may have been, have similarly brought their own presuppositions to it. One who seeks to interpret biblical prophecy, therefore, cannot be indifferent to the ways in which these remarkable writings have influenced theology, shaped ecclesiastical policies, and nurtured both the hopes and fears of ordinary people over many centuries.

This is remarkably true in the present, even though most of those who cling most passionately to interpretations of biblical prophecy as a guide to modern political history and its complexities have largely shunned relating those interpretations more directly to a serious critical understanding of it. Nevertheless the contemporary popular ecclesiastical scene would appear to be as strongly attached to distinctive, speculative, and in most cases, palpably misdirected, interpretations of the great biblical prophets as any previous period has been. Perhaps only the remarkable upheavals of the civil conflicts of seventeenth-century Britain have been more deeply embroiled in specific ways of interpreting them. So it has been a valuable, if sometimes seemingly esoteric task, to look more closely at the ways in which men and women of the past sought to find in prophecy both insight into the theological purposes of God and a message that could unlock the secrets of what would be the outcome of troubled and uncertain times.

Two primary themes have inevitably stood at the top of the agenda for this undertaking. The first of these is the awareness, so strongly present to the reader of the New Testament, that the prophetic foretelling of the meaning, circumstances, and consequences of the life, death, and resurrection of Jesus of Nazareth had all been foreseen in prophecy. This "argument from prophecy" was both a central plank of the christological argument of the earliest Christians concerning the person of Jesus as the Messiah—the Christ—and also of the christological formulations of the church. It was, as it was inevitably bound to become, a central reason for the Christian retention of the Old Testament, which saw in the two Testaments two witnesses to the status of the Redeemer. So, from a Christian perspective, and by an inevitable reciprocal response on the part of Jewish scholars, the role of biblical prophecy in foretelling the coming of the messiah has been of great significance.

Not until the early eighteenth century, and then largely in the wake of the major philosophical insights of John Locke into the nature of human knowledge and his placing of the claim that Jesus was the Messiah as the earliest and most basic Christian confession, did this central position begin to be challenged. For a period a rather dualistic approach to the meaning of the central "messianic" foretellings of the Old Testament held sway in Great

Britain. Then, in the wake of the fundamental shift in the whole foundations of Christology led by F.D.E. Schleiermacher, the question of the messianic message of prophecy reawakened. Perhaps not surprisingly the consequence of this renewal of interest in the subject at the beginning of the nineteenth century ultimately led to a sharpening of the divide within Christian hermeneutical traditions. The conservative and critical paths of interpretation became widely divergent, so much so that by the end of the nineteenth century the more critical expositions of biblical prophecy had almost entirely lost interest in the question of its messianic significance.

To trace this development has proved an interesting and rewarding task, since it places the study of the prophets back in the larger context of Christian theology and of the importance of Jewish-Christian debate of these fundamental issues.[54]

Even more surprising, and rather more seriously neglected by scholarship until recent years, has been the extent to which the interpretation of prophecy in Great Britain sought to find within it a "sacred calendar" of world history. The highpoint of this hermeneutical approach is to be seen in its impact upon seventeenth-century England, giving rise to stormy political debates and awakening hopes of the imminent breaking-in of a new heavenly kingdom. From this there emerged in the nineteenth century a renewal of attention to it and a new perspective that has contributed greatly to the rise of modern fundamentalist movements.[55]

So the study of Old Testament prophecy has not remained without a much wider range of interest, touching upon some of the most central questions of Christian theology and cutting deeply into the hopes and expectations that have shaped the most energetic and influential areas of modern church life.

Part 1

PROPHET, KING, AND MESSIAH

1   Amos and the Politics of Israel

The message of the prophet Amos represents a decisive no to the future of Israel.[1] This is summed up succinctly in the interpretation of the fourth of the series of five visions of chapters 7—9:

The end has come upon my people Israel; I will never again pass by them. (Amos 8:2)

It is echoed, with a comparable degree of finality, in the prophetic lamentation:

Fallen, never to rise again,
is the virgin Israel. (Amos 5:2)

The emphasis with which the message is put leaves no doubt as to its decisive import, yet uncertainty prevails when we endeavour to spell out in precise political terms what exactly the prophet was implying about the future political destiny of the kingdom of Israel. In the broad context of the events of the eighth century B.C. it must appear that the terrifying fulfilment of this threat occurred with the collapse of the Northern Kingdom of Israel under pressure from Assyria during the final quarter of the century.[2] Yet there are no indications that Amos the prophet openly foresaw Assyria as the divine agent which would bring about the fulfillment of his threats. Furthermore the rhetorical appeal of 3:9 would seem, on the surface at least, to indicate that Assyria was regarded by the prophet as no more than one of several potentially threatening foreign powers.[3] In any case, since Amos was evidently active during the reign of Jeroboam II (786–746 B.C.E. according to W. F. Albright's chronology), his prophecies are usually dated between 760 and 750 B.C.E. How and why would they have been remembered, if their message had not become directly relevant until at least a quarter of a century later?

Within the book itself the answer to the question of what Amos envisaged by the "end" of Israel is spelled out, at first explicitly and secondly by implication, in the interpretation and narrative sequel that is given to the third of Amos's visions, that of the "plumb-bob" (Amos 7:7–8) in 7:9–17. This consists of a threefold declaration in verse 9 of what the threat of the vision of Yahweh standing holding a plumb-bob means in political and religious terms. This is then followed by an account in verse 10 of how this message was conveyed to the court of Jeroboam II, and this in turn calls forth a response by Amaziah the priest of Bethel to Amos and Amos's rejoinder to him. It is in the course of this response that what is implied by the prophet's threat is yet more fully spelled out (v. 17), and it is only at this point that clear allusions to the depredations brought about by the Assyrians become fully evident.

This narrative of verses 10–17 has become a central feature of the interpretation of the book of Amos, and the preceding verse 9 also enjoys special significance as the first clear indication of how the prophet envisaged that his threats would achieve fulfilment. Although no mention by name is made of Assyria, the nature of the misfortunes described point to the sufferings inflicted by this power upon the Northern Kingdom from 733 B.C.E. onward. We are certainly entitled to conclude that an informed Israelite reader from a time after the end of the eighth century could have been expected to recognize from the fate threatened to Amaziah and his family that it was Assyria's actions in the last third of that century which had marked the fulfilment of Amos's threats and which showed Assyria to be the agent of the divine wrath of which Amos had prophesied.

In recent research the entire section comprising the third of Amos's visions and its narrative sequel has been the subject of fresh investigation and has led to demands for a substantial reappraisal of its origin and significance.[4] Our immediate concern is to elucidate what exactly was thought to be implied by Amos's threat that "the end" was about to befall Israel and to clarify what light is shed upon this question by Amos 7:9, which interprets the plumb-bob vision, and the encounter with Amaziah which follows this. In order to do this it is necessary first of all to examine the literary relationships between the vision account of Amos 7:7–8 and the interpretation of this in verse 9. Then we can proceed to consider the narrative which follows this to see how this adds a further layer of interpretation.

The image that is central to 7:7–8, which constitutes the third of Amos's series of five visions, is of Yahweh standing beside (or upon) a wall, holding in his hand a "plumb-bob." This, at least, is the usual translation of the Hebrew word 'ănāk, which appears both in the account of the vision itself (v. 7) and in its initial interpretation in verse 8. However, in spite of its established position in all the major English versions, this rendering of the Hebrew noun is scarcely supportable from the linguistic evidence, as both G. Brunet[5] and W. Beyerlin[6] have shown. The Akkadian cognate shows that the metal that is referred to here is most probably tin, or possibly iron (LXX has "steel"). The most direct association of this was with military weapons, rather than with a builder's measuring instrument. However, W. Rudolph has sought to recognize that iron or tin is referred to and has suggested the rendering "pickaxe."[7] If we accept that a military connotation is the more probable, we can then take this to indicate that the symbolism of the vision should be understood to declare that Yahweh was seen with a weapon in his hand and so was about to let loose "weapons of warfare," and so more abstractly "warfare" upon his people Israel.

What region Amos was referring to as "Israel" must certainly be understood to be the Northern Kingdom, rather than a more ideal entity comprising Israel and Judah.[8] This can be ascertained from other passages in this prophet and from the pre-Deuteronomic background of usage more generally. This is important in trying to unravel the political implications of Amos's message since there is no reason to suppose that he was, at this stage, declaring that both Israel and Judah would be overrun by a major foreign power. The few indications which appear to point to the contrary conclusion, that Amos thought of a larger Israel which included Judah, can be confidently ascribed to later editorial work.[9] Hence there is no solid reason for doubting that Amos's vision of Yahweh holding in his hand an instrument described as 'ănāk expresses a threat that warfare was soon to break out within the Northern Kingdom of Israel from an unspecified quarter.

Since the prophet's activity is ascribed to the reign of Jeroboam II (Amos 1:1; cf. 7:9), this would have marked the end of a long, and clearly highly successful, reign in the Northern Kingdom by one of the most resourceful of its kings. Such a long period of power and prosperity has given rise to the introduction of some special words of explanation from the historian of 2 Kings, 14:26f., who, from his point of view, clearly did not regard Jeroboam II as deserving of such success.

The verse which elaborates upon the initial interpretation of Amos's third vision (v. 9) presents a fuller explanation of its meaning, and has frequently been taken to belong structurally to the original vision account. Yet there are strong reasons for questioning this, on the grounds of both form and content. As P. R. Ackroyd points out,[10] the reports of all five visions show a certain formal similarity and are equally brief (7:1, with a prophetic response in vv. 2–3; 7:4, with a response in vv. 5–6; 7:7–8, with no prophetic response, unless the narrative of vv. 10–17 is thought to provide this; 8:1–2 and 9:1). However it is more especially in matters of content that doubts arise as to whether 7:9 formed a part of the original vision report. Most important here is the fact that verse 9 reveals demonstrable connections of material content with the narrative account of verses 10–17 which follows. These are to be found in the highly distinctive references to the tradition of "Isaac" ("The high places of Isaac," v. 9, and the "house of Isaac," v. 16) and even more strikingly in the fact that the threat against "the house of Jeroboam" in verse 9 is referred back to in verse 11, although in an imprecise way as simply "Jeroboam."

There is, however, a yet more striking feature about the way in which these later verses interpret the significance of what the vision of Yahweh's bringing "tin" (= warfare) upon Israel will mean. This concerns the summary report that Amaziah is said to have sent to the royal palace of Jeroboam II in verse 11:

Jeroboam shall die by the sword,
and Israel must go into exile away from his land.

It is in this that we hear for the first time about exile as a major part of the doom that Yahweh is announcing through his prophet. This is then made even more clear by Amos's reply to Amaziah, in which he insists that Amaziah will be disinherited from his land. He then proceeds to reaffirm the threat of exile for Israel as a nation:

. . . and Israel shall surely go into exile away from its land. (Amos 7:17)

We could, at first glance, simply regard this as a point of little distinctive importance since it could be considered inevitable that some victims of war, especially prisoners taken after a battle, would be rounded up and taken off to be sold as slaves. They would therefore suffer a fate of exile. However, it is a point of major historical importance that the Assyrian conquest of the Northern Kingdom of Israel brought something far more drastic than this conventional form of exile to individuals. This took the form of forcible deportations of large sections of the population, which have left a deep legacy of bitterness in the biblical literature (2 Kings 17:24–28). It is this emphasis upon the fate of exile in Amos 7:17 that provides one of the strongest indications that the report in which it appears has taken account of the historical experience of Israel in the latter years of the eighth century at the hands of Assyria. It is not warfare alone that is being referred to here, with its inevitable sufferings for the defeated, but the cruel and prolonged policy of oppression practiced by the suzerain power of Assyria. Such oppressive rule used as a major instrument of policy the wholesale deportation of large established communities.[11]

The interpretation that is placed upon the message of Amos's third vision in the narrative of 7:10–17 can then be seen to mark a considerable extension of meaning beyond what was directly implicit in the symbolism of the vision itself. As verse 9 has spelt out the political message of the vision, so the narrative of verses 10–17 has served to extend and reinforce this yet further.

This raises, as we have already noted, serious doubts whether verse 9 can be regarded as an intrinsic part of the original report of the vision. Its links with the narrative that follows it are too close for this to have been the case. We could then draw the conclusion that verse 9 has been specifically composed in order to provide a bridge between the original vision report, with its undefined threats of warfare, and the narrative account of verses 10–17 which shows more clearly what this threat was to mean in historical reality.[12] However, such a conclusion also runs into difficulties since, in spite of the connections between verse 9 and verses 10–17, it is virtually impossible to suppose that priority attaches to the narrative and that verse 9 has been composed as an introduction to this.

In the first instance it is noteworthy that the pronouncements of verse 9 comprise a distinctive threefold pattern:

1. The high places of Isaac will be made desolate.
2. The sanctuaries of Israel will be devastated.
3. Yahweh will bring violent conflict ("the sword") upon the household of Jeroboam.

This threefold pattern reflects concerns which came to prominent attention in the Deuteronomic Reform movement, and they might easily be described as constituting a "Deuteronomistic" level of interest: The non-Jerusalem sanctuaries were to suffer ruin and the non-Davidic royal house of Israel (Samaria) was to suffer violence. However since the existence of both the sanctuaries and royal house of the Northern Kingdom were the subject of prolonged opposition and polemic in Judah, it is far from clear that the special attention that is accorded to both here could only have arisen as late as the time of the Deuteronomists. Quite evidently these were issues which the Deuteronomists inherited from the political and religious history of Israel's past and with which they sought to deal in their own radical fashion.

It is hardly necessary therefore to conclude that verse 9 represents a Deuteronomistic interpretation of Amos's vision. Nevertheless the affinities with the Deuteronomistic concerns are evident and there are sound reasons for concluding that the interpretation of the meaning of Amos's message that warfare would be unleashed upon Israel which is given in verse 9 is secondary to what was contained in the original report. It interprets that broad threat in two very specific directions: against the sanctuaries of the Northern Kingdom and against its royal house.

It is helpful at this point to consider the light that is shed upon Amos's vision and its interpretations by the immediate political context in which it was given. This is shown up clearly by the account of Jeroboam's successful and long reign that is given in 2 Kings 14:23–29 and the immediate sequel to this in the violence that erupted shortly after Jeroboam's death (2 Kings 15:8–16). Zechariah reigned a mere six months before being assassinated in a coup. However, Shallum, the successful usurper, reigned only one month before being, in turn, murdered and displaced by Menahem (2 Kings 15:14). So in a single year Israel had three kings, the royal house of Jeroboam II was removed, and by this event the dynasty founded by Jehu had been brought to an end. The sword had struck with great force in the very heart of Israel's political life.

All these factors indicate strongly that these events must surely have been felt as the most direct and immediate fulfilment of Amos's words. To what extent foreign powers and foreign policies had any part to play in such inner turmoil in Israel remains unknown. Nor can we do more than guess whether Amos himself had any knowledge of the existence of the conspiracies and hostility which engendered such violence. We are, however, given some grounds for recognizing where some major points of friction had arisen and which continued to be keenly felt as points of conflict throughout the next two decades. Jeroboam II is remembered as having "restored the border of Israel from the route up to Hamath as far as the Sea of the Arabah" (2 Kings 14:25).

How Israel's ruler had achieved this success in reestablishing such a broad territorial extension of this kingdom is not made clear. Undoubtedly military conquest would have played some part. Nevertheless much may well have been achieved through skillful diplomacy and through establishing favourable links with the various chiefs and family heads who controlled their own individual regions. Jeroboam II had evidently been a shrewd diplomatist who, in achieving his ends, had left Judah seriously weakened and isolated. There are sound reasons for believing therefore that the expansion of territory which Jeroboam II achieved was largely at Judah's expense and left a lasting legacy of antagonism which eventually contributed substantially to the outbreak of the Syro-Ephraimite war a decade later.[13] Indeed it seems likely that the appeal by Ahaz of Judah to Assyria (2 Kings 16:7), and the alliance of Israel with Syria, which sought to depose him, were late developments in a prolonged period of conflict and hostile diplomacy.

In the light of such a background of political turmoil and conflict we have strong grounds for believing that a certain continuum of political ambition and policy making linked the violence that swept away the royal house of Jeroboam II in 745 with the eventual appearance of Assyria as a major factor in Israelite-Judean affairs during the following decade.

So far as the origin and significance of Amos 7:9 is concerned, this has a direct bearing upon the question of its purpose. An observant scribe, mindful of all that had transpired so rapidly after Jeroboam's death, has incorporated into the account of Amos's threatening vision some more specific detail regarding the events which could be regarded as its "fulfilment." Nor need we conclude that this addition was made at any great interval of time after the first preservation of Amos's message in writing. It shows some affinities with central concerns of the Deuteronomic movement, but these simply reflect issues that continued to torment Israelite and Judean relationships for more than a century.

Much discussion has focussed upon the unique reference in Amos: 7:9 to "the high places of Isaac." It is noteworthy that the name of the patriarch is spelt in a distinctive fashion here which led the ancient versions to attempt some dissociation from the person presented as the son of Abraham and the father of Jacob. Yet this patriarch of the nation must be the figure who is alluded to, which points us to conclude that the sanctuaries referred to must have been those which claimed to have been founded by this ancestor of Israel. This points us unmistakably to Beersheba and its vicinity (cf. Gen. 24:62; 25:11; cf. Gen. 16:13f.) in the far south. Not surprisingly, if this is the case, it fits remarkably well with the fact that Jeroboam II had been successful in extending his territorial control as far south as the Dead Sea. On this point too, therefore, the historical allusions of Amos 7:9 suggest that it represents an interpretation that was added relatively early to the report of Amos's vision and which took full account of the political situation that marked Jeroboam's final years and their bloody aftermath. A specific aspect of its import was that the region in the far south of Israelite territory would suffer devastation. At the same time a distinctively religious note was given to Amos's vision by drawing attention to the impending destruction of ancient shrines, greatly revered within the nation, but which stood as rivals to the major sanctuary of Jerusalem. In this respect Amos 7:9 anticipates central concerns of the Deuteronomic movement.

When we compare the wholly unique reference in 7:9 to "the high places of Isaac" with the broader reference in verse 16 to "the house of Isaac," the priority of the former becomes clear. As the preceding line of verse 16 shows, "house of Isaac" has simply become a synonym for "Israel," and the specific reference of verse 9 has become broadened into a very general one. We can see that a closely similar proceeding has taken place in regard to the specific reference to "the house of Jeroboam" in verse 9, as compared with the more general "Jeroboam" of verse 11. The precisely aimed threat against Jeroboam's royal house in verse 9 has been viewed against a very changed set of political eventualities in the narrative of verses 10–17.

In verse 9 the prophetic message is presented as a warning that "the house of Jeroboam" will suffer violence by the sword. This threat accords well with the circumstances of the uprising that transpired shortly after Jeroboam II's death. It should no doubt be taken to mean that the entire dynasty of which Jeroboam II was a representative, which had begun with Jehu's uprising, would be removed from its privileged position. In the narrative of verses 10–17, however, it is Jeroboam who is threatened (v. 11), which indicates that the author of the narrative was no longer thinking in any direct way of the violent events that erupted after Jeroboam's death. By the time verse 11 was written, these events lay in the past and were no longer of immediate dynastic interest so far as the fate of the Northern Kingdom was concerned.

Rather attention had now come to focus on the question whether Israel's kingship could survive at all. The historically imprecise assertion "Jeroboam shall die by the sword" has then simply been broadened to represent the ending of kingship in the Northern Kingdom. Appropriately therefore it has been combined with the pronouncement that all Israel will be taken into exile. Taken together, the treatment of the two subjects, "the high places of Isaac" and "the house of Jeroboam" in verse 9 are strongly indicative of the conclusion that the narrative of verses 10–17 was composed later than the more precise definitions of verse 9.[14] Furthermore it appears equally certain that the author of the narrative has worked on the basis of the material given in verse 9 and has developed his broader interpretation of the message of Amos's vision upon his awareness of what transpired later in the eighth century.

We can then accept the conclusion that verse 9 was composed prior to the narrative of verses 10–17, and formed the primary text on which the narrative was based. Such a literary evaluation is further reinforced when the overall character of this latter report is examined in detail. The detailed nature of this account requires to be looked at carefully in view of the fact that the incident at Bethel in which Amaziah rebuked Amos, and to which the prophet responded by appealing back to the circumstances of his call, has become a central feature of the interpretation of the book.[15]

Peter Ackroyd has pointed out the distinctive character of the preservation of a narrative of this kind in a prophetic book and has raised the question of its specific purpose.[16] Narratives reporting action involving prophets are rare in the prophetic books of the Old Testament, although they appear quite frequently in the historical books. Accordingly Ackroyd has suggested that this narrative too may once have existed independently and formed an episode within an edition of one of the historical books. Its apparent links with both the prophetic episode of 1 Kings 13 and the narrative of 2 Chronicles 24 could point to such a conclusion. Yet our contention is that this conclusion should be ruled out altogether. The degree of dependence shown by the narrative upon Amos 7:9 shows that it has been composed to fit in its present position as a feature of the interpretation of Amos's vision of Yahweh standing holding in his hand 'ănāk.

Throughout it is clear that the intention of the Amos narrative is wholly to provide support for the interpretation of Amos's prophecies and to reinforce the claim that a unique divine authority attached to him and to his message. The purport of the conflict between Amaziah and Amos is to show that Amos was a true spokesman of God. The action recorded in the narrative therefore is wholly minimal and, as has been consistently noted, offers no clear outcome for the confrontation described. What happened to Amos after he had been addressed by Amaziah remains wholly unknown. It was of no interest to the author of the narrative, who has instead been concerned to focus all attention upon the nature of the message which Amos brought. The following main features stand out.

(1) The report of how Amaziah sent word to Jeroboam concerning what Amos had said, combined with the heavy attention that is drawn to the fact that Bethel was a royal sanctuary (v. 13), places the greatest emphasis upon the political implications of Amos's pronouncement about the future of Israel's kingship. No longer, as in verse 9, are the sanctuaries themselves singled out as the subject of coming destruction, but attention is focused instead upon the fact that it is the royal house of the Northern Kingdom of Israel that is threatened. The mention of the threat to the sanctuaries of Israel has been adapted to show that it represents a threat to Israel's royal house. This is in line with the feature that the threat to Jeroboam's dynasty has been enlarged into a threat to the entire future of the monarchy of the Northern Kingdom.

(2) The origin of Amos from Judah is especially highlighted in the narrative (v. 12). In historical fact it is not clear to what extent this was an issue of any major significance in the original prophecies of Amos. Undoubtedly Amos came from Tekoa, but it is not at all to be taken for granted that this meant that he embraced a pro-Jerusalem, pro-Davidic, political stance. He may have done, but it seems unlikely, and the highlighting of Amos's Judahite origin in verse 12 can best be explained as due to the author's awareness that Judah fared less badly under the Assyrians than did Israel. We may compare the similar intent of the comment in Hos. 4:15. This point therefore has been introduced out of an awareness of the differing fates that befell Israel and Judah in the last quarter of the eighth century. A hint is thereby given that Judah was to be spared the totality of political eclipse that became the fate of Israel at the hands of the Assyrians.

(3) The conflict between Amaziah and Amos, together with the dialogue in which it is expressed, appears to draw upon some brief narrative report of a conflict between a prophet and a priest, and Ackroyd has instructively drawn attention to these elements. This observation is used to support his suggestion that the narrative may rest upon an older one which may once have belonged within the tradition of the historical books.[17] Certainly it is possible that some earlier narrative elements have been employed in reporting this encounter. Yet such a conclusion is far from essential, since the whole confrontation scene between prophet and priest is so stereotyped as to be readily explicable from a popular store of tales designed to magnify the direct "charismatic" authority of the prophet. As we have noted, the concern is wholly to demonstrate Amos's divine authority and the truth of his message. There is no "plot" as such, since no sequel is provided.

(4) The most marked characteristic of the narrative account in Amos

7:10–17 is that it serves to develope the political implications of Amos's third vision of Yahweh standing with *'ănāk* in his hand. It shows that this threat was thought to have been fulfilled by the destruction of the Northern Kingdom of Israel at the hands of the Assyrians. It achieves this end in a number of ways. First, as we have noted, it uses both the "high places of Isaac" and the "sanctuaries of Israel" references from the interpretation given in verse 9 to demonstrate that these implied the ending of a separate monarchy for the Northern Kingdom altogether. Second, it has treated the "house of Jeroboam" reference in the same way by broadening it into a threat against "Jeroboam." The reigning king of Amos's day simply stands for the kingship of Israel and all specific dynastic connotation is dropped.

Third, and most strikingly of all, the narrative introduces in no less than four explicit pronouncements the fact that Israel is to be dispossessed of its land and taken away into exile. This is mentioned first in verse 11, "Israel must go into exile away from his land," and is then repeated in closely similar words at the conclusion of the whole narrative in verse 17. Alongside these two direct pronouncements we find two more expressed in regard to the personal fate threatened to Amaziah. He is to be dispossessed of his land—"your land shall be divided out by line (to others)" (v. 17c)—which is followed by the declaration "you yourself will die in an unclean (i.e., foreign) land" (v. 17d). There can be no doubting the fact that exile is presented as the major disaster that is to befall Israel.

These considerations regarding the content of the narrative report of Amos 7:10–17 show that Amos's threats found their political focus in the ending of a separate political identity for the Northern Kingdom and the exiling of a large part of the population. These were the terrible consequences of Assyrian intervention in the Levant that befell Israel during the last quarter of the eighth century and from which it never recovered. We cannot doubt that the author of the narrative knew of these tragic events and has linked them directly with Amos's prophecy of Yahweh rising up in conflict against his people.

Taken together we can discern a clearly identifiable threefold pattern emerging in the series of interpretations placed upon Amos's third vision. The original report of this is given in Amos 7:7–8 and foretold that Yahweh was about to bring violence and bloodshed upon his people Israel. What precise form this violence and bloodshed would take is not spelt out, and this we can assume to have been typical of much ancient prophecy. The character of coming events was foretold, but their precise details and timing were left open. Nor was the prophet in any deep sense a fatalist, since he allowed that Yahweh's action could be revoked if the people showed penitence and a change of attitude (cf. Amos 7:2, 5f.).

The openness and brevity of the original pronouncement of Amos's third vision, however, contains a grim warning that judgment has become inevitable ("I will never again pass by them," v. 8). It has then been given much more precise and political direction by the addition of verse 9. In this the internal conflicts and political violence that erupted shortly after Jeroboam II's death, and which are fully reported by the historian of 2 Kings, have been set in the forefront. It is these events, which caused major instability to the Northern Kingdom after 745 B.C.E., which are viewed as the fulfilment of Amos's threat. In spelling out the details of this, the author of Amos 7:9 was mindful of how those events had put an end to the royal house of the king who ruled when Amos prophesied, and how the large territorial gains made by Jeroboam II had been lost.

A third level of interpretation, however, has been added by the author of the narrative of Amos 7:10–17. The author of this has based his account upon the prophetic interpretation given in verse 9 and has sought to understand this in relation to the events which overtook Israel and Judah from 735 B.C.E. onwards. The conflict between these two sister kingdoms had flared into open war, worsening their relationship yet further. This in turn had led to the Syro-Ephraimite alliance and its attempt to remove Ahaz, the king of Judah, in order to reestablish a coordinated front in the face of a threat from Assyria. The disastrous outcome of this was that Ahaz had "bought" Assyrian aid to prop up his position and both kingdoms had fallen inescapably under the power of Assyrian domination. Further rebellion had brought complete ruin to the Northern Kingdom, involving the ending of its separate monarchy and the eventual exiling of a large segment of its population. It is these later events, which took place between 722 and 701 B.C.E. which are reflected in the narrative of Amos 7:10–17.

This review of the political interpretation of Amos's warning that "the end" was about to come upon Israel offers an instructive instance of the way in which the compilers of the prophetic books have sought to weave together a record of the prophet's original words and pronouncements with some indication of how they were thought to have taken effect in regard to specific political events. The prophet was certainly not concerned to "predict" the course of events in any simplistic and naive fashion. It was fundamental to his role as a prophet that his task to was warn and exhort people, so that they might maintain the support and protection of Yahweh their God. The final course of history could only be determined by God himself, and this was never a fixed fate. All that the prophet could hope to do was to see some glimpses of the divine purpose and pass on what he saw to his people. Yet events themselves provided an "interpretation" of the prophet's message, and it was wholly in order that, in recording the prophet's words, either he himself or his followers should indicate how events themselves confirmed his message. To some extent this entailed the incorporation of historical information *post eventum*. Yet this was in no way a falsifying of prophecy, or a fabricating of its truthfulness, but rather a way of drawing out its fuller meaning.

Our contention is that this process is clearly evident in the unfolding pattern of political interpretation accorded to Amos's vision of Yahweh standing holding *'ănāk* in his hand (Amos 7:7–8). In such a process of developing interpretation we can also discern how a sense of divinely controlled purpose and interconnection was traced in events. Amos's warning of violence could lend to the events that took place with Zechariah's murder a sense that one continuing purpose, issuing from Yahweh's anger against his people, bound together the disastrous last years of the Northern Kingdom of Israel. Amos was believed to have foreseen the "end" coming upon Israel, even though that end did not fully materialize until fully half a century after the prophet's warnings had been given.

2   The Prophecies of Isaiah to Hezekiah concerning Sennacherib

2 Kings 19:21–34 // Isa. 37:22–35

The narratives concerning the role of Isaiah in the confrontation between Hezekiah and Sennacherib (2 Kings 18:17–19:37 // Isa. 36:1–39:8) have commanded considerable attention as expressions of a highly distinctive "Zion theology" of Jerusalem, and, by implication, of the kingdom of Judah as a political entity. They also reflect very directly a prominent aspect of the royal Davidic dynastic theology of Judah from which the "Zion theology" cannot be separated. Taken as a whole the three incidents which provide the thematic basis of the sequence of narratives of 2 Kings 18:13–20:19 (// Isa. 36:1–39:8) present a striking interpretation of the special significance of the Davidic royal house and of its relationship to Jerusalem.

The inclusion of these narratives in 2 Kings indicates a degree of connection with the Deuteronomistic circles who were responsible for the composition of the extensive history of the rise and fall of Israel (DtrG). At the same time their appeal to the prophet Isaiah points to their further relationship with the *traditio* of the prophecies of this prominent figure.

Since our concern in the present study is with only one aspect of these narratives, namely the prophecies ascribed to Isaiah announcing the forthcoming defeat and humiliation of Sennacherib in his assault on Jerusalem (2 Kings 19:21–34 // Isa. 37:22–35), we may begin summarising some conclusions about their larger narrative context that have been argued for elsewhere.[1]

The first of these is that the group of narratives extending from 2 Kings 18:13–20:19 (// Isa. 36:1–39:8) form a connected whole.[2] The accounts concerning Hezekiah's sickness (2 Kings 20:1–11 // Isa. 38:1–22) and the visit of the Babylonian emissaries (2 Kings 20:12–19 // Isa. 39:1–8) are intended to illuminate the fact of Hezekiah's piety and to draw attention to the contrasting fates of Jerusalem at the hands of the Assyrians and Babylonians.

A second point is that the account concerning Jerusalem's deliverance from Sennacherib's forces in 701 B.C.E. (2 Kings 18:13–19:37 // Isa. 36:1–37:38) is, following a critical analysis initiated by B. Stade,[3] made up from at least two separate literary strands (sources A and B).

A third major conclusion is that this narrative relating Jerusalem's miraculous deliverance from Sennacherib was composed at some considerable interval after 701 B.C.E. and displays a markedly theological character. All of these points require further discussion and examination in view of continued attention to their composition and purpose.

The Isaianic Prophecies in their Narrative Context

Our immediate concern is with the prophecies ascribed to Isaiah in 2 Kings 19:21–34 (Isa. 37:22–35). The wider issues which concern the interpretation of their narrative setting can only be touched upon briefly. However, the significance of these prophecies, and the question of their literary affiliations, are necessarily related to conclusions reached regarding this narrative setting. A feature of considerable significance is that the account of the threat to Jerusalem mounted by Sennacherib's forces and of the subsequent divine protection of the city possesses a highly distinctive narrative structure. The only major military action that is recounted relates to the slaughter of 185,000 of the Assyrians by the angel of Yahweh (2 Kings 19:35 // Isa. 37:36). Consequently, the extent to which this account can be correlated with other historical information concerning the events of the year 701 B.C.E outside Jerusalem is strictly limited.[4] For the rest the central focus of interest lies in the speeches ascribed to the Assyrian Rabshakeh (2 Kings 18:19–25, 28–35 // Isa. 36:4–9, 13–20) and the prophecies of Isaiah which serve directly as a rejoinder to these (2 Kings 19:21–34 // Isa. 37:2–35).

Certainly a historical *dénouement* is required by the speeches and the prophecies, since the divine intervention which concludes the account serves to show the falseness of the claims of the Rabshakeh, who has spoken on behalf of the Assyrian king. Correspondingly, the dramatic defeat of the Assyrian forces proves the truth of Isaiah's prophecies, which were addressed to Hezekiah but which concerned Sennacherib and his claims. The broad theological contention, that it is Yahweh, the God of Israel, who is controlling world events, determines the entire structure of the narrative. That this is the primary issue is fully anticipated by the prayer of Hezekiah in 2 Kings 19:14–19 // Isa. 37:14–20. We can draw the conclusion therefore that the speeches of the Rabshakeh and the prophecies of Hezekiah occupy a constitutive place in the narrative, which can scarcely be said simply to have been composed in the interests of reporting an event.

There are, however, a number of features relating to both these speeches of the Rabshakeh and the prophecies of Isaiah which give cause for reflection.[5] It becomes clear from the report given of Sennacherib's defeat outside Jerusalem that this far exceeds in scope and severity what either the speeches of the Rabshakeh or the prophecies of Isaiah had led the reader to expect. The primary focus of the former is the claim that none of the gods of other nations defeated by Assyria had availed to save their worshippers. Correspondingly the assurance of the latter is that Sennacherib will be unable to take Jerusalem and will return to his homeland frustrated of his purpose, since Yahweh will certainly defend his city.

It comes as a singular surprise therefore to learn that a crushing defeat, wrought by the direct intervention of God, was inflicted upon Sennacherib's army outside Jerusalem.

I have argued earlier that the fact that this action exceeds the expected conclusion that is anticipated by the prophecy ascribed to Isaiah points to its being a relatively late intrusion into the account as a whole. Clearly, some action is required to demonstrate Sennacherib's inability to enter Jerusalem, but the massive destruction of his army represents an extreme expression of such inability. All the indications are that the account has been built up through an extended period of literary growth, with a consequent tendency to heighten the element of miraculous divine intervention.

It would appear probable therefore that the report of this angelic slaughter belongs to the very latest stage in the formation of the story. Moreover, since it is this verse which marks the sharpest departure from what is otherwise known of the events of 701 B.C.E., we must also conclude that it represents a quite exaggerated estimate of these events. Accordingly, I have argued in my earlier study that this verse was most probably added at a stage when the two narratives which Stade designated as A and B were already combined.[6] Those who would locate it in one of these literary strands ascribe to it source B.

However, we need probably to go further than this and to regard Stade's all-inclusive division of the report of Jerusalem's deliverance between two closely parallel literary sources as no more than a provisional assessment.

Clearly we are faced in this narrative with the literary deposit of a tradition concerning a major event in Judah's history which was extensively reflected upon and which has left its mark, not only on the final form of the Deuteronomic History (DtrG), but also upon the book of Isaiah.[7] Once these wider affinities are taken fully into consideration it would seem virtually certain that the historical and theological concerns which have given rise to the composition of the narrative regarding Jerusalem's deliverance were concerns which were keenly felt over a prolonged period of time. They have been given expression in more than one way and are prominently to be seen in a major strand of redactional work woven into the collection of Isaiah's prophecies in Isaiah 1—35 (notably in Isa. 8:9–10; 10:27b–34; 14:28–32; 29:5–8; and 31:5).[8]

From the perspective of authorship and origin therefore we must conclude that the process of formation which has given rise to the narrative of 2 Kings 18:13–19:37 // Isa. 36:1–37:38 was an extended and wide-ranging one.[9] The authors who have been responsible for developing this narrative did not work in isolation, nor can it have been composed simply to form a self-contained addition to the Deuteronomistic History.[10] At many points it deviates considerably from established concerns of the Deuteronomistic School. Furthermore, its authors can clearly be seen to have drawn extensively upon a written collection of Isaianic prophecies.

Several additions and expansions have been made to the narrative in the process of its composition, and, in its finished form, it cannot be separated from the story of Hezekiah's sickness which follows it. This story illustrates the king's piety and faith, a feature which has a strong bearing upon how the story of Jerusalem's deliverance from Sennacherib is to be understood. Compare 2 Kings 20:6; Isa. 38:6. In a similar fashion, the emphasis upon the need for total trust in Yahweh, especially when contrasted with the faithlessness of Ahaz at the time of the Syro-Ephraimite crisis (cf. Isa. 7:9), is reflected in a number of passages preserved in Isaiah 1—35.[11]

Nor is the final form of the story of Jerusalem's escape from the clutches of Sennacherib in 701 B.C.E. to be understood apart from the account of the visit of the Babylonian emissaries sent by Merodach-baladan in 2 Kings 20:12–19. Quite evidently, this account, with its advance warning of a humiliating defeat for the royal house of Judah at the hands of a future Babylonian aggressor, has a major theological purpose. It has been designed to assist the reader to understand why Jerusalem and the Davidic monarchy suffered more severely under the Babylonians in 598 (and 587) B.C.E. than was the case in 701 B.C.E. when Sennacherib planned to attack Jerusalem (so especially 2 Kings 20:17–18 // Isa. 39:6–7). The contrast between the two situations has called forth the inclusion of the warning given to Hezekiah after the visit of the Babylonia emissaries, and has also contributed greatly to the composition of the account of Jerusalem's deliverance in 701 B.C.E.

Overall, therefore, it would appear to be the case that the narrative of Jerusalem's miraculous deliverance from Sennacherib in 701 B.C.E. is built up from several component elements which have been composed over an extended period of time. This period certainly extended beyond the time of crisis for Jerusalem and the Davidic monarchy in 598 and 587 B.C.E. Prominent among these elements in the composition of the narrative would appear to be two loosely parallel accounts of the course of events relating to the confrontation between Hezekiah and Sennacherib. However these have undoubtedly received additions and expansions which are in line with the interests which have led to the addition of the two narrative sequels as well as some prominent redactional work evident in the formation of Isaiah 1—35.

What we have in these narratives, therefore, is the result of the bringing together and expansion of a cluster of traditions which had as their focal centre the recognition that, when seen in the light of later events, Jerusalem and its royal house had experienced a remarkable deliverance in 701 B.C.E. This recognition, that experience of events which occurred long after those of 701 B.C.E. is reflected in the account of what happened then, has an important bearing on the interpretation of both the contents of the speeches ascribed to the Rabshakeh and to the prophecies ascribed to Isaiah.

The claim that a massive disaster overtook Sennacherib's army in 701 B.C.E. is fully in line with a number of prophecies threatening such an eventuality ascribed to the prophet Isaiah and contained within Isaiah 1—35. Accordingly, the account of this event, which reflected so signally upon the importance of Jerusalem and the Davidic dynasty in the divine purpose, does not stand isolated from a literary point of view, but must be related to the question of the origin of these prophecies.

The Origin and Date of the Narratives

The conclusions that we have reached so far lead us to recognize that additions appear to have been made to the narrative account of Jerusalem's deliverance in 701 B.C.E. at more than one stage. Furthermore, these additions are not simply to be understood as the consequence of a desire to heighten the significance of what happened in 701 B.C.E. in the context of the literary composition of the Deuteronomistic History, but relate closely to the editing of the collection of Isaiah's prophecies.

Since the work of W. Gesenius and B. Stade the conclusion has been widely maintained that the report of Jerusalem's deliverance in 701 B.C.E. was originally composed for incorporation into 2 Kings, from whence it has been borrowed and secondarily incorporated into the collection of Isaiah's prophecies.[12] However, the close connection with the editorial strand in the latter collection, which anticipates a massive defeat for Sennacherib outside Jerusalem, indicates the importance of this link with the Isaianic corpus. Furthermore, there are features of the narrative which demonstrate beyond question that it fits only awkwardly and somewhat obliquely into the general framework of the Deuteronomistic History. A number of scholars have therefore argued that it is an expansion of the original DtrG and the extent to which it can be called "Deuteronomistic" is very questionable.[13] Certainly its appeal to direct divine intervention through the action of the angel of Yahweh is markedly out of character with the subtle and hidden understanding of divine providence which otherwise pervades that history. Although its prominent concern with Jerusalem and the Davidic royal house is broadly in keeping with major features of the Deuteronomistic ideology, we must conclude that it has been incorporated at a relatively late stage into the Deuteronomistic work. The question arises, therefore, whether all three of the Hezekiah-Isaiah narratives formed a complete unit in their present form when added to DtrG, or whether further additions were introduced after this incorporation had taken place. Such issues have a particular bearing upon the question of the origin of the prophecies ascribed to Isaiah. If the link between the narratives and the scroll of Isaiah's prophecies is given full weight, then it is most easy to conclude that the incorporation into DtrG took place when all three of the narratives were virtually in their extant shape.

Overall, the question whether the narrative concerning Jerusalem's deliverance belongs more originally and directly to DtrG than it does to the book of Isaiah does not have a simple answer. The widespread assumption that the relationship to DtrG is primary is not at all borne out by the facts. The fact that DtrG already contained a report of the events that took place between Hezekiah and Sennacherib in 2 Kings 18:13–16 has been a long-standing cause of difficulty for historians. Over against this the more extended, and more controversial, account of Jerusalem's deliverance shows every sign of its having been incorporated into DtrG later, probably in a form close to that which it now has. In any case the assumption that the narrative account of Jerusalem's deliverance was composed for inclusion in the Deuteronomistic History has led to a serious tendency to ignore the importance of the connections which the Isaiah-Hezekiah narratives have with the Isaianic corpus of prophecies.

The Meaning of the Prophecies

When we look closely at the prophecies ascribed to Isaiah in 2 Kings 19:21–34 // Isa. 37:22–35, we find that they are of a threefold character. The first of them in 2 Kings 19:21–28 (//Isa. 37:22–29) is addressed directly to Sennacherib as the king of Assyria and sharply rebukes him for his claim as a world-conqueror which reveals the sin of *hybris*.

The condemnation implicit in this prophecy compares closely with the rebuke and threat in the prophecy ascribed to Isaiah in Isa. 10:5–15 and also with the rebuke of the Babylonian tyrant in Isa. 14:4–21 (cf. also Isa. 2:12–22).

The second prophecy in 2 Kings 19:21–28 (// Isa. 37:30–32) affirms the giving of a sign to Hezekiah the king of Judah that he will be delivered from his Assyrian oppressor. It gives the reason for this in Yahweh's special regard for Jerusalem and the dynasty of David, not in any specific blasphemous affront that the Assyrian ruler has perpetrated against Yahweh. The giving of a "sign" recalls the fact that the report of Hezekiah's sickness also involved the giving of a "sign" (2 Kings 20:8–11 // Isa. 38:7–8). Furthermore there are strong echoes of the similar giving of a sign to Ahaz by Isaiah in Isa. 7:11, 14. There is no direct connection with the rebuttal of Sennacherib's boastful claims, although the form of the prophecy indicates that it has been designed to reinforce an already known assurance from God which looks for Jerusalem's restoration after ruination.

Undoubtedly, the notion of a remnant has been taken from the name of Isaiah's child Shear-jashub mentioned in Isa. 7:3, but the significance attached to the name has been considerably changed. Further reinterpretations of the Shear-jashub name are to be found in Isa. 10:20–23, which may, or may not, be closely contemporaneous with the usage in 2 Kings 19:30, 31.

The third of the Isaianic prophecies of the narrative we are concerned with is set in 2 Kings 19:32–34 (// Isa. 37:33–35) and is the easiest of the three to interpret. It is addressed "concerning the king of Assyria" and affirms categorically that he will not enter the city of Jerusalem but will return home by the way that he came:

> Therefore thus has Yahweh said concerning the king of Assyria: He shall not come into this city, or shoot an arrow there, or come before it with a shield, or cast up a siege-mound against it. By the way that he came, by the same he shall return, and he shall not come into this city, says Yahweh. For I will defend this city to save it, for my own sake and for the sake of my servant David. (2 Kings 19:32–34 // Isa. 37:33–35)

Virtually all those critics who have recognised the complex and piecemeal literary structure of the narrative account of Jerusalem's deliverance in 701 B.C.E. have seen this prophecy as the most original and fundamental of the three. At one time it must have stood alone as the report of Isaiah's reply to Hezekiah, serving as a rejoinder to the boasts of the Rabshakeh on behalf of Sennacherib. It is therefore undoubtedly to be recognised as the most original of the three prophecies and the one that belongs structurally to the earliest form of the Isaiah-Hezekiah narratives.

In its own way this prophecy is noteworthy since, from a literary point of view, it fits smoothly and necessarily into the expanded account of what happened in 701 B.C.E. It is also noteworthy that, from an historical point of view, it raises no serious problems concerning the course of the military action that took place which led up to Hezekiah's surrender (2 Kings 18:13–16).

Since I have already drawn attention to the surprise occasioned by the subsequent report in the narrative (2 Kings 19:35 // Isa. 37:36) of a remarkable defeat of Sennacherib's forces, we may say little more about this prophecy here. It belongs in a fundamental way to the narrative since the Rabshakeh's speech and Hezekiah's prayer undoubtedly call for some response from God. Its role in the account is wholly appropriate, although its presence serves to draw attention to the fact that the other two prophecies ascribed to Isaiah which precede it are clearly less homogeneous in their context.

The most informative feature of this prophecy therefore would appear to lie in the fact that it belonged to the narrative structure before the highly dramatic report of the destruction of Sennacherib's army was added. It sticks closely to the historical facts and draws its awareness of Yahweh's control over the events of 701 B.C.E. from the fact that Sennacherib did not enter Jerusalem nor wage any battle in the city.

Contrastingly, we may conclude that the other two prophecies represent additions which were made later, most probably when the narrative was close to its final form. In this case, these additional prophecies may be assumed to have known about the claim that Yahweh had acted through his angel to destroy the forces that threatened Jerusalem. However, they are not intrinsically necessary to the story that unfolds, and both of them point to concerns and interests which lie beyond the narrative itself. The first rebukes Sennacherib's *hybris* and affirms that Yahweh is in control of all historical events, even when a far superior military power (Assyria) confronts a very weak one (Judah). The second of these additional prophecies presumes that Judah and Jerusalem have suffered a major military defeat and destruction and proceeds to give assurance that there will be a surviving remnant for the house of Judah and that this will be based in Jerusalem.

The Prophecy concerning Sennacherib's *Hybris*

The question of the time of origin of the prophecies ascribed to Isaiah concerning Sennacherib's threat to Jerusalem in 701 B.C.E. requires close attention. In many respects these prophecies show features which are closely related to those of the speeches ascribed to the Assyrian Rabshakeh. These have now been the subject of a good deal of close attention in the light of known Assyrian military and propagandistic practices and the extent to which they reflect details of religious reforms introduced by Hezekiah. Overall, however, we may reaffirm positions that have been outlined earlier.[14] These are that the speeches have been composed to provide a basic feature of the narrative concerning Jerusalem's deliverance and reflect an awareness of the situation that developed in Judah long after 701 B.C.E. They are not firsthand reports, therefore, but have been composed at some considerable interval after the event they report.

Clearly much the same is true, as we have already noted, of the prophecies ascribed to Isaiah. The "original" prophecy is that of 2 Kings 19:32–34 (//Isa. 37:33–35), which presents in quite brief compass a divine response to the Assyrian ruler's boastfulness expressed through the Rabshakeh. It belonged to the narrative from its earliest form and requires no further analysis other than what has already been noted concerning its historically restrained expectation of the manner of Sennacherib's divine humiliation. What occasions surprise is that two further prophecies have been added to the narrative at all, since they are not strictly necessary for the successful completion of the story.

Since the most original of the prophecies already contains a rebuttal of Sennacherib's boastful pride, the addition of a much enlarged condemnation of his *hybris* appears at first sight to be excessive. However, it presents a powerfully ironic rebuttal of Sennacherib's claims to be the author of his victories and to be in control of events. His very claims to success are a condemnation of his sin of pride, for which he must necessarily suffer punishment:

> This is what Yahweh has spoken concerning him:
> She despises you, she scorns you—
>   the virgin daughter of Zion;
> she wags her head behind you—
>   the daughter of Jerusalem.
> Whom have you mocked and belittled
>   Against whom have you raised your voice
> and proudly lifted up your eyes?
>   Against the Holy One of Israel!
> By your messengers you have mocked Yahweh,
>   and you have said, With my many chariots
> I have gone up the tops of the mountains,
>   to the furthermost parts of Lebanon;
> I felled its tallest cedars,
>   its choicest cypresses;
> I came to its remotest hideout,
>   its densest forest,
> I dug wells and drank foreign waters,
>   and dried up with the sole of my foot
>   all the streams of Egypt.
> Have you not heard
>   that I determined it long ago?
> I planned from ancient times
>   what I now cause to happen,
> that you should make fortified cities
>   into heaps of ruins,
> so that their inhabitants, devoid of strength,
>   are confounded and ruined,
> and have become no stronger than plants of the field
>   of feeble grass,
> like grass on the housetops,
>   withered as soon as it grows.
> I know when you sit down
>   and when you go out and come in,
> and how you have raged against me.
> Because you have raged against me
>   and your arrogance has come to my attention,

I will put my hook in your nose
   and my bit in your mouth,
and I will turn you back on the way
   by which you came.
(2 Kings 19:21–28 // Isa. 37:22–29)

Since we may regard it as certain that both prophecies have been added at a stage subsequent to the composition of the original prophecy, both of them represent quite late intrusions into the overall material of the narratives. Since the first prophecy must have been added at quite a long interval after the occurrence of the events of 701 B.C.E. this prophecy condemning Sennacherib's *hybris* must have been composed later still.

In my study of the Isaiah narratives published in 1980 I adopted the view that the belief that a great defeat had been inflicted upon Sennacherib's forces outside Jerusalem could best be interpreted against the background of Josiah's attempt to reestablish a united kingdom of Israel in the wake of the collapse of Assyrian control in the region.[15] Certainly the upsurge of a strong "Zion theology" during Josiah's reign is intelligible as an interpretation of Judah's survival under Assyrian pressure when contrasted with the collapse and dismemberment of the Northern Kingdom.

However, the evident desire in the narrative to use the story of what happened in 701 B.C.E. to provide a basis of theological reasoning to uphold resistance against the sixth-century threat from Babylon needs now to be more fully considered. Not only has C. Hardmeier interpreted the material in the light of resistance to Babylon in Zedekiah's reign, but both K.A.D. Smelik and F. J. Gonçalves have noted the extent to which the narrative reflects awareness of the disasters of 598 and 587 B.C.E. of Jerusalem. It is also important that we should bear in mind a significant feature of the account of the visit of the Babylonian emissaries of Merodach-baladan which I noted in an earlier study.[16] This concerns the striking fact that, although a very detailed fortelling is made of the disaster that was to befall the Davidic royal house in 598 B.C.E. when Jehoiachin was taken into Babylonian exile, surprisingly, no hint is given of the far worse catastrophes that befell both royal house and city in 587 B.C.E..

All the indications are that, after the downfall of the Northern Kingdom in the last quarter of the eighth century B.C.E., a political theology that was strongly pro-Judah, pro-Davidic dynasty, and pro-Zion emerged in a very aggressive and nationalistic form in the court circles of Judah during the reign of Josiah. It then continued, with shifts and modifications, during the subsequent reigns of Jehoiakim and Zedekiah. The fact that it survived for several decades means that it can only be a matter of relative significance and conjecture to determine at what stage particular aspects of its claims arose. The most urgent and important question, therefore, is not whether such a

Zion-centered political theology emerged as a major factor in Judah's political and religious life as early as Josiah's reign, but whether such a theology could have continued after 587 B.C.E. It is altogether credible that a strong belief in Zion's inviolability, and the related assurance that Yahweh could protect his people, if necessary, by the intervention of an angel from heaven, could remain a part of Judean life after the catastrophe of 587 B.C.E..

Already, and in line with the suggestions of Smelik and Gonçalves, I have suggested that this was the case.[17] Far from the ruination of the Babylonian destruction of 587 B.C.E. leading to the abandonment of all hope surrounding Jerusalem's role as Yahweh's chosen abode, the opposite was the case. Accordingly it seems perfectly credible that the most extreme affirmations of Yahweh's special protection for Jerusalem in 701 B.C.E. arose *after*, rather than *before*, the disasters of 587 B.C.E..

If this was the case, then this situation provides us with the best clue to uncovering the origin and purpose of this additional prophecy rebuking Sennacherib's *hybris* ascribed to Isaiah. Its presentation of an extremely sharp rebuttal of Sennacherib's claims to power and its distinctive ironic style match closely the ironically presented boasts of the Assyrian ruler conveyed through the Rabshakeh's speeches.

By the skillful use of hyperbole, drawing upon the recognition that no human being can usurp the throne of God, the author of this prophetic condemnation discloses the absurdity of the Assyrian ruler's claims. May we not then conclude that this prophecy, which rebuts all human pretensions to possess the power to determine events, has been added because there was a felt need to reinforce yet more forcibly the assertion that Yahweh was in control of all human events? In other words should we not conclude that this further prophecy attributed to Isaiah has been added in the wake of 587 B.C.E. in order to strengthen the force of the basic theological argument of the narrative? The original narrative drew confidence from the knowledge that Sennacherib had not entered Jerusalem in 701 B.C.E. However, once the catastrophes of 598 and 587 B.C.E. had taken place, a stronger basis of hope was sought after. This led on the one hand to a reaffirmation of the argument that all human claims to power must ultimately surrender before the supreme power of God. It is this that the condemnation of Sennacherib expresses. At the same time, a conviction emerged that a supreme demonstration of Yahweh's power had already been made outside Jerusalem in 701 B.C.E. Both developments were a form of response to the disaster brought upon Jerusalem in 587 B.C.E..

In 587 B.C.E. Yahweh had clearly not defended his city, so that some element of theodicy was needed to explain why this had occurred. By emphasising the necessity of faith on the part of the king some element of conditional human response was introduced. This is then well expressed through the story of Hezekiah's sickness and subsequent recovery. At the same time, by introducing a heightened emphasis upon Yahweh's intolerance of all human pride, the author of the prophecy rebuking Sennacherib's *hybris* added a further note of explanation why the action of 701 B.C.E. had been unique. At the same time he reaffirmed his conviction that Yahweh alone determined the course of historical events. No human being could withstand the plan and purpose of Yahweh.

The Significance of the Prophecy of the Remnant

The content of the "sign" in the second of the Isaianic prophecies is striking:

> And this shall be the sign for you; this year you shall eat what grows of itself, and in the next year what grows up from this; then in the third year sow, and reap, and plant vineyards, and eat their produce. For the surviving remnant of the house of Judah shall again take root downward, and bear fruit upward; for out of Jerusalem shall go forth a remnant, and out of Mount Zion a band of survivors. The determination of Yahweh will achieve this. (2 Kings 19:29–31 // Isa. 37:30–32)

Not only does it appear that the concern that Hezekiah should receive a "sign" from Yahweh has been suggested by Isaiah's offer of a sign to Ahaz, but the content of the sign appears to have arisen directly on the basis of the threat reported in Isa. 17:4–6. This consisted of a warning by Isaiah of national ruin threatened upon the house of Jacob at the time of the Syro-Ephraimite crisis. In this threat the imagery of a destroyed harvest with only gleanings left is used as an indication of impending judgment. In the prophecy of 2 Kings 19:29–31 the imagery of the gleanings left after a harvest is taken up and redeveloped as a sign of hope. From this the idea that the gleanings constitute the "remnant" of a harvest has led on to the use of the concept of a remnant of a people which is turned into an assurance that such a remnant will survive in Jerusalem. This compares very closely and directly with the isolated assurance set in Isa. 14:32, a brief note which concludes a most significant section in the book of Isaiah (Isa. 13:1–14.32).

The concern with a remnant of the house of Judah, located in Jerusalem, is the most striking feature of this prophecy. If the case for recognizing that the prophecy which condemns Sennacherib's *hybris* has been added after 587 B.C.E. carries considerable plausibility, then the case for a similar dating of the prophecy concerning the remnant in Jerusalem (2 Kings 19:29–31) is stronger still. That there was a community of some kind which survived in Judah after 587 B.C.E., at first with its centre at Mizpah, is shown by the reports of Jeremiah 40—43. That the temple site, too, continued to be regarded as of major significance after 587 B.C.E. is highlighted by the report of the pilgrimage to the temple site by men from Shechem, Shiloh, and Samaria, mentioned in Jer. 41:5.

However, in some ways even more noteworthy from a sociopolitical standpoint is the evident conviction with which the narrative reports of Jeremiah 40—43 seek to discredit the community that survived in Judah after 587 B.C.E.[18] As is widely evident from the edited form of the prophetic books of Jeremiah and Ezekiel, the entire focus of hope expressed in these books is of a return from exile, led by those who had been taken to Babylon. They are claimed to form effectively the remnant—the body of survivors of the former kingdom of Judah—from which the new Israel will emerge.

All of this draws very considerable attention to the strikingly contrasted view presented in the "Isaianic" prophecy of 2 Kings 19:29–31 (// Isa. 37:30–32). Moreover, such a view of the central position occupied by the concept of Zion in this remnant theology is further supported from Isa. 14:32 and Isa. 4:2–6. These prophecies, which are certainly to be ascribed to a post-587 B.C.E. date, set the concept of a remnant located in Zion (see especially Isa. 4:3–4) in the forefront of the hope of restoration. In broad terms the original Zion concept of a holy mountain of Yahweh, replete with all the overtones of an older mythological interpretation, has been recast into a prophetic assurance about the political and religious leadership to be exercised by a company of survivors in Jerusalem. May it not therefore be the case that the addition of the prophecy concerning the remnant in 2 Kings 19:29–31 (// Isa. 37:30–32) marks a very important shift in the extension and development of the political theology of the Isaiah narratives? The Davidic-Zion orientation that formed its original nucleus has been modified and reminted in the light of the tragic events of 587 B.C.E. to incorporate a new doctrine of the remnant. This remnant, however, is emphatically not a remnant of survivors scattered among the nations, which otherwise occupies the centre stage of the books of Jeremiah and Ezekiel. Instead it is strikingly, and apparently exclusively, a remnant located in Jerusalem. The necessity and importance of this location has been dictated by the origins of its basis in the earlier Zion-David political theology which flourished in the latter days of Judah, and which has been given its most important literary expression in the book of Isaiah.

If this is the correct explanation for the fact that the original prophecy ascribed to Isaiah in the narrative of Jerusalem's deliverance in 701 B.C.E. has been expanded by the addition of two further ones, then two additional points may be made. In the first place, such a conclusion strongly reinforces the contention that the formation of the narratives of 2 Kings 18:17–20:19 has been made in close relationship to the editing of the book of Isaiah. Not only are materials drawn from the collection of Isaiah's prophecies, but quite central themes which have served to shape that collection are set in the forefront of the narratives. In general perspective, although connections with Deuteronomistic interests are recognisable, the narratives are quite centrally concerned to show how Isaiah's prophecies are to be understood in the light of events, especially the events of 598 and 587 B.C.E. attendant upon Babylonian imperial oppression of Judah.

The second point is less evident, but potentially even more significant. This concerns the fact that one of the most marked characteristics of the prophecies of Isaiah 40—55 is their extraordinary extension and development of the concept of "Zion" (Isa. 40:9; 41:27; 46:13; 51:11, 16; 52:7f.). In particular the apparent concern to address the exiles in Babylon as themselves still constituting part of Yahweh's "Zion" is remarkable. The concept has been so extended that its theological significance has overridden most of its original geographical significance. Should we not explain this as a consequence of the fusing together of the ideas of "remnant" and "Zion" which we find in 2 Kings 19:31 (// Isa. 37:32)?

Undoubtedly, such a combination of thematic ideas is exceptional, since in origin the ideas of divine protection associated with the Zion concept were at the opposite end of the semantic spectrum from those associated with the threatening connotation of the idea of "remnant." Yet by combining them together, a workable image of religious tradition and faith was formed which offered a basis for the hope of the restoration of Israel. In turn, the combination of such thematic concepts has required a significant reminting of the Zion ideology in the prophecies of Isaiah 40—55 so as to include a hope for the survivors of Israel scattered among the nations.

3

The Messianic Hope
in the Old Testament

Anyone who comes to the Old Testament from a Christian perspective is likely to do so with a strong expectation of finding in it a clear and positive message concerning the promise of a coming messiah. The reason for this is to be found in the way in which the writings of the New Testament refer back to passages from the Old Testament in which they discern such a message, and most of all because of the centrality of the title "Messiah" for the interpretation of the person of Jesus of Nazareth. The familiar title "Christ" applied to Jesus is simply an interpretation, by means of a latinized form of the Greek *chrestos*, of the Hebrew word *mashiah*, anointed one.

We have only to look at a number of passages in the gospel story to see how central a place is given to this belief that God had, centuries before the actual birth of Jesus, foretold of his coming. We can simply point to the question posed to Jesus by the disciples of John the Baptist in Matt. 11:3: "Are you he who is to come, or shall we look for another?" The answer given to these disciples is clearly intended the make reference back to the prophecy of Isa. 35:5–6 and to imply the affirmative sense that Jesus is the long-expected messiah. In a wholly similar vein the account in Matthew 21 of Jesus' triumphal entry into Jerusalem on Palm Sunday, riding on a donkey, is shown to be a fulfilment of the prophecy of Zech. 9:9. Jesus is the messiah, and the promise that such an "Anointed One" would come at God's appointed time is understood to be fundamental to the meaning and purpose of the Old Testament. It is not simply that such a promise is assumed to be present in the Old Testament, but that it is taken to be the central and dominant feature of it, most of all in the books of prophecy, but certainly also in the Psalms and even in the Law.

Such a broad general perspective upon the theological meaning of the Old Testament is fully supported by other aspects of Christian teaching and tradition. The ever-sustained popularity of G. F. Handel's oratorio *The Messiah* since it was first performed in 1742 can be readily backed up further by looking at a number of widely adopted liturgical practices. The entire season of Advent in the ecclesiastical year is maintained under the claim that the preparation for the celebration of the birth of Jesus of Nazareth mirrors

49

the long centuries during which the Jewish people awaited the coming of the messiah. Such a claim is then readily illustrated by a number of passages taken from the Old Testament which are presented as expressing such a hope. They comprise a corpus of texts which are taken to constitute, with little further question, the Jewish doctrine of the messiah.

There can be no questioning the fact that, throughout much of the history of the Christian Church, interest in the Old Testament has largely centred upon attention to such a doctrine of the messiah as the most significant way in which the two parts, or Testaments, of the Bible are related to each other. It is easy enough to put this in a slightly more abstract way in terms of Promise and Fulfilment,[1] but in general, even when this is done, the general theme of Promise, as applied to the Old Testament, requires to be focused more directly into that of the promise of a coming messiah.

It may then come as something of a surprise that virtually all of the major books on Old Testament theology say very little at all about such a messianic hope and, even when they do, do so in a very guarded and circumscribed way.[2] Many centuries of sharp, and often bitter, debate between Jews and Christians over the interpretation of the most familiar of the biblical passages concerned in the discussion necessarily urge us to caution. Moreover, it was largely as a consequence of controversies and arguments that deeply rocked the English church during the early eighteenth century that Christian biblical scholarship felt itself compelled to drop the primary form of its claim that the Old Testament presented a promise of the coming of a messiah.

During the nineteenth century the debate entered a new phase and took on a new form through a quite striking clash of approaches adopted by two markedly different scholars, who were both teachers at the same university. This was the newly founded Prussian university of Berlin, and the two scholars concerned were the celebrated F.D.E. Schleiermacher (1768–1834) and E. W. von Hengstenberg (1802–1869). The latter had been appointed to Berlin to succeed W.M.L. de Wette (1780–1849) in the hope of giving to the theological faculty there a more conservative image.

It is not too much to claim that the clash of approaches and methods that came to light in von Hengstenberg's attempt to rebut certain of the basic contentions of Schleiermacher has remained a very significant dividing line in Christian Old Testament scholarship. One approach appeared to be modern, rational, and liberal, whereas the rejoinder to it has appeared conservative, traditional, and uncritically believing in its emphasis.

Of course the arguments of neither scholar would be repeated today precisely in the form used at the time, but nevertheless, once a sharp division has occurred, it is often difficult to remove afterwards the feeling that a choice has to be made between two irreconcilable alternatives. It is in any case clear that, after the initial form of the debate had lapsed, the subject of messianic hope and the Old Testament became a particularly difficult and divisive one to deal with. It is undoubtedly significant that A. F. Kirkpatrick, in his very influential and popular Warburton lectures of 1886–90 under the title *The Doctrine of the Prophets*,[3] could virtually ignore the question of the messianic hope completely. It could be replaced by a short chapter showing that the coming of Jesus marked the goal of prophecy.

However the fact that the major books on Old Testament theology which have appeared during the twentieth century have had very little to say about a messianic hope in the Old Testament must be regarded as surprising. It is true that many of the issues that affect Jewish-Christian dialogue do not so much arise from the strictly Old Testament side but may be thought instead to belong to the field of New Testament and Intertestamental studies. In this an investigation into the political circumstances of the first century A.D. which led Jews to look for a coming deliverer figure can be traced. That they did so after the image of the archetypal figure of David the king, and so drew inspiration from certain passages of the sacred scriptures which portrayed the role of the king in exceptionally brilliant colours, should not occasion surprise.

There are, however, two factors which made it appropriate to rethink some of the basic issues concerning the significance of the messianic hope in the Old Testament. (1) It is especially true in this subject that the methods used by scholars in interpreting the text of the Bible have a very considerable impact upon the meaning arrived at (and perhaps more significantly the level of importance attaching to the meaning). The changing attitudes to the subject of messianic expectation in the Old Testament have been strongly reflective of changing methods in studying it. (2) Much discussion of the past twenty years has focused on the question whether or not it is appropriate to strive for a distinctively "biblical" theology that would be neither simply "Old" nor "New" Testament in its historical and literary commitment, but would instead endeavour to deal with the Bible as a literary whole. If such is possible and desirable, then it would seem clear that the question of the messianic hope ought to have a prominent place in such a biblical theology.

We can present a very brief sketch of the way in which the subject has come to engage modern biblical scholarship. After the tensions, bloodshed, and deep divisions of the period of the Civil War in seventeenth-century England, the eventual restoration of the monarchy (1660) led on appropriately to the passing of an Act of Toleration (1689) which excluded only Roman Catholics and Unitarians from the national church. Since religion had been a major ingredient in the division of the nation, the removal of excessive religious distinctions was a necessary step towards recovering a new basis of national unity. John Locke (1632–1704) put forward the idea that

"Jesus is the Messiah" was the simplest and minimal Christian commitment. More than this could lead to argument and division, even though most would wish to express a commitment to much more. Yet how could one test and prove that Jesus was the messiah, if the issue was disputed? It was this that led to the debates of the early eighteenth century and to the critical re-examination of those biblical texts which were believed to have foretold the coming of a messiah, in many cases several centuries before they were fulfilled.[4] The upshot of these debates was to force the Christian church to recognize that in no single case did the passages concerned bear the interpretation that had been later placed upon them.

In order to accommodate such a difficult and unwelcome conclusion the more critical minds of the church argued that prophecy could have a "double meaning"—an original literal one in which the fuller messianic significance of the message would not have been known and a later "spiritual" one which would only become plain in the passage of time. This was how the situation lay until the time of Schleiermacher when, in his reconstruction of the doctrine in *The Christian Faith*,[5] he argued that Christianity possessed only an accidental and historical link with Judaism, not a necessary and theological one. That Jesus should have been described and understood as the messiah awaited in Judaism was therefore peripheral and dispensable, even though it was historically accurate and valid. This was the position that von Hengstenberg tried so hard to counter in his extensive work entitled *The Christology of the Old Testament* and first published in three volumes in Berlin between 1829 and 1835.[6] In spite of its ability to appeal to what had always been regarded as a central tenet of Christian doctrine, von Hengstenberg's presentation resorted to a wholly arbitrary and artificial pattern of biblical interpretation. Individual elements of the doctrine of the messiah were treated as disclosed by God in an arbitrary and random fashion throughout the long history of Israel. It was an attempt at a *tour de force* in biblical exegesis, but it foundered on its complete inability to reconcile its conclusions with the equally secure foundations in Christian tradition of the principle that biblical interpretation must be based on a truly historical and literal understanding of the text. There could be no circumventing the conclusions that had been arrived at in the debates of a century earlier.

Although conservative scholarship attempted to retain some features of an earlier messianic doctrine to be found in the Old Testament, the whole trend for the remainder of the nineteenth century was in the direction of abandoning it. Perhaps more strictly we should say that the aim was rather to replace it by the notion that the entire history of Israel, including the experience of prophecy, could be regarded as a "preparation" in the Old Testament for the coming of Jesus.[7] How effectively this was done may be a matter for debate, but, in general, it is clear that history, rather than messianic prophecy, became the key to understanding how the Old Testament could be thought to find its completion and goal in the New. Messianic prophecy no longer appeared to be particularly necessary, so that nothing seemed to be lost by conceding the point that passages in prophecy and psalmody that had at one time been thought to foretell the coming of such a messianic figure could not, in their original and literal sense, be said to do so.

As the belief was largely that prophets had, long in advance of the event, foretold the coming of the messiah, so scholarship found it possible to recognize a new area of importance for understanding Christian interpretation of Jesus as the messiah. This lay in the Jewish world of thought and political expectation that formed the immediate background to the emergence of Christianity. It is evident from the Gospels that the evangelists wrote in the conviction that it was well known that the Jewish people were expecting a messiah. Most early Christian polemic against the Jews centreed, not upon whether Jews were expecting a messiah, but rather upon whether Jesus was that figure. The study of the Jewish background to the New Testament, itself a very complex and demanding field of study, thereby provided something of a replacement for the older attempts to trace the hope of a coming messiah in the prophecies of the Old Testament.

Nevertheless this opening up of the whole new area of Jewish background to the New Testament, most exemplified in the monumental work of Emil Schürer (1844–1910),[8] did not of itself dispose of the subject so far as the Old Testament was concerned. Clearly the Jewish exegetes and scholars of the first century A.D. had worked on the assumption that they were developing a doctrine that was truly to be found in the Old Testament. If the manner of their exegetical reasoning and techniques was mistaken, it had, nevertheless, undoubtedly been based on certain basic assumptions which are to be found in the Old Testament. A great gap needed to be filled therefore in demonstrating how Jewish messianic expectations of the New Testament period had emerged out of older hopes and affirmations which are demonstrably present in the Old Testament literature.

We may, nevertheless, sum up the position at the turn of the century so far as interest in messianic expectation was concerned. Critical interpretation of the Old Testament prophets had largely abandoned it on the understanding that the passages which had been central to establishing it could not support the meanings that had been claimed. Over against this there was a deep recognition that the historical development of the Old Testament religion of ancient Israel had been mediated to the early Christian church by the Judaistic background of the New Testament. It was here that the real seedbed of messianic doctrine was thought to be found. The questions that remained to be explored then seemed largely to focus on tracing whence this late Judaistic circle of ideas had originated.[9]

The first efforts at carrying the study further and seeking to rehabilitate the doctrine of the messiah as worthy of a major place in biblical interpretation are to be found almost entirely within the sphere of what we have come to term the "History-of-Religions" method of approach. This was largely a Göttingen-based group of scholars, among whom the most famous are Ernst Troeltsch, Hermann Gunkel, and Wilhelm Bousset.[10] That it was this group of scholars who revitalized scholarly interest in messianic expectation in ancient Israel should not surprise us in view of the fact that it was their approach which played a large role in emphasizing the importance of Intertestamental Judaism as the intellectual bridge between the two Testaments.

The subject, and the new methods of approaching it, attracted attention outside Germany so that, in a dissertation submitted for a doctorate in divinity at Cambridge and published in 1908 as *The Evolution of the Messianic Idea: A Study in Comparative Religion*,[11] W.O.E. Oesterley presented a fresh case for seeing the messianic idea as important to the Old Testament. His starting point was provided by a number of assumptions concerning ancient mythology and its preservation, albeit in fragmented remnants, in the Old Testament. Oesterley argued that such a mythology had shown a common pattern throughout the ancient Near East and that it projected forward into the future the idea of a "Golden Age." Within this coming idyllic era a divine "saviour figure" was to appear as an agent of the divine rule and a herald of the kingdom of God. Oesterley saw many variations in the way in which this mythological notion was presented. At times, as in Isa. 2:2–4, God was to be the messianic ruler, but in general Oesterley accepted the fundamental conviction that either a purely human ruler, as in Isa. 11:1–5, or a divine-human figure, as in Isa. 9:5–6, was expected to come. Overall Oesterley embraced the idea, widely accepted in the history-of-religions movement, that the coming golden age was portrayed as a return of an idyllic primeval age of the world's dawning.

It is symptomatic that Oesterley's book was influenced by the history-of-religions movement in biblical scholarship since much of the major interest in the subject in the twentieth century has been similarly affected. This is certainly the case with the posthumously published magmum opus from H. Gressmann (1877–1927) entitled *Der Messias*.[12] The work is far more detailed, and is more guardedly presented, than Oesterley's work, but it follows a closely similar path. What it introduces is a fuller realization that the primary textual focus for many of the ideas that appear in the messianic expectation is to be found in certain of the royal psalms. Gressmann singles out particularly Psalms 2, 72, and 110. Israel's kingship, which is assumed to have drawn many of its images and themes from the Amorites, and ultimately from Egypt, presents the king as a semi-divine ruler. He brings salvation, justice, and prosperity to his people. In the postexilic period, the disappointments and frustrations with the present political order led to a strongly focused projection of this picture of the ideal king into the future.

It is probably not necessary to dwell extensively upon the influence of other contributions from scholars along the lines which were originally marked out by Oesterley and Gressmann, and which belong to the influence of the history-of-religions movement more generally. This is the case with the work of A. Bentzen, *King and Messiah*,[13] originally published in German in 1948, and S. Mowinckel, *He That Cometh*,[14] originally published in Norwegian in 1951. The latter volume must certainly be regarded as the most important work on the subject published to date. Behind these two works, and a large number of shorter essays on the subject, lie the very voluminous discussions and controversies that took place among scholars on the subject of the nature and ideology of Israel's kingship.[15] It is quite impossible to survey such a large range of material at this point. Its relevance for the study of messianic hope in the Old Testament was twofold. It is established beyond question that the imagery and titles accorded to the messiah were drawn from earlier titles applied to the reigning king of Israel. It also was able to show, at least in substantial measure, that most of the passages in psalmody and prophecy which had been taken by later Jews and Christians as fortellings of the messiah's coming were either directly addressed to the reigning king of Israel, or were assurances concerning the restoration of such a monarchy after its collapse in 587 B.C. I. Engnell, in particular, was eager to describe every king of Israel as a "messiah," or at least potentially so.[16] However this has only led to confusion in the use of terminology and certainly does not account for all of the features of the Jewish expectation of a messiah. It is in any case singularly worthy of note that none of the other nations which cherished such a high doctrine of kingship, in many cases far more pretentious and ideologically exalted than that of Israel, carried this forward into the formation of a messianic expectation. This, so far as we know, was a unique achievement of the Old Testament.

If it is the case that most of the imagery and many of the themes of what came to be understood as the messianic hope of ancient Israel originated in the elaborate, and mythologically oriented, ideology of kingship nurtured in the days when Israel had a king, then it still remains open to question what other factors so acted upon this ideology that it was projected forward in such a unique fashion. Undoubtedly the removal from office of Zedekiah, the last of the line of Davidic kings, by the Babylonians in 587 B.C. was a significant factor in this development.

This was clearly seen by S. Mowinckel, and it is a point that is given considerable weight in the more recent study by J. Becker, *Messianic Expectations in the Old Testament*.[17] Becker notes that a singularly important feature of

Old Testament messianic expectation lies in its inseparable connection with the dynasty of David. This cannot, however, simply be a consequence of what Becker calls "The Davidic monopoly," but must be linked to other factors, more genuinely prophetic in their character, than the political and historical considerations that shaped the course of the Davidic dynasty. Nevertheless it is a matter of very considerable importance that the mainstream of messianic expectation in the Old Testament period, right up to New Testament times, came to be far more concerned with the scion of the house of David than with the restoration of the kingship as such. Indeed, the restoration of a Jewish kingship under the Hasmoneans appears to have served only to encourage messianic expectation in a nonroyal direction, rather than to have satisfied it. Furthermore it became very important for the early Christian claims to the messianic office of Jesus that the messiah was not a king in any formal, or rigidly political, sense (cf. John 18:33–39).

This brings me to a point where it is possible to summarize the half-century of research which sought in the reconstruction of ancient Israel's ideology of kingship, prompted initially by the history-of-religions approach, the key to understanding the origin of messianic hope. This approach was able to shed light on many of its features, but certainly not upon all. Moreover, it could put forward only very broad speculations as to why that hope focused almost entirely upon the Davidic family of kings and why it could embrace some strongly anti-monarchic features. Clearly if there is one passage in the Old Testament which can deserve the title of the seedbed of the messianic hope it is that of 2 Sam. 7:1–17 and especially verse 16 itself: "Your house and your kingdom shall endure forever before me, your throne shall be established forever." Much scholarly debate has been devoted to seeking to unravel the oldest elements of what is stated in this celebrated passage and its links with the age of either David or Solomon.[18] This need not directly concern us, since it is the central role accorded to this promise in the Deuteronomistic History (Joshua–2 Kings) which has given to it so far-reaching a significance. This point was noted by Dennis J. McCarthy in an essay published in 1965,[19] and it has continued to draw extensive attention since then. In many ways it is this promise from the mouth of the prophet Nathan which has acted as a pivotal point around which the entire narrative tradition of the Old Testament has been built up. Nor is it without its significance upon later prophecy since, as J. Vermeylen has persuasively argued,[20] the key passages from the prophet Isaiah concerning the birth of the Immanuel child (Isa. 7:10–17) and the coming ruler of the house of David (Isa. 9:2–7; Heb. 1—6) have been influenced by a knowledge of this prophecy set in 2 Samuel 7. Moreover, this is also quite certainly the case in regard to those prophecies concerning the hope of restoring the Davidic monarchy after the Babylonian exile which are now to be found in all the major prophetic collections (cf. Isa. 11:1–5; Jer. 33:14–26; Ezek. 34:23f.; 37:24–28). We should certainly also note the importance of 2 Sam. 7:1–17 for the expectations that surrounded Zerubbabel and the work of rebuilding the temple in 521 to 516 B.C. (Ezra 3—6).

If we are to think of the royal ideology concerning the unique status of Israel's king as the "Son of God" as providing the bricks and mortar out of which the messianic hope emerged, then undoubtedly 2 Sam. 7:16 is the foundation on which it rested. Of course this prophetic promise was not messianic in its original sense, but rather a basic element of the political theology of the Israelite state. It has, however, through the exigencies of history and the way in which Israelite prophecy reacted to them, become a part of the projected shape of the restored Israel of the future. Even this projection into the future did not take place all at once, but by a series of steps. First the expectations of restoring the Davidic monarchy once the period of Babylonian exile had ended; then, as these hopes were disappointed and modified during the Persian era, the hope reappeared in a new form. The full evidence for this new form is not found until much later when we have the evidence of the New Testament and the Qumran community.

It is in respect of the formative role played by 2 Sam. 7:1–17 in the development of Israel's messianic hope that we can see why it has been so difficult for Old Testament theology to incorporate an effective treatment of the subject into its main structure. It is only when the foundational themes of the historical narratives of the Old Testament are examined as to their theological witness, and when the so-called secondary passages of the great prophetic collections are given due weight,[21] that the subject is set in a better perspective. On this front it would certainly appear that the aim of presenting an Old Testament theology within the framework of the full canonical scope of the Old Testament literature, such as B. S. Childs recommends should be attempted, ought to give more room for the emergence of Israel's messianic hope. In particular we can also see that, in such a connection, the recognition that, in acquiring their present canonical shape, many important passages of Old Testament prophecy have been subjected to a process of rereading and reinterpretation has a significant contribution to make. By the redactional setting that has been accorded to them in the extensive prophetic corpora of the Bible, many prominent sayings regarding the coming restoration of the Davidic kingship have been given a greatly extended meaning. This is very clearly the case, as Vermeylen has pointed out, in regard to the prophetic promise of Isa. 11:1–5. This saying was itself assuredly given its present position at some time during, or shortly after, the Babylonian exile. In itself it has been designed to take up, and carry forward, the more central promise given earlier in Isa. 9.1–6 (Eng. vv. 2–7). It is an assurance concerning the restoration to the throne of a Davidic heir after the ending of the line of Davidic kings in Jerusalem in 587 B.C. However there has now been added to it an even more striking passage in verses 6–9 concerning the paradisal conditions which the new Davidic heir will bring to all the earth when he comes to reign. It now means that this promise of the messianic age in its expanded form gives voice to the most elaborate and far-reaching portrayal of what the messianic era means. In this instance the literary evidence would appear to be reasonably clear that a particular prophecy, given in one set of historical circumstances when the hope of restoring the Davidic monarchy seemed near to attainment, has subsequently been reread at a later age, perhaps as much as two centuries later, and given a very different and much expanded meaning. Nor is this all, since the original prophecy was itself intended to link up with what had been declared in the earlier prophetic passage of Isa. 9:1–6.

In fact the entire sequence of prophecies from Isa. 6:1 to 11:16 has been evidently subjected to a series of expansions and interpretative notes which demonstrate how a continuing effort at updating was taking place as the literary form of the prophetic corpus of the canon was in process of formation. If we are to use the New Testament imagery, new wine was being poured into old bottles (cf. Matt. 9:17).

This not only applies to the prophetic writings of the Old Testament, however, since other parts of the canon were undoubtedly also being affected by the drawing together of a larger body of literature. Long before it became an established principle of biblical interpretation that scripture should be interpreted by scripture, such a pattern of exegesis was imposing itself upon the actual formation of the Bible. The effect of this is very much apparent in regard to psalmody when we consider what can have been the purpose of retaining such a relatively large number of royal psalms for a religious community that had no king and was compelled to live under the jurisdiction of foreign rulers. Surely we have here, as B. S. Childs has argued,[22] a strong indication that these ancient compositions, which had themselves originated in a period when Israel had a reigning king, were being reinterpreted in expectation of a time when a new Davidic ruler would appear. The psalms themselves were being reinterpreted as prophecy.

I realize that I am here drawing together two lines of modern critical approach to the Old Testament which are not necessarily connected. The first of these is that of a redaction criticism in which full attention is to be given to the final editorial shape of each of the biblical books. The second is that of "canon criticism," as B. S. Childs has labelled it. Clearly there is some advantage in keeping the two aspects of the literary growth of the Old Testament separate from each other, since they are not exactly the same. Nevertheless there is to be seen very markedly in the way in which the prophetic writings of the Old Testament have been given their final shape, the feature that a series of overall patterns has been imposed on the literature.[23] These patterns are certainly not unrelated to the conviction that all true prophecy ultimately derives from God.

Nor can we leave out of reckoning the point that the present division of the Old Testament into books is a largely artificial division. This is abundantly evident in respect of the Pentateuch, where the present fivefold division is a very superficial feature of the whole composition. There are also clear indications that the present arrangement of the Latter Prophets into four collections does not mean that these were four wholly independent works.[24]

It may at first appear that what I am pointing to here as a prominent feature of the editorial history of the major prophetic collections of the Bible is something of a return to the argument put forward by Thomas Sherlock and others in the eighteenth century that prophecy could have a double meaning—an original meaning dictated by the prophet's own situation and a later, spiritual and fuller, meaning imposed by God and revealed only at the time of its fulfilment. No doubt there are similarities, but the evident unsatisfactoriness of this earlier argument was that it reduced prophecy to near meaninglessness since the true meaning of a prophecy could only be discovered in its fulfilment. In this way it allowed the fulfilment to determine what the original prophecy meant. What Vermeylen and others are pointing to in this complex pattern of rereading and reinterpreting a prophecy is the fact that, already within its literary context, the original prophecy can be seen to have been accorded a more elaborate, and larger, signification.

This seems to me to be important because it brings to our attention the fact that the type of interpretation of these royal prophecies which is found in later Judaism and in the New Testament does not stand isolated and distinct from what has preceded it. Rather it marks the end of a long process of what we have come to describe as "inner-biblical" exegesis.[25] The New Testament does not impose a wholly fresh way of understanding the writings of the Old. It is itself the product of the continued work of rethinking, reapplying, and revitalizing the promises, threats, and assurances which the Old Testament contains. That such a continued work of updating the sacred text has taken place in respect of the formulation of a manual of divine law, or instruction (Heb. *torah*), is plain. Its postbiblical results are to be seen in the Mishnah and Talmud, and are not unrelated to what we find in the New Testament in the Sermon on the Mount. What has taken place in regard to prophecy therefore, and in particular in regard to the development of the messianic hope, is yet another aspect of the way in which there is a discernible and highly significant process of development during which the originally short prophetic utterances have been compiled into larger collections, and ultimately into major books of considerable length.

This does not, of course, mean that the way in which the new Testament interprets the "messianic" prophecies of the Old can now be seen to represent precisely the meaning that had already come to be attached to each of them before the New Testament era. It does, however, mean that we are no longer faced with a simple and clear-cut contrast between one original literal meaning and a later expanded, or spiritual, one. The fact would appear to be that a very extended and wide-ranging process of reflection and elaboration upon the manner and mode of God's work in Israel is being worked out by the literary shaping of these prophecies in the building up of the canon. What the new Testament has to say can then be seen to fit in some recognizable way into such a scheme.

We may now return to a point that I mentioned at the beginning of this chapter. One of the striking features of the subject of messianic hope in the Old Testament is the way in which interest in it has reflected a changing pattern of method and approach in biblical scholarship. It was, in the early eighteenth century, almost the first casualty of the emergence of more rigorous techniques of exegetical work that began what we have come to think of as the critical era of scholarship. Paradoxically too it shows how one side of the legacy of John Locke came to be set in opposition to another side of his great contribution to human understanding. Then in the early part of this century the interest in a history-of-religions approach to the Old Testament reawakened concern with the doctrine of the messiah. Since then both redaction criticism and the so-called canon criticism have opened up new ways of thinking about, and understanding, how Israel's messianic hope came to emerge from within the Old Testament.

We may fittingly conclude then by noting the prominent place that such a doctrine of the messiah can expect to have in the more recent attempts to establish a genuinely biblical theology. This would move beyond the conventional separation into an Old and a New Testament theology and would properly seek to include within its range the many issues concerning the relationship between the two Testaments. Much of the impetus for this interest has stemmed from the essay by H. Gese, dating from 1970, entitled "Considerations on the Unity of Biblical Theology."[26] It is not necessary to follow the many details of Gese's argument, and their conclusions, in their totality in order to appreciate the significance of opening up the discussion about the theological use of the Bible in this way. The publication by H. Graf Reventlow of a survey, *Problems of Biblical Theology in the Twentieth Century*,[27] has further shown that, in such a setting, the rise of messianic expectation in the Old Testament deserves a significant place. The impulse for doing this would seem to me to be important for enabling Old Testament studies in an academic context to relate positively and critically to wider areas of theology. Not least also it would help to reduce the kind of confused bewilderment that arises when critical study of the Old Testament writings appears to ignore, or even to refute, popular expectations about their meaning fostered by many centuries of Christian use and liturgical practice. At the same time, it is also important, when every branch of theological study is being subjected to fresh scrutiny, to be able to show that Old Testament studies can take a full and constructive place within the larger framework of biblical and theological study.

Part 2

ISAIAH

4

The Immanuel Prophecy of Isaiah 7:10–17 and Its Messianic Interpretation

The problems of the interpretation of the celebrated Immanuel prophecy of Isa. 7:14 do not begin with this verse alone but are intimately bound up with a number of separate questions relating to its literary setting. The justification for attempting yet another reexamination of this much-discussed prophecy is that some significant new perspectives have arisen in relation to a number of redaction-critical approaches to the study of Isaiah 1—39. Among these are valuable contributions made in regard to the specific prophecy of Isa. 7:10–17, as well as constructive reevaluations which concern the part played by the Davidic royal ideology in the preaching of Isaiah and the editing and structure of the book which bears his name.[1]

In considerable measure the study of the Immanuel prophecy of Isa. 7:10–17 and of the royal accession oracle of 8:23–9:6, with which, from a literary perspective, it is closely connected, has been dominated for almost half a century by researches into the royal ideology of Judah and its origins. In this regard a significant new development came with the recognition that neither the prophecy concerning the birth of the Immanuel child, nor that making the announcement of the coming of a triumphant Davidic ruler, originally conveyed the transcendent messianic expectation that later generations of Jews and Christians found in them.[2] Nevertheless, in regard to the attempts to establish the date and precise historical significance of these prophecies, the recognition that an elaborate royal mythology, focussed on the Davidic dynasty, flourished in Judah in Isaiah's time provides only a very partial solution to the difficulties that they present. Other questions of a literary and redaction-critical nature also require careful consideration.

In this study it is helpful to break the questioning down into three separate issues and to look at each of them in turn. The first of these concerns the extent to which the belief that it is possible to trace the existence of an Isaianic "memoir" (Ger. *Denkschrift*) in Isa. 6:1–9:6 provides a basis for resolving some of the apparent inconsistencies and difficulties in this section. In particular we are concerned with the light it can shed on establishing the historical context of the prophecy of Isa. 7:14. The second question follows on from this since it concerns the attempt to find a literary narrative core to this memoir in 7:2–8:4 built around a sequence of three sign-names given to three separate children. If this point is established, then we are entitled to assume that the interpretations of all three names can be expected to display a substantial measure of inherent consistency. Without going so far as to insist that this literary context must wholly determine the meaning of the Immanuel prophecy of 7:14, we can at least expect it to set the parameters within which the meaning must be sought.

The third issue concerns the nature of the relationship between the prophecies which centre upon the three sign-names given to children and the prophecy of a royal accession in 8:23–9:6. Clearly if this latter oracle belonged to, and formed the conclusion of, an original "Isaiah memoir," then the case for perceiving some relationship to the prophecy of the birth of the Immanuel child is strengthened. However, if there are reasons for believing that this royal accession prophecy has been added to the narrative of the children's sign-names at a later stage, the significance of the latter narrative will be affected. In either case it must be admitted that it is the close proximity to the Immanuel prophecy of this declaration of a royal birth and accession to the throne which has had the effect of suggesting by association that the Immanuel child of 7:14 is a royal son and heir. Whether or not it was the intention of the original editors to imply this, it appears that it is the connection between the birth announcement in 7:14 with the announcement of a royal birth in 9:5 that has suggested to many interpreters that both of them derive from the royal ideology.

The first question we are to deal with concerns whether or not there is preserved in Isa. 6:1–9:6 the elements of an original first-person memoir composed by the prophet himself. Such a thesis goes back to the study *Jesajas Erleben* by K. Budde of 1928,[3] but, as H. Graf Reventlow has pointed out,[4] such a theory is in fact already substantially implicit in the celebrated 1892 commentary on Isaiah by Bernhard Duhm.[5] Certainly the first-person narrative form which appears in chapters 6 and 8 is highly distinctive in prophecy, but, on account of its very spasmodic and partial appearance, it must on a critical evaluation be regarded as having undergone considerable addition and modification. Moreover some features of a first-person narrative form already appear in Isaiah 5. Accordingly, not all of the present text of 6:1–9:6 can possibly have formed part of such an original memoir, and a substantial amount of subsequent expansion must be regarded as having taken place. Brief glosses, such as the references to "the king of Assyria" in 7:17, 20 and 8:4, have been made, but so also have many more extended enlargements. Moreover a major difficulty for the hypothesis is caused by the fact that the first-person form is found in 6:1–11 and 8:1–18, but not at all in chapter 7. Yet in content chapters 7 and 8 have greater connection with each other than do chapters 6 and 7. It is necessary to argue therefore, as

Budde does,[6] that the first-person form of the original memoir has been adapted in chapter 7:3 to speak of the prophet Isaiah in the third person. If Budde's thesis of an original Isaianic composition of a memoir faces several literary criticisms, we might modify it to follow O. Kaiser[7] in regarding the presence of the autobiographical memoir form as the work, not of the prophet himself, but of a later editor. He may himself have followed only inconsistently his own chosen literary form. More radically Reventlow[8] has argued that we must now set aside altogether the case for seeing the elements of such a prophetic memoir underlying the text of Isa. 6:1–9:6.

The case, from a purely form-critical perspective, is certainly not very clear when we attempt to define the extent of such a memoir. Nevertheless it remains true from the perspective of redaction history that it is much easier to understand why the form of such a memoir should have become distorted and partially obliterated in the course of subsequent editing than that, as a construction of later editors, it should have been employed only in a very clumsy and limited fashion. Still less is it easy to explain why, if there had never existed such a memoir at all, the first-person autobiographical form can still be found in chapters 6 and 8. The case for recognizing that a written testimony from the prophet, composed at some stage in the period of the Syro-Ephraimitic conflict, did form a foundational nucleus of Isaiah's book and that some remnants of it still appear in the text appears on balance to be a reasonable and helpful one.

However, if the literary arguments for recognizing the existence of such a memoir encounter difficulties, the case is much assisted by a broader attention to some other features of the message of 6:1–9:6. It is these to which O. H. Steck[9] has pointed in several studies, and which have received the more recent support of the Danish scholars Kirsten Nielsen[10] and Jesper Høgenhaven.[11] The central question here relates to the basic determination of whether the pronouncement of the Immanuel birth in 7:14 is to be understood as a threat to Ahaz, to whom it is addressed, or as a promise, with reassuring connotations for the king and the dynasty he represents. Undoubtedly, as Gese points out,[12] the anger expressed in verse 13 by Isaiah at the king's refusal to ask a sign anticipates that that sign, when it is given, will serve to condemn the king's lack of faith. Yet, in apparent contrast to this, the interpretation of the sign-name Immanuel given in verse 16, "the land before whose two kings you are in dread will be deserted," reads quite decisively as a message of assurance in the face of the threat from the Syro-Ephraimite coalition.[13]

This is a point that A. Laato, in advocating the existence of an Isaianic memoir, has taken up and has sought to resolve by seeing in the Immanuel birth a royal messianic figure who will bring deliverance to Judah, but who will, at the same time, replace the faithless house of Ahaz.[14] Hence good news for the nation is not good news for the king. The Immanuel message is therefore both salvation and judgment. However, this is not the only way in which the tensions inherent in the Immanuel message can be resolved. Such an interpretation becomes suspect precisely because it has to construct a very questionable and wide-ranging meaning for the Immanuel birth as the declaration of the founding of a new royal dynasty in order to accommodate the threatening expectation aroused by Isaiah's anger towards the king referred to in verse 13. It allows the overall interpretation to be dominated by a single feature of its literary setting against the witness of the explicit interpretation that is given. It is noteworthy, and decisively significant, that the pattern of an ambiguous sign-bearing name, followed by an interpretation which is quite unambiguous as to its intent, is found with all three of the Isaianic sign-names; Shear-jashub (7:3) is interpreted in 7:7–9; Immanuel is interpreted in 7:15–17; and Maher-shalal-hashbaz is interpreted in 8:4. All three interpretations have undergone some expansions, and only the third of them appears to be relatively intact in its original form with only the minor addition of the reference to "the king of Assyria." Nevertheless, even with these expansions an underlying consistency in the message of all three names can easily be discerned.

This message is clearly reassuring in content and this is in line with what we find in 7:16. We are faced therefore in the case of the interpretations of all three names with three versions of the same message. The second and third differ from the first by the addition of a cryptic indication of the timescale between the birth of the child bearing the name and the expected deliverance which the name signifies. In the case of all three children it needs to be positively asserted that the sign consists of the name that is given and not in the manner or nature of the birth itself.

It is in this respect that the theological features of the case for recognizing an underlying "Isaiah Memoir" to which Steck has pointed prove helpful.[15] In this a certain distance both of time and experience can be seen to have elapsed between the actual oral delivery of the prophet's messages and the recording of these together with a recognition of the response that they had elicited from the king. The content of the significance of all three sign-names was of assurance and security for Ahaz and his dynasty, but these had been refused by the king as the memoir clearly shows. It is the rebuff to the words of promise that has aroused the prophet's anger, turning promise into threat. This is well brought out in the paradoxical play on the idea of God as a "Rock" in 8:14.

If this is a helpful line of critical investigation, then it would seem that the belief that an original Isaianic memoir, even if in a much-edited form, underlies Isa. 6:1–9:6 has an important bearing on the understanding of the Immanuel prophecy of Isa. 7:14. It clarifies two issues: first that this prophecy is reassuring in the meaning that is attached to the name, and secondly that this meaning is more or less identical with the message of the Shear-jashub and Maher-shalal-hashbaz names. A redaction-critical observation concerning the literary context can then assist towards ascertaining the interpretation of one of the most heavily disputed verses of biblical prophecy.

The second of our lines of questioning follows on directly from this, for, if there were an original Isaianic memoir, then the narrative of the three children with the sequence of three sign-names given to them would appear to have formed the central part of it. It is undoubtedly true that the arguments here are in danger of becoming somewhat circular, since this narrative forms a major reason for recognizing that there was a written memoir from the prophet. In form, however, it is not uniform since it is couched partly in the first-person form and partly in the third. Nevertheless this sequence of three sign-names followed by their interpretation offers the most clearly connected, and chronologically sequential, feature of Isa. 6:1–9:6.[16]

There is then a further feature of considerable literary significance in that the note concerning the role of these children's names as "signs" in Isa. 8:18 reads very much as though it were the conclusion of the entire memoir: "Behold, I and the children whom Yahweh has given me are signs and portents in Israel from Yahweh Sabaoth, who dwells on Mount Zion." This sums up very adequately the central structural component of the preceding narrative. This perception is adopted by several scholars,[17] and it must surely be correct. It then provides us with an important basis for elucidating the scope and purpose of such a memoir. This did not originally extend as far as 9:6, but was concluded at 8:18.

We are therefore compelled, when we adopt this conclusion, to accept that the royal accession oracle in 9:1–6, and its introduction in 8:23, did not form a part of the original prophetic memoir. Nor did this originally include the rather obscure sequence of comments in 8:19–22 which have proved such a headache for translators. Overall it points to the conclusion that the memoir comprised an account of the prophet's call in 6:1–11, the narrative of the sign-names and their interpretations in 7:2–17, 8:1–4 followed by the threatening pronouncements of the ruin that would ensue for both Israel and Judah as a result of Ahaz's refusal to accept the message of the names in 8:5–8, 11–15.[18] The results of such a reconstruction leave us with a clear and coherent account of the prophet's message at the time of the Syro-Ephraimite conflict and a convincing explanation as to why this message was formally assuring in content, but ultimately threatening in its implications once it had been rejected by Ahaz. Very significantly it points to a meaning which was wholly clear and intelligible in the historical and political situation that Ahaz's policies had initiated.

If we recognize this to have been the main scope of Isaiah's memoir, then we are faced with the task of understanding in this context the precise import of the Immanuel prophecy of Isa. 7:10–17 and its connection with the threat to Ahaz's continued retention of his throne. The narrative context shows that both had been placed in jeopardy by the Syro-Ephraimite alliance, whereas the interpretations added to the sign-names offer reassurance to the king in this regard. Nor is it hard to perceive that the introduction into the memoir of the accession oracle of 9:1–6 by a later editor has been specifically aimed at strengthening this message of assurance by pointing to the promises that belonged intrinsically to the political theology of the Davidic throne.

Once the sequence of three sign-names belonging to the children is viewed in isolation from the accession prophecy of 9:1–6, we can see that, just as all three of the names bear a closely similar message content, so were all three children offspring born to the prophet. This would not necessarily require that they were born to the same woman, although this is certainly not to be excluded in the light of the chronology and time-scale involved. However Høgenhaven does not draw this conclusion, but instead finds only the first and third of the children to have been born to the prophet. The second, bearing the name Immanuel, whose birth is announced in Isa. 7:14, he regards as an expected royal son and heir. This he does because he finds in the narrative introduction to the prophecy in 7:10–13 indications that the future of the royal house is the central issue which the sign of the name must address. On this he is assuredly correct, but, more particularly, he finds in the form of the birth announcement itself, distinctive royal-mythological traits which lead him to conclude that this second child must be of royal blood. Hence Isaiah's pronouncement must, he thinks, refer to an imminently expected royal birth. That this cannot possibly, for chronological reasons, be a reference to the birth of Hezekiah has already been fully recognized in earlier critical discussions.[19]

It is a similar conviction that Isa. 7:14 refers to a royal birth that leads Laato to conclude that the prophet must have been referring, not to the birth of Hezekiah who was to be Ahaz's actual successor, but to the emergence of a wholly new royal dynastic line that would eclipse the one represented by Ahaz.[20] Yet this leads to even greater difficulties since, in the event, we know that Hezekiah did eventually succeed his father Ahaz. Laato, in admitting that the Immanuel child cannot possibly be a reference to the birth of Hezekiah, has looked for some other line of interpretation in which the Immanuel child is taken to be of royal blood, without being a son to Ahaz. It is a consequent part of his interpretation therefore that Isaiah's prophecy proved to be startingly mistaken on this occasion.

All of these are simply needlessly strained and difficult attempts at interpretation which are eliminated once we adhere to the eminent sense of J. J.

Stamm's conclusion that Immanuel was a child of the prophet's.[21] This remains my own position,[22] which current attempts to reestablish the belief that the Immanuel child was of royal blood have only served to strengthen. Such a conclusion finds its strongest support in the recognition of the central role played by the sequence of three sign-names in 7:2–8:4.

However, in maintaining this position, it is necessary to look more closely at those considerations which have led so many scholars to conclude otherwise and to examine the cogency of these. Among these we must set the recognition that the question of the security of Ahaz's royal house is raised, not only by the historical context of 7:1–13, but also by the introduction of the accession oracle of 9:1–6. This serves to announce the coming of a royal successor to Ahaz, who, unlike this faithless king, will bring greatness to his people (9:6) and the overthrow of the yoke of the foreign oppressor (9:3). So then it is to the question which forms the third of our main lines of investigation concerning the relationship between the Immanuel prophecy of 7:14 and the accession oracle of 9:1–6 that we must now turn.

We may recall as of first importance in this connection that the reference to a royal birth in 9:5 is best understood, following A. Alt's influential essay,[23] as that of a royal "rebirth" or "divine adoption" in line with the affirmation of Ps. 2:7. The origins of such metaphorical language lie deeply rooted in the inherited mythology of the divine foundation of the royal throne. The notion of the birth of the Immanuel child of 7:14 therefore, which points to a real birth, requires to be understood quite differently from the royal "rebirth" of 9:5.[24] Nevertheless there is little doubt that the metaphor of birth has been very important to the editor who has placed the accession oracle in its present position, on account of its appropriateness in pointing to the coming of a ruler who will achieve the greatness which Ahaz's lack of faith had denied to him. This editor therefore has fully taken into account the knowledge that the Syro-Ephraimite alliance posed a direct threat to the royal dynasty of Judah, and has deliberately drawn attention to the promises linked to that dynasty.

However this does not prove the point that the Immanuel child must have been a royal child. What it does show is that, by making this insertion, the editor has brought about a shift of emphasis in the interpretation of the Immanuel prophecy to a point where the sign no longer consists solely of the name of the child, but is also reflected in the circumstances of his birth.

The addition of the accession oracle in 9:1–6 by an editor has given added emphasis to the original prophetic birth announcement of 7:14 with the intention of reinforcing the reader's awareness that the reputation and future of the Davidic dynasty was at stake. This might have been regarded as a somewhat arbitrary and needless proceeding had there not been a very profound reason why an editor should have been so concerned to condemn

Ahaz, while at the same time reaffirming the greatness and splendour of the Davidic dynasty. This profound reason lies in the editor's concern with the figure of Hezekiah to whom the accession oracle of 9:1–6 points.

Before looking in more detail at the manner in which the editorial interest in the figure of Hezekiah has led to the introduction of the accession oracle of 9:1–6, it is open to suggest that, at the same time as adding this oracle, the same editor has also made significant additions to Isaiah 7. These were designed to point the contrast between Ahaz and his successor. We can note first of all therefore that there appear to be two significant insertions in chapter 7 which belong together with the introduction of Isa. 9:1–6. The first of these has been the introduction in Isa. 7:2 of the reference to the panic which overtook Ahaz when he learnt of the threat to depose him. This points forward to the unbelieving response to Isaiah's message and highlights the reason for the king's treacherous action in seeking help from Assyria. The second insertion is the addition of the concluding element of the interpretation of the sign-name Shear-jashub in verse 9b: "If you will not believe, surely you shall not be established." Without this allusion back to the dynastic oracle which marked the foundation of the Davidic dynasty in 2 Sam. 7:16 the interpretation of the Shear-jashub name is much closer in form to that of the other two names.

In this connection we need to bear in mind that the question of the faith of the royal occupant on the throne of David cannot have been an issue which belonged intrinsically to the form of the original dynastic prophecy made to David. The very essence of constitutional dynastic monarchy is the element of unalterable divine givenness to which it is able to appeal. It has nevertheless been introduced here in Isaiah 7 with startling prominence. Thereby an unexpected element of conditional promise has been introduced as a central part of the royal ideology where it is, in a constitutional sense, strangely out of place. Gerhard von Rad has therefore been wholly correct in drawing attention to the great importance of the concept of "faith" for the Isaiah tradition[25] which has now been made central in Isaiah 7. However whether this originated, as von Rad claimed, with the tradition of "holy war" appears less clear. It is precisely this concern with faith which belongs as a highly distinctive feature to the layer of "anti-Assyrian" redaction in the Isaiah collection.

We draw the conclusion then that both the insertions in Isa. 7:2 and 9b have been made in order to indicate that Ahaz's refusal to respond positively to the message of Isaiah arose from a lack of faith. Should we not then also draw a further most significant conclusion on the basis of this recognition of the presence of substantial editorial reworking in Isa. 7:1–17? This is that, as a consequence of this redactional activity which has introduced the accession oracle in 9:1–6, the Immanuel prophecy itself has also been reinterpreted. This has pointed to the presumption that the child that bears this name is now understood to be a royal child. In fact must we not now conclude that it has been this editor's quite deliberate intention to relate the Immanuel prophecy directly to the accession oracle of 9:1–6? He has done this in order to make the announcement of the child who carried such an auspicious name a foretelling of the accession of Hezekiah who would revive the fortunes of the Davidic dynasty. The prophet's child has been turned into a royal prince.

It is not difficult to see that there were features of the prophecy of Isa. 7:14 which lent themselves to such editorial treatment. We have already noted that the message attached to the child's name was intended as an assurance to Ahaz that the attempt to usurp his throne would fail. Moreover the name itself, with all its overtones of divine power and victory, must have appeared wholly appropriate for a royal prince. Perhaps too the rather mysterious oracular form which introduces the young mother and her expected child carried with it certain overtones of a unique divine event.[26] At any rate it appears that it has been the editor's intention to reinforce the condemnation of Ahaz by making the very prophecy which, by its rejection, condemned him, into a foretelling of the coming of his successor. The fact that there were chronological reasons why such a prophecy could not have been an announcement of the birth of Hezekiah, since he was already a youth of some years, has not hindered such a step. Possibly the exact dates of the succession of Hezekiah to the throne were in confusion already at this time, as they have remained ever since.

When we ask why this special emphasis upon the lack of faith displayed by Ahaz in appealing for protection to Assyria has been introduced by an editor into a central place in Isaiah 7, we find the answer in the broader Isaianic presentation of the figure of Hezekiah. If, as we have argued, Isa. 9:1–6 was intended from the outset to refer to Hezekiah's succession to his father Ahaz, we have the essential key to understanding the redactor's purpose. This lies in the way in which Hezekiah is elevated in a number of passages throughout Isaiah 1—39 to become an exemplary model of a king of David's dynasty on account of his resistance to Sennacherib in 701 B.C.E.

This emphasis upon Hezekiah as faithful king and hero is the central theme of the narratives of Isaiah 36—39, where it is especially Hezekiah's faith in Yahweh's power to deliver him that is stressed. In line with this we have the emphatic assurances ascribed to Isaiah in connection with Hezekiah's revolt in 705 to 701 B.C.E., which declare that Yahweh has purposed to inflict a humiliating defeat upon "the Assyrian" (Isa. 10:5–15, 16–19, 33–34; 14:25; 31:5). Hezekiah's faith in Yahweh's power to defend him and his city contrasts markedly with Ahaz's total lack of faith and his pathetic willingness to seek to secure his throne by appealing to the king of Assyria.

We can see therefore that the editor who introduced the accession oracle into Isa. 9:1–6, and who reinterpreted the Immanuel prophecy of Isa. 7:10–17, stood very close to the authors of the narratives of Isaiah 36—39. Together they express a consistent stratum of interpretation which has striven to present Hezekiah and the events of 701 B.C.E. in the most favourable possible light.

It is then this desire to emphasize the contrast between the actions of Ahaz and Hezekiah which has brought about such a major editorial reworking of Isa. 7:1–17. The aim has been to highlight the contention that it was through a lack of faith in Yahweh that Ahaz stooped to his treacherous action.

Since I have argued elsewhere in my study *Isaiah and the Deliverance of Jerusalem*[27] that this Isaianic presentation of Hezekiah's triumphant victory of faith over Sennacherib in 701 B.C.E. represents a relatively late and retrospective account of what took place in that year, there is no necessity to reiterate the arguments for that assessment here. Its importance in regard to the Immanuel prophecy is that it serves to explain two of its most prominent features. First that the original account in the Isaianic memoir of the confrontation between Ahaz and Isaiah has been supplemented by the addition of the accession oracle of 9:1–6. This addition was, from the beginning, intended to point forward to Hezekiah as a worthier occupant of the throne of David than Ahaz had been. Secondly it has brought about an editorial reworking in Isaiah 7 to highlight the lack of faith which had brought about Ahaz's action in appealing to the Assyrian king for protection. It is in the course of this reworking that the shift has been made in the form of the prophet's narrative record of the event, obscuring the fact that the Immanuel child, like the other two who bore sign-names, was also a child of the prophet's. The birth of the child has become a part of the sign, together with the name that he bore.

It would certainly appear to be the case that the motivation that led to this development and reinterpretation of the Immanuel prophecy was largely informed by a concern to set a distance between Ahaz's reprehensible action in appealing for help to the king of Assyria and the central ideology of the Davidic royal house. By condemning the king's action as one engendered by a lack of faith, room was left for a more acceptable portrayal of Hezekiah as a king who displayed faith. Thereby the reputation of the Davidic dynasty could be preserved, at the cost of affirming that its promises could only be realized through kings who dared to show trust in Yahweh.

All of these considerations point to the recognition that, once an editor felt the need to defend the reputation of the Davidic dynasty by drawing attention to the contrast between Ahaz's lack of faith and Hezekiah's victorious faith, the whole character of the Immanuel prophecy was changed.

We need also to consider that this may have given rise to a rewording of the prophecy itself, especially in the direction of obscuring the identity of the child's mother,[28] although this can only be a matter for conjecture. We have already claimed that both Isa. 7:2 and 9b were additions introduced as a consequence of this editorial revision. Certainly also we should note here that the addition of the concluding comment in verse 17 averting back to the division of the united kingdom of David and Solomon after the latter's death must have been introduced as a consequence of this reworking. By making such a reference the reader's attention was drawn to recognize that the coming of the new king would have direct relevance to the question of the unity of Israel. Beside this verse, however, it is also attractive to think that the address to the king as "the house of David" in verse 13 was made at this time, in line with the comment in verse 2. May it not also have been that it was during the course of this reworking that the very significant literary fact that the basic narrative of Isa. 7:1–17 had belonged to the Isaiah memoir was obscured by the introduction of the change to refer to the prophet in the third person in verse 3? By this means the awareness that the Immanuel child was the prophet's son was even further obscured.

Such an attempt to find a thoroughgoing reworking and reinterpretation of the original form of the Immanuel prophecy of Isa. 7:10–17, and its immediate preface in the Shear-jashub prophecy of Isa. 7:1–9, may at first appear to be rather highhanded. Yet when we look closely we can see that the redactional process which has been at work here has moved in a consistent path and is wholly consonant with a major editorial feature which has been widely recognized in Isaiah 1—39. In introducing the royal accession oracle of 9:1–6 in order to show that the successor to Ahaz, Hezekiah, would do much to restore the damaged reputation of the Davidic dynasty, the basic groundwork for the reinterpretation of the Immanuel prophecy was established. Once this had taken place, it was a simple step to form an even closer connection between the promise of the Immanuel name in 7:14 and the dynastic promises of 9:1–6 by suggesting that the Immanuel child would be a royal child and to point to this identification through the imagery of "birth" in 7:14 and 9:5.

It is worthwhile to note at this point, as Laato does,[29] that early Judaism did understand the oracle of 9:1–6 as a reference to the accession of Hezekiah. In view of the fact that this king succeeded Ahaz on the throne of Judah this is in any case the most straightforward way in which its relevance as an accession oracle for a new king of the Davidic line would have been grasped. This understanding would then appear to be wholly correct in its perception. Accordingly we should set aside the otherwise attractive proposal of Hermann Barth[30] and others who conclude that the oracle of 9:1–6 can best be understood as a reference to the accession of Josiah to the Davidic throne.

It may be helpful at this point to consider further the question of the origin of Isa. 9:1–6, since this must already have existed in a finished form when it was adopted by the redactor and is unlikely to have been his own composition. We may even consider whether there are any grounds for thinking that Isaiah was its author. This, however, appears very improbable. In origin it is an ancient coronation psalm which has particularly suited the editor's purpose on account of its imagery of coronation as a divine rebirth. He has introduced it at this point in order to reassert the political theology of the Davidic dynasty and he has done this quite deliberately in order to point to the realization of these promises through Hezekiah.

Once we recognize that the insertion of this royal accession oracle was intended to point to Hezekiah's succession to Ahaz, we can see how this has brought about a significant reinterpretation of the Immanuel prophecy of Isa. 7:10–17. We can also see why this prophecy subsequently became obscure in its complexity. It originally referred to a child shortly expected to be born to the prophet's wife and stands second in the sequence of three such names which formed a major core of the Isaiah memoir. However, once Isaiah's prophecies came to be edited with a view to presenting a very favourable picture of Hezekiah, and more significantly still a favourable picture of the outcome of events in 701 B.C.E., then we have the major key to understanding why this prophecy has undergone such a major reinterpretation. The concern to reinforce the condemnation of Ahaz, and to contrast this with Hezekiah's faith, has found in the Immanuel prophecy a suitable vehicle for such an end. Both such concerns, however, were simply a part of the wider interest in reestablishing a favourable portrayal of the Davidic dynasty and of relating this directly to the deliverance of Jerusalem from Sennacherib in 701 B.C.E. In a sense therefore the more distant point of reference is Jerusalem and its temple with a desire to understand the difference between the city's fortunes in 701 and 587 B.C.E.

Perhaps such a conclusion may serve as a modest attempt at resolving the conflict of interpretations that has existed for so many years as to whether the Immanuel child was a son expected to be born to the prophet or to the king. In some degree both interpretations are present in the text.

Furthermore, once the tragic events of 587 B.C.E. had brought an end to the royal status of the Davidic dynasty in Jerusalem, a quite new situation developed. That there arose a strong hope and expectation that there would be a restoration of the Davidic monarchy is attested in Isa. 11:1–5, which must belong to the late sixth century B.C.E. Later still it is evident that an even larger hope emerged in which something more than the reclaiming of the monarchic crown by an ancient dynastic line was anticipated. This hope concerned the coming of an eschatological deliverer who would free Israel from the yoke of foreign oppression. For this hope the accession oracle of Isa. 9:1–6, now reinterpreted in the sense of the promise of an eschatological ruler of this kind, served as a foundational text.

When this reinterpretation of the prophecy of 9:1–6 occurred, then it carried with it a yet further reinterpretation of the Immanuel prophecy of 7:10–17. This was now understood to foretell the coming of a deliverer whose origin was shrouded in mystery, and to whom the mysterious birth oracle of 7:14 lent added dignity. Evidence of this further rereading of the Immanuel prophecy is found in Isa. 7:15 in another addition to the interpretation of the Immanuel name. This points to the prosperity and wealth which will spring up on the land when the time of renewal arrives. It is in line with the picture of paradisal peace which has been appended in 11:6–9 to the prophecy of 11:1–5.

This late postexilic re-reading of the Immanuel prophecy as witness to the coming of a mysterious divinely appointed deliverer is attested additionally by the introduction of the cryptic words "when she who is about to give birth has brought forth" (Micah 5:2b) into the oracle of Micah 5:1–5. This is a glossator's comment,[31] but there can be no doubt that it is a direct allusion back to the Immanuel prophecy of Isa. 7:14 and its interpretation as a foretelling of the mysterious circumstances surrounding the birth of the eschatological messiah. To this extent the text of Isa. 7:14 can be seen to hide within itself not one single interpretation but no less than three different interpretations. It is in a sense a theological palimpsest containing a vital key towards understanding the complex history of one of the major themes of prophecy in Israel.

In paying tribute to Professor Rolf Rendtorff, who has worked hard to draw the attention of scholars to the necessity of a "holistic" exegesis of the text of the Hebrew Bible, I hope that it is not inappropriate to focus upon the way in which a single text can contain within itself evidence of a long history of interpretation. So much difficulty within Jewish and Christian apologetic, and within the ambition of arriving at a clear modern critical understanding of the meaning of Isa. 7:14, has arisen through a failure to recognize the way in which a redactional process of "re-reading" can alter and extend the original sense of a prophecy. It is greatly to be hoped therefore that Professor Rendtorff's "holistic" approach to the interpretation of the Hebrew Bible will continue to bring a larger frame of reference to the message of prophecy.

5   Beyond Tradition-History

Deutero-Isaianic Development of First Isaiah's Themes

An Analysis of Methods and Their Underlying Assumptions

The book of Isaiah has come down to us as a work of sixty-six chapters, and it is noteworthy that our earliest complete Hebrew manuscript of an Old Testament text of this size, namely, the famous Isaiah Scroll found at Qumran (1QIs[a]), is of this book, and presents it to all intents and purposes in the form in which we know it. Yet concerning this book, unlike many old Testament literary works, there has emerged something akin to a consensus among critical biblical scholars that the book does not derive from a single author, the eighth-century Isaiah of Jerusalem, and that the presence of material from much later than the eighth century B.C. is unmistakably evident. Earlier scholars, such as the mediaeval commentator Ibn Ezra and the seventeenth-century Dutch philosopher B. Spinoza (1632–1677), had inferred that chapters 40ff. of the book derive from a sixth-century B.C. Babylonian background, and firm arguments for this were set out in 1788 by the German scholar J. C. Doederlein in a critical review.[1] This theory gained for itself a modest following, but with the publication of Bernhard Duhm's famous commentary of 1892 the case, both for this and for the further separation of chapters 56—66 as of still later origin, became widely accepted. So a kind of rough-and-ready characterization of the book as deriving from at least three prophets—First Isaiah, Second Isaiah (Deutero-Isaiah), and Third Isaiah (Trito-Isaiah)—has arisen, although this was never more than a very marginal and improbable explanation of the origin of the book. The extent to which the last eleven chapters (56—66) had a unified origin in themselves has consistently been seriously questioned, as has also the extent to which these chapters evidence a relationship of some kind to those ascribed to "Second Isaiah."[2] Some scholars have upheld the claim that at least some parts of chapters 56—66 share a common authorship with "Second Isaiah." Nevertheless, within this overall critical breakup of the assumption of the unity of the book based on a common historical setting and single prophetic author, the view that the sixteen chapters that form the present chapters 40—55 of the book are a literary and historical unity has been widely adopted. In fact so confident has scholarship felt in its identification of the work and activity of the unnamed author of these chapters that, not only have commentaries been published on them alone, isolated from the remainder of the book,[3] but it has become customary in reconstructing the overall chronology of prophetic activity in ancient Israel and Judah to describe the work of the unnamed prophet of the exile to whom we owe Isaiah 40—55 as quite independent of its preserved literary setting.

Nevertheless we may note some significant points which have remained unresolved questions concerning this critical reconstruction of the work of the so-called Second Isaiah.

In the first place there have always been some scholars who have challenged the hypothesis altogether on the grounds of a very conservative literary and theological approach to the Old Testament, pointing to a number of thematic and stylistic connections which link the various parts of the book of Isaiah together. So, in spite of the difficulties so carefully noted by scholars, a unity based on common authorship has been defended by, among others, O. T. Allis[4] and E. J. Young.[5]

This approach has convinced few critical minds for the clear reason that the difficulties do not lie with matters of vocabulary and style, but rather with even more important issues relating to the very nature of prophecy and its historical relationships. The sixth-century Babylonian background of chapters 40—55 is so explicit that to deny its relevance for an understanding of their contents is to ask for a totally different understanding of prophecy from that which clearly pertains elsewhere in the Old Testament prophetic books. We can cite even so important a figure as Martin Luther himself for a recognition of this important "historical" context to prophecy.[6] More attractive, therefore, has appeared the argument that the connection of chapters 40—55 with the work of the eighth-century Isaiah of Jerusalem may be explained by positing the existence of a group of "disciples" of this prophet, among whom eventually "Second Isaiah" emerged.[7] Yet this approach seems to claim more than it properly explains, since it retains the idea of a connection based on authorship, only now it is a "school" of authors, without requiring any truly intrinsic connection of content between the various blocks of material. So far as it goes, it may be correct, but it does not really explain anything very much; it merely projects a hypothesis to account for the fact that chapters 40—55 of the book of Isaiah now appear as part of a larger work.

We may pause now to note the attraction that has been given afresh to the unique literary problems of the book of Isaiah by the method of "canon criticism" advocated by B. S. Childs.[8] This recognizes that, alongside the evident historical context which has a bearing on the interpretation of Isaiah 40—55, there is also a literary context in which chapters 1—39 form for the reader an indispensable part of the context of meaning by which they should be interpreted. When "Second Isaiah" speaks of "former things" therefore (Isa. 41:21; etc.), the reader will naturally recognize that things prophesied in chapters 1—39 are being referred to.[9] I should not wish here to comment upon the many wider issues raised by the whole approach which Childs advocates under the name of "canon criticism." From the perspective of the book of Isaiah it seems highly improbable that the process of "canonization" had anything at all to do with the reasons the book of Isaiah acquired its present shape. From the evidence, not only of the Qumran manuscript and the references in the New Testament, but also from the intrinsic contents of the book, it is virtually certain that those who ultimately adopted the book of Isaiah, along with the other prophetic books of the Old Testament, into the canon already found them in their present form and that their intentions in establishing the shape of the canon cannot, and should not, be assumed to have been identical with the intentions of those who shaped the present book of Isaiah.[10] Our problem is a literary and theological one of redaction-criticism, not the larger and more problematic one of canon criticism, which we may set aside for discussion in the realm of hermeneutics. The most that we can properly say in regard to canon criticism is that only when we can resolve some of the problems concerning how the book of Isaiah acquired its present shape may we have something to contribute towards the larger issues relating to the canon. We should assume that the problems of the book of Isaiah need to be clarified and resolved first of all in relation to that book, rather than in relation to a wider set of questions concerning the canon of the Old Testament.

We may conclude this part of the broader survey of modern critical approaches to the book of Isaiah by noting some relevant points, if only to remove them from clouding our discussion. The first of these is that to assume that ancient scrolls needed to be of a certain length; that nothing more than a question of literary convenience (and a saving of expensive materials) accounts for the current length and shape of the book of Isaiah must be looked upon as a counsel of despair. More than this certainly appears to have been at issue, and there are sufficient signs of a deeper concern with questions of meaning and interpretation that stretch across all sixty-six chapters to rule out such an approach based on purely external, material, factors.

It is also very striking that chapter 35, for instance, which H. Graetz[11] and C. C. Torrey[12] thought belonged along with chapters 40ff., consciously anticipates and summarizes the major themes of chapters 40—55. This fact seems best explained as a conscious attempt to introduce later themes at this point in the book for some deliberate editorial and interpretative function. It is all of a piece with the fact, which I have myself drawn attention to elsewhere, that chapter 39 serves as an important editorial "bridge" between the threat to Jerusalem posed by the Assyrians and that which was later posed by the armies of Babylon.[13]

It is also in order for us to bear in mind that no mere process of simply "adding on" more and more prophecies to the Isaiah scroll can account for its present shape. By a wide scholarly consensus chapters 24—27 are regarded as the latest chapters in the book, later even than chapters 56—66, and other late material is to be found in chapters 34—35, and is certainly also scattered in other parts of chapters 1—21. Some process of editorial shaping has taken place, however much we may also be led to recognize that sometimes more arbitrary factors may have served to form the book into its final sequence of material.

So far, this survey of scholarly methods and their underlying assumptions has had the rather negative intention of showing that little has up till now been achieved in explaining the purpose and shape of the book of Isaiah as comprising the material which makes up the sixty-six chapters it now possesses. It is, I firmly believe, one of the most complex literary structures of the entire Old Testament. The ascription of it to Isaiah has created a rather dangerous assumption that it is a unity because it derives from a single author. Such a view prevailed both in Judaism and Christianity down to the end of the eighteenth century, although in practice it had very little impact upon the book's interpretation, which was governed by other considerations than the more strictly historical ones. It was not until the work of Doederlein and those who came after him that a rigidly historical approach led, of necessity, to the breakup and abandonment of the idea of a unity of the book based on single authorship. Yet questions remain, since the book does not have a common author. What were the literary factors which gave rise to its present overall shape, and does this overall shape offer anything that might properly be called the message of the book of Isaiah? What we are concerned with is then quite properly an essay in editorial history, or more technically, an essay in redaction criticism. Given that the extant work is a unity, if only in the sense that it is a unified "collection," we shall be asking whether it does not also possess a unity of theme and content. After all, even an anthology of texts such as we may produce in the modern world may usually be expected to display some overarching unity of background and theme.

We may pause over a further couple of general points. The method that has come to be known as "redaction criticism" has initially first arisen in biblical studies in relation to narrative texts, such as the Gospels of the New Testament or the supposed Yahwist source of the Hexateuch. Where such narrative texts are concerned we may expect the chief redactional interests to show themselves in relation to an overarching "plot" by which much shorter narrative units are brought together. It is less clear that anything of this nature can, or should, be looked for in relation to a prophetic text. Rather we may start our investigation here with a prior assumption that the redactional elements will show themselves in regard to the way in which the prophecy was believed to have been fulfilled, or to be awaiting fulfilment.[14] It is this aspect of an expected fulfilment of prophecy which lends to the question about what prophecy "means," a peculiar, but fascinating, difficulty. The fulfilment was understood in relation to events, but these events were merely alluded to, often under the guise of vague symbols or word imagery, so that we cannot now recover a very clear picture of what precise events they were, or were expected to be. The second general point lies in the problems relating to the whole method of redaction criticism and the kind of text that it was designed to deal with. Religious texts of many kinds have an extraordinary multi-dimensioned and multi-faceted character, but none more so than the Old Testament books of prophecy. Just as they have been centuries in being formed, so, during that time, many different interpretations, and kinds of interpretation, have been woven into them. Much recent discussion has centred, in part sparked off by B. S. Childs's method of canon criticism, upon whether the earliest, or the latest, level of meaning is the most important and authoritative for us. I do not wish to take sides over this broad issue, except insofar as it is very markedly evident that such a scholar as Duhm, with his analytical method, was entirely, and almost obsessively, concerned with the problems of original meaning. Such would be in order if the books of prophecy were merely collections, or anthologies, in which the original sense has been retained and the role of the editor, or editors, reduced to a minimum. On the other hand, if the work of the editors has been substantially more than this, then we may expect that they will themselves have injected a great degree of their own understanding into the work. Even at a prima facie level it would certainly appear that the very complexity of the final shape given to the book of Isaiah points us to this latter conclusion. The later, redactional, stages in the formation of the book have contributed more to an understanding of what it means than can usefully be gleaned by modern attempts to reconstruct the story of the "life and times" of Isaiah of Jerusalem in the eighth century B.C.

My purpose from this point on is a relatively straightforward one: accepting that chapters 40—55 of the book of Isaiah originated from the sixth century B.C., when Judah and Jerusalem were under the domination of Babylon, what have these chapters to do with the earlier prophecies of Isaiah of Jerusalem preserved in chapters 1—39 of the book? Three broad possibilities present themselves: (1) The prophetic author of chapters 40—55 had nothing to do with the original Isaiah and neither did his prophecies. For unknown reasons a later scribe came to associate them with the earlier sayings of Isaiah and thus they came to be linked in a literary fashion. Only later, at a level that we might relate to the period of canonization of the prophetic literature, were serious attempts made to understand the book as a whole.

(2) A second possibility would, more plausibly, offer a modification of this and would arise if, once the quite independent author of chapters 40—55 had left his material in literary form, a scribe recognized its eminent suitability to form a sequel to the earlier prophecies of Isaiah. Thus the two parts of the book—the "Assyrian" part and the "Babylonian" part—would have become linked together and, from this time onwards, further material would have been added developing the sense of interconnectedness still further.[15]
(3) Yet a third possibility, however, should also be considered. This is that, from the outset, the material in chapters 40—55 was intended to develop and enlarge upon prophetic sayings from Isaiah of Jerusalem. In this case the later material was intended to supplement the earlier and to influence the way in which it was understood. In this case a further consideration arises, although I shall not deal with it in the course of the present examination. It will have to remain as an issue for further investigation. This is the question whether the contents of chapters 40—55, if they were not at one time an independent body of prophecies from the person of the otherwise unknown "Second Isaiah," should be regarded as forming the unity that has so widely been maintained during the present century.

My present concern is to try to show that this third possibility concerning the origins of the so-called Second Isaiah material is the most probable one, and that it calls for fuller and more serious investigation than it has hitherto received. This position is that, from the time of their origin, the prophetic sayings of Isaiah 40—55 were intended as a supplement and sequel to a collection of the earlier sayings of the eighth-century Isaiah of Jerusalem. I shall certainly not be able to argue that all the material of Isaiah 40—55 can be explained in this fashion, but this is not of itself necessary. Rather I should wish to proceed along the lines of separating the more certain from the less certain aspects of such a conclusion. A few concluding remarks may then be in order concerning what further direction of research such deductions may be pointing us to.

Two Fundamental Themes

We may begin our more detailed investigation by looking at two prominent and fundamental themes to be found in Isaiah 40—55 where a conscious allusion back to themes from the collection of Isaiah's prophecies appears to be intended. The first of these concerns *Israel's blindness and deafness;* three passages call for immediate attention, and a fourth will need to be looked at. The first of these is in Isa. 42:16.

> Then I will lead the blind along the road [. . .][16]
> I will guide them in paths they have not known.
> (Isa. 42:16)

A few verses later a much longer section expressing the same contention appears, making it clear that "spiritual" blindness is what is being referred to:

> Here, you deaf;
>> and look, you blind, that you may see!
> Who is blind except my servant,
>> or deaf as my messenger whom I send?
> Who is blind as the one with whom I am at peace [or, 'who fulfils
>> my purpose']
> or blind as the servant of Yahweh?
>
>> (Isa. 42:18–19)

The following verses (42:21–25) then elaborate further upon this deafness as a failure to listen to, and obey, Yahweh's *tôrâ*.

A third passage with the same theme of blindness and deafness then follows in 43:8:

> Bring forth the people who are blind, yet have eyes,
>> who are deaf, yet have ears!
>
>> (Isa. 43:8)

The following section which enlarges upon this theme then concerns Israel's role as Yahweh's witnesses. This is followed by a kind of "excursus" on the theme of the folly of idolatry in verses 9–20 during the course of which the fourth reference to those who are blind and those who are deaf appears:

> They do not know; nor do they understand; for he has covered over their eyes, so that they cannot see, and their hearts, so that they cannot understand.
> (Isa. 44:18)

This verse clearly intends the reader to understand that the practice of idolatry is a major consequence of the blindness and deafness which has befallen Israel and raises the possibility that we should understand the entire prose excursus on the folly of idolatry as an elaboration of the theme of blindness. It is, in effect, a homiletical discourse showing how spiritual blindness affects people, and could very well be a subsequent elaboration upon the original prophetic text.

The theme of Israel's blindness and deafness, understood in a metaphorical and spiritual sense, is clearly of central importance to Isaiah 40—55. Not only so, but it makes its point in a way which assumes that this deafness and blindness is already known to be the case. Nor do I think that we can properly doubt its source of origin, since it derives from the call narrative of Isaiah and the terms by which he was commissioned with a divinely given task towards Israel:

And he [God] said, "Go and say to this people;
　　Listen carefully, but do not understand;
look intently, but do not perceive.
Make the mind of this people dull,
　　and their ears deaf,
　　and cover over their eyes;
lest they see with their eyes,
　　and hear with their ears,
and understand with their minds
　　and repent and be healed.
　　　　　　　　　　　　　　　(Isa. 6:9–10)

Not only do we have here language so strikingly related to the otherwise unanticipated references to blindness and deafness in chapters 42 and 43 that we should not doubt that the later instances are dependent on the earlier, but the central importance of the original occurrence in the call narrative must further confirm this conclusion.

In case we should remain in any doubt that this is an instance where later prophetic sayings have been modelled on an earlier one, the further taking-up and development of the theme of blindness and deafness in still later prophecies introduced into the book should assist still further in persuading us. The most notable instance of this is to be seen in Isa. 35:5. We have already had occasion to mention that, seen from an editorial perspective, this chapter serves as a kind of summary anticipation of themes and assurances which are found more fully set out in chapters 40—55. Nor can there be very much doubt, I believe, that, in spite of its location within chapters 1—39, the material of chapter 35 is later than, and dependent on, the contents of chapters 40ff. We read in Isa. 35:5:

Then [in the coming time of salvation] the eyes of the blind shall
　　be opened,
and the ears of the deaf unstopped.

It proceeds further to declare the great life-enriching healing and vitality which will mark this new age by affirming that the lame man will leap like the hart and the dumb will speak. All of this rather suggests that the imagery of deafness and blindness is being understood in a literal, and not a metaphorical, sense.

A further, and possibly even later, development of the theme of the ending of the era of blindness and deafness appears in 29:18:

On that day the deaf shall hear the words of a book,
　　and out of their gloom and darkness
　　the eyes of the blind shall see.
　　　　　　　　　　　　　　　(Isa. 29:18)

A point of further interest in this is that the reference to gloom and darkness appears to allude back to Isa. 8:23, thereby linking this imagery with that of blindness. Certainly, if we can reconstruct the chronology of the development of this theme in the book of Isaiah we arrive at the following picture. First Isaiah's call-account used the imagery of Israel's blindness and deafness to signify the refusal of the people to listen and respond to the prophet's message. In chapters 42 and 43 the unknown exilic prophet has taken up this imagery to affirm that it describes a condition which still prevails, but in spite of it God's salvation will quickly come. Further development of the imagery in 35:5 and 29:18 then uses the idea that the ending of (physical) blindness and deafness will characterize the coming great era of salvation. It would seem here that we have a very strong case indeed for regarding the prophetic author of Isaiah 42—43 as familiar with the actual words recorded of Isaiah's call in a section which is usually ascribed to the "Isaiah Memoir."

I should like now to turn to another group of passages in chapters 40—55, which are usually reckoned as the work of "Second Isaiah," where a conscious allusion back to the language of Isaiah of Jerusalem appears intended. This concerns the varied expressions which are employed to affirm *the divine election of Israel;* to stress that Yahweh really has chosen it, in spite of all appearances to the contrary, and to make plain that God has not rejected it. So we find the following:

> Comfort, comfort my people,
>   says your God.
>   (Isa. 40:1)

> But you, Israel, are my servant,
>   Jacob, whom I have chosen,
>   the descendants of Abraham, my friend;
> you whom I took from the ends of the earth,
>   and called from its remotest parts,
> saying to you, "You are my servant,
>   I have chosen you and not rejected you."
>   (Isa. 41:8–9)

> I will say to the north, Give up,
>   and to the south, Do not withhold;
> bring my sons from afar
>   and my daughters from the end of the earth,
> every one who is called by my name,
>   whom I created for my glory,
>   whom I formed and made.
>   (Isa. 43:6–7)

> But now hear, O Jacob my servant,
>   Israel whom I have chosen!
> Thus says Yahweh who made you,
>   who formed you from the womb and will help you:
> Do not be afraid, Jacob my servant,
>   Jerusalem whom I have chosen.
>
> (Isa. 44:1–2)

We could easily go on to multiply many more instances of this theme which is such a prominent one in chapters 40—55 of Isaiah (cf. especially 42:1–4; 43:20–21, 44:5, 21–22; 45:4, 9–10; 51:4, 16; 52:5). So in fact scholars have usually written concerning the distinctive doctrine of Israel's election which is to be found as a new feature in the teaching of Second Isaiah.[17] But, we must ask, is it only the circumstances of the plight of those exiled and imprisoned in Babylon which has given rise to the idea that Yahweh appeared to have rejected his people? This might be sufficient reason for the development of a special doctrine of Israel's divine election by the supposed Second Isaiah. Yet I think that we cannot set aside the evidence that it is precisely in the prophecies of the earlier Isaiah of the eighth century that language is used which clearly affirms that Israel no longer is God's people and that he has indeed rejected her. So it is a distinctive feature of the language of Isaiah, one which has received perhaps insufficient attention from the commentators, that Israel is described as "this people," in a manner which is designed to show that Yahweh is no longer prepared to speak of it as "my people" (so Isa. 6:9–10; 8:6, 12; 28:14; 29:13; cf. further 30:9). Isaiah 10:6 describes Israel as "the people with whom I am angry" (literally, "people of my wrath"). Most prominently Isa. 2:6, which commences the admittedly difficult and heavily overworked unit of 2:6–22, asserts:

> For thou hast rejected thy people,
>   the house of Jacob.
>
> (Isa. 2:6)

Can there be any real doubt here, in view of the clear nature of the original language in Isaiah affirming that God has rejected his people, that this highly distinctive aspect in the teaching of Deutero-Isaiah has arisen in conscious awareness that the opposite had earlier been affirmed? The later prophecy is making unmistakably plain that the time of rejection is now past and that a new age is about to dawn in which the closeness of Yahweh's relationship to his people will be especially evident.

That the prophecies of Isaiah 40—55 should have arisen in a situation where access to a written collection of the prophetic sayings of Isaiah of Jerusalem was possible should in no way surprise us. Hermann Barth has made out a very good case, which I have elsewhere given written support to, that a carefully edited and compiled edition of Isaiah's prophecies had been prepared during the age of Josiah (639–609 B.C.).[18] In this the ending of the time of Assyrian domination over Israel and Judah, which had been central to the historical understanding of Isaiah's prophecies, was affirmed. Yet, it would appear that the view here presented, that particular themes from chapters 40—55 have arisen in conscious development of and response to earlier Isaianic sayings, indicates rather more than a peripheral feature of their origin. It strongly suggests that the concern to carry forward the message of Isaiah of Jerusalem was a significant part of the intention of these chapters from the beginning. All the more is this so in view of their highly distinctive lyrical and psalmlike quality. This would appear to represent more than a rather unusual degree of influence from the tradition of cultic psalmody and to belong closely to the way in which these lyrical sayings were designed to counterbalance the more traditional forms of prophecy which are to be found in chapters 1—32. In any case it certainly suggests that chapters 40—55 should no longer be regarded as the self-contained and independent body of material that it has so widely been thought to be in recent years. The "life and times of Second Isaiah" would appear to be a highly problematic reconstruction on the part of the modern critic!

Other Themes Possibly Developed from Isaiah

So far we have considered only two fundamental themes where a prominent saying from the tradition of Isaiah's prophecies has occasioned developments of them in chapters 40—55. We now come to consider some other possible themes where this feature is also present. In order to establish the general method of approach it seems important that we should endeavour to keep the more certain examples apart from those which are less clearly so. In general we should note in regard to "First Isaiah" the quite extraordinary way in which individual themes based on particular words and verbal images in Isaiah are given later interpretative treatment. So we find that the "briars and thorns" from Isaiah's Song of the Vineyard (Isa. 5:1–7) is a verbal image which is taken up several times subsequently (the original occurrence in Isa. 5:6, followed by 7:23–25; 9:18; 10:17; 27:4). Other images are similarly dealt with, of which probably the most important is that of the "Remnant" implicit in the name of Isaiah's child, Shear-jashub (Isa. 7:3; cf. further 10:20–22; 11:11, 16).

Yet other verbal imagery is given interpretation in this fashion, and it is open to explore whether some of "Second Isaiah's" language may not display similar characteristics. Here immediately comes to mind the mention of Yahweh's "witnesses" which appears in Isa. 43:10, 12 and 44:8 and, most enigmatically so far as its proper significance is concerned, in Isa. 55:4 in a retrospect on the role of David among the nations. We may consider also whether the reference in the "Isaiah Memoir" regarding the conferring of a sign-name on the prophet's son Maher-shalal-hash-baz has not been an influence here. From a reference to those whose task it was to act as "reliable witnesses" (Isa. 8:2) to the inscribing of the child's intended name upon a tablet, the idea has developed that the whole of Isaiah's prophecy is a "witness" to God's action and intentions towards his people. From this has arisen further the idea that all Israel, which is in possession of this prophetic word of testimony from God, can serve as his witnesses (cf. especially 43:10–13). Such an idea might appear far-fetched and unnecessary were it not for the fact that the concern with "witnesses" in Isa. 43:9ff. occurs in immediate sequence to the reference to the blind and the deaf in 43:8.

A further possibility also presents itself in that in Isa. 8:16 the child's name, Maher-shalal-hash-baz, is described both as a "testimony" (*te'ûdâ*) and a "teaching" (*tôrâ*). In 42:4 and 21 the term *tôrâ* = "teaching" is used in a very unusual fashion, since it can hardly be intended as a reference to Yahweh's "law" in the later sense. Rather it appears to refer to Yahweh's "purpose," which is shortly to be realized and which has been declared beforehand by the prophets. With such a wide-ranging and important term such as *tôrâ* it might seem to be special pleading to suggest that an allusion back to Isa. 8:16 may have been intended. Yet it certainly seems to be the case that, so far as its meaning is concerned, a connection with the earlier prophetic usage serves greatly towards a better understanding of its significance in chapter 42.

We may note some further possibilities. It is in Isa. 44:26 that the message of "Second Isaiah" takes on a truly prophetic character where it makes a clear pronouncement about God's future action:

[He it is]
who confirms the word of his servant,
    and performs the counsel of his messengers;
who says of Jerusalem, "She shall be inhabited,"
    and of the cities of Judah, "They shall be built,
    and I will raise up their ruins."

(Isa. 44:26)

Such a saying might appear to be wholly explicable from within the historical context which has been reconstructed for the origin of Isaiah 40—55. Yet once again a most striking counterbalance is achieved to the central terms of the prophetic commission that was given to Isaiah at his call:

Then I said "How long, O Lord?" And he said:
"Until cities lie waste without inhabitant,
    and houses without men,
    and the land is utterly desolate . . ."

(Isa. 6:11)

89

The later passage achieves a very clear effect of declaring that the terms of the original prophetic commission given to Isaiah have been fulfilled, so that the time to restore and rebuild can now begin. Once again it is not merely the fact of interesting verbal connections that catches our attention, but that, both in the terms of the original threat and of the subsequent reversal of it, its centrality to the overall message that is being declared is so evident. In this case too we cannot let pass unnoticed that the later prophecy is insisting that God does "confirm the word of his servant," which may here then refer, not simply to the message that is being given, but to that which has already been given and is now fulfilled.

One further possible instance may be looked at. In the close redactional structure of Isaiah chapter 5 the pronouncement of how Yahweh intends to carry out his punitive purpose upon his people is declared in a passage which pictures him summoning a hostile army from afar, in which there can be no doubt that a reference to the army of Assyria is intended. This act of divine summoning is to be carried out by Yahweh's raising a "signal," or "flag," to them:

> He will raise a signal to a distant nation,
> and whistle to it at the ends of the earth;
> then behold, swiftly, speedily, it comes!
> (Isa. 5:26)

This has a very close counterpart in the unit of Isa. 49:22–23 which declares that Yahweh will raise a signal to the nations to send back his scattered people from among them. The very leaders of the nations, their kings and queens, will assist Israel to make their return. We might have considered this imagery of the raising of a signal flag to have been so established a part of contemporary military practice that it could easily have provided a suitable image for two quite independent prophetic speakers to have adopted it. Yet the theme of this "signal flag" evidently became one of importance to the later, more deeply eschatological development, of the prophetic theme of the great "return" from the nations. Isaiah 11:10 interprets it of the house of David and then 11:12 uses it to designate the time when Yahweh will act to bring about the great return of his people from among the nations. Since these two later developments appear, with near certainty, to be developments based upon the imagery used in 49:22, is it not logical to suggest that, in turn, the usage there has been based upon the original Isaianic saying in 5:26?[19]

It could be argued that, even if all that I have said regarding the conscious allusions back to Isaianic prophecies in chapters 40—55 of the book of Isaiah is conceded, this still does not dislodge the secure position of the widely adopted hypothesis of an unknown prophet, the so-called Second Isaiah, who was active in Babylon during the years between 546 and 538 B.C. This is indeed possible, for it is certainly to be reckoned with that such a prophet may have been in possession of a collection of Isaiah's sayings. Yet such an hypothesis would appear to be less and less likely the more closely the material is investigated. Since the work of Begrich showed the heavy dependence of "Second Isaiah" upon the forms and language of psalmody,[20] the distinctive literary characteristics of this material have been widely remarked upon. The distinctive form of address to "Zion," even apparently for those who were in Babylon, has elicited special comment and attention.[21] Persistently too questions have arisen whether scholarship has been correct in positing for all of chapters 40—55 an origin in Babylon. The place of origin would seem to be a question that is not so readily capable of resolution as may at first appear. In any case my own purpose will have been achieved if a strong case can be made to show that the evidence that the prophecies of "Second Isaiah" reveal a conscious dependence on earlier sayings of Isaiah of Jerusalem is firm and reliable. This in itself would be sufficient cause for those who have preserved the material to have combined the material of chapters 40—55 with the earlier prophecies.[22] In turn this can be shown very clearly to have had a profound influence upon the shaping of the book, since a number of themes, as I have already mentioned, are then taken up still further in its later contents.

A further point deserves mention at this juncture. Since the studies of Gerhard von Rad, a great deal of attention has been given to the so-called traditio-historical method of approach to such a book as that of Isaiah. So, in his interpretation, the presence of elements of the "Zion" and "David" traditions in chapters 40—55 can be explained on the prominence of both within the cultic tradition of Jerusalem upon which both Isaiah, and the later "Second Isaiah," drew.[23] No doubt in the latter case this was at some remove on account of his time of exile in Babylon. Yet what I have been arguing for is essentially of a rather different nature from such an influence from established cultic and political traditions which may be assumed to have had a long and widespread influence in Israel. The distinctive connections that are observable in the formation of the book of Isaiah, where one prophetic saying provides a basis for the development of further sayings related to it, appears as a distinctively prophetic feature. It related to the very nature of prophecy itself, in which particular words and images could be regarded as fraught with special power and significance. So they could be reapplied, reinterpreted, and even recast altogether, so as to provide further images of God's purposes for his people. In time the more intricate and elaborate consequences of this type of prophetic interpretation gave rise to apocalyptic, which cannot properly be isolated from prophecy itself.

If we are also to press the questions concerning the origin of the material in Isaiah 40—55, which has come conventionally to be ascribed to "Second Isaiah," then it would seem that the case for recognizing the contribution made by cultic personnel, the so-called cult-prophets, from Jerusalem is very strong. This has been argued for by J. Vincent, and it appears to be an increasingly probable deduction to make from so much of the recent research into the origin of these enigmatic chapters.[24] Whether this must imply an actual origin in Jerusalem appears to be less certain, and the possibility of a Babylonian setting, as so widely advocated, may be correct for at least some of the material.

A further consequence also appears to be worthy of further consideration and investigation. If the sixteen chapters which have usually been ascribed to "Second Isaiah" are really the work of one man, then they stand unique within the otherwise intricate web of prophecy and prophetic interpretation which constitute the remainder of the book. Nowhere else do we have such a solid and undisturbed block of material left intact. This is not in itself a reason why it should not be the case here. Nevertheless there do appear to be indications that in respect of some material, as in the admonitory rejections of idolatry, later hands have been at work. Overall the formation of the Old Testament books of prophecy has been a remarkably complex sequence of literary and theological developments of ancient written texts. The assumption, which was really never more than an assumption until the end of the eighteenth century, that the unity of these books can be explained as a unity of authorship is clearly mistaken. Yet they do possess a certain kind of unity which belongs to the nature of prophecy itself and the various ways in which it was applied to historical events, which alone could provide its fulfilment, and so, in a real sense, which alone could establish its true meaning.

We might be disposed to describe the processes of unravelling the intertwined threads by which such a book as Isaiah has taken shape as "redaction criticism." Yet, if this is to be so, it behooves us to keep in mind that this is concerned with very different kinds of redactional operations from those which pertained to narrative texts, where the combination of smaller units and themes has been undertaken from quite different perspectives from those which belong to prophecy.

The Unity of the Book of Isaiah

The Book of Isaiah comes to us as a single literary whole, comprising sixty-six chapters, and this given datum of the form of the book must be regarded as a feature requiring explanation. It establishes a basis for the interpretation of the individual sayings and units of which it is made up and provides a literary context which must inevitably affect the interpretation of the several parts of the whole. Furthermore modern critical scholarship has become accustomed to the working principle that the long process of formation of such an ancient literary text reflects a number of levels of interpretation. The examination of features relating to the editorial structure of the book carries with it a number of important considerations and expectations regarding the situations to which its sayings were related and, not least, to the delicate task of establishing some reasonably convincing chronology of the origin of its various component parts. At times we may assume that the literary order of the collection of prophetic sayings points to varying stages in the chronological order of their inclusion in the overall collection. At other times, however, it appears probable that the order has been determined by editorial considerations in which certain literary and theological interests must be postulated in order to account for the positioning of the material. It is several years ago now since Georg Fohrer drew attention to the importance of this factor in accounting for the distinctive structure of Isaiah 1, which has been put together in order to provide a general thematic introduction to the book.[1] It is largely built up from authentic Isaianic sayings, but these must certainly have appeared originally in different parts of the collection where their historical setting would have been more clearly apparent. As it is, their extant form establishes a broad appeal for repentance, rather than pointing to a particular historical epoch of the ministry of the prophet Isaiah.

In an earlier age of scholarship the opening reference (Isa. 1:1) to "Isaiah the son of Amoz" was taken to indicate that all of the prophecies which it contains were given in the eighth century B.C. A few commentators have continued to defend such an assumption, seeking to relate each of them to the ministry and thought of the great prophet of Jerusalem.[2] Yet the development of a historical-critical method of analysis has shown that only by doing violence to a reasoned and meaningful interpretation of many passages can such an assumption be defended. By the time of the publication in 1892 of Duhm's classic commentary on the book[3] all the evidence that is reasonably necessary for the task of literary-critical analysis had been assembled to show that the contents of chapters 40—55 must be ascribed almost entirely to the era of the Babylonian exile in the sixth century B.C. and the contents of chapters 56—66 must be later still. As a consequence the ascription of these sections to a Deutero-Isaiah and Trito-Isaiah respectively has been adopted by a number of scholars. Especially in the case of chapters 40—55 their interpretation has been undertaken with little or no consideration for their setting within the book as a whole. More recently some attempts have been advanced to relate chapters 56—66 to the preceding chapters 40—55, with a consequent questioning of the hypothesis of a "Trito-Isaiah,"[4] but little at all to explain their connection with chapters 1—39. For the most part the book of Isaiah has been interpreted as comprising two separate parts which bear little real relationship to each other. Frequently it has not even been felt necessary to explain how these two parts came to be linked, and when an explanation has been forthcoming it has taken the form of an argument based on literary convenience. It is argued that a leather scroll would be of a certain length, and it would be an economic necessity to make full use of this. Later prophecies might therefore be added in order to fill up a scroll with little concern for the mutual relationships of the content of the various sayings, save in the broadest possible way.

A second possibility, however, has at times been aired by scholars, based upon an argument put forward by the Norwegian scholar Sigmund Mowinckel.[5] This is that the book as a whole should be regarded as the work of "Isaiah's disciples" (cf. Isa. 8:16), so that the unnamed prophets who stand behind chapters 40—66 should be claimed as, in some sense, the disciples of the earlier Isaiah of Jerusalem.[6] The argument here is essentially an adaptation of the earlier assumption that the unity of the book is based upon a certain unity of authorship, with the modification that the author is no longer a single individual but rather a "school," or body of "disciples." Their existence over a period of at least two centuries is postulated without any clear identification of where, or how, such a group maintained itself. The argument in fact rapidly becomes completely circular in that the existence of such a group is attested from the book, the structure of which is assumed to be illuminated by the identification of such disciples. The value of such a hypothesis, therefore, becomes gravely vitiated in the absence of any clear indication of what constituted membership of such a body of prophetic disciples. We have no information to confirm that such a circle actually existed, and to postulate their existence for such a long period of time after the original prophet's death renders the concept of a "disciple" virtually meaningless. What entitled a later figure to claim to be such a disciple, and how far could such a later figure introduce new prophecies of his own alongside the task of preserving and interpreting those of the original master? In the end such a hypothesis seems almost exclusively designed to defend the assumption that the unity of the book can be explained as based upon a form of community authorship. If the historical evidence is so overwhelmingly clear that the book cannot be understood as the product of a single author, then it is assumed that it can nonetheless still be defended as the work of a single identifiable group of authors. Mowinckel himself, who did not in his later work develop this suggestion concerning the circle of Isaiah's disciples, understood the hypothesis in so broad a compass as to separate it from the composition of the book of Isaiah. Such "disciples" were held to have been so central a group in the formation of the Old Testament as to have composed a significant number of psalms, the Decalogue, and the book of Deuteronomy. In other words they were identified by him as a major circle of Jerusalem scribes and legislators.

In reality, however, it is not the questionable character of the hypothesis concerning Isaiah's disciples that should concern us, but rather the questionable nature of the assumption that the unity of the book of Isaiah is to be explained somehow as a unity based on authorship. When we look at the book of Isaiah as it now exists, we can discover a considerable number of indications that it has been assembled over a long period, but with a very clear concern to group prophecies in a thematic fashion. This is more noticeable, for example, in the case of the "Babylon" prophecies of Isaiah 13:1–14:23 where we have a whole series of separate prophecies brought together under the general heading of Israel's encounter with Babylon, dating from the eighth to the sixth centuries B.C.[7] Whether any of the prophecies derived from the eighth-century figure of Isaiah of Jerusalem is uncertain, but it is quite certain that most of them did not. What is clear, however, is that Judah's political involvement with the neo-Babylonian empire began during the period of Isaiah's ministry, as the narrative incident recounted shows (chap. 39). This was eventually to lead to the political submission of Judah to Babylonian power and the destruction of the temple of Jerusalem and the cessation of the rule of the Davidic monarchy from there. The sequence of "Babylon" prophecies (13:1–14:23) is then to be explained as a kind of commentary on Judah's fortunes *vis-à-vis* Babylon over a period of two centuries, rather than as the work of a single author. In a not dissimilar fashion we can see that the attempt on the part of editors to build up an extensive group of prophecies concerning foreign nations and cities (chaps. 13—23) marks a related attempt to establish a measure of editorial unity and connectedness. What we see to be the case in regard to the Babylonian prophecies (13—14) is, in a larger and more complex fashion, true of the book as a whole. Where these two chapters reflect Israel's fortunes at the hands of the neo-Babylonian empire, the book as a whole covers the wider political fortunes of Israel from the eighth to the fifth centuries B.C. Possibly a few prophecies are to be dated later still, but in all essentials the main contents belong to the period of just over two centuries which began with the prophet Isaiah's call in 737 or 736 B.C.

When we look at the literary structure of the sixty-six chapters, some considerations stand out with relative clarity. In the first place, chapters 36—39 have evidently been taken from the corresponding sections in 2 Kings 18—20, with the main addition of Hezekiah's psalm (38:9–20).[8] They have been inserted before chapter 40 at a relatively late stage in the compilation of the book and thereby assist the reader in making the transition from the "Assyrian" part of the book (1—35) to the "Babylonian" part (40—66). In fact the report of the visit of the Babylonian emissaries to Hezekiah (chap. 39) makes a very convenient transition to this Babylonian background by introducing the question of what is to be the fate of Jerusalem and its Davidic monarchy in the face of the threat posed by Babylon. Such a conclusion becomes all the more convincing once we recognize that chapter 35, with its theme of the transformation of the wilderness and the appearance of a highway in it for the return of Yahweh's people to Zion, is basically a summarized "digest" of the main content of the prophecies of chapters 40—55.[9] In other words it makes a suitable conclusion for the first half of the book by introducing an abbreviated summary of the message of hope which occupies the second half.

All of these considerations are sufficient to indicate that the overall structure of the book shows signs of editorial planning and that, at some stage in its growth, attempts were made to read and interpret the book as a whole. There are also many indications, however, to show that the contents of the book have passed through a number of stages of ordering and redaction and that what we now have is the result of a process of editing and addition. It would be possible to suppose therefore that the kind of editorial unity which now binds chapters 1—39 with chapters 40—66 belongs to a late, and relatively superficial, stage in the book's compilation. Yet this appears unlikely, and a number of significant points can be adduced to suggest that the overall unity belongs more prominently to the understanding of the book as a whole rather than it being a superficial stage of development. In the first place it is not just in chapter 35 that the message of chapters 40—55 is introduced into the earlier part in order to balance out the predominantly threatening note of chapters 1—35. There are earlier, similar summarizing assurances of the return of Yahweh's people to Zion (11:12–16; 19:23; 27:12–13), which are based upon the prophecies from chapter 40 on. Even more strikingly, a promise is made (18:7) that the people of Ethiopia will bring gifts to Yahweh's people in Zion, which must certainly have been taken from the prophetic promise given in Isaiah 45:14. Brief as such sayings are, their location and their character point to a clear and concerted attempt to provide certain interim summaries of the overall message of hope so that the separate parts of the book may be appropriately rounded off.

More important than the existence of these brief summaries, however, is the further fact that the overall structure of chapters 1—35 is an unusually complex one, so far as its chronological growth is concerned. By comparison, chapters 40—55 provide the longest single coherent block of prophecies in the whole book. Any process of literary agglomeration, such as is usually postulated, whereby later material was simply added on at the end of an established literary collection, fails to account for the structure of this material. Whereas chapters 40—55 form a reasonably coherent and unified whole, and are usually dated with confidence in the period 546–538 B.C., chapters 56—66 are much less clearly to be assigned to so compact an historical period. Nevertheless, even here, it is highly likely that the various sayings are in a rough chronological sequence and that all are to be dated later than chapters 40—55.[10] This is certainly not so with chapters 1—35, however, where not only do we have sayings which are clearly dependent on the contents of chapters 40—66, but other indications show us that it is within these chapters that we have the latest parts of the book. Most notably chapters 24—27, which are often described as the "Isaiah Apocalypse," must belong to the Persian period and are to be understood as a very late section.[11] Moreover these chapters should certainly not be regarded as forming a self-contained unit which can be read in isolation from the rest of the book. Rather they can be better interpreted as a late apocalyptic recasting and development of earlier prophetic images and themes. This is fully borne out by the large number of references and allusions which are to be found in them, drawn from earlier prophecies.[12] Most prominent in this respect is the New Song of the Vineyard of 27:2–5,[13] which undoubtedly alludes to the earlier Song of the Vineyard (5:1–7). Unfortunately the textual problems and difficulties of Isa. 27:2–5 prevent a very full and clear comparison between the two songs, the first of which is undoubtedly a complex allegory, or *māshāl*. Noteworthy too is the fact that the allegorical interpretation of the theme "thorns and briars" (27:4) has been taken from 5:6 by way of a whole sequence of intervening interpretations which are to be found elsewhere in the book (Isa. 7:23–25; 10:17; 32:13). However the indications are sufficiently firm and impressive to show that there is material present in chapters 1—35 which points to a process of adaptation, reinterpretation, and development in the build-up of the book.

Within recent years two major works have been devoted to the study of the redactional history of Isaiah 1—35.[14] At some stage chapters 36—39 were added to this earlier Isaianic collection, but if we follow the indications which we have already noted, it would appear most probable that this step was taken at a time when much of the material of chapters 40 and following had already been joined to this earlier prophetic book. Recent study of chapters 56—66 has tended to reinforce the awareness that these chapters are closely related to chapters 40—55, even though it is highly improbable that they derive from the same prophetic author. Rather they belong to the period of the late sixth and early fifth centuries B.C. when the restoration of religious and political life was taking place in Judah under Persian imperial supervision. To that extent these chapters highlight the way in which the promises and rich assurances given by the exilic prophet of chapters 40—55 began to take effect. The connection of chapters 56—66 with 40—55 can therefore be regarded as certain and clear, whether the chronological gap which separates these two parts was a very wide one or a narrow one. All of this shows that the major question about the unity of the book of Isaiah concerns the relationship of chapters 40—55 with 1—35. It could be that this relationship is a relatively late feature which emerged only when the separate collections of material were fairly close to their present shape. On the other hand, since we have already been able to note a number of passages in chapters 1—35 which show a literary dependance upon some of the themes of the subsequent chapters, it may well be that we can discover some clues to suggest that the linking of the prophecies of chapters 40 and following with the tradition of Isaiah's prophecies belongs more fundamentally to the structure of the book. Perhaps more important even than this, however, is the recognition that careful examination may be able to show the basis of the connection between the two main parts of the book. That a difference of authorship and of historical setting lies between what we have called rather loosely the "Assyrian" and the "Babylonian" parts of the book is undoubted. Only a very forced and artificial mode of exegesis can associate the prophecies of these chapters directly with the person of Isaiah, whose latest prophecies must be dated very shortly after 701 B.C. The most likely conclusion for us to draw from these facts is that, at some stage in the growth and compilation of the book, the contents of the prophetic message of chapters 40 and following were felt to be an appropriate, and even necessary, complement to the message given earlier in chapters 1—35.

It is not necessary here to reexamine the contentions of those scholars who have sought to trace the collecting, preserving, and editing of the prophetic sayings of Isaiah of Jerusalem whose ministry spanned the years between 737 and 701 B.C. These were the years of Assyrian imperial expansion and aggression which brought an effective end to the old Northern Kingdom of Ephraim (cf. esp. Isa. 9:8–21; 5:24–25) and which left a much-reduced kingdom of Judah as a small surviving vassal kingdom under Assyrian rule (cf. Isa. 1:8). The central message of Isaiah therefore was concerned with the circumstances and reasons for this political ruination, and it was very rightly addressed, in the first instance, to the sister kingdoms of Israel and Judah. Israel and Judah formed Yahweh's vineyard, which had proved unprofitable and which was now about to be laid waste (Isa. 5:1–7). The Song of the Vineyard therefore quite appropriately serves as an introduction to the prophet's message and must once have formed an introduction to a primary collection of his prophecies which is now included in the unit 5:1–14:27. Undoubtedly, a number of additions have been made to this, but we can detect that it began with a warning of the arrival of the Assyrians (5:26–30) and concluded with an assurance of their eventual demise (14:24–27).

That Isaiah had foretold the eventual overthrow of the Assyrians and the removal of the threat which they posed to Yahweh's people Israel (Isa. 10:5–15) appears certain, even though the elaboration of this prophetic assurance of the overthrow of the Assyrians appears to have been undertaken later, building on the prophet's own language.[15] This is the main thrust of the argument presented by Hermann Barth for recognizing a Josianic anti-Assyrian redaction of a collection of Isaiah's prophecies.[16] Since the thesis proposed by Barth has now been widely described and discussed, it is not necessary to examine its major contentions at this stage. It is sufficient simply to note that it sets out a very strong case for recognizing that a major written collection of Isaiah's prophecies was extant before the death of King Josiah in 609 B.C., and that this prophetic corpus was edited and shaped in such a way as to show how Yahweh's purpose had been fulfilled *vis à vis* Israel and the Assyrians in judgment and eventual deliverance and vindication. All of this renders it perfectly possible and feasible that the great unnamed prophet of Isaiah 40—55, who appeared with a message of hope during the latter years of the Babylonian exile, could have known and made allusion to the earlier prophetic collection now embedded in Isaiah 1—35.

Such a conclusion is argued in a rather brief fashion by J.F.A. Sawyer.[17] It must certainly be regarded as a possibility, although it is by no means a necessary conclusion. Apart from the rather indecisive arguments put forward by Sawyer, two individual considerations should be noted. The first of these concerns the much-discussed question of the identification of the "former things" to which the prophet refers (Isa. 42:9; 48:3). It must be held as possible that by such references the prophet was alluding to earlier prophecies of judgment upon Israel, Judah, and Jerusalem which had been fulfilled.[18] That these were specifically the subject of earlier prophecies of Isaiah is a possible explanation of these claims, although it is difficult to determine whether the prophet himself, or his subsequent editor, made such a conscious connection.

Rather more direct and imposing in their support for the belief that the exilic prophet of Isaiah 40—55 did know and allude to the prophecies of Isaiah are two references to the unresponsiveness of Israel to the divine message (see 42:18–20; 43:8). The explicit declaration of the blindness and deafness of Israel described there echoes very strikingly the words of the prophetic commission of Isaiah (found in Isa. 6:9–10).

The metaphors of blindness and deafness used to describe spiritual insensitivity may appear sufficiently obvious and straightforward, so that we could conclude that it has been purely a fortuitous chance which has led to their being adopted by two quite independent prophetic figures. Nevertheless, the very strong and unanticipated way in which they appear in Isa. 42:18–20 and 43:8 suggests that their employment here is due to a conscious allusion to the commissioning speech of the prophet Isaiah. Furthermore, the metaphors of blindness and deafness used to describe the condition of Israel which made it unable to respond to the divine warning through the prophet Isaiah are given a unique emphasis in the call narrative. It would be quite understandable, therefore, that a later prophet, who had come to view the entire period of Israel's subjugation to the Mesopotamian powers of Assyria and Babylon as one of national blindness and deafness, should have deliberately picked up such a theme in stressing the joyousness of his new message.

Nor is this all, since, in a short redactional passage (Isa. 32:1–8) which must derive from the Josianic editors of Isaiah's prophecies, it is the theme of blindness and deafness which is expressly picked up (see Isa. 32:3). If Deutero-Isaiah had access to a written collection of his predecessor's prophecies, it would have been most natural that the theme of Israel's blindness and deafness should have appeared in it as a very striking feature of the prophetic explanation for the catastrophes which had overtaken Israel. Nor is this the end of the matter, since we find that in the hopeful summary of the message of Isaiah 40—55, which is set out in chapter 35, once again it is the theme of Israel's blindness and deafness which is pointedly referred to (35:5).

Looking at it overall we can see that a striking instance of unity in the book of Isaiah is provided by the idea that the prophetic message from God falls upon deaf ears and is set forth to people who are unable to comprehend what their own eyes see. It marks a theme which was introduced by Isaiah himself in his account of his call. It was thereafter taken up by the later prophet of the Babylonian exile and by at least two groups of editors who used it to shape and interpret the material which they helped to compile. In particular, it is the manner in which that theme reaches across the major division of the book which marks it out.

This brings us back to the leading issue that confronts us in studying the structure of the book of Isaiah and which has in reality remained a pressing question ever since a technique of literary-historical criticism came to be applied to it. What is the fundamental connection between the predominantly hopeful message of chapters 40—55 and the largely threatening one of chapters 1—39?

Primarily, we must recognize that prophecy was a message about Israel and its destiny, so that the factors which have led to the bringing together of its various sections and sayings were essentially thematic and religious rather than literary or biographical. In this regard it is evident that Isaiah of Jerusalem had delivered a sharply threatening announcement of judgment and disaster upon Jerusalem. Most of all this is to be seen in Isaiah 2:6–4:1, although other passages, too, appear with a similar note of threat. I have argued fairly extensively elsewhere for a recognition that these threats came to be linked with the capture and destruction of Jerusalem by the Babylonians in 587 B.C.[19] Although it may at first appear strange to associate the prophecies of Isaiah with an event which took place more than a century after the latest of his sayings had been delivered, it would not have appeared so to ancient scribes and editors. Prophecy was regarded as a "living" word from God which could take effect in more than one way and at more than one time. There are, in any case, a significant number of glosses and additions in the book which show that a significant revision was made in the wake of the destruction of Jerusalem in 587 B.C.

Alongside this phenomenon, we already have in the book of Jeremiah a most instructive narrative instance showing the way in which a prophecy concerning the fate of Jerusalem (Jer. 26:16–24) given more than a century before could be cited to help illumine a later event. We can add to this the point already made, namely, that Isaiah 39 was incorporated into the book of Isaiah precisely to associate the fate of Jerusalem and the Davidic monarchy at the hands of the Babylonians with the prophecies of Isaiah. Taken together, these factors point to the conclusion that the body of Isaianic prophecies which had taken shape by the time of Josiah's death in 609 B.C. came subsequently to be used in order to obtain some understanding of why the catastrophes of 598 and 587 B.C. had happened.

In broad measure the prophecies of Isaiah had provided a divinely given insight into the reasons for the judgments which had befallen Israel and Judah at the hands of the Assyrians since the beginning of the Syro-Ephraimite crisis in 736 B.C. Out of this series of disasters Judah had at first survived with a Davidic ruler still on the throne and its chief city Jerusalem relatively intact. It is small wonder that the institution of the Jerusalem temple, as well as that of the Davidic monarchy, should have become regarded as especially favored by God (cf. Isa. 37:35). Yet the events of 598 and 587 had overthrown even these convictions, which certainly were not part of the message of Isaiah himself, but which had nonetheless come to be associated with his prophesying and with the events of his prophetic ministry. Once the Jerusalem temple had suffered destruction and the Davidic dynasty had been removed from Judah, a renewed urgency and severity attached to Isaiah's prophecies which had warned of judgment even upon the city of Jerusalem itself. It is entirely understandable in the light of this that a further revision of the written Isaianic collection was made.[20] We have good reason, therefore, for concluding that the prophecies of Isaiah came to be used and interpreted by the survivors of 587 B.C. in order to understand the reasons for what had befallen them. To this extent the book of Isaiah was set alongside the books of Jeremiah and Ezekiel, both of which, in the hands of different scribal groups, came to be focused sharply upon the fate that had befallen Judah and Jerusalem.

Once the connection between the prophecies of Isaiah and the destruction of Jerusalem is recognized as a factor in the way the book of Isaiah came to be developed, we have the single most essential clue towards understanding why the prophecies of chapters 40 and following came to be incorporated into the book. It was a fundamental aspect of the motives and interests which influenced the scribes who have preserved and ordered the various prophetic collections that they have sought to ensure that divine threats be followed and counterbalanced by divine promises. With this in mind, it is not difficult to see why prophecies which had foretold Jerusalem's destruction should have been followed by the much warmer and reassuring note found in Isa. 40:1–2.

In the absence of any other note concerning the historical background of this exilic prophet, or of the reasons for the punishment which Yahweh had inflicted upon Israel, it would appear intentional that these reasons should have been found in the prophecies and forewarnings of doom which abound in the earlier part of the book of Isaiah. Far from Deutero-Isaiah having an entirely independent and self-contained message of his own to declare, his message can quite properly be understood as a complement to that which has preceded it in the earlier chapters of the book. Whether the original prophet of the exile saw this, or whether it was a circle of later editors who felt the appropriateness of adding his message to that of Isaiah, makes very little difference to its distinctive meaning. The main point is that the earlier, and more primary, collection of prophecies in which the fate of Jerusalem figured prominently was seen to be effectively filled out and complemented by those from the exilic age. In a similar fashion the threat of the Day of Yahweh in the "Babylonian" prophecy (13:6–8) must refer to the day in which the Babylonian armies destroyed Jerusalem. Yet this was subsequently complemented by a prophecy of the overthrow of Babylon (13:17–22).

Our major contention here, therefore, is that the conjunction of the prophecies of chapter 40 and those following with those that precede them was a deliberate step taken by the scribal redactors of the book for a profoundly religious reason. It had nothing to do with matters of literary convenience or assumed identity of authorship but was designed to clarify and fill out the divine message given to Israel, and especially to Jerusalem. In this regard we find that this thematic connection between the two major parts of the book of Isaiah was especially concerned with the fate of Jerusalem and with the Davidic dynasty.

The relationship of chapters 56—66 of the book with its preceding parts is still a topic requiring fresh investigation and discussion. Nevertheless, it is reasonably clear that these eleven chapters, with their proto-apocalyptic character, were intended to be understood, not as a fresh and entirely self-contained declaration from Yahweh to the postexilic community, but rather as a carrying forward of the divine word as it had been declared on the eve of the overthrow of Babylon by the unnamed prophet of chapters 40—55.[21] Its central concern with Jerusalem, instead of with the wider political entity of Israel, marks the bringing of the divine message into the changed circumstances of the new era. Even so, in chapter 62 (vv. 6–12), it manages to retain an effective link with the earlier prophecies of the book in which the fate of Jerusalem, Zion, and the temple that stood there had occupied a prominent place.

This passage (62:6–12), declaring in colorful and vivid imagery the glories of the rebuilt and restored Jerusalem, develops and rounds off fittingly the promise given earlier (55:11–17). This in turn redresses the note of warning and threat to Jerusalem which is to be found in a number of earlier passages in chapters 1—32. It can hardly be satisfactory, therefore, to seek an interpretation of a passage such as this as though its literary context made little difference to the way in which we are to understand it. It stands at a significant endpoint in a series of declarations of Yahweh's word concerning Jerusalem. To this extent there is a measure of connectedness and unity imposed upon the book of Isaiah. This is not in any way to minimize the achievements of those scholars who have shown how varied are the component parts of the book and who have sought to trace the particular historical contexts to which each unit belongs. Nevertheless, such a process has tended to highlight the disunity that abounds and has encouraged a pattern of interpretation which has paid too little attention to the links and interconnections which are also present. Not least it has often led to the treatment of passages in isolation which were never intended to be so understood since, from the outset, they took the form of additional interpretations and applications of more primary units.

To trace the process of literary growth by which the book of Isaiah came to assume its present shape is a task which cannot yet be regarded as completed. The useful essays into tracing the redactional history of such a large and primary work have not yet achieved anything approaching a consensus regarding the relative dating of each of its component parts and sayings. Nevertheless, it must be claimed that the recognition that such a redactional history was undertaken by ancient scribes and interpreters for profound spiritual and interpretative reasons is an important factor for us to bear in mind. The prophetic word of God is essentially a divine message concerning his actions and intentions towards his people, and it should not be surprising for us to discover that it has been the continuity and connectedness of this divine purpose which provides the proper basis of unity in the four major prophetic collections.

Part 3

JEREMIAH

7

Jeremiah 1—25 and
the Deuteronomistic History

To a significant extent the prophetic books may be regarded as collections of collections in which the primary material consists of prophecies that were originally orally delivered and most of which were originally short in length. They have been preserved in writing by unknown editors, and in this process of written preservation some degree of grouping and structuring of the prophecies has certainly taken place. By what principles this structuring occurred is far from clear. The inclusion of short superscriptions (as in Jer. 1:1–3; 2:1; 3:1; 7:1; 11:1; 21:11; 25:1–2) has served to offer some brief contextual setting for the prophecies, and there appear also to be appropriate closures (so Jer. 5:18–19; 9:12–16). It is possible that other units were intended to mark transition points in the collection. Since we do not know in what context the prophecies were read, whether by small groups of trained scribes, or by larger communities in more formal acts of public confession and worship, the role of these beginnings and endings is not clear. They do little more than provide a bare minimum of historical information for the elucidation of the prophecy. They are, however, sufficient to indicate that we cannot be altogether dismissive of the role of the book's editors.

Alongside this we can note that there sometimes appear to be signs of a chronological sequencing of material, although this is not consistently carried through and the context of many prophecies remains obscure. Such a chronological scheme, even though very incompletely maintained, seems likely to reflect the processes of transmission. Further to this we may note that the classification of material on formal grounds, best linked with the name and work of Sigmund Mowinckel,[1] contains some implications for the editorial shaping of the book. Mowinckel himself appears strongly to have hinted in the direction of assuming that the different classes of material were preserved in different transmission strata, although he later modified this conclusion substantially.[2] Yet the nature and content of the so-called Source C material fails to support the conclusion that it derives from a separate transmission "source" as such. It appears rather to have been intended to be read in conjunction with other material in the book, on which it is partly dependent.

All of this suggests that we are faced either with assuming (1) that there is no very clear structure at all to the grouping of prophecies in Jeremiah 1—25, other than a very loose one or (2) that whatever structure there may originally have been had undergone significant disturbance in the course of the book's further preservation and transmission.

What I wish to do here is to suggest one avenue of investigation, which appears to me to be sufficiently defensible to be worth serious consideration, and which does have some bearing upon the historical and literary context in which the book of Jeremiah was formed.

Prophecy in the Deuteronomistic History

There exists in 2 Kings 17:7–23 a very noteworthy reflection upon the final collapse of the Northern Kingdom, under Hoshea, before the power of King Shalmaneser of Assyria. It is listed by Martin Noth as one of the key passages, otherwise set out in the form of speeches or prayers, by which the Deuteronomist directly injects an element of meaning and explanation into the events narrated concerning Israel's rise and fall.[3] We may summarize the main contents relatively concisely:

1. The people of Israel had sinned against Yahweh their God. . . . They had worshipped other gods. . . . They set up for themselves pillars and sacred poles. . . . They served idols, of which Yahweh had said to them, "You shall not do this" (vv. 7–12).
2. Yet Yahweh warned Israel and Judah by every prophet and every seer, saying, "Turn from your evil ways and keep my commandments and my statutes, in accordance with all the law that I commanded your ancestors and that I sent to you by my servants the prophets." They would not listen but were stubborn, as their ancestors had been. They went after idols and became false. . . . They rejected all the commandments of Yahweh their God . . . (vv. 13–17).
3. Judah also did not keep the commandments of Yahweh their God, but walked in the customs that Israel had introduced . . . (vv. 19–20).
4. When he had torn Israel from the house of David, they made Jeroboam son of Nebat king. Jeroboam drove Israel from following Yahweh and made them commit great sins. The people of Israel continued in all the sins that Jeroboam committed; they did not depart from them. . . . So Israel was exiled from their own land to Assyria until this day (vv. 21–23).

The four central themes are the following: (1) The Northern Kingdom of

Israel had been disloyal to God, and this is proven by its idolatry. (2) Yahweh had warned of God's anger through prophets, but the people rejected the prophetic warnings. (3) Israel was punished by being sent into exile, but Judah also has disobeyed God. (4) Disloyal kings, who followed the path of Jeroboam and disobeyed God's law, were primary causes of Israel's downfall.

What is worthy of note is that this reflects very closely indeed the central themes of the structure of Jeremiah 1—25. We can outline these as follows and note the correspondences. It is evident that this overall structural pattern is introduced by the opening call and commissioning narrative of Jer. 1:1–9 and is provided with a summarizing conclusion in Jer. 25:1–14. These two units provide an outer framework for the whole larger structure. The call narrative, with its appended visions, reflects a certain stylizing, but almost certainly draws on authentic elements of the Jeremiah tradition. It serves both as an affirmation of the divine origin and authority of the message that is given in the book that follows, and also as a key to its central message. This latter is then the subject of Jer. 25:1–14, which is unusual in that it makes reference to the written scroll of the prophecies (25:13), but, by doing so, clearly betrays its role as a formal ending to a literary collection. It must undoubtedly have been composed to perform this function.

The recognition that the material characterized by Mowinckel as "Source C" had its origins in a Deuteronomistic circle of authors has gained convincing recognition among recent scholars.[4] The purpose of the present study is to extend this towards a recognition that the structural shape accorded to Jeremiah 1—25 also betrays a strongly Deuteronomistic origin. By demonstrating this shape, it is hoped to suggest ways in which the use of the Jeremiah prophetic tradition contributed a major, and final, component of the Deuteronomistic theological development of the exilic era.

Both the opening and concluding sections of Jeremiah 1—25 contain explicit summaries of the purport of Jeremiah's prophecies (so especially 1:14–19 and 25:8–14). Such summaries reveal their purpose of serving as editorial guides to the comprehensive written collection of Jeremiah's sayings referred to in 25:13. They have been designed from the outset to introduce, explain the historical relevance of, and summarize the message of the prophet Jeremiah. Their message, put briefly, is that God has called for hostile nations to come from the north to threaten and punish Judah for its many and grievous sins. These nations will set their thrones against Jerusalem to accomplish God's judgment upon the city (Jer. 1:14–16). This enemy from the north has materialized in the person of Nebuchadrezzar, who is Yahweh's "servant" to punish Judah (25:9), so that the whole land will be left a ruin (25:11).[5] While this enemy comes to inflict God's punishment, the faithful prophet, within the walls of Jerusalem, will be threatened but not overwhelmed (1:17–19).

Judah and Israel

Jeremiah 2:1–3:5 follows the call narrative with a long, and broadly based, indictment of Israel as a whole, but specifically addressed to the citizens of Jerusalem (Jer. 2:2). The nature of the indictment and the appeal back to the national origins in the wilderness make it clear that it is still "all Israel" that is the subject of this prophetic condemnation. However, the immediate sequel in 3:6–11, which is, unexpectedly, specifically ascribed to "the days of King Josiah" (3:6), affirms that the punitive lesson meted out to the Northern Kingdom had not been learned by Judah. "Yet for all this her false sister Judah did not return to me with her whole heart, but only in pretense, says Yahweh" (Jer. 3:10). On the contrary, Israel's disobedience was not as bad as that of Judah: "Faithless Israel has shown herself less guilty than false Judah" (3:11). The central features here are consistent with a Deuteronomistic origin.[6] The appeal to Israel to return to Yahweh, which follows in 3:12–4:2 (interrupted by the reassuring insertion of 3:15–18) then establishes the possibility of repentance and renewal. What follows this in 4:3–6:30 is then very explicitly addressed to "the people of Judah and the inhabitants of Jerusalem" (Jer. 4:3; cf. also 4:5, 11; 5:1, 20).

All of this suggests that there is an overall structure extending from 2:1 to 6:30 which pivots upon the basic assertion of 3:10–11 that Judah was more guilty of disobedience to God than its sister kingdom in the north. This links up closely with the Deuteronomistic assertion of 2 Kings 17:7–23 that the Northern Kingdom's downfall was an act of Yahweh's punishment upon her. Although it is true that this concerns what happened to the Northern Kingdom in the eighth century, the lesson that it teaches was evidently intended to be a lesson learned by Judah. If Yahweh punished Israel so harshly, how much more did Judah and Jerusalem deserve to be punished since their sins were greater than those of the sister kingdom in the north! Jeremiah's prophecies were addressed to a specific community in a particular crisis situation. The structural setting has provided this warning with a larger context by establishing that the threat to Judah was fully justified and vindicated by comparison with the fate of its sister kingdom in the north. When the Northern Kingdom had suffered at the hands of the Assyrians, Judah had failed to heed the implicit warning this had provided.

That the overall structure of Jer. 2:1–4:2 endeavours to make this the lesson to be learned from the fate of the Northern Kingdom in the eighth century B.C.E. can then be better understood if precisely the opposite conclusion was the one widely held. Study of the presuppositions of Josiah's cultic reform, of the rise and development of the Deuteronomic reform movement as a whole, and of the kind of hot-headed counsel that appears ultimately to have swayed Zedekiah into rebellion against Babylon—all these point to the conclusion that this was indeed the case in Judah.[7] Judah's survival in the

eighth century, which contrasted with the ruination of the Northern Kingdom, had been widely interpreted as a mark of Judah's loyalty to Yahweh, in
contrast to Ephraim's faithlessness. It is possible to go on from this to suggest that, at the heart of the reform movement which motivated Josiah, there
lay such an interpretation of the events of the eighth century. It has left an
imposing legacy in the collection and redaction of Isaiah's prophecies, and
not least in the elaborated accounts of what had happened when Sennacherib confronted Hezekiah in 701 B.C.E. Judah's reprieve from Sennacherib's threat was understood as a consequence of her faithful allegiance to
the Davidic dynasty (cf. 2 Kings 19:34). Therefore, a primary problem of
theodicy lay before the Deuteronomic movement—that of showing why the
"favoured" deliverance of Judah at the time of Ephraim's near destruction
should have turned out merely to have been a temporary reprieve. What was
thus necessary was to demonstrate that Judah's sins were as great as, and indeed even worse than, those of its sister kingdom in the north. This is precisely the central point of the section that follows in Jer. 7:1–10:25.

Idolatry—The Worst of Sins

If we turn next to consider the question "What was the evidence that the
Northern Kingdom's downfall was an act of punishment from God?" we
have a clear answer set out in 2 Kings 17:7–12, with its decisive summarizing conclusion: "they served idols, concerning which Yahweh had said to
them, 'You shall not do this'" (v. 12). This is then precisely the controlling
theme which holds together the larger unit of Jeremianic prophecies in Jer.
7:1–10:16. It is introduced by the Deuteronomistic prose address concerning the Jerusalem temple in 7:1–15,[8] an affirmation regarding the useless-
ness of animal sacrifice as a means for removing sin (7:16–26), and a denun-
ciation of the evil nature of the child-burning cult on the high-place of
Topheth, which defiled the very temple area itself (7:30–34). The Jerusalem
cultus had become no better than a form of idolatry, alongside which the
overt practice of idolatry was widespread among the people (Jer. 10:10–16).
The final unit of Jer. 10:12–16, which is didactic in character, reasserts the
folly of idolatry as a form of human delusion. It would certainly appear that
this admonition, with its psalmlike formulation, was originally of independent origin. Nevertheless the theme that it expresses, that idols are a delusion, that they characterize the worship of Gentile nations, but Yahweh is
the true God, is a significant summing up.

The accusation of idolatry and its inevitable punishment holds together
overall the unit of Jer. 7:1–10:16 and points directly to the central Deuteronomistic polemic regarding the downfall of the Northern Kingdom in
2 Kings 17:7–12. Not only are Judah's sins worse than those perpetrated by

its sister kingdom in the north, but they are essentially of the same character, namely idolatry. The detailed evidence given in support of this argues, as in Ezek. 8:1–18, that the temple of Jerusalem had become the setting for such idolatrous acts (Jer. 7:30–34). Even worse, this temple of Yahweh had been made into an idol (Jer. 7:4), for the people had trusted in its physical actuality rather than in the God who was worshipped there (Jer. 7:8–11).

The short unit of Jer. 10:17–25, which follows this extended affirmation concerning the idolatrous character of Judah's religion, concludes the section by offering a summary concerning the prophet's message and the divine judgment that it foretold. That there is an overall structure to the section of Jer. 7:1–10:25, which has been loosely built around the theme of idolatry, appears certain. So also does the fact that it is markedly Deuteronomistic in character. Where the reformist tendencies on which this movement was built had adopted a progressively more restrictive attitude towards the temple cultus, now the Deuteronomistic editors have affirmed that the entire cultus of Jerusalem had become unacceptable to God. First Hezekiah's age had witnessed the rejection of the Nehushtan image (2 Kings 18:4). Then later the Asherah symbol within the temple had needed to be condemned (2 Kings 21:7). The line of polemic was now drawn to an endpoint by the comprehensive condemnation of the temple cultus as idolatrous because of the way in which worshipers trusted in it falsely. Certainly much of this must be regarded as reflective apologetic made in the wake of the catastrophe of 587 B.C.E., but no doubt authentic Jeremianic material can be found in it. The important point is that the accusation of idolatrous practices has been built up to provide an explanation for a religious disaster of immense proportions. God had to destroy the sanctuary where the name of Yahweh was invoked, because of the manner in which it had been abused. In defense of such a claim the earlier example of the fate of Shiloh is cited (Jer. 7:14).

The Prophet as Covenant Mediator

The lengthy section extending from Jer. 11:1–20:18 begins with a general introduction concerning the covenant nature of Israel's relationship to Yahweh and evidences a strongly Deuteronomistic character (Jer. 11:1–8).[9] This feature has been widely recognized, not least on account of its forthright covenant language and ideology. However, it is not simply the Deuteronomistic nature of this piece by itself, but the fact that it appears clearly to have been designed in order to establish a covenant framework for the larger unit it introduces. It is followed directly by a presentation of the prophet's role as a mediator of this covenant. The painful nature of this mediatorial role is illustrated by the first of Jeremiah's "confessions," which immediately follows it (Jer. 11:18–20). This appears as a response to the threat upon his life made by the people of Anathoth (Jer. 11:21–23). At the beginning of the larger unit, therefore, a certain structural pattern is established: the prophet of God is a mediator of the covenant between Yahweh and Israel, but this mediatorial role is threatened by popular rejection.

Jeremiah is presented as the intermediary established by God to summon the people back to obedience to the covenant. However, not only had the people broken this covenant (Jer. 11:10) but their actions in threatening Jeremiah's life now served as proof of their rejection of the prophetic mediator. As the larger unit unfolds, punctuated by the further pain expressed through Jeremiah's confessions, we find that the experiences of the prophet parallel closely those of the "founder" of the covenant—Moses. Yet, whereas Moses' intercession had availed to avert final disaster for Israel's ancestors in the wilderness before their entry into the land (Deut. 9:8–29), this could not now be repeated. Jeremiah's prayers could not avail to avert the inevitable consequences of the people's total rejection of Yahweh as Israel's God (Jer. 11:14–15). Israel's refusal to hearken to the prophet's words is demonstrated by the rejection of the message-bearer.

The theme of mediation, which provides a structure to the whole unit, is then further exemplified by additional signs of the people's rejection of the prophet (Jer. 15:15–21; 17:14–18; 18:19–23) and intensified warnings of the judgment that must follow. The entire sequence of Jeremiah's so-called confessions finds its theological context in the understanding that the prophet is, like Moses, a mediator of the covenant. His likeness to Moses is spelled out for all to recognize in that he suffers pain and rejection as Israel's founding leader had done.

In case this point might be overlooked it is given explicit declaration in the brief introductory unit of Jer. 15:1–4. The Deuteronomistic character of this is clear[10] and is strikingly reinforced by the cross-linkage to 2 Kings 21:10–15, which refers to the period of Manasseh's reign, with all its fearful brutalities, as explanation for the fact that even Josiah's reforms could not avert the final downfall of Jerusalem and Judah. If we follow the suggestion of F. M. Cross,[11] then this use of Manasseh's reign as explanation of the final catastrophe was a late feature introduced into the Deuteronomistic History. It helped to turn the original more hopeful narrative composed in Josiah's reign into one coloured by awareness of ultimate disaster at the hands of the Babylonians.

This covenant theology has an oddly dual character. On the one hand it makes clear that judgment is not a predetermined and fixed fate, but affirms that room for mediation and reconciliation exists. On the other hand it introduces a conditional factor that does not shrink from envisaging that Israel might finally be destroyed. The story of Moses' intercession in the wilderness serves to demonstrate this point. That prophets served Israel's needs as intercessors, in the manner of Moses and Samuel, is expressly made clear in Jer. 15:1:

> Then Yahweh said to me: "Though Moses and Samuel stood before me, yet my heart would not relent concerning this people." (Jer. 15.1)

Overall it is clear that the historical figure of Moses has exercised a powerful role on the part of the editors of Jeremiah 1—25 in shaping a portrait of the office and role of Jeremiah as a prophet.[12] At the same time a reverse influence is also evident on the part of the Deuteronomists in which the portrait of Moses has been shaped according to Judah's encounter with prophets such as Jeremiah. "Deuteronomy saw Moses as the first of the prophets. Intercession was an integral part of his prophetic vocation."[13]

The conclusion of the entire larger unit comprising Jeremiah 11—20 finds its climax with a violent outburst from Jeremiah in which the prophet complains against the total rejection of his message by the people (Jer. 20:7–12). The full extent of this rejection, and the ultimate cry of pain with the prophet's recognition of its irreversible nature, are revealed in Jeremiah's curse upon the day of his birth (Jer. 20:14–18).

All of this parallels very closely indeed the highly distinctive Deuteronomistic presentation of the prophets as the rejected mediators of God's covenant set out in 2 Kings 17:13–14:

> Yet Yahweh warned Israel and Judah by every prophet and every seer, saying, "Turn from your evil ways and keep my commandments and my statutes, in accordance with all the law that I commanded your ancestors and that I sent to you by my servants the prophets." They would not listen but were stubborn, as their ancestors had been, who did not believe in Yahweh their God. (2 Kings 17.13–14)

What is especially significant in this, and what links it so closely with the Jeremianic material, is that it not only presents the work of prophets as that of covenant mediators, but it presents the rejection of such prophets as an accomplished reality. This marriage between the idea of popular rejection and of the "true" prophet marks a formative stage in the development of the notion that God's faithful prophet is a martyr figure.[14] Such a development has provided a central feature of the Deuteronomistic interpretation of prophecy in the divine economy of Israel.[15] Admittedly such earlier figures as Amos and Hosea were "rejected" prophets of this kind, but not until the time of Jeremiah could it be fully recognized that prophecy had "failed" in the sense that it had been unable to avert the final collapse of the surviving part of Israel as Yahweh's people. Until that time the hope could still be entertained that God's appointed prophets would summon the people back to their ancestral loyalty.

Jeremiah is, in fact, the paradigmatic illustration of the degree of total national rejection of the message of the prophets which is described in this

Deuteronomistic reflection. The theology of covenant shows the conditional nature of Israel's continuance before God; the prophets are portrayed as reaffirming the terms of this covenant. Now the figure of Jeremiah, typified in his rejection, serves to make plain that Israel has not kept the covenant and must suffer the inevitable curse spelled out in Jer. 11:1–8. More than any other prophetic figure he is presented as the classic exemplar of "the prophet like Moses" who is ascribed an ongoing place in the life of the nation in Duet. 18:15–22.[16]

If these observations are correct, to the effect that there is a close correlation between the structure of Jer. 11:1–20:18 and the portrayal of Jeremiah as an outstanding exemplar of the Deuteronomistic conception of a prophet "like Moses," then some significant features must be related to them. Not only are there passages of an undoubtedly Deuteronomistic flavour within the larger unit as a whole, as has been widely recognized, but the overall framework bears a Deuteronomistic character. The individual "confessions" of the prophet are located so as to highlight this covenant-mediatorial role. Kathleen O'Connor notes this vital structuring role of the so-called confession passages within their larger setting:[17]

> The arrangement and distribution of materials, the development of the theological argument, the placement of the confessions and the unifying function of both the call account and closing summary show that the final form of cc. 1–25 came from a writer.

Overall the structure of Jeremiah 11—20 demonstrates, in a comprehensive fashion, an important presupposition of the covenant theology that the Deuteronomists had come to embrace. Disobedience could push Israel beyond the brink of disaster. Whereas Moses had interceded successfully with Yahweh on Israel's behalf,[18] such intercession could now no longer hold back the nation from catastrophe.

Undoubtedly all of this has been given its final shape in the aftermath of 587 B.C.E., as we should expect. It uses fundamental elements of the Deuteronomistic theology to develop a theodicy. The confessions attributed to Jeremiah have been incorporated by the prose writer in order to illustrate the indictment of Israel and to explain the disaster that finally overtook the nation.[19] Nevertheless it is not simply a backwards-looking review, justifying an irremediable situation of the past. Rather it is forward-looking in that it ties the explanation of past tragedy to concepts of covenant, and to the realities of prophecy and *tōrâ*, which were to carry the remnants of the nation into a new future.

The Faithless Shepherds

We can move on then to a further observation in respect of the concluding part of the structure of Jeremiah 1—25. The final section in Jer.

21:1–24:10 has, as its central core, a series of prophecies concerning the fate of the various kings of Judah who ruled, sometimes only briefly, during Jeremiah's ministry. These prophecies are introduced in 21:1–10 by a prose section, with a broadly based announcement to Zedekiah, the last of the Davidic kings to rule in Jerusalem, that the city will fall to the king of Babylon. The collection of prophecies that deal with the Davidic kingship therefore begins chronologically at the end with the last of such rulers, but in a way that is thematically appropriate since it draws attention to the fact that it is the fate of the dynasty as a whole that is at issue. That this was an issue that lay close to the centre of the Deuteronomic movement as a whole is shown by the fact that the notion of a dynastic promise to the royal house of David provides the Deuteronomistic History with a pivotal centre (2 Sam. 7:1–17).

The sequel to the introduction in Jer. 21:1–10 concerning the fate of Judah's royal house is a sharp condemnation of an unnamed "king of Judah" in Jer. 21:11–14. This monarch is addressed in 21:13 as "You who are enthroned above the valley." It is likely that one specific ruler was originally intended (Jehoiakim?), but, as it now stands, a larger framework has been accorded to it showing that it is the entire "house of David" that is threatened (cf. the address in v. 12). As it now reads, the threat serves to draw out the important feature that the reproof, raised against an individual ruler in Jerusalem, places in jeopardy the future of the entire Davidic dynasty.

This feature is even more fully brought out in the passage that follows, which has served as something of an exemplary illustration of the manner in which the prophet's Deuteronomistic editors have developed the message of his prophecies. There stands in verses 6–7 a short poetic threat, addressed to an unnamed king of Judah:

> For thus says Yahweh concerning the house of the king of Judah:
> You are like Gilead to me,
>   like the summit of Lebanon;
> but I swear that I will make you a desert,
>   —cities without inhabitants.
> I will prepare destroyers against you;
>   all of them with their weapons,
> will cut down your prime cedars
>   and hurl them into the fire.

(Jer. 22:6–7)

The authentic Jeremianic origin of this unit can be reasonably defended, with its poetic play on the imagery suggested by the impressive House of the Forest of Lebanon (cf. 1 Kings 7:2; 10:17, 21). The link with 21:13–14 through the imagery of "forest" and "fire" is clear.[20] However, the threats of 21:11–14 and 22:6–7 addressed to the contemporary Davidic ruler have been given a Deuteronomistic elaborative interpretation in 22:1–5 that reinforces the threat and provides it with a fuller explanation.[21] W. Holladay opposes the Deuteronomistic ascription of this material, while largely conceding the strength of the arguments for it.[22] The kingship, even that of so august a dynasty as that of David, is to serve the welfare of the people by upholding justice (v. 3). It must operate within the requirements of the divine covenant made at Horeb between Yahweh and Israel.

This point is then spelled out further, and quite explicitly, by the Deuteronomistic editors in 22:8–9:

> When many nations pass by this city and say among themselves, "Why has Yahweh treated this great city like this?" Then they shall answer, "Because they abandoned the covenant of Yahweh their God and worshipped other gods and served them." (Jer 22:8–9)

In this manner the threat directed against a specific ruler in Jerusalem, most probably Jehoiakim, is broadened by the book's editors into a condemnation of the dynasty which he represented. The behaviour of one individual king is drawn upon to demonstrate that the future of the entire dynasty had been put in jeopardy. The God-given grace of a royal house could not override the necessity for each king to rule with justice and fairness. Where, in the past, such failure of individual kings had brought condemnation upon themselves, the message is now extended to threaten the continuance of the Davidic dynasty.

That the monarchy was a conditional institution in Israel is a point explicitly made by the Deuteronomistic historian (cf. 1 Sam. 12:25), and this is fully in line with the concessionary nature of the institution of kingship in Israel set out in Deut. 17:14–20. Jeremiah 22:9 makes the same point by insisting that the royal throne of David was subordinate to the covenant that Yahweh had made with his people. So we come to see that the editorial framework which has been given to Jeremiah's royal prophecies displays a strongly Deuteronomistic character. The Davidic kings were to be regarded as mediators of Yahweh's covenant with Israel, but only if they themselves obeyed the conditions of this covenant (cf. especially vv. 4–5).

Following on these primary oracles dealing with the Davidic kingship we have pronouncements concerning the fate of Shallum-Jehoahaz (Jer. 22: 10–12), Jehoiakim (Jer. 22:18–19, preceded by sharp invective in vv. 13–17), and Jehoiachin (Jer. 22:24–30).

We can then relate this point to the observation that the structure of Jer. 21:1–24:10 appears to display a distinct interest in the fate of the Davidic dynasty in general, over and above the question of the personal fates of the last individual rulers of Judah. This more comprehensive concern with the final collapse of what had survived as a remnant kingdom of Judah, epitomized in the fate of its royal rulers, is further shown by the placing of 24:1–10 as a concluding element. Whether or not this unit, with its lessons from the good and bad figs, really goes back to a saying from Jeremiah has been disputed. J. Unterman summarizes a very probable conclusion thus: "It cannot be denied that 24:4–7 has all the signs of an authentic Jeremianic prophecy."[23] W. Holladay would locate the saying in 594 B.C.E. Yet this is not to deny that there has been some Deuteronomistic elaboration of Jeremiah's words, and the placing of the unit in its present position appears to fulfill a particular editorial role.[24]

The symbolic fate of the good and bad figs comes to a meaningful end with a warning that King Zedekiah of Judah, together with those who had remained with him in Jerusalem, were all doomed (vv. 8–10). The significant point for the overall structure of Jeremiah 1—25 is that the characterization of the Judaean community as "bad figs" has been given a larger significance in the wake of subsequent events and thereby has served to orient the hope expressed in the book towards the community exiled in Babylon. The threefold agents of death—sword, famine, and disease—link together the opening and closing sections concerning the disastrous nature of Zedekiah's reign from its beginning to its end (so especially 21:9 and 24:10, see also 29:18).

By the use of such opening and closing declarations, the prophecy of 24:4–7 concerning the fate of the "bad figs" who remained in Judah after 598 B.C.E. is related to an awareness of the tragic events of 587 B.C.E., which had brought the kingdom of Judah, and the royal dynasty which had given it a divine foundation, to an end. This is then repeated in 29:17. The final rounding off of the whole collection in Jeremiah 1—25 is then given in 25:1–38, with a remarkable summary statement of what was regarded as the divine plan determining the world events relating to Jeremiah's ministry in 25:8–13.

Clearly it cannot occasion surprise that a prophet such as Jeremiah should have made forceful pronouncements concerning the various kings who ruled Judah after Josiah's death in 609 B.C.E. Undoubtedly these rulers carried a primary level of responsibility for Judah's ultimate downfall. What is surprising is the extent to which the Deuteronomistic framework that is given to these royal prophecies invests them with a larger theological and political significance. Not only is the Davidic monarchy, as a primary institution of Israel, accorded only conditional approval, but the fate of the Davidic dynasty as a whole is placed in question. We cannot be in doubt that it is the Deuteronomistic editors of the book who have imposed this broadened layer of meaning onto Jeremiah's prophecies, and that they have done so in the light of what they knew had taken place in 587 B.C.E., with as much help as they could obtain from Jeremiah's authentic prophecies. At the same time they have used these prophecies to address issues that lay open, and unresolved, in the major history-work they had compiled.

The conditional interpretation of the kingly office compares closely with the Deuteronomistic historian's explanation of the role of the monarchy in contributing to the downfall of the Northern Kingdom:

> When he [Yahweh] had torn Israel from the house of David, they made Jeroboam son of Nebat king. Jeroboam drove Israel from following Yahweh and made them commit great sin. The people of Israel continued in all the sins that Jeroboam committed; they did not depart from them until Yahweh had removed Israel out of his sight . . . (2 Kings 17:21–23)

In this evaluation the importance of the kingship as an institution is affirmed, its role in the downfall of the Northern Kingdom recognized, and the central significance of the Davidic dynasty implied. Defection from allegiance to the Davidic dynasty is presented as the beginning of Ephraim's misfortunes. These assertions fit smoothly with the points which the editorial framework of Jeremiah's prophecies to Judah's kings seeks to bring out. Kingship only existed within Israel in order to serve the needs of the Mosaic covenant.

Conclusion

It remains to draw some basic conclusions from this examination of the structures of Jeremiah 1—25. First of all we may note again the primary point that there is a broad structural shape to these chapters, which fall into four major sections. These deal respectively with the coming downfall of Judah, rendered inevitable because it had failed to heed the warning implicit in the fate of the sister kingdom of Ephraim more than a century earlier. Second, the question of the temple of Jerusalem is focused upon, and the necessity for its destruction is explained in terms of the idolatry practised there. The historical sanctuary had served as a cover for idolatrous practises, but worst of all, the temple itself had been made into an idol because it had been treated as a false basis of security. The belief that human beings could "possess" the presence and power of deity, and could thereby be assured of divine protection, was precisely what made an image of God an offence and an illusion. The house of Yahweh in Jerusalem had been regarded by the people of Judah in the same manner that worshipers of an idol believed that it gave them assurance of divine protection.

The third and fourth sections of the prophetic collection of Jeremiah 1—25 focus respectively upon two types of divine mediation. The first is that of Israel's prophets whose task had been to warn Yahweh's people of the divine anger when they departed from obedience to the divine order. The second was that of kingship, and more particularly that of the dynasty of the royal house of David, which had ruled in Jerusalem for almost four hundred years.

These are all issues of prime significance for the Deuteronomistic movement, the origins of which are to be traced back to Josiah's reign, and perhaps even earlier still to the time of Hezekiah. It is a well-nigh classic expression of the situation outlined by Max Weber that the words of a "charismatic" prophetic leader have led to a process of "routinization" in order to make his words accessible and adaptable to a larger community and their ongoing needs.[25] However, in the structure given to Jeremiah 1—25 the shaping of the units does not simply reassert familiar, and firmly established, features of Deuteronomistic theology. Instead it uses these central themes as a tool for accommodating, interpreting, and applying Jeremiah's prophecies. This literary process illustrates very clearly the way in which a prophet's editors provide the record of his sayings with a context of historical, theological, and institutional references by which the enduring meaning of his prophecies is to be grasped. It illustrates the aims of such a work of "routinization" by which the unique and extraordinary elements of the prophet's preaching are set within a larger context in which they are to be applied and understood.

The Final Days of the Deuteronomistic Movement

If these observations are correct regarding the structural shape that has been accorded to Jeremiah 1—25, then they provide us with an important clue to the origin and purpose of many of the Deuteronomistic elements to be found within this impressive collection. From the outset this material was written, and was designed to serve, a literary and theological purpose. Its intention is to be seen in the literary and structuring role which it serves in its surviving location in the Jeremiah scroll. This at least would appear to be the case for such passages as Jer. 3:6–12, 15–18; 7:1–15; 11:1–8; 21:1–10; 22:1–9; 24:1–10; 25:1–14. There is therefore no need to posit a separate stratum of supposed Deuteronomistic homilies, composed independently and subsequently incorporated into the scroll of Jeremiah's sayings. The aim rather has been to elucidate and elaborate the meaning of Jeremiah's prophecies, seen in the painful retrospect of the events of 587 B.C.E. The Deuteronomistic authors were writers, not preachers, a characteristic which is wholly in line with the observations of M. Weinfeld regarding the wisdom-scribal aspects of the Deuteronomistic literature.[26]

A further conclusion deserves serious consideration. If, as is argued here, Jeremiah 1—25 displays a clear structure, a coherent attachment to central Deuteronomistic themes, and an overall conformity in its theological ideas, then it is this work which constitutes the original "Deuteronomistic" scroll of Jeremiah's prophecies.[27] Admittedly some subsequent additions have been made to this, but these are not extensive, and essentially the work has survived as a coherent and consistent unity. When we turn to Jeremiah 26—52, however, the situation is substantially changed. Not only are the literary forms significantly different, with much narrative reportage (Mowinckel's "Source B"), but the theology and political outlook are very much modified. Most notably this is evident on three key issues: kingship, covenant, and Israel's future hope. It would extend the present study too far to explore these in detail, but we may note some basic points.

In the first instance the hope of a restoration of the Davidic dynasty has been accorded a major role (Jer. 33:14–26), whereas the original "Deuteronomistic" edition of Jeremiah's prophecies was indifferent to this, and even basically negative in its attitude to such an expectation. Secondly, the covenant theology of Jeremiah 1—25 has been wholly changed and recast with the introduction of the hope of a "new" covenant in Jer. 31:31–37. Thirdly, and perhaps most remarkably, the original hope of Jeremiah 1—25, which looked for a survival and renewal within Judah of a chastened and penitent community, has been abandoned. All hope for the future now rests with a return from Babylonian exile of those who had been taken there in 598 B.C.E. and later (Jer. 29:1–31.26).

Clearly much authentic reminiscence of Jeremiah's part in the events of Judah's final collapse has been preserved and much echoing of "Deuteronomistic" language and theology is still to be found. Nevertheless the move beyond the central ideas and themes found in the Deuteronomistic History and Jeremiah 1—25 is very marked. The original Deuteronomic movement has clearly collapsed, and new expectations and ideas have taken over the centre stage in the light of new events!

What we have is essentially an original book of Jeremiah's prophecies, edited by the Deuteronomic circle most probably at a time close to the completion of the History (c. 550 B.C.E.?) and an extensive addendum to this in Jeremiah 26—52. This was forced upon the Deuteronomic traditionists in the wake of major upheavals that took place in Judah after 550 B.C.E., and part 2 of the present Jeremiah book undoubtedly reflects this. We may go on to speculate that the original editorial composition of Jeremiah 1—25 took place in Judah, where all the Deuteronomistic literary ventures had their home. The location where the revised book (Jeremiah 1—25 plus 26—52) was completed is no longer clear, although a Babylonian setting would seem to be most plausible.

If these conclusions regarding the origin of Jeremiah 1—25 and its connections with the Deuteronomic movement are valid, then we may venture a further comment. Since the study by Noth of the overall shape and composition of the Deuteronomistic History, scholars have noted the seeming abruptness and enigmatic nature of its conclusion in 2 Kings 25:27–30.[28] If our conclusions regarding the involvement of the Deuteronomic circle in the editing of Jeremiah's prophecies are correct, then we can see in the major shift between the shape of Jeremiah 1—25 and that of Jeremiah 26–52 some important clues as to how this enigma came to be resolved.

There is also an unresolved question concerning the strange pessimism of the work, if it held out no clear line of hope for Israel's restoration in the future.[29] The awkwardness and seeming unlikelihood of such perceptions are considerably reduced once we recognize the closeness of the connections between the History and the Deuteronomistic edition of Jeremiah's prophecies. They were both products of the same scribal-theological circle. Positions left unresolved in the History, particularly those regarding the uncertain future of the kingship and the restoration of national life in Judah as God's people,[30] are much clarified by the original Deuteronomistic book of Jeremiah (Jeremiah 1—25). At the time when this was made there was still room to hope that the Judaean community, penitent and spiritually furnished with the Mosaic *tôrâ*, would lift itself up from amidst the ruins of Jerusalem and rebuild the city and surrounding countryside. This was a hope that Jeremiah personally clearly shared (Jer. 40:1–12). By the time that the revised scroll of Jeremiah appeared (Jeremiah 1—52), all such expectation had been abandoned and the idea of "Return" (Heb. *šûb*), both spiritually and physically to the land of Judah and to its cultic centre Jerusalem, remained the only effective line of hope that appeared practicable.

If the claim is correct, therefore, that the original Deuteronomistic edition of Jeremiah is to be found in Jeremiah 1—25, then we are able to shed considerable fresh light upon the contrasting patterns of future hope which took time to achieve resolution after the catastrophe of 587 B.C.E.

Jeremiah: Prophet of Hope

In a quite striking fashion Jeremiah, who has in popular estimation been re-membered as "the weeping prophet," was the prophet through whom the message of hope for the rebirth of Israel came to the fore. Although it is true that we do not have from him anything like the sustained sequence of prophetic promises and assurances that we find in Isaiah 40—55, we do en-counter a remarkable message of hope, founded on the nature and purpose of God himself and declared to Judah in a time of nightmare, horror, and desolation. It is as if Jeremiah had looked into the abyss of Judah's total ruin and destruction and had then, almost in contradiction of his own feelings of despair, heard God's word of hope given to him in the very hour of deepest darkness. In order to reconstruct the time and situation in which this glow-ing divine assurance came to light, we must first examine two basic features which affect very greatly the overall interpretation of the book of Jeremiah. These concern the literary structure of the book, especially insofar as this relates to the prophecies of hope which it contains, and the historical back-ground of the prophet's career. In the latter connection we are, of course, concerned in particular with recognizing those periods of his ministry when a message of assurance and hope can most readily be explained and under-stood.

The Literary Problem

Jeremiah's prophecies of hope are primarily grouped together in chapters 30—33, which has led to the description of these chapters as "the Book of Consolation," especially in view of the obvious heading that is given to them in 30:1-3. Even here we find that the group of prophecies breaks apart into two quite clear sections, comprising chapters 30—31, most of which is in po-etic form, and chapters 32—33, almost all of which is in prose. Much of chapter 32 is made up of a narrative relating an incident which can be pre-cisely dated to the time of the siege of Jerusalem in 588/7 B.C. There can be no reason for doubting that this collecting together of the prophecies of hope has been an intentional action on the part of an editor, so it cannot be implied that all of the prophecies which are to be found there were given at roughly the same time. In fact, it seems clear that the narrative incident of 32:1–15 has provided a point of anchorage for the drawing together of other prophecies of hope to this position. When we look at the contents of the Book of Consolation in Jeremiah 30—33, we find that it consists of prophetic material representative of all three main categories which are to be found in the book as a whole. There are in chapters 30—31 a number of beautiful and memorable prophecies set out in poetic form, which have generally been classified as the primary basis of Jeremiah's recorded preaching.[1] Besides this we have in the narrative of 32:1–15 an account in which Jeremiah is referred to in the third person, which belongs alongside similar narrative reports preserved in Jeremiah 26—29, 34—45.[2] This material is sometimes referred to as the "Baruch Narrative" on the assumption that Baruch was either the author, or at least the primary informant, of the narrative. There are also some homiletical prose passages which show a distinctive preaching style and which make extensive use of language and ideas elsewhere employed in the book of Deuteronomy.[3] What is clear, therefore, is that the collection of the hopeful prophecies into a single group was achieved at a fairly late stage in the process of compiling the book of Jeremiah's prophecies and that it drew upon different source collections. This, as we shall see, has a bearing upon their interpretation.

Two points have special bearing upon our immediate task. The first of these is that the narrative source from which 32:1–15 has been drawn shows evidence of having been edited and revised in the light of the destruction of Jerusalem in 587 B.C.[4] For this reason we can understand that it puts a very special emphasis upon the role of the exiles who had been taken to Babylon. They are viewed explicitly as the group of Israelites through whom the restoration and rebirth of Judah would be achieved. The second point is of a similar nature and concerns the prose homilies, which also display a marked post-687 coloring.[5] Such homilies look back upon Jeremiah's actual prophetic utterance and record it after some interval of time. J. Bright has described such reports of prophecies as prophetic "reminiscence," since they do not record the actual words which Jeremiah is likely to have used, but rather focus upon the main "gist," or central theme.[8] Opinions among scholars have varied over the closeness with which such "reminiscences" stand to Jeremiah's own words, with some, like J. P. Hyatt, virtually refusing to accept any Jeremianic content,[7] while others affirm that Jeremiah can be regarded as the effective author of the material.[8]

From our point of view what is most important is to recognize the way in which such reminiscences look back upon earlier prophecies, which evidently had a very reproving and threatening character, and combine them with a message of hope concerning the rebirth of Israel from among the

Babylonian exiles, which quite certainly took its origin in the time around 687 B.C. This must be true of the account of Jeremiah's visit to the potter's house in 18:1–12, where the hopeful message implicit in verses 8–9 appears to draw upon this note of assurance from after 587 B.C. So too the prophecy concerning the two baskets of figs (Jeremiah 24), which was addressed by Jeremiah to those citizens of Jerusalem who had remained in the city after the first deportation to Babylon in 598 B.C., has been expanded with a hopeful reference to the fate of those in Babylon (vv. 4–7). We find a similar rounding out of Jeremiah's original prophecy, couched in a very distinctive homiletical style, in the account reporting the sending of Jeremiah's letter to the exiles in Babylon (29:1–32). When we look at this letter and its contents in close detail we find that its primary purpose and intent was to warn those who had been taken to Babylon that their stay there would be a long one. Against the false advice of the prophets in Babylon who had been promising a speedy return to Judah, Jeremiah insisted that these people would spend their entire lifetime—seventy years (29:10)—in Babylon. The message to them from God, therefore, was that they should settle down in Babylon and build their homes there:

> Build houses and live in them; plant gardens and eat their produce. Take wives and have sons and daughters; take wives for your sons, and give your daughters in marriage, that they may bear sons and daughters; multiply there and do not decrease. (Jer. 29:5–6)

When we look at the more hopeful message, centering upon the possibility of the repentance of these exiles and their eventual return to their homeland (vv. 10–14), we find that it clearly refers, not to an immediate possibility, but to one that will eventually become real, after the seventy years have elapsed:

> For thus says the LORD: When seventy years are completed for Babylon, I will visit you, and I will fulfil to you my promise and bring you back to this place. For I know the plans I have for you, says the LORD, plans for welfare and not for evil, to give you a future and hope. Then you will call upon me and come and pray to me, and I will hear you. You will seek me and find me; when you seek me with all your heart, I will be found by you, says the LORD, and I will restore your fortunes and gather you from all the nations and places where I have driven you, says the LORD; and I will bring you back to the place from which I sent you into exile. (Jer. 29:10–14)

Although we cannot rule out the possibility that this message forms a part of Jeremiah's original letter to those deported to Babylon, it seems much more probable that, in establishing a final written presentation of Jeremiah's message, the note of hope and assurance which properly came to light during the crisis of 588–87 B.C. has been combined with prophetic messages given before that time. In this way the most important of Jeremiah's prophecies have been given a more comprehensive and rounded form. On the other hand, if such a message of hope had been made so explicitly by Jeremiah before 587 B.C., it is difficult to understand why its coming appears to take him so unawares and to challenge his despairing resignation to Judah's final destruction. Rather than portray the prophet as a figure alternating between periods of hope and despair, it seems that we can best see his message of hope as arising at a quite specific time in his career. In any case we must also add that there are a number of features of a literary and theological kind which indicate that the message of hope contained in such prophecies as 18:1–12, 24:1–10, and 29:1–32 represents a post-587 revision of prophecies that originally belonged to an earlier phase of the prophet's career.

The Historical Problem

We can be somewhat briefer in looking at the bearing which some questions concerning the historical background of Jeremiah's career have upon his message. The superscription in Jer. 1:2 dates the time of the prophet's call in the thirteenth year of Josiah's reign, 626 B.C. Yet we have few, if any, prophecies which can be certainly dated to the years of Josiah's reign, which continued until 609 B.C. with that king's untimely death in battle. One of the few prophecies firmly ascribed to Josiah's reign is found in Jer. 3:6–14, a prophecy of some concern to us since it is an appeal to the remains of the Northern Kingdom of Ephraim to return to God. The important story of the compilation by Baruch of a scroll of Jeremiah's prophecies in the fourth year of Jehoiakim (Jer. 26:1), 605 B.C., shows that the formation of a book of Jeremiah's prophecies did not begin until relatively late in his career. It is not surprising, therefore, that very different scholarly estimates have been expressed on the question whether we have many, or even any, prophecies from Jeremiah which are to be dated before 609 B.C. In the classic work of John Skinner, *Prophecy and Religion*,[9] as well as in the reassessment of Skinner's positions advocated by H. H. Rowley,[10] the position is argued that we do have a number of prophecies stemming from the reign of Josiah, that is, from before 609 B.C. On the other hand the position adopted by Hyatt, that Jeremiah's call did not come until 609 B.C., rules out such a possibility.[11] We may note something of a mediating position advocated by Norman Gottwald in placing the date of the prophet's call in 616 B.C.[12]

All of this has very direct relevance for the question of the prophet's message of hope since it is virtually impossible to think that Jeremiah could have proclaimed messages of hope and assurance to Judah during the reign of Jehoiakim (609–598 B.C.), whose attitude and policies he so bitterly condemned. Since the commentary of Paul Volz on the book of Jeremiah, published in 1922,[13] the view has been pressed that Jeremiah did have a message of hope, combined with an appeal for an immediate return to Yahweh, from early in Josiah's reign, probably from a time close to that of the great reform of religion. This position has been taken up and advocated by W. Rudolph in his commentary on Jeremiah's prophecies.[14] Not only does Rudolph regard the prophecy of Jer. 3:6–18 as belonging to this early, Josianic stage of Jeremiah's activity,[15] but he places the original basis of Jer. 30:1–31:40 here also.[16] Furthermore, he regards the primary addressees of these prophecies as the survivors of Ephraim, the old Northern Kingdom of Israel, which had been broken up under Assyrian imperial rule. Certainly we cannot altogether rule out the possibility that Jeremiah had viewed the time of Josiah's reformation as one of renewed hope for both Israel and Judah.

There is also a later period, which can only have been brief and short-lived, when we can credibly fit a number of hopeful prophecies from Jeremiah into the general framework of Judah's history during his lifetime. This period was after 598 B.C., when Jerusalem had been captured by the armies of Babylon and when Jehoiachin, along with many of the leading citizens of Judah, had been deported to Babylon (Jer. 52:28). When Zedekiah was then placed on the throne of Judah there appeared a time of respite from the agonizing trials that had marred the preceding decade since Josiah's death. Such at least would appear to be the most straightforward interpretation and implication of the prophecy which makes a heavy play of the meaning of the royal name Zedekiah:

> Behold the days are coming, says the LORD, when I will raise up for David a righteous Branch, and he shall reign as king and deal wisely, and shall execute justice and righteousness in the land. In his days Judah will be saved, and Israel will dwell securely. And this is the name by which he will be called: "The LORD is our righteousness." (23:5–6)

The giving of the name "The LORD is our righteousness," which is a direct interpretation of the name Zedekiah, points clearly to this king's reign (598–587 B.C.), and the character of the formulation shows that it has been modeled upon the auspicious "coronation oracle" form for a new king. It must therefore have been given at the beginning of Zedekiah's reign, at the time of, or shortly after his accession. Many commentators, however, including Skinner,[17] regard the prophecy as heavily ironic, intended to direct attention away from Zedekiah, who is regarded as unworthy to bear his name, and to point to the future coming of a new king who will more truly live up to the promises implicit in his Davidic ancestry. In many ways this seems too subtle an explanation of the passage since there is no clear indication that it is intended to be an ironic dismissal of Zedekiah and the possibility for the rebirth of Judah which his accession marked. On the other hand, the authenticity of the prophecy to Jeremiah is not above question,[18] and in any case the hopes which may have flourished briefly with the submission of Judah to Babylon after Jehoiakim's act of rebellion quickly evaporated away.

An examination of Jeremiah's prophetic career in the light of its historical background shows, then, that, even before the great turning point of 587 B.C. when Jerusalem suffered massive destruction at the hands of the Babylonians, there were two periods when some message of hope from God may be fitted into Jeremiah's preaching. Yet even having conceded this point, it seems that neither is a very strong or firmly secured attestation of his prophetic message. They are possibilities and no more, and such a conclusion leads us to recognize that it was during the great crisis brought on by Judah's defeat and destruction in 588–587 B.C. that Yahweh's word of hope became clear and incisive to Jeremiah. As such it marks one of the great turning points in the entire corpus of the prophetic literature of the Old Testament.

Jeremiah's Message of Hope

We can turn now to look at the passage which must of necessity hold the central position in any consideration of Jeremiah's assurance for the rebirth of Israel, Jer. 32:1–15. The passage is a narrative recounting an incident which happened to the prophet during the time of the siege of Jerusalem by the Babylonian forces in 588–587 B.C. Bright boldly affirms that this narrative "is of the utmost importance for the light that it casts on the hope that Jeremiah held for the future."[19] The action took place in the tenth year of Zedekiah's reign when Jeremiah was held as a prisoner in Jerusalem and was visited by a relative from his native town of Anathoth. Since Jeremiah was attempting to visit Anathoth when he was arrested (Jer. 37:11–14), it appears probable that news of the situation in Anathoth had already become known to the prophet. The matter of the relative's visit concerned Jeremiah's right, under Israelite legal practice (cf. Lev. 25:25), to purchase (literally, to "redeem") land belonging to the family which had become open for public disposal. In order to retain such family property within the wider confines of the ancestral group, the right of "redemption" was conferred primarily upon the next-of-kin in a clearly defined line. For the person upon whom such a right was conferred there was a corresponding obligation to maintain the family's property inheritance by such means as a way of preserving its honor and protecting its long-term interests:

> Jeremiah said, "The word of the LORD came to me: Behold, Hanamel the son of Shallum your uncle will come to you and say, 'Buy my field which is at Anathoth, for the right of redemption by purchase is yours.' Then Hanamel my cousin came to me in the court of the guard, in accordance with the word

of the LORD, and said to me, 'Buy my field which is at Anathoth in the land of Benjamin, for the right of possession and redemption is yours; buy it for yourself.' Then I knew that this was the word of the LORD." (32:6–8)

The way in which the incident unfolds provides us with a dramatic understanding of the manner in which ordinary life situations could suddenly become filled with new meaning and significance as the prophet recognized within them "the word of the LORD." As the situation unfolds further, so the content and character of God's word become more precise and explicit:

And I bought the field at Anathoth from Hanamel my cousin, and weighed out the money to him, seventeen shekels of silver. I signed the deed, sealed it, got witnesses, and weighed the money on scales. Then I took the sealed deed of purchase, containing the terms and conditions and the open copy; and I gave the deed of purchase to Baruch the son of Neriah son of Mahseiah, in the presence of Hanamel my cousin, in the presence of the witnesses who signed the deed of purchase, and in the presence of all the Jews who were sitting in the court of the guard. I charged Baruch in their presence, saying, "Thus says the LORD of hosts, the God of Israel: Take these deeds, both sealed deed of purchase and this open deed, and put them in an earthenware vessel, that they may last for a long time. For thus says the LORD of hosts, the God of Israel: Houses and fields and vineyards shall again be bought in this land." (32:9–15)

The content of the message of hope is clear, that there will one day be a return to normal life and business and all the processes of work and agriculture in the land that was at that time so ravaged and threatened by the armies of Babylon. The ominous and fearful setting, made all the more poignant by the fact of Jeremiah's own personal imprisonment at the hands of his own people, makes a great contrast to the simplicity and certainty of God's word of hope. At a time when Jeremiah could feel the cold grip of near despair and hopelessness, he found that the word of God alone provided a new assurance for the future. Nor at this stage is there any indication as to how soon the return to normality would come about, nor even in what specific political context it would be realized. It is simply a clear and firm assurance that the word of God alone is the ultimate ground and certainty of hope.

The sealing of the deed is then made the subject of a beautiful and moving prayer from Jeremiah (32:16–25) in which the prophet reflects upon the nature of God and on the way in which this merciful and saving nature has been revealed in the history of the sinful and undeserving people of Israel. God had indeed been merciful and gracious, and in this simple commercial act of the purchase of a field, Jeremiah had encountered for himself the element of hope which that divine mercy brought. Yet it was not a hope which was valid for himself only, but for all the people who would survive to take their place in this new Israel that would one day be born.

We must turn now to look at two prophecies from Jeremiah, contained in "the Book of Consolation" (chaps. 30—33), which are addressed to the survivors of the old kingdom of Ephraim. Volz, Rudolph, and Bright all locate these early in Jeremiah's career,[20] from a time close to the reform of religion in Jerusalem sponsored by Josiah in 622 B.C. They are to be related, therefore, to the appeal for the return to Yahweh of these survivors set out in 3:6–13. Such a date would certainly fit the prophecies quite well, but we ought not to rule out the possibility that these two prophecies stem from after 587 B.C., during the brief period of Gedaliah's governorship.[21] It is quite conceivable that, staring at the ruins of Judah and Jerusalem, Jeremiah should have become very conscious that the promises of God concerned all Israel, and so have turned his attention to the remains of the Northern Kingdom. In fact, as a native of Anathoth, it is possible that Jeremiah felt himself to belong to Israel as a whole, rather than to the narrower political interest of Judah.[22]

> Thus says the LORD:
> "The people who survived the sword
>   found grace in the wilderness;
>   when Israel sought for rest,
>   The LORD appeared to him from afar.
> I have loved you with an everlasting love;
>   therefore I have continued my faithfulness to you.
> Again I will build you, and you shall be built,
>   O virgin Israel!
> Again you shall adorn yourself with timbrels,
>   and shall go forth in the dance of the merrymakers.
> Again you shall plant vineyards
>   upon the mountains of Samaria;
> the planters shall plant,
>   and shall enjoy the fruit.
> For there shall be a day when watchmen will call
>   in the hill country of Ephraim:
> 'Arise, and let us go up to Zion,
>   to the LORD our God.'"
>
> (31:2–6)

The meaning is clear, since the essential content of the hope for the future of Israel consists in the return to normal life, with security and prosperity for agriculture and vinedressing, that had been denied to Israel for so long. That "the hill country of Ephraim" is addressed, and that its citizens are to go up to worship God in Zion, is not a mark of the subservience of the Northern Kingdom to Judah but of the reunion of the two kingdoms. To some degree Josiah's reformation had endeavored to establish such a reconciliation of the two kingdoms, but in a number of respects a date for this prophecy during Gedaliah's governorship would appear the more probable when, with both Ephraim and Judah lying in ruins, the truth became clear to Jeremiah that only in harmony with each other could the purpose of God for Israel be achieved.

The prophecy in Jer. 31:15–22 must be closely allied with that of 31:2–6 and located at the same point in Jeremiah's ministry. It is among the most poignant and vivid poetic expressions of hope in the Old Testament. It pictures Rachel, the ancestral mother of the nation, weeping over her dead children until God commands her to wipe away her tears and to recognize the great future that now awaits those who have been scattered among the nations:

> Thus says the LORD:
> "A voice is heard in Ramah,
>   lamentation and bitter weeping.
>   Rachel is weeping for her children;
>   she refuses to be comforted for her children,
>   because they are not."
> Thus says the LORD:
> "Keep your voice from weeping,
>   and your eyes from tears;
> for your work shall be rewarded,
>   says the LORD,
>   and they shall come back from
>   the land of the enemy.
> There is hope for your future,
>   says the LORD,
>   and your children shall come back
>   to their own country.
> I have heard Ephraim bemoaning.
> 'Thou has chastened me, and I was chastened,
>   like an untrained calf;
> bring me back that I may be restored,
>   for thou art the LORD my God.
> For after I had turned away, I repented;
>   and after I was instructed, I smote upon my thigh;
> I was ashamed, and I was confounded,
>   because I bore the disgrace of my youth.'
> Is Ephraim my dear son?
>   Is he my darling child?
> For as often as I speak against him,
>   I do remember him still.
> Therefore my heart yearns for him;
>   I will surely have mercy on him,
>   says the LORD.

"Set up waymarks for yourself,
   make yourself guideposts;
consider well the highway,
   the road by which you went.
Return, O virgin Israel,
   return to these your cities.
How long will you waver,
   O faithless daughter?
For the LORD has created a new thing on the earth:
   a woman protects a man."
                              (31:15–22)

    As in Jeremiah's other hopeful prophecies it is important to note how emphatically the source and certainty of this hope is found in God himself and not in any specific historical or political eventuality. Its certainty is divinely guaranteed, although no explicit timescale is introduced, nor does the prophet leave his hearers to suppose that it will be an immediate possibility for them.

    The two prophecies in verses 7–9 and 10–14 which stand between these two unquestionably genuine Jeremianic ones contain language and ideas very similar to those in Isaiah 40—55. Bright's verdict is no doubt correct: "They seem to represent an adaptation and application of Jeremiah's prophecies to the situation of the exiles."[23] Once we bear in mind that prophecy was understood and recorded as a comprehensive message from God, rather than a record of the sayings of individual prophetic figures, we can see how important it was for the editors of the prophetic literature to strive for some coordinated and interconnected picture of the hope that God had set before his people. In the light of this it makes good sense that Jeremiah's message of hope should have been amplified in the context of the fuller message of the return given in Isaiah 40—55:

For thus says the LORD;
"Sing aloud with gladness for Jacob,
   and raise shouts for the chief of the nations;
proclaim, give praise, and say,
   'The LORD has saved his people,
      the remnant of Israel.'
Behold, I will bring them from the north country,
   and gather them from the farthest parts of the earth,
among them the blind and the lame,
   the woman with child and her who is in travail, together;
   a great company, they shall return here.
With weeping they shall come,
   and with consolations I will lead them back,
I will make them walk by brooks of water,

in a straight path in which they shall not stumble;
for I am a father to Israel,
and Ephraim is my first-born."

(Jer. 31:7–9)

A further filling out of the message of hope from Jeremiah in the light of the prophecies of Isaiah 40—55 is to be seen in the immediately following verses, which picture the glorious return to Zion:

Hear the word of the LORD, O nations,
and declare it in the coastlands afar off;
say, "He who scattered Israel will gather him,
and will keep him as a shepherd keeps his flock."
For the LORD has ransomed Jacob,
and has redeemed him from the hands
too strong for him.
They shall come and sing aloud on
the height of Zion,
and they shall be radiant over the goodness of the LORD,
over the grain, the wine and the oil,
and over the young of the flock and the herd;
their life shall be like a watered garden,
and they shall languish no more.
Then shall the maidens rejoice in the dance,
and the young men and the old shall be merry.
I will turn their mourning into joy,
I will comfort them, and give them gladness for sorrow.
I will feast the soul of the priests with abundance,
and my people shall be satisfied with my goodness,
says the LORD.

(31:10–14)

It is not difficult to see how closely the prophecy echoes the language and themes of the later chapters of Isaiah, which certainly suggests that we are not dealing with the exact words of Jeremiah here. Rather, it is his message of hope filled out and given sharper focus by the prophecies of Isaiah 40—55 concerning the return of the Babylonian exiles to Jerusalem. The future of Judah is presented in Jer. 31:23–38. Once again, the passage affirms that this hopeful future will only be realized when the exiles return to their homeland, and there is a further emphasis upon the ultimate reunion of Judah and Israel.

From here we can proceed to consider the best known, and in several respects the most original, of Jeremiah's prophecies of hope. This concerns the establishing of a new covenant between God and Israel which will supersede the old covenant made on Mount Sinai. Only here in the Old Testament, in fact, do we encounter such bold language about a new covenant and its implication that the old covenant was valid only within a certain limited historical timescale, which makes it an important theme for giving a perspective to the entire Old Testament. The language and the specific terminology used are very closely related to that of the book of Deuteronomy, so that it is very unlikely that we are dealing here with the exact words of Jeremiah. Rather, the passage is Jeremiah's message of hope concerning the rebirth of Israel looked at and interpreted from the perspective of the Deuteronomic editors of his prophecies. They have attempted to give theological precision and direction to the poetic images of hope which Jeremiah's own prophecies had employed:

> In those days they shall no longer say:
> "The fathers have eaten sour grapes
> and the children's teeth are set on edge."
> But every man shall die for his own sin; each man who eats sour grapes, his teeth shall be set on edge.
> "Behold, the days are coming, says the LORD, when I will make a new covenant with the house of Israel and the house of Judah, not like the covenant which I made with their fathers when I took them by the hand to bring them out of the land of Egypt, my covenant which they broke, though I was their husband, says the LORD. But this is the covenant which I will make with the house of Israel after those days, says the LORD: I will put my law within them, and I will write it upon their hearts; and I will be their God, and they shall be my people. And no longer shall each man teach his neighbour and teach his brother, saying, 'Know the LORD,' for they shall all know me, from the least of them to the greatest, says the LORD; for I will forgive their iniquity, and I will remember their sin no more." (31:29–34)

The particular proverbial saying that is cited at the beginning is mentioned also in Ezek. 18:2, where, in a rather different fashion, the prophet presents his message in such a way as to rebut the implied note of despair and of resignation to an unavoidable fate which it asserts. It is not, at least in the first instance, a proverb about responsibility so much as about life and the possibility of repentance and renewal. In the proverb the children simply assert despairingly that they did not bring their misfortunes upon themselves and that they are now powerless to escape from them! The prophet rejects such a fatalistic resignation by asserting that each individual can seek God for himself or herself, and then find the divine grace in his or her own life (cf. Jer. 29:12–14).

So far as the law is concerned Jeremiah's new covenant is not promised to contain a new law which will replace the old laws of Moses and the Decalogue. Instead, it promises a new power and possibility of obedience to the law, made real because God will inscribe the laws on the heart of every Israelite. With this dramatic language the prophet perceives the inwardness

134

of true religion and the necessity for a personal response to God and a personal commitment to obedience to him. External laws remain an external authority until they are taken up and written upon the heart.

The two concluding prophecies of Jeremiah 31 take the form of two short appended comments affirming the certainty and fullness of the salvation that is promised to Israel. The first of them has a splendid doxological quality, reiterating the basic truth that God alone is the source and ground for hope for his people:

> Thus says the LORD,
> who gives the sun for light by day
> and the fixed order of the moon
> and the stars for light by night,
> who stirs up the sea so that its waves roar—
> the LORD of hosts is his name:
> "If this fixed order departs
> from before me, says the LORD,
> then shall the descendants of Israel cease
> from being a nation before me for ever."
> Thus says the LORD:
> "If the heavens above can be measured,
> and the foundation of the earth
> below can be explored,
> then I will cast off all the descendants of Israel
> for all that they have done,
> says the LORD."
>
> (31:35–37)

The passage has a twofold character which shows that it has been designed to fit into its present position immediately after the great prophecy of "the New Covenant." It is in part a doxology for the greatness of God as exemplified by his power in and through the created order; on the other hand, it is a divine oath affirming the implicit assurance contained in the promise of the new covenant: God will never completely cast off his people Israel.

The final promise of Jeremiah 31, set out in verses 38–40, asserts the sacredness which will belong to all Jerusalem in the coming days of Judah's restoration. The prophecy is certainly not from Jeremiah in its present form, but has been inserted to show that a central feature of the rebirth of Israel will be the rebuilding and exaltation of Jerusalem.

When we turn back to consider the message of hope that is contained in the prophecies of chapter 30, a much more complex literary structure reveals itself to us. In 30:5–7 (excluding the last line) we have a prophecy warning Israel and Judah of judgment that is coming upon them. Bright regards its origin from Jeremiah as unquestionable, and would date it in Josiah's reign.[24] In fact, there is little that it contains which enables us to locate it precisely in any one period of Jeremiah's ministry. To this has been added in prose in verses 8–9 a hopeful assurance about the ultimate restoration of all Israel. A further supplement in poetic form in verses 10–11 gives a more distant warning of God's final judgment upon the nations, in which Israel too will be punished but not entirely destroyed. These verses mark an interesting aspect of the transition from prophecy proper to apocalyptic, with their more radical eschatological message of a great judgment upon the nations.

A similar pattern, of a prophetic word addressed to Israel and Judah which is full of threat, supplemented by an assurance that those who had threatened Israel will eventually themselves be punished by God, is to be found in Jer. 30:12–17. The original prophecy is to be seen in verses 12–15 and leaves no doubt that it is a warning that Israel is about to be brought into dire distress and that this will be a just punishment for its misdeeds. Then suddenly the whole tone of the prophecy is changed, and verses 16–17 show that those who have been the agents for God's judgment upon his people will themselves be judged:

> Therefore all who devour you shall be devoured,
>   and all your foes, every one of them, shall go into captivity;
> those who despoil you shall become a spoil,
>   and all who prey on you I will make a prey.
> For I will restore health to you,
>   and your wounds I will heal,
>   says the LORD,
> because they have called you an outcast:
> "It is Zion, for whom no one cares!"
>
> (30:16–17)

We certainly cannot suppose that both prophecies were proclaimed at the same time, since this would only have given a confused and contradictory message. There is no reason, therefore, for doubting the genuineness of the threat of verse 12–15 to Jeremiah, perhaps also from the early period of his ministry. The two verses containing the assurance would then have been added in order to give a fuller and more complete presentation of Jeremiah's message. This addition was probably not the work of Jeremiah himself, but undoubtedly relates to the message of Babylon's downfall contained in the prophecies of chapters 50 and 51.

There is one further prophecy of hope and assurance in Jeremiah 30 which we should consider, one which is concerned primarily with the rebuilding of the city of Jerusalem. Found in Jer. 30:18–22, its content shows clearly that it originated after 587 B.C. when Jerusalem suffered considerable physical destruction. It is probably to be dated around 550 B.C., and al-

though an origin from Jeremiah cannot be ruled out altogether, this is unlikely. More probably, it is a further example of the way in which Jeremiah's
fundamental message of hope has been amplified and related to specific
problems and concerns of the small community that survived in Judah:

> Thus says the LORD:
> "Behold I will restore the fortunes of the tents of Jacob,
>   and have compassion on his dwellings;
> the city shall be rebuilt upon its mound,
>   and the palace shall stand where it used to be.
> Out of them shall come songs of thanksgiving,
>   and the voices of those who make merry.
> I will multiply them, and they shall not be few;
>   I will make them honored, and they shall not be small.
> Their children shall be as they were of old,
>   and their congregation shall be established before me;
>   and I will punish all who oppress them.
> Their prince shall be one of themselves,
>   their ruler shall come forth from their midst;
> I will make him draw near, and he shall approach me,
>   for who would dare of himself to approach me?
>   says the LORD.
> And you shall be my people,
>   and I will be your God."
>
> (30:18–22)

The prophecy raises the question of the future government of Israel and
Jerusalem through the person of "the prince." This clearly became an issue
of considerable importance after the removal of Zedekiah, the last of the
kings of the Davidic line. Gedaliah, who fulfilled the role of "governor" for
a brief period after 587 B.C., was not of Davidic lineage, which must certainly
have been a factor contributing to the dropping of the title "king." During
the period in which the present prophecy originated, which was so important for the production of a collected "edition" of Jeremiah's prophecies, it
becomes evident that the question of the future government of Israel, and
the possibility of the restoration of the Davidic monarchy, became points of
controversy.[25] It was out of this period of uncertainty, and the eventual failure to reestablish the Davidic monarchy in its original governmental role,
that the messianic hope was born. We shall find a further significant
prophecy concerning this question in Jeremiah 33.

The final three verses of chapter 30 of Jeremiah (vv. 22–24) repeat a
threat that is found earlier in 23:19–20, and no truly convincing explanation
presents itself to account for its inclusion here. Its Jeremianic origin is assured, but its purpose at this point, coming after an assurance of the rebuilding of Jerusalem, is not clear.

We come now to consider chapter 33 of the book of Jeremiah, which completes the Book of Consolation. It is made up of two prophecies or, more precisely, collections of prophetic sayings, 33:1–13 and 33:14–26. The second of these prophetic collections is not found in the Septuagint translation, and this is probably a good indication that it entered the book of Jeremiah at a relatively late stage. Neither of the prophecies can have originated from Jeremiah himself in their present form, and they can best be regarded as applications and amplifications of Jeremiah's message of hope to the situation in Judah during the years of exile. The first group of sayings is very much in the form of an expansion of Jeremiah's words found in 32:15, to which it has quite clearly been directly related in verses 4–5. The passage promises that, in spite of the appalling destruction and devastation of the city of Jerusalem and the great carnage among its citizens, the city will be rebuilt. It surveys the city, already lying in ruins, when everything appears to be hopeless and God seems totally to have abandoned it. Nevertheless, it finds complete assurance in what God has promised and the healing that this will bring:

> The word of the LORD came to Jeremiah a second time, while he was still shut up in the court of the guard: "Thus says the LORD who made the earth, the LORD who formed it to establish it—the LORD is his name: Call to me and I will answer you and will tell you great and hidden things which you have not known. For thus says the LORD, the God of Israel, concerning the houses of this city and the houses of the kings of Judah which were torn down to make a defense against the siege mounds and before the sword: The Chaldeans are coming in to fight and to fill them with the dead bodies of men whom I shall smite in my anger and my wrath, for I have hidden my face from this city because of all their wickedness. Behold I will bring to it health and healing, and I will heal them and reveal to them abundance of prosperity and security. I will restore the fortunes of Judah and the fortunes of Israel, and rebuild them as they were at first. I will cleanse them from all the guilt of their sin against me, and I will forgive all the guilt of their sin and rebellion against me. And this city shall be to me a name of joy, a praise and a glory before all the nations of the earth who shall hear of all the good that I do for them; they shall fear and tremble because of all the good and all the prosperity I provide for it.
>
> "Thus says the LORD: In this place of which you say, 'It is a waste without man or beast,' in the cities of Judah and the streets of Jerusalem that are desolate, without man or inhabitant or beast, there shall be heard again the voice of mirth and the voice of gladness, the voice of the bridegroom and the voice of the bride, the voices of those who sing, as they bring thankofferings to the house of the LORD:
>> 'Give thanks to the LORD of hosts,
>> for the LORD is good,
>> for his steadfast love endures for ever!'
> For I will restore the fortunes of the land as at the first, says the LORD.

"Thus says the LORD of hosts: In this place which is waste, without man or beast, and in all of its cities, there shall again be habitations of shepherds resting their flocks. In the cities of the hill country, in the cities of the Shephelah, and in the cities of the Negeb, in the land of Benjamin, the places about Jerusalem, and in the cities of Judah, flocks shall again pass under the hands of the one who counts them, says the LORD." (33:1–13)

The meaning of the passage, which is in prose, is perfectly clear, even though a number of obscure words and phrases occur, as the marginal notes in the RSV show. The promise looks back upon Jeremiah's momentous word of assurance during such a calamitous hour of Jerusalem's history. Surveying the ruins of the city which the Babylonian armies had left, it sees in the rubble no sign of hope that a return to the happiness and vitality of normal city life can ever take place. Yet what is impossible in terms of human potentiality is possible with God, and even things which the human mind finds difficult to comprehend are assured through the word of God. The picture of Jerusalem's restoration is thereby seen as a marvelous instance of the way in which God's providential care for his people is worked out.

The last two verses expand the scope of the divine promise to all the cities of the land of Israel, and make plain that its message of hope is not confined to Jerusalem only.

The second of the prophetic assurances set out in chapter 33 concerns primarily the promise that a line of Davidic kings will be established to rule over Israel. This was a deeply rooted tradition which appears in the very forefront of the concerns which have governed the account of the last decades of Judah in 2 Kings (especially 2 Kings 22—25). Jeremiah's own specific message about the fate of Jehoiachin (Jer. 22:30) had ruled out the possibility of the continuation of the Davidic kingship with Jehoiachin or his descendants. Yet, with the removal of Zedekiah, after his capture, from the royal throne in Jerusalem (Jer. 39:1–7), the possibility of any restoration of Davidic kingship seemed to have been thrown into serious doubt. Although it is couched in broad and general terms, the promise of Jer. 33:14–26 clings firmly to the belief that the Davidic covenant will be upheld, although it hints that this may not necessarily be in its original kingly form (cf. the "prince" of Jer. 30:21):

"Behold, the days are coming, says the LORD, when I will fulfil the promise I made to the house of Israel and the house of Judah. In those days and at that time I will cause a righteous Branch to spring forth for David; and he shall execute justice and righteousness in the land. In those days Judah will be saved and Jerusalem will dwell securely. And this is the name by which it will be called: The LORD is our righteousness."

"For thus says the LORD: David shall never lack a man to sit on the throne of the house of Israel, and the Levitical priests shall never lack a man in my presence to offer burnt offerings, to burn cereal offering, and to make sacrifices for ever. (33:14–18)

The relationship of the prophecy to that of Jer. 23:5–6 is shown by the emphasis upon the name of the coming king, "The LORD is our righteousness," which makes a play on the name of Zedekiah, the last of the kings of Judah. The date at which this renewed interest in the restoration of the Davidic monarchy arose cannot be certainly determined, but it would appear to be during the middle years of the Babylonian exile, perhaps around 550 B.C. Although the prophecy came later to be understood in a fuller "Messianic" sense, that is clearly not its intention here. It simply reaffirms the hope of the restoration of the line of Davidic kings to Israel, at the time after Zedekiah's removal and death, when this had been placed in doubt. Initially the hopes for such a restoration of the kingship to Israel focused upon Jehoiachin's descendants in Babylon (cf. 1 Chron. 3:17ff.).

The following two prophecies in Jeremiah 33 (vv. 19–22 and 23–26) have clearly been added as further supplements to that of verses 14–18 in order to give added emphasis to the note of assurance and certainty concerning the Davidic dynasty and Levitical priesthood in Israel. The fact that the title "king" is avoided in verses 19–22 and that the stress is placed on a line of descendants, rather than upon one individual, shows how the exact nature of the role that the Davidic family would play in the future Israel was an issue still filled with many uncertainties during the exilic years and immediately thereafter. Complex as the questions were, we can find in such passages important evidence for the transition from a hope based on the restoration of the Davidic monarchy to a hope of a coming Davidic "Messiah" who could fulfil a unique saving role in the future. We may look first at the assurance of verses 19–22:

> The word of the LORD came to Jeremiah: "Thus says the LORD: If you can break my covenant with the day and my covenant with the night, so that day and night will not come at their appointed time, then also my covenant with David my servant may be broken, so that he shall not have a son to reign on his throne, and my covenant with the Levitical priests my ministers. As the host of heaven cannot be numbered and the sands of the sea cannot be measured, so I will multiply the descendants of David my servant, and the Levitical priests who minister to me." (33:19–22)

That the question of the restoration of the Davidic family to the government of Judah and the hoped-for exaltation of one of Jehoiachin's descendants to a restored kingship were matters of great controversy is revealed by the presence of a further prophecy in Jer. 33:23–26. Its broad and certain note of confidence in God and his promises to Israel makes it a fitting conclusion to "the Book of Consolation":

The word of the LORD came to Jeremiah: "Have you not observed what these people are saying, 'The LORD has rejected the two families which he chose'? Thus they have despised my people so that they are no longer a nation in their sight. Thus says the LORD: if I have not established my covenant with day and night and the ordinances of heaven and earth, then I will reject the descendants of Jacob and David my servant and will not choose one of his descendants to rule over the seed of Abraham, Isaac, and Jacob. For I will restore their fortunes, and will have mercy upon them." (33:23–26)

In surveying the message of hope in Jeremiah it is clear that the dramatic revelation which came to the prophet with the purchase of the field of Hanamel (Jer. 32:1–15) marks the great turning point. In the hour of greatest crisis, when the human supports for hope appeared to have been swept away by the calamity that engulfed Judah in the years of 588–87 B.C., Jeremiah became aware that the true ground for hope lies with God himself. The city that human ambition had vainly brought to ruin could, nevertheless, be rebuilt and glorified through the grace of God.

Part 4

EZEKIEL

9   The Ezekiel Tradition: Prophecy in a Time of Crisis

There exists an inevitable measure of ambivalence in any prophecy, since it requires a certain matching up of what was actually said by a prophet with particular events in which these words could be regarded as fulfilled for a satisfactory interpretation to be achieved. Peter Ackroyd has drawn attention to the way in which a specific prophetic saying could be developed and reapplied to new situations over a period of time, since it was regarded as a "living" word of God.[1] This essay drew my attention to a facet of biblical prophecy that has increasingly commanded attention as a key to understanding the peculiar structure of the major prophetic books of the Old Testament. It is clear that in no case are we here presented with a series of prophecies preserved simply as the original prophet received or preached them. Instead, they have passed through a substantial process of editing during which additional material has been introduced to amplify and expand upon the original sayings and records. There is, therefore, a kind of commentary, which is often very complex and difficult to identify because it has become woven into the text of the book itself. In some cases this expansion of an original prophetic collection has continued over a very long period and can be seen to have passed through several stages of quite major reorganisation of the material, besides the incorporation of additions to it. This is most marked in the case of the book of Isaiah, where different stages in the redactional expansion can still be detected. Hence scholars have noted the importance of an edition made during Josiah's reign, and a further important stage added in the wake of the destruction of much of Jerusalem in 587 B.C., with the removal of the Davidic monarchy from the throne of Judah.[2] The later stages in the growth of the book of Isaiah show all the main characteristics of the transition from prophecy, as it was originally understood, to apocalyptic.[3] This is most marked in regard to Isaiah 24—27 and 56—66, but is also to be found in some other smaller sections of the book.

However, when we turn to consider the books of Jeremiah and Ezekiel, we find that the situation is not nearly so complicated and that a far greater degree of homogeneity and planned application can be seen to have existed in the way in which this redactional shaping has taken place. More particularly we can see that a far greater homogeneity of theological outlook and institutional affinity exists in the work. I am not here concerned about individual glosses or minor textual developments, which undoubtedly continued after this major work of literary shaping took place. My concern is rather with what I might term the literary and theological shape of the major prophetic collections. Although it lies outside my immediate concern here, we might also note that a similar redactional shape has also been imparted to the Book of the Twelve Prophets, although, for obvious reasons, the degree of diversity within the unified structure is more obtrusively apparent.[4]

In the twentieth century, once critical scholarship had firmly established the case for recognising that our prophetic books are not simply collections of the original sayings of the prophets but contain a great deal of secondary material, two theories have tended to hide the proper appreciation and evaluation of this theological redaction of these literary collections. The first has been the belief that the formation of the books has been the result of a process of continuous, and more or less unrelated, agglomeration of material. For example it was taken for granted that the contents of Deutero- and Trito-Isaiah had essentially nothing at all to do with the prophecies of the original Isaiah of Jerusalem. An almost limitless number of stages during which individual glosses and additions were made could then be posited. The second hypothesis has been that each of the great prophets, but most especially Isaiah and Ezekiel, gave rise to the organisation of a body of "disciples," who would then have been responsible for the preservation of the original prophet-master's sayings and for the addition of further prophecies to these. A most extreme example of the pressing of this hypothesis has been offered by I. Engnell,[5] who uses it to virtually set aside any possibility of distinguishing between what the original prophet said and what his disciples added to this. In effect a theory of collective composition of the great prophetic books has been posited, with the assumption that something of the stamp and theological outlook of the original prophet would have remained impressed on the material that only arose later. Attractive as such a theory has been, because of its apparent ability to account for the retention of an ascription of authorship to the original prophet, it results in a great deal of vagueness and uncertainty in our evaluation of the secondary material in the particular books concerned. So long as a vague umbrella of identity as the work of a "disciple" was maintained, quite markedly varied and disparate material could be assumed to belong to a book. Even more, such a hypothesis strains our credulity to an impossible extent, if we are required to believe that a body of Isaiah's disciples could have existed, as an identifiable and functioning entity, through a period of almost four centuries, without leaving any proper record of their existence, save for the book in which they manage to preserve their cover of anonymity.

Even more than these objections, however, the theories either of a random agglomeration of material, or of a progressive process of addition by disciples, fail to account satisfactorily for the extant shape of the major prophetic collections. This concerns the issue of respect for the original integrity and significance of the sayings of the great prophets. Both a process of random agglomeration and that of additions by disciples assume that the progressive building-up of the collections of sayings shared the same level of inspiration and consequent authority between prophet-master and disciple or scribe. All is assumed to partake of the same authority as the declared word of God, irrespective of the precise agency of its origin. Yet this conflicts with one of the most important points noted by Ackroyd.[6] This pointed to the fact that it is precisely the special nature, and consequent special authority, of the original prophetic saying that was believed to make it applicable to a whole series of situations. It was because it was regarded as uniquely meaningful that a prophetic saying given by one of the great figures of Israel's prophetic movement could be applied and reapplied in a whole sequence of situations, many of which were entirely unrelated to that of the original prophet. We have only to consider the way in which the themes of "thorns and briers" (Isa. 5:6; 7:23–25; 10:17; 27:4) or the names Shear-jashub and Immanuel are used in the development of Isaiah's prophecies (Isa. 7:3; 10:20–23; 11:11, 16; 7:14; 8:8, 10) to see that a very considerable authority was felt to pertain to the actual words of the master's prophecy. In this respect it is precisely their possession of a unique authority that has led to their reapplication to new situations far beyond those which could have been envisaged by Isaiah himself. If we are to think of the editors and expanders of the prophetic material as disciples of the original prophet, it can therefore only be with a marked awareness of the difference between the role of the prophet and the role of his disciples. They become merely his interpreters. This is a very different situation from that envisaged by Engnell, in which he implies that no essential difference existed between the authority of the prophet and that of his disciples.

In reality, however, it seems that little real gain is achieved by positing a band of prophetic "disciples," who may be presumed to have remained in a separately identifiable existence after the original prophet had died. Obviously there were tradents of the prophetic sayings, and all the indications are that these tradents kept the contents of the three major collections of Isaiah, Jeremiah, and Ezekiel as self-contained literary wholes. The evident degree of cross-connection and overlapping between the contents of the books is quite minimal. Another reason for doubting whether the definition of "disciples," or of a "prophetic school," adequately describes the character and work of the tradents and interpreters of the prophets who have contributed towards the formation of their books is found in the affinities between their work and that revealed in other parts of the Old Testament literature. Once we find that the work of collecting, shaping, and interpreting the sayings of a great prophet has been undertaken in the language, thought-forms, and situations that are related to other literary works of the Old Testament, then it seems clear that the aim of such men was more than simply to preserve a prophet's sayings. Rather it was more evidently intended to relate what the prophet had said to a particular situation and to the needs and concerns of a central religious group within the life of the nation. Nowhere is this more openly to be seen than in the case of the book of Jeremiah. Here the preserved literary work shows an extraordinary degree of connection, in certain of its parts, with the work of what we have come to know as the Deuteronomic school.[7] This was evidently extensively active in Judah, at least from the middle period of Josiah's reign (640–609 B.C.) until the middle of the sixth century B.C. So close are the literary and theological affinities between these parts of the book of Jeremiah and the book of Deuteronomy, as well as with the Deuteronomistic History (Joshua–2 Kings), that a fundamental connection between the authors of the respective works must be posited. This applies especially to the narratives contained in the book of Jeremiah (Mowinckel's source B) and to the prose sermons (Mowinckel's source C).[8] Clearly we have in both groups of material a direct link with the preaching and activity of Jeremiah himself. At the same time, so close are the connections of thought and theological vocabulary with those of the Deuteronomic school that we must conclude that what we are presented with here is a view of Jeremiah's work seen through the eyes of Deuteronomistic interpreters. A point of particular importance is that this presentation of Jeremiah's preaching has been particularly coloured by the fact that the Jerusalem temple had been destroyed in 587 B.C. and that, after the murder of Gedaliah, all hope of the renewal of Israel had switched to the exiles in Babylon.

The question of the date and provenance of this Deuteronomistic edition of Jeremiah's preaching falls into several separate issues. The fact that, within the preserved book, this Deuteronomistic material is spread across the primary collection of prophecies in Jeremiah 1—25 and the narrative accounts of 26–28; 34–45, as well as the prophecies of hope collected together in 31–33, shows that this Deuteronomistic affiliation was influential at several stages. It is not our purpose here to reopen the discussion concerning this important feature of the study of the book of Jeremiah, except insofar as it reflects upon the character of the prophetic literature as a whole. I have argued elsewhere that a most important connection exists between an early stage of the collection of Isaiah's prophecies and the formative period of the Deuteronomic movement during Josiah's reign.[9] What is important, therefore, is not simply the theological character imparted to the respective literary collections by the tradents of the prophetic sayings but the time and the situation to which they have addressed them. What is most striking as far as the Jeremiah sayings are concerned is the fact that they are viewed by the Deuteronomistic editors from a post-587 B.C. standpoint. This is most evident in the instances of the Temple prophecies of Jer. 7:1–15; 26:1–19, where it is beyond question that the destruction of the temple in 587 B.C. has been allowed to influence the tradition of Jeremiah's authentic prophecy warning against a false trust in the temple. It provides an excellent illustration of the way in which the sense of how a prophecy was fulfilled has been allowed to affect the formulation of what it actually pronounced. This cannot be regarded as a process of "falsifying" a prophecy *post eventum*, but must be seen rather as an attempt to show how the fulfilment took effect. In this case it was evidently of unique importance to have been able to cite Jeremiah's prophecy, since, as we know from elsewhere (e.g., Lam. 2:6f.; 4:13), the physical destruction of the Jerusalem temple appeared to contradict all notions of Yahweh's power and sovereignty.

That the Deuteronomistic editing of the Jeremiah material was a post-587 B.C. undertaking appears to be beyond any question, as soon as we look in detail at what it contains. Not only in detailed matters of content, but more broadly in its whole theological direction, it shows this colouring. In broad outline it uses Jeremiah's prophecies to provide a kind of theodicy for the tragic events that took place at the hands of the Babylonians in that momentous year. This is further borne out when we examine this Deuteronomistic material in relation to the two earlier major compositions from this movement: the book of Deuteronomy and the Deuteronomistic History (Josh.–2 Kings). As P. Diepold has shown in respect of its theology of the land as Israel's inheritance,[10] there can be little cause for doubting that the Deuteronomistic material in Jeremiah represents the latest stage of Deuteronomistic theological development of this major theme.[11] All in all, therefore, we can see that it is a matter of considerable importance that we should view the way in which Jeremiah's prophecies have been edited and addressed to a particular situation as of great concern to understanding the final stage of Deuteronomistic theological development. The issues are not simply relevant to determining the authenticity, or otherwise, of the contents of the book of Jeremiah but are related to formative theological developments during the exilic age. Not least is this so in respect of the way in which an Israelite theology of covenant (Heb. *berit*) was built up.[12]

If these observations are established, then it greatly strengthens the conclusion that this Deuteronomic theological movement, or school, undertook its work in Judah during the late seventh century and the first half of the sixth century B.C. Since the law book of Deuteronomy and the Deuteronomistic History were two works that must have been composed in Judah, where along the literary source material for such an enterprise was available, this is obviously also the most probable setting for the editing of Jeremiah's prophecies. All the more does this appear to have been the case, since Jeremiah himself remained in Judah after 587 B.C., until his compulsory removal to Egypt (Jer. 43:6). Before leaving this question of the literary affinities of the book of Jeremiah, we may consider a further fact. If the Deuteronomistic material was added to the collection after 587 B.C., which must be regarded as certain, then the latest date for these additions and the accompanying editorial shaping cannot have been much later than 550 B.C. This is borne out by the fact that there is no hint of the political possibilities of a return engendered by the rise of Cyrus, which became prominent after 546 B.C. Similarly the expectations of an eventual return of the Babylonian exiles appear vague and ill defined. Their certainty is based upon theological conviction, not imminent political expectations related to the situation of either Judah or Babylon. We are led therefore to locate this editorial shaping and development of Jeremiah's prophecies in the period between 580 and 550 B.C. as the most probable time of its origin. In the face of the lack of any strong evidence to the contrary, we should also place it in Judah, where the other Deuteronomic-Deuteronomistic compositions originated. We are not therefore faced with indications of a period of progressive and protracted building-up of material in the book of Jeremiah over an extended period but rather with an important attempt to relate Jeremiah's prophecies to a specific historical situation. As long as the analysis and consequent literary evaluation of the different types of material in the book of Jeremiah were regarded solely as an aspect of understanding the transmission of this particular prophet's sayings, then the critical questions appeared baffling and difficult to resolve. Yet as soon as we relate the literary and theological phenomena of the book to the wider questions concerning the Deuteronomic movement in Israel and Judah, a much clearer picture emerges. The key to this understanding has been available to scholars since the commentary of Bernhard Duhm (1901),[13] but only in recent years has the value of his observations been satisfactorily explored. To think of the tradents of the prophecies as disciples of the original prophet reveals only one very partial side of their work and identity. Much more meaningful is their close association with the Deuteronomic movement and its theology. Furthermore, the particular situation to which they addressed their interpretation of the prophecies is especially important for understanding the way in which they have gone about their task.

So far my considerations regarding the formation of the prophetic books have dealt mainly with the book of Jeremiah, rather than with Ezekiel. Yet this may be defended as a necessary way of proceeding for two reasons. The first of these is that the book of Jeremiah provides a particularly clear instance of the title "disciples," offering a very misleading characterisation of the aims and intentions of those who have shaped a major prophetic book. Their affiliations were clearly wider than this, so that their work must be understood in connection with the history of Judah during the sixth century B.C. and the special concern that these tradents felt for the major religious institutions of Israel, especially the Jerusalem temple, but also including the Davidic monarchy. Secondly, the problems concerning the literary and theological structure of the book of Ezekiel are greatly illuminated by a comparison with what is to be seen in the book of Jeremiah. If Jeremiah, both as a prophet himself and as the originating figure of the book that derives from him, is to be regarded as the prophet of Judah during the sixth century B.C., then Ezekiel is certainly to be seen as the prophet of the Babylonian exiles. Moreover, whereas all the theological connections of the book of Jeremiah are with the Deuteronomic movement, those of Ezekiel are to be found in the work of the emergent Priestly school. This may be used as a broad, and admittedly loosely defined, title for the authors of the Holiness Code (Leviticus 17—26) and the Priestly Document. There are, in any case, other grounds for asserting that the major theological and historical affinities of these literary works are with the world of the Babylonian exiles, and with their successors who returned to Judah after 538 B.C.

In recent years the book of Ezekiel has been the subject of a very marked change of outlook on the part of critical scholars. Beginning with the work of G. Hölscher,[14] there was a growing inclination to recognise that the coherence and homogeneity that was at one time thought to have characterised the book could not be sustained under critical examination. There are marked variations in the formal and stylistic features between different parts of the book, and some significant changes of theological emphasis. A further turning point was then reached with the attempt of V. Herntrich[15] to show that the original prophet Ezekiel had lived and worked in Judah throughout the period of his ministry and that the Babylonian background of the book was a later overlay imposed on this. From this there emerged, almost as an inevitable critical afterthought, the claim that Ezekiel had experienced a dual ministry, as argued by A. Bertholet, H. W. Robinson, and others.[16] For a period this belief that Ezekiel had initially worked in Judah between the years 593 and 587 B.C. and had then been taken to Babylon, where he entered upon a second phase of his prophetic activity between the years 587 and 571, assumed the proportions of something approaching a critical consensus. Yet, beginning with the publication in 1955 of Georg Fohrer's commentary on Ezekiel,[17] this critical assessment has been compelled to give way in favour of the position that recognises that all of Ezekiel's ministry was conducted in Babylon. There are no overriding objections, therefore, to accepting the dates and setting that the book itself presents, which suggest that Ezekiel was a member of a Jerusalem priestly family who was taken to Babylon in 597

B.C. He then received his call to prophesy in the year 593 (Ezek. 1:2) and continued his prophetic ministry until the time of the latest of the prophecies, which are dated in 571 B.C. (Ezek. 29:17).

However, this return on the part of biblical scholarship to a recognition of the reliability of the evidence of the setting of Ezekiel's ministry that the book itself provides has not meant a complete return to the *status quo ante* Hölscher of critical investigation. It is clear that the book does show an impressive degree of theological homogeneity and a remarkable element of planned literary structure. The major divisions of the book between chapters 1—24, 25—32, 33—39, and 40—48 are all undoubtedly the consequence of an attempt to give some literary and theological "form" to the book as a whole. Yet this shape is also quite clearly not something that the original prophet could have imposed; nor are the broad theological features of the book all to be ascribed to the particular theological outlook of Ezekiel himself. The way in which even the most devastating invective against Judah has been rounded off with words of hope and assurance (e.g., in 16:53ff.; 20:33ff.) is evidence enough that a considerable amount of development and reworking of the original Ezekiel prophecies has taken place. It is for this reason that Walther Zimmerli[18] has posited the existence of an Ezekiel "school," who must be looked to as the body responsible for imparting this literary and theological structure to the book. It cannot be, therefore, that the original prophet has been responsible for the extant book that bears his name; nor can we ascribe all the material within it to his authorship. In a number of instances it is clearly very difficult to ascertain whether the material that can be seen to be "secondary," as defined by its present position, is from the original prophet or from the "school." Such difficulties only highlight still more emphatically the point that the question of "authenticity" is not always the major question regarding the setting of a passage, except insofar as it bears upon the issue of time of origin. Perhaps it is not altogether surprising, therefore, that the belief in the existence of an Ezekiel "school," and the willingness to recognise that a measure of secondary material is to be found in the book, has been capable of being carried to quite extreme lengths. Thus, for example, J. Garscha has renewed the demand for a more radical approach to the questions of the literary structure of the book and has argued that only a relatively small proportion of the extant prophecies come from Ezekiel, the prophet of the exile.[19] Yet such a position appears extreme, and goes a considerable way beyond what is necessary to explain the evidence of redactional development and elaboration. Overall, the much more cautious approach shown by Zimmerli would appear to be justified, and the conclusion may be drawn that a quite remarkable part of the general homogeneity and uniformity of the book stems from the contribution of Ezekiel himself.

However, it still remains open to question whether the assumption of an Ezekiel "school" is the best and most satisfactory way of explaining how the original prophecies of Ezekiel have been developed and edited. This is because scholarship has for long recognised that another dimension of affiliation also exists for Ezekiel's prophecies. This, as we have already noted, is to be found in the connections that exist between the theological outlook of Ezekiel and those of the Priestly Document, and more particularly the Holiness Code of Leviticus 17—26. It is obviously a quite unsatisfactory assumption to suppose that it was the "school" of Ezekiel that was responsible for the composition and theological outlook exemplified in these works. In fact the measure of theological and literary connection that can be shown to exist between them is not such as to suggest any immediate community of authorship. With the widespread application of a traditio-historical method of study to the literature of the Old Testament, especially to the Old Testament prophets, as exemplified in the work of Gerhard von Rad,[20] it has appeared possible to explain much of the commonality of outlook and interest between the book of Ezekiel and the authors of the Holiness Code and the Priestly Document as due to the dependence on the Jerusalem cult tradition that all three works shared. Ezekiel was born and brought up in the priestly traditions of the Jerusalem temple, and this must certainly be taken to imply that he was a descendant of the Zadokite family and that he had most probably already taken an active role in that cultus before his deportation to Babylon. Such at least would appear to be the most probable explanation of his being singled out for deportation in 597 B.C. If we had not been told of this priestly derivation in Ezek. 1:3 we should in any case certainly have deduced it from the character and content of the prophecies that his book preserves.[21] Valuable and helpful as this traditio-historical method of analysis and criticism has been, it is open to suggest that it is capable of being pressed too far in its effort to explain the features of theological overlap between literary works that show many common features of language and thought. The reason for suggesting this is provided by what we have already noted in connection with the literary shape afforded to the book of Jeremiah. As it is now preserved, this prophetic book reveals a most instructive example of the way in which the work and sayings of a particular prophet have been remembered and applied to a particular situation at the hands of a very distinctive theological circle. It is neither Jeremiah's "disciples" nor the figure of Baruch that has imparted the special stamp to the book of Jeremiah that we now have. Nor yet is it the Deuteronomic school who have simply wrested the sayings of Jeremiah from their original setting and added their own words under the guise of the preaching of Jeremiah. Rather it is the consequence of a most fruitful marriage of the *traditio* of Jeremiah's prophecies with the situation that the Deuteronomic school found itself faced with in

Judah after 587 B.C. What we find is Jeremiah's preaching seen through Deuteronomic eyes and applied to a unique situation that was understandably of paramount significance to the aims and concerns of the Deuteronomic school of Judah. It may be suggested, therefore, that we have a roughly comparable situation in respect of the prophecies of Ezekiel.

The material from the book of Ezekiel that we are especially concerned with here is to be found in chapters 40—48, in what has come to be known as the Reconstruction Programme. That this programme is based upon an authentic vision of the prophet Ezekiel, which is dated in Ezek. 40:1 to the twenty-fifth year of exile (i.e., 573 B.C.), must be held as certain. At the same time it has come to be widely recognised, by H. Gese (1957) and others,[22] that this original vision has undergone substantial expansion in order to incorporate a number of provisions for the administration of the cultus, especially in respect of the role of the priests and the Levites. This Reconstruction Programme, therefore, can be seen to have developed the Ezekiel tradition in a particular way and in regard to a specific issue, that of the restoration of the Jerusalem temple and its cultus, which had an authentic basis in the prophet's message.

When we consider the literary and theological affinities of the Ezekiel tradition from another aspect, we find that some further valuable light is brought to bear upon how it has developed. This concerns the question of the relationship of the book of Ezekiel, and especially of its Reconstruction Programme, to the Holiness Code (H), which has now been incorporated into the book of Leviticus to form chapters 17—26. We may leave aside here the further question whether this Holiness Code was incorprated first, as a self-contained entity, into the Priestly Document, or was only subsequently added to the Tetrateuch (Genesis–Numbers), after the Priestly Document had already been combined with the earlier narrative materials of JE.[23] What is very clear is that there is an undoubted relationship between Ezekiel and H, but this is not one that can be reduced to any one simple formula. That Ezekiel was the author of the Holiness Code must certainly be set aside as altogether too simplistic and improbable a solution to carry conviction. Yet neither can we make the deduction that the Holiness Code is later than Ezekiel at all points, as J. Wellhausen concluded.[24] As the broad examination undertaken by Zimmerli shows,[25] there are some points where the dependence appears to be in one direction and others where the reverse is true. What we have in the two literary works of the book of Ezekiel and the Holiness Code are compositions that have undoubtedly exercised a mutual influence upon each other.[26]

We may limit our attention to two particular issues concerning the priesthood. In Ezek. 44:10ff. the Levites are precluded from the enjoyment of full priestly status in the renewed sanctuary and instead are reduced to the level of providing a kind of "second rank" clergy. The full priesthood, which is regarded as enjoying levitical descent, is to be restricted to the Zadokites, who must certainly be identified with the descendants of the Jerusalem priests of the preexilic era. As we know, many of these had been deported into exile in Babylon in 597 B.C., among them Ezekiel himself. Neither of these administrative regulations can be regarded as originating with Ezekiel himself, but there is every reason for supposing that they represent a point of view that emerged among the body of tradents of Ezekiel's prophecies whilst they were still in Babylon. At the latest we should date these regulations in the period shortly after the fall of Babylon to the Persians in 538 B.C. Most probably it arose before then.[27]

As has been widely noted, this view of the role to be enjoyed by the Zadokite priesthood presented in Ezek. 44:15ff. finds no echo in the Priestly Document, or its later additions, where the qualification for the priesthood is to be one of "the sons of Aaron." This latter rule must certainly be a later formulation than that of the Ezekiel Restoration Programme, and in any case represents that which came finally to be accepted for the Jerusalem priesthood of the postexilic era. What particular controversies needed to be fought and resolved before such a formula could be agreed upon can only be the subject of speculation and hypotheses. Yet one thing is clear, and this is that it was the restoration of full sacrificial worship in the rebuilt Jerusalem temple in 516 B.C. (Ezra 6:15) that necessitated a satisfactory resolution of the issue. That it marks one aspect of the many conflicts that provoked tension between the community that returned from Babylon and that which had survived in Judah at the commencement of the Persian era can reasonably be assumed. There are good grounds, therefore, for regarding the regulations governing the priesthood that are presented in Ezek. 44:15ff. as having been compiled before 516 B.C. After that date it would appear that such a formulation would have become progressively obsolete.

A number of other features have also provided pointers to indicate that we can trace a most interesting triangle of development between the preaching of the prophet Ezekiel, the work of the "school" who have given us the Reconstruction Programme of Ezekiel 40—48 and the Holiness Code of Leviticus 17—26. Particularly is this detectable in the way in which the concept of holiness itself is understood.[28] There is much, therefore, that can be adduced to justify the conclusion drawn by Zimmerli that "The circles which have given to H its (pre–Priestly Document) form must not be sought too far from the circles which transmitted the book of Ezekiel."[29] Not only is this so in regard to the major theological and linguistic affiliations that the relevant literary compositions display, but it must also be regarded as true in respect of the time at which they worked. It is surely extremely unlikely that the authors of the Ezekiel Reconstruction Programme are to be placed any later in time than 516 B.C. The completion of the work of rebuilding the Jerusalem temple must indicate the most probable *terminus ante quem* of their work.

What we have so far considered in regard to the identity of the circles who have been responsible for the preservation and literary shaping of the Ezekiel tradition is simply a fuller elaboration of the point, already established by Zimmerli, that these circles must be sought in close proximity to those who have produced the Holiness Code. This work is itself not a fully uniform composition but shows every sign of having been composed and developed over a period of time.[30] Parts of it appear to be older than Ezekiel, whilst other parts are from a time after that of the prophet of the exile. In the case of the development of the Ezekiel tradition, however, the period of its literary shaping cannot have been very extended, since the great bulk of it, including the Reconstruction Programme, must have been completed by 516 B.C., and very probably before 538 B.C. What we have is a form of literary commentary and adaptation of Ezekiel's prophecies particularly directed towards the hope of restoring the Jerusalem cultus. It emerged among the Babylonian exiles, and very probably from within the circles of the exiled Zadokite priests of Jerusalem. Understandably enough it found its inspiration and divine authority in the prophecies that Ezekiel had given. Yet it did more than simply preserve these prophecies in the manner that might be posited of disciples. Rather it extended and applied them to provide a mandate for the restoration of the Jerusalem temple cultus in anticipation of the time when it would once again become necessary. This work is probably to be dated, therefore, to the period between 571 and 538 B.C.

It is at this point that we may draw into the discussion a further issue that has a direct bearing upon the identity and aims of the bearers of the Ezekiel tradition. This concerns the relationship that must be assumed to have existed between the Holiness Code of Leviticus 17—26 and the *torah*-book of Deuteronomy. This has been the subject of an independent study by A. Cholewenski[31] and has given rise to a picture of a very complex interconnectedness extending to various levels of literary composition. The precise details of Cholewenski's thesis do not directly concern us, whether or not they can be sustained in every detail. What is of primary significance is the fact that the Holiness Code can be seen to offer some kind of "corrective" and reworking of cultic rulings and practices that are dealt with in the book of Deuteronomy. Evidently these were felt to go too far in abandoning many of the older cultic rulings and interpretations of Israel's worship in favour of a more reasoned and theological approach. It cannot escape our attention, therefore, that, of the two great prophets of the final collapse of Judah, the Jeremiah tradition has received its shape at the hands of the

Deuteronomic school, whereas the Ezekiel tradition has been fashioned within the circle of the authors of the Holiness Code and the nascent Priestly school. Furthermore it seems clear that, at least until the time of Gedaliah's murder, the Deuteronomic school was located in Judah. Against this we must set the fact that the Ezekiel tradition was certainly preserved in Babylon, at least up to the time of the Persian conquest in 538 B.C. and possibly for some little time after that.

In the light of all this it must certainly appear that we continue to recognise the important role played by distinctive circles of tradents in preserving and shaping the great prophetic collections of Jeremiah and Ezekiel, and certainly of Isaiah also, although in a rather different fashion. Perhaps "school" is the most appropriate term by which to describe the work of these editors. In the case of Ezekiel it is clear that what they have done is to elaborate and apply the original prophet's message to the time and situation in which they found themselves placed. Nor is this situation difficult to identify, since it is quite evidently that of the latter half of the sixth century B.C., at a period when the cultic life of Jerusalem lay in ruins, and when a particular hope of its restoration had begun to take shape. In some sense they were "disciples" of the original prophet, yet such a description fails to take adequate account of other interests and loyalties that this circle of tradents so evidently shared. Their setting has for long been recognised to be that of the priestly circles who compiled the Holiness Code.

If our thesis is supportable, then it would suggest that our prophetic literature has not been the subject of a more or less continuous and indiscriminate process of elaboration, commenting, and glossing. Rather a very much more restricted activity has been undertaken, which can for the most part be assigned a relatively precise chronological location. In the case of the books of Jeremiah and Ezekiel this can be identified with relative clarity and confidence. The case of the Book of the Twelve is necessarily somewhat different, and so also is that of the book of Isaiah. Yet even in this latter case, if the thesis of Hermann Barth[32] is to be followed, a quite precise and relevant edition of Isaiah's prophecies was made in Josiah's reign that has left a profound mark upon the shaping of the book.

So far as the Ezekiel tradition is concerned, we find that virtually all the substantive material in the book belongs to the sixth century B.C., even though it does not all stem from the prophet Ezekiel himself. The shape that has been given to it has made it into a charter for the rebuilding of the Jerusalem temple and for the restoration of its cultus after the disaster of 587 B.C. That Ezekiel had himself proclaimed the divine word that authorised such a charter is not to be doubted and is, in any case, evident from the way in which Ezekiel's great vision of 573 B.C. has been reported and expanded.

Thus, out of a sequence of prophecies that forewarned how God would deal with his people, there has emerged a book that is far more than a conventional prophecy and is a divine sanction for the renewal and revitalising of worship in Jerusalem after the tragic events that had brought it to an almost complete end in 587 B.C. Thereby the prophetic word itself acquired a much more durable and lasting significance.[33]

10   The Chronology of Redaction in Ezekiel 1—24

We may begin our consideration of the question of the chronology of redaction in Ezekiel 1—24 by identifying as clearly as possible the nature of the questions that present themselves to us. My initial concern has been especially prompted by issues raised in M. Greenberg's commentary to Ezekiel 1—20 in the Anchor Bible series.[1] Prior to the publication of this volume in 1983 there was a marked and discernible trend in Ezekiel studies which began as far back as 1952 with Georg Fohrer's examination of a number of outstanding literary-critical questions in the book.[2] The publication of Walther Zimmerli's masterly volumes in the Biblischer Kommentar series[3] lent widespread support and popularity to this trend which saw in the book of the prophet a substantial core of authentic prophecies from Ezekiel which had been edited and expanded in the circle of the "Ezekiel School." The book therefore was essentially the literary product of this Ezekiel school, but stood in direct relation to the original prophet. Not only was this school of prophetic disciples responsible for the preservation and literary shaping of the original material, but such disciples had also undertaken a specific type of developmental exegesis in which they had added to the body of prophetic sayings to form more extensive structured units.[4] The book can be seen to consist therefore of original Ezekiel units, set with considerable confidence and precision in a precise chronology of the prophet's career, coupled with later material from the Ezekiel school. This must be classed as secondary, both in a temporal sense that it arose at a later, less precisely definable, stage in the formation of the book, and also in that it displays a derivative and dependent status in its attachment to the original prophetic sayings.

The positing of such a developmental type of exegesis, together with its ascription to a body of disciples of the original prophet, has carried wide support and has its origins in a belief in the formation of circles of prophetic disciples as a widespread feature of ancient prophetic activity.[5] It has the merits of recognising the complex and composite nature of the larger units of written prophecy while at the same time retaining an awareness of the primacy and high authority accorded to the original sayings of the prophet. It has also encouraged the view that there is no sharp division to be drawn between the oral features of prophecy, as it was originally publicly declared, and the literary features of what has been preserved within the larger corpus of scripture.

Such conclusions, however, regarding the formation of the prophetic book of Ezekiel leave a number of major issues unresolved. In particular the question of the chronology of this developmental elaboration of the prophetic material left by Ezekiel has remained very unclear, both in relative and in absolute terms. It is widely recognized that Zimmerli himself argued that such a process of elaboration and enlargement of the original prophecies began with Ezekiel and so, in several instances, it is impossible to discern whether the original prophet was responsible for a particular secondary addition, or whether it was the work of one of his later followers. Furthermore, in the type of developmental exegesis posited by both Zimmerli and F. L. Hossfeld, little endeavour was made to attempt any consistent cross-referencing of the developmental additions to see whether any coordinated layering of the material has been undertaken. Even more frustrating from the scholar's perspective who is concerned with the wider developments of Israel's faith in the postexilic period, is the lack of any utilisable "anchor points" by which to correlate the stages in the growth of the literary collections of Ezekiel's prophecies with other identifiable developments in the life of the postexilic community. All the more is this regrettable in the light of the fact that the detailed elaborations regarding the ordering of the cultus given in the Reconstruction Programme of Ezekiel 40—48 have been widely seen to bear closely upon the events concerning the rebuilding of the Jerusalem temple in the years 520–516 B.C.[6] The somewhat paradoxical situation has therefore arisen in which much accord has been given to the recognition that the book of Ezekiel was a text of outstanding importance to the life and restoration of worship in the postexilic Jerusalem community, and yet the precise directions in which its authority was felt to operate have remained vague and unclear.

There are some further issues which require general reflection before looking in more detail at some instances of the chronology of redaction in Ezekiel 1—24. In an earlier essay[7] I have drawn attention to the quite marked way in which, allowing for all the many nuances and variations which are possible within a broad circle of themes and ideas, there are very marked affinities between the redaction of the book of Ezekiel and that of the Holiness Code and the Priestly Document on the one hand, just as there are affinities between the Dueteronomic school and the editing of the book of Jeremiah on the other. The tensions and conflicts between the D-school and the P-school, if we may broadly describe these movements, would appear to have been a central and prominent framework of theological and religious reasoning which moulded the life of the postexilic community in Jerusalem. The ultimate outcome would seem to have represented some form of compromise between the two. The extent to which the Jeremiah tradition has been affected and moulded at the hands of the Deuteronomistic school has received a considerable degree of attention from scholars.[8] This is not to endorse the idea that Jeremiah's literary editors can be wholly identified with the authors of some part of the Dueteronomistic History, or even some layer of editing in the book of Dueteronomy. Nevertheless the cross-connections and contacts between the extant literary form of the book of Jeremiah and other writings which bear the Dueteronomistic stamp are such as to make it pointless to posit a "Jeremiah School." Contacts with other parts of the Old Testament literature are sufficiently strong to establish the point that some larger group of literary and theological scribal activists has been at work. There are, however, as J. W. Miller has shown,[9] a number of significant points of contact between Jeremiah and Ezekiel, and these are particularly strong where the sayings concerning future hope and restoration from exile appear. Probably S. Herrmann has been wrong to lay so much emphasis upon the "Deuteronomistic" character of this elaborative work.[10] Nevertheless clearly much of it is evidently not from Ezekiel himself and shows considerable likelihood of representing part of a fairly widespread attempt during the late exilic, and early postexilic, periods on the part of a small community to formulate the essential agenda for Israel's future restoration. The return from Babylon, the rebuilding of the temple, and the restoration of the Davidic monarchy would all appear to have figured in this hope.

These broad considerations are sufficient for us to formulate a number of propositions regarding the aims, manner, and purposes of the redaction of Ezekiel's prophecies. First of all we may suggest that the hypothesis of a distinctive "Ezekiel School" lays too much weight on the role of the redactors as preservers of Ezekiel's prophetic sayings, rather than upon the concern to relate and interpret them in the light of other major interests which faced the Jewish community in exile. Indications are that there was a felt need, not so much to produce independent prophetic books, but rather to produce a comprehensive and coordinated corpus of written prophecy with which to confront the existing religious dilemmas. The very assumption of the divine origin and authority of prophecy militated against any over-preoccupation with maintaining the separateness and individual distinctness of what one individual prophet had said. There are good grounds for supposing therefore that much greater interest attached to establishing a harmonised and reasonably consistent portrayal of what shape God had decreed through his prophets for Israel's future, than for positing a jealously guarded copyright over each individual prophet's preserved sayings.

A second point also requires more reflection than has often been accorded to it. This concerns the fact that the area of elaboration and addition to such a book as Ezekiel, as in reality to all the prophetic collections, shows a very heavy and marked emphasis in the direction of affirming ultimate return, restoration, and salvation for Israel. Without wishing to return to the rather wooden critical dogma that all preexilic prophecy was prophecy of judgment and doom, nevertheless this viewpoint does contain a substantial truth. The areas where the greatest level of subsequent addition and elaboration of prophetic sayings has taken place is that of hope of salvation and eventual triumph over the nations. This is in any case clearly what we should expect from our knowledge of the political and social context of the postexilic era, in which all four of the great canonical prophetic collections took shape. It belongs to the needs and circumstances of this historical context that the literary shaping of the books of prophecy has been undertaken in the way that it has. It is not the moods and convictions of Ezekiel's disciples that have determined the character of what Zimmerli has called the phenomenon of *Fortschreibung* in the book of Ezekiel, but rather the necessity for interpreting the original prophet's threats and promises in the light of the changed situation that had arisen once the fateful acts of judgment had befallen Israel. In so many ways it is the similarities between all the formulations of hope and assurance that have been woven into our prophetic literature that strike the reader most forcibly, rather than their distinctiveness and isolation. The impression is forced heavily upon us that, working on the basis of highly distinctive individual prophecies, the editors of the canonical prophetic collections have worked hard to establish a consistent and coherent pattern to them.[11] It is not surprising therefore that this coordinating and harmonising tendency has at times been identified as a kind of comprehensive Deuteronomistic pattern of editing. The essential truth of such a viewpoint, which can easily be exaggerated, is that the various stimuli which accorded to prophetic literature a canonical, or proto-canonical, status in ancient Israel tended towards the harmonising of central issues and the minimising of significant differences.

A third point is relevant here. When we consider the kind of expansions and additions that are the essential mark of the *Fortschreibung* in the book of Ezekiel, then it is noteworthy that this appears as an essentially "literary" activity, in contrast to the markedly "oral" character of the original prophet's sayings and situations. There is much to support the contention therefore that it has been primarily the formation of written prophetic collections that has occasioned an essentially new treatment of prophecy. It is noteworthy that, as set out by such scholars as Herman Gunkel[12] and Claus Westermann,[13] the most basic forms of prophetic utterance are readily identifiable as oral forms. Even the first written collections of prophecy appear largely to have retained these characteristic features of oral formulation. It is however the uniquely literary form of prophecy in the Old Testament that marks such an important religious development in the life of ancient Israel. Just as the transition from orality to literacy can be seen to have affected the folklorist and storytelling arts, and to have had a profound impact upon patterns of human thinking,[14] so also must the transition from oral to written prophecy be recognized as fraught with extensive theological consequences. The possibility of assembling out of various disparate prophecies a knowledge of a divine "plan," of coordinating prophecies so as to construct a coherent picture of God's purposes and actions, all emerged once prophecy acquired the relative fixity and stability that written recording afforded it. This strongly suggests to my mind that the kind of *Fortschreibung* that is to be found in the book of Ezekiel must be understood as a consequence of the preservation of the original prophet's sayings in writing. Whether Ezekiel himself began this, or whether from the outset Ezekiel's adherents and associates undertook this makes little difference. The essential point would seem to be that the work of the original prophet still retains much of the oral characteristics of prophecy, whereas the work of elaborating and enlarging upon these prophecies displays features that are more easily intelligible as a scribal literary activity.

When we examine the characteristic methods and set formulae used in this process of enlarging upon the original prophetic sayings, the more self-evidently literary character of it is indicated. The detailed embellishment of allegories, fresh applications of metaphors used earlier, the use of simple repetitive connective formulae, all serve to suggest that, once prophecy had become a text, then it became possible to enlarge and develop it in ways that had not been open to it in its original preached form. Most striking of all in this regard is the feature displayed by the Old Testament in which prophecy is regarded as susceptible of fulfilment centuries after it had originally been given. However it is particularly the literary features of this further development of prophecy that are of primary concern in regard to the redaction of Ezekiel's prophecies.

It is in this connection that I find myself sharing both important areas of agreement and disagreement with Greenberg's commentary in the Anchor Bible series. In attempting what he has described as a "holistic" type of exegesis Greenberg has drawn far more attention than has previously been given to the presence of patterns, structures, and recurrent themes that are to be seen in the larger exegetical units. There is at times a kind of contrapuntal technique, a careful balancing of themes, and the presence of what he has described as the "halving" pattern.[15] Such structures appear to be evident in such a way as to extend right across the separate units and divisions which have been noted by Zimmerli and others in their conviction that a progressive build-up and elaboration of the units has taken place. For Greenberg the presence of these "holistic" patterns is taken as indicative of a complex planned structure, a feature which has increasingly engaged the attention of literary poetic approaches to the Old Testament literature. This leads Greenberg to suggest that we should allow this evidence to point in the direction, not of positing a gradual agglomerative development of the text, but rather of subtly planned poetic units which may be credited to the original prophet.

That such units are to be seen, and that such features of careful echoing and repetition of themes in later sections which first appear in earlier ones plays a significant part in the compositional technique, may be granted. Yet, in disagreement with him, I would suggest that these patterns do not properly constitute a *prima facie* case for arguing that they are the result of a carefully planned structure which originated with the prophet himself. Rather, it would appear, they can be adequately accounted for, and more satisfactorily explained, as a mark of the technique and interests of the scribal circles to whom we owe the extant literary form of the book. Hence I would agree that the evidence of structure and carefully formulated patterns in such chapters of Ezekiel's book as 16, 17, and 20 has proved a valuable and useful insight. At the same time it is neither clear nor probable that it is the work of the original prophet that has occasioned this, but rather the distinctive interests and procedures of the circle to whom we owe the formation of this literary work. In particular it would appear very markedly to be the case that such intricate, and often very lengthy, structural patterns are a decisively literary stage in the book's development. It is hard to believe that, even to a very carefully attuned ear, such patterns and nuanced allusions would readily be grasped if the text were merely heard. It is the written form of it, and the consequent possibility of pausing, making reference back to specific words and verbal images, and offering multiple interpretations of them, which renders them meaningful as a component of interpretation.

Before exploring this theme in a little more detail we may note a further important consideration. Although it has not by any means been the only criterion for separating the original prophetic unit from later additions to it, a quite major factor has been the sudden and unexpected transitions from threat and bitter invective to assurance and hope of ultimate salvation. Whereas there is no difficulty in supposing that this could provide an intelligible and meaningful programme for an outline of Yahweh's future actions towards Israel, it is well nigh impossible to believe that the prophet, in all the bitter turmoil and conflict of the situations in which he was called upon to preach, could have made any convincing impact upon his hearers by confusing them in this way. They needed to know what was going to happen to them, not to some far off generations in an indeterminate and unknown future. It is in fact once again the literary preservation of prophecies, which are thereby torn from their original real life situations (decontextualised), which has occasioned the need for a more rounded and onward-looking sketch of the long-term future. It is supremely the sharpness, and psychological incongruity, of such transitions from threat and impending doom to assurance and ultimate hope that has called for a substantial chronological separation of sections within the larger units. In chapter 16 of Ezekiel, for instance, how could hearers have taken to heart the utter indictment of the *māshāl* of the Foundling Child in verses 1–34 if the hearer carried away in his, or her, mind the mellow and forgiving words of verses 59–63? Clearly some other factor, unconnected with the needs and urgency of the situation to which the original prophetic *māshāl* was addressed, has arisen and has called for a substantially changed note in the completed literary unit. The case may not be so markedly clear in regard to the intervening units of verses 35–43 and 44–58, but even here the introduction of new themes and complex qualifying interests points to the recognition that, viewed as a single intricate composition, this exceedingly long unit of sixty-three verses makes a confused impact. In view of the intensity and vigour of the prophet's language it is impossible to believe that he would so heavily have compromised the impact of what he had to say by becoming so discursive. What may be acceptable as interesting and engaging poetic style, when read as literature, cannot be regarded as effective and moving preaching when viewed as addressed to a specific situation and audience. Once again therefore there are strong indications that it has been the fact of a written preservation of the original *māshāl* that has called forth a substantial degree of modification and expansion of it in order to accommodate it to the changed situation presupposed by the formation of a prophetic book. The original prophetic message possessed a clear and firmly defined context dictated by the historical and political situation in which it was given. As a written prophecy, however, preserved through a period when that original context had receded into the past, it acquired a new context, partly provided by the new historical situation that had arisen, but also very substantially affected by the larger literary context in which it was now placed.

In defining what he understands by the process of *Fortschreibung* in Ezekiel 16, Zimmerli speaks of a "successive supplementation of a kernel element."[16] He considers that the prophet himself may have contributed to this development, but that, in any case, it can safely be ascribed to the work of the Ezekiel school. What I am suggesting here in order to grasp the character and purpose of this extensive elaborative work, not only in the book Ezekiel but in all the prophetic literature of the Old Testament, is that it can no longer adequately be described as "prophetic" in the fullest and pristine sense of inspired oracular utterance. It is a type of secondary undertaking, in many ways more akin to a commentary, or *pesher*, than to a further additional prophecy which might be considered by itself. This is not to say that it does not exercise an important function within the overall nature of the prophetic book, but it cannot be understood simply as a process of adding on new prophecies to those that are already there. Rather it has the purpose of adapting and harmonising the prophetic message in order to enable it to fit in coherently to the larger corpus of prophetic literature.

This alone appears to provide an adequate explanation of the most striking feature that pertains to this editorial process. The constant, and at times almost doctrinaire, rounding off of dire and fearsome threats with words of hope and assurance, which appears so prominently in Ezekiel 16, 17, 20 as well as widely in other parts of the prophetic literature, cannot be overlooked. The stimulus towards this feature, which often becomes most marked where the original threat appears most sharp and incisive, must have originated as a literary device made necessary by the manner in which the prophetic texts were being read, possibly liturgically. It surely cannot be the case that the original prophet's disciples were inevitably more genial and optimistic in their expectations for the future of their people than was the original prophet! It is the literary preservation and continued use of the prophetic texts that has prompted this distinctive structural shaping of the material.

This also directs our attention to a further feature concerning this elaborative development of the prophetic literature which bears directly upon Greenberg's observation. Where in the original prophecy the threatening nature of the prophecy can be understood as directly related to the threatening political nature of the situation in which it was given, this is nothing like as clearly evident in the secondary material that has been added to it. In the years between 593 and 587, when Ezekiel's warnings of doom were proclaimed, both for Judah and Jerusalem, the threatening situation was matched by the threatening prophecies. This becomes progressively less clear in the character of the elaborations that have been made to them. Even the note of indictment and warning, as for example in Ezek. 16:35–43 when added to verses 1–34, raises broader religious issues. Throughout Ezekiel there is totally lacking any firm indication that a changed political scene has suggested, either to the prophet or his disciples, that the grounds of hope are to be found in the new possibilities occasioned by this changed historical context. Not even the accession of Amel-Marduk and the release of Jehoiachin from prison has left any firm trace in the book of Ezekiel. Possibly Ezek. 17:22–24 is an exception to this, but it is noteworthy that there are few, if any, clear indications of the occurrence of major political events reflected in the secondary material which constitutes the *Fortschreibung* of Ezekiel's prophecies. On the contrary there is a recognisable phenomenon which characterises this material so that its context, so far as this is made up of specific ideas and themes, is provided by the original authentic saying of the prophet. This must surely be regarded as a decisively literary characteristic in its composition, since it presupposes the earlier prophetic unit and has been designed to be read, rather than heard, in conjunction with it.

There are, it is true, indications of some important shifts and vacillations regarding the expected future of major political institutions. So, for example, where Ezekiel himself appears to have been essentially negative in his expectations regarding the future of the Davidic dynasty and kingship (cf. Ezek. 19:14), the secondary elaborations dealing with this theme are quite categorically optimistic (Ezek. 17:24–28), and a further modification is evident in the references to the "prince" in the Reconstruction Programme (Ezek. 45:7, etc.). No doubt it would be possible to explain this as a special issue of importance to the supposed Ezekiel school, yet it is much more probable that it was the primary importance of the issue to the wider body of men and women concerned with Israel's restoration that explains its presence in the book. This is simply one among many indications that the written collections of prophecy, which came to enjoy canonical status in the Old Testament, were made the subject of an extensive literary editorial activity. The purpose of this was to formulate on the basis of the prophetic collections that already existed a coherent and tolerably harmonised picture of the future hope that awaited Israel. Herrmann has identified this as essentially a Deuteronomistic movement,[17] but it represents an activity which has contributed a dominant share of the shaping and preservation of much of the Old Testament literature during the exilic, and early postexilic, periods. It would seem therefore that it is mistaken to explain the elaboration of Ezekiel's prophecies as the consequence of an extended agglomerative technique in which new prophecies from Ezekiel's disciples were simply added on to those already in existence. Rather the character of this editorial and elaborative work would appear to have been more directly concerned to adjust the received prophecies in order to accommodate to the wider religious and political interests of a central group of exiles. In particular a certain consistency of viewpoint had to be established and an accommodation to a number of central themes and issues undertaken. We find therefore that the books of both Jeremiah and Ezekiel deal firmly and decisively with the hopes about the restoration of the Davidic monarchy, even though this introduces tensions with the views of the original prophetic deposit. The question of the return from exile, the expected ending of the period of exile, and the fate of other nations also deeply affected by Babylonian imperial expansion, all required to be considered and added to the corpora of prophetic sayings. All of this became possible precisely because prophecy had assumed a written form, had been cut off from the context of events which had called forth the original sayings, and needed to be adjusted to relate to a very large and sub-stantial collection of prophecies of many kinds. Essentially this implies that prophecy had to be edited in a literary fashion, and by the addition of a num-ber of basic interpretative themes and guidelines, to render it suitable as a canonical text. It required to be adapted to the future needs of Israel in which the situation of "exile" was imperceptibly changing into one of a more pro-longed and indeterminate "diaspora." We cannot therefore separate out the processes of canonical shaping and authorisation of certain prophetic texts, among which we include the book of Ezekiel, from the purely literary process of preservation of the original utterances of the great prophets. The transition from an oral to a literary stage of prophecy belongs to this process, and its literary character is clearly marked by the introduction of a number of didactic themes. The sharp indictments of particular offences, which are the hallmark of the great prophets, become transformed into the broad ac-cusations of disobedience against the *torah* of Yahweh and the disloyalty im-plicit in all idolatry and idolatrous activity. As a canonical text prophecy has, of necessity, had to divest itself of much of the historical specificity which it originally possessed. It had to be made more broadly applicable and widely relevant. Most especially, once it was intended that it should be read beyond the time when the threats and warnings of disaster facing Israel had been turned into horrifying reality, then it became essential that the messages of hope, which also belonged to prophecy, should be more adequately set out. Some account also needed to be taken of the way in which prophecy would be read and studied, so that it could be accommodated into convenient lit-erary units.

All of this suggests that prophecy, which in its origins was an essentially preached oral form of religious utterance closely tied to specific situations, had to submit to the work and interests of the scribes. In the process it had to become more didactic and admonitory in character and less precisely threatening. One aspect of this accommodation of prophecy to a new liter-ary setting would appear to be the opportunity it provided for more com-plex literary and poetic patterns of the kind that Greenberg has noted in commenting upon Ezekiel 1—20. It would nevertheless seem questionable, in recognizing that this literary elaboration took place after Ezekiel had ceased prophesying, whether its authors can properly be described as con-stituting a prophetic school of the kind envisaged by Zimmerli. Their inter-ests would appear to have been much wider than this, and their techniques more consciously scribal, than to be suitably thought of as prophetic in the normal sense. For too long the heavy Scandinavian emphasis upon schools of prophets with an ongoing process of memorising orally delivered poetic utterances has coloured the study of the prophetic literature. Opposition on dogmatic grounds to the late nineteenth-century literary criticism of the prophetic books, and the desire to replace this with a criticism more attuned to the oral character of early prophecy, has moved too far in the reverse direction. Emphasis upon a kind of corporate authorship preserved carefully within a closely defined band of prophetic disciples has been allowed to blur attention to the question of discovering the original prophet's words. The recent attention, as in the work of Greenberg, to the larger literary units of prophecy and their self-evidently literary structuring may provide a basis for renewed interest in the theological and religious consequences of the formation of the prophetic literature of the Old Testament.

The reduction of a corpus of prophecy to a written deposit was inevitably affected, and to some extent controlled, by the needs of the community who would provide its readers. These needs were in most cases very different from those of the prophet's original hearers. All the indications are, not only from the book of Ezekiel but from the entire prophetic corpus of the Old Testament canon, that these needs extended far beyond that of simply recording and preserving the original prophet's words exactly as he had uttered them. The concerns to interpret, clarify, and draw out the implications of prophecy for future generations of the people of Israel have inevitably reflected themselves in the way in which this prophetic literature has been compiled. Too often scholars have acted as though the purpose of the individual book was simply to provide an anthology of a particular prophet's sayings.

So far as the chronological aspects of this transition from the time when the original prophet had been active until the time when a fixed book of his prophecies came into being, no wholly definitive criteria appear to be available. Yet all the indications are that the main part of such as task was completed within a space of no more than two generations from the time of the original prophet's death. There is little reason therefore for allocating this part of the formation of the book of Ezekiel beyond the end of the sixth century B.C., by which time most of the material contained in it can be satisfactorily explained.

Part 5

THE RISE OF APOCALYPTIC

11 Apocalyptic, Literacy, and the Canonical Tradition

There occurs in Mark 13:14 a brief clause amounting to no more than three words which have had, in spite of their brevity, a considerable impact upon the study of biblical eschatology. Not least they proved to be of considerable importance to G. R. Beasley-Murray's early and still profoundly significant study of Mark 13 and of Jesus' expectations for the future.[1] The words are ὁ ἀναγινώσκων νοείτω, "Let the one who reads understand." In his early (1864) study of the messianic hope of Jesus, the Strasbourg scholar T. Colani found in these words evidence that the "Little Apocalypse" of Mark 13 was based on an earlier written text which had come to be incorporated into the Gospel tradition and to be understood as the teaching of Jesus. The short rubric to the reader betrayed the fact that an already extant written document lay at the back of the Gospel report of the eschatological teaching of Jesus. A considerable number of scholars took up this view that the phrase did reflect the prior existence of a written eschatological discourse, several of them suggesting that it may have been a Jewish apocalyptic text that had been adapted to the Christian message.

However, since the substantial part of Mark 13:14 makes reference to τὸ βδέλυγμα τῆς ἐρημώσεως, "the sacrilege that makes desolate," with its connections with Dan. 9:27, 11:31, and 12:11, it may also be contended that the purport of the short rubric to the *reader* to take careful note was to draw attention to connection with these other scriptural passages.[2] It could then be understood to be a device to alert the reader to the special significance of the pronouncement regarding the desolating sacrilege as marking an event already foretold in earlier scripture as a sign of the end of time. Both possibilities need certainly to be considered and are not wholly exclusive of each other. The written form of the apocalyptic discourse of Jesus is then coupled with earlier written prophecy from the Old Testament.

Beasley-Murray is sharply critical of the argument that the address to the reader provides evidence of an already extant apocalyptic document. He comments: "More than any other single factor it has given rise to the view that the unknown apocalyptic writer has here nodded, forgetting that such as exhortation is inappropriate in the mouth of Jesus *speaking* (so Colani and

173

a multitude of followers)."[3] Elsewhere he had earlier written, "It would be hard to find in the whole New Testament a better case than this for adducing the hypothesis of gloss!"[4] Since the Markan evangelist does himself introduce a number of comments and interpretations for the reader (e.g., Mark 5:41; 7:3, 11, 19), it certainly cannot be ruled out that the comment is the work of the Gospel writer designed to assist in the understanding of the teaching that he conveys. However, the issue concerning at what stage this short note was introduced into the text is one that cannot be resolved with more than varying degrees of probability, whether the evangelist himself introduced it or a later scribe. That the intention is to draw the reader's eye to recognize the special import of the message contained in the verse and the allusions that it contains to earlier passages of scripture in the book of Daniel and elsewhere in the writings of the Old Testament would appear to be highly likely.

Besides the possibility that the gloss, if it be such, draws attention to the wider scriptural context in which the words of Jesus are to be understood, it also raises two further issues that have assumed growing importance to biblical scholarship. The first of these concerns the importance of literacy, and of the implications of literacy, for the interpretation of the biblical tradition. The second concerns the relevance that such a phrase has within the frame of reference of what has come to be described as "canon criticism."

As far as the first point is concerned it should certainly be borne in mind that the earliest Christian communities were only semi-literate and that many of them almost certainly contained only a small proportion of fully skilled and literate leaders and teachers. Among the Galilean and Judean communities to which the teaching of Jesus was first made known, it is probable that the degree of literacy that prevailed was not particularly high. Even those who could write may often have attained only a limited skill in doing so; thus their habits of mind and conventions of practice were those that belonged to a society in which information was largely conveyed orally. That the skill of the fully literate scribe was still something of a rarity made his expertise of great value to the early Christian churches, where the reading, copying, and interpretation of scripture came to be held in very high regard. If this were the case, and it is highly probable, even though we lack precise statistics to ascertain the details, then it is necessary to understand this brief comment to the reader in Mark's Gospel in the light of it. What the illiterate person cannot fully understand because of his or her inability to perceive the connections with earlier scriptural passages, the literate person can pursue with greater skill. The comment therefore cannot be regarded as a relatively minor and unimportant one, but as a serious and necessary pointer to the deeper significance of the teaching that has been given.

It is noteworthy that in the initial stages of the form criticism of the

Gospel tradition, attention was drawn most fully to those characteristics that reflected forms of oral teaching and communication.[5] The more recent development of redaction criticism has naturally served to complement this by paying more attention to the written nature of the Gospels as texts. Even so, at least in their early development, the transition from orality to literacy has been considered primarily from the perspective of accurate preservation.[6] Undoubtedly written formulation of the Christian message and teaching, once the church had spread throughout the Roman Empire, became a matter of key importance to the preservation of its integrity. The difference between orality and literacy, however, is far more than a difference in the manner and reliability of the preservation of important material. "Writing restructures consciousness," claims Walter Ong,[7] and certainly the many studies that have been devoted to the impact of literacy upon the way people think bears this out.[8] The very nature of language, the use of repetition and figures of speech, and the way in which words and verbal images are related to ideas are all deeply affected by written preservation. Writing not only provides a more fixed and durable mode of disseminating truths, avoiding the pitfalls of a continued series of subtle changes being introduced, but it enables connections and meanings to be conveyed that would not be readily perceptible to the nonliterate mind. There would seem therefore to be little reason for doubting that the short phrase in Mark 13:14 is not an intended, or inadvertent, pointer to the existence of an apocalyptic source document, but a witness to the differences of understanding available to the literate, over against the nonliterate, person.[9] The significance of all that is implied by the reference to "the sacrilege that makes desolate" will only be understood by the person who can *read* the Old Testament scriptures.

The importance of traditions of textual exegesis current among Jewish rabbis and employed in the exegetical tradition of the synagogue for an understanding of apocalyptic, especially in the book of Revelation, was argued for by A. Schlatter.[10] The deep respect Beasley-Murray retained for Schlatter's biblical exegesis and his advocacy of it should certainly not pass unremarked; however, it has been very much to the credit of the Swedish scholar Lars Hartman to have shown the importance of this tradition of rabbinical textual exegesis for the interpretation of Mark 13. We may cite Hartman's general position:

> We get a certain idea of how the creative mind of the author worked with the material it had learned when we are able to determine which OT passages are echoed in the text and then consider how it came about that the author recalled these particular passages and why his "intuition" or his exploring mind sought out just this or that passage in the OT.[11]

The development of Jewish apocalyptic was, therefore, very markedly a scribal activity, developed with the aid of written texts and dependent upon the ability of the interpreter to recognize specific allusions and to make certain verbal connections that would not be obvious to the nonliterate person. Yet it should certainly not be assumed that the import of what was to be conveyed through these allusions was without interest to such a person. The skilled literate person, well-versed in the art of picking up this complex range of contextual images and ideas, would be expected to explain and assist the less skilled in appreciating their value. It would then appear that it is precisely this situation which has occasioned the rubric to the reader in Mark 13:14. What is being conveyed by the eschatological discourse of Jesus is not simply a prophecy about forthcoming events, but at the same time a vitally significant evaluation of the import and meaning of those events for all who look to the Hebrew scriptures as the ground and guide of their hope. This fact will become evident to the skilled reader of the scriptures, especially the book of Daniel, but will need to be explained to the nonexpert who will be unable to achieve this.

I have elsewhere, in the article "Prophecy as Literature: A Re-Appraisal,"[12] drawn attention to the way in which written prophecy differed from the forms of orally delivered prophecy from which it emerged. We may single out three main characteristics of the way in which this difference manifested itself and of the importance of each of them to the rise of apocalyptic literature. The first of these is what we may describe as the formation of paradigms, or patterns, so that prophecy relating to one set of historical circumstances came to be adapted to apply to others. We may cite as an example of this the allusion to the powerlessness of the "rod and staff" of the Assyrians referred to in Isa.10:24–27. The reference is back to Isa. 9:4 (Heb. v. 3), with its mention of "the day of Midian," but already by way of earlier developments of the "rod and staff" metaphors in Isa. 10:5, 15. It must be accepted, therefore, that the "Assyrians" of Isa. 10:24 no longer refers to the imperial power of that name but has become a hidden code name for some later oppressor of Judah.[13] The original situation has been adapted to a later age, probably a very much later one.

The second point is a close development of this since it concerns the removal of the prophecy from its original historical context and its replacement by a larger context, primarily derived from other prophetic texts. The historical context of the original prophecy is set aside so that as it becomes a paradigm of the divine purpose and activity it receives its new context from the body of prophetic literature in which it is set. This does not mean that it loses all historical reference, since it does, in fact, take on the possibility of being applied to a whole series of further historical events. Nonetheless, the uniqueness of the initial historical context is abandoned, and the prophecy or prophetic theme becomes a part of a much wider scheme of divine revelation. In this sense it truly becomes "apocalyptic"; that is, revelatory of a wide segment of the divine purpose. It should be noted, as K. Koch has done,[14] that this development of a prophecy often took bizarre and sometimes dangerous directions, but we may still recognize it as a feature that came to be firmly attached to written prophecy. Just as the very nature of a written document made open the possibility of interpretation on the basis of new literary contexts, so was the original historical context and meaning of the prophecy submerged beneath this.

The third feature whereby written prophecy differed from earlier oral prophecy is already evident within the example cited. Words and metaphors, in this case that of the "rod and staff," originating in Isa. 9:4 (Heb. v. 3), become connectives to provide a multiplicity of meanings. Even more clear in this regard is the development of the "remnant" motif in Isa. 10:20–23, where the notion of "remnant" has originated from the name of the prophet's child Shear-jashub in Isa. 7:3. This brief section in the book of Isaiah, which in itself so clearly demonstrates the emergence within the prophetic books of techniques of scribal exegesis that were later applied much more freely and extensively in the formation of apocalyptic and other forms of midrash, is of special interest. The reference to the idea of a remnant has occasioned a need to relate this to the threat of a "full end" (Heb. *kalah*) upon all the earth: "For Yahweh, Yahweh of Hosts, will make a full end, as decreed, in the midst of all the earth" (Isa. 10:23). This is noteworthy because it is repeated with near verbal exactness in Isa. 28:22 and is then taken up as a part of a more intricate picture of the end time in Dan. 9:27. In all three instances great significance is attached to the belief that such destruction has been "decreed" by God through the voice of prophecy. This undoubtedly implies prophecy that had become written down and was, therefore, available for the reader to consult. It is the literary aspect of prophecy that has made possible such a range of further interpretation of it. The question as to where the primary locus of this decree of destruction was to be found is not made completely clear. Probably, since two instances of its development are to be found in the book of Isaiah, we should refer to Isa. 6:11. Later associations with the message of Amos may then have encouraged such a development further (cf. Amos 8:2).

The rise of apocalyptic, therefore, was only possible because prophecy had come to take on a written form. With this written form there was opened up the possibility of new forms of interpretation based on scribal techniques of word association, etymologizing and the like. Moreover, the establishing of a written form resulted in a corpus of literature from which further guidance might be sought. One scripture could be interpreted with the aid of another scripture, and it was evidently not long before scribal interpretation gave rise to harmonizations, supplementations, and even more intricate literary connections. The original historical context, which was recorded in relation to prophecies, receded into the background. In its place there emerged the literary context provided by other literature which quickly took on the character of a literary canon of texts. We may cite Hartman again in regard to the literary background of the emergence of Jewish apocalyptic texts:

> This authoritative function of the OT was the point of departure from which the Scriptures were interpreted and applied in Judaism. The reason why I mention this is that the way in which these texts use the OT seems to be akin to that in the *midrashim*, partly owing to the fact that the *midrashim*, with their *Sitz im Leben* in the rabbinical schools and the synagogues, probably contributed in various ways to the material worked on by the creative imagination of the authors and partly owing to the actual technique.[15]

It is not difficult to appreciate that it was chiefly the use of such scribal techniques that drew together the otherwise very different interests of apocalyptic speculation and wisdom. Both depended on the elaboration of subtle literary techniques, such as the scribes had developed, for an adequate appreciation of their meaning. Apocalyptic became a form of prophecy intelligible to scribes. Nor is it difficult to see how much of the fascination of such developments, so far as prophecies about the end time were concerned, owed not a little to a deep feeling for the power and mysterious intensity of the written word, especially among those who were either illiterate or only partially literate.

It is this feature of apocalyptic, both in its Jewish and Christian forms, which leads us to the final consideration of the present discussion. The past fifteen or so years of biblical scholarship have witnessed the advocacy of a variety of forms of "canon criticism" as a serious alternative to earlier forms of historico-critical exegesis of the Bible.[16] The range of the discussion and the various ways in which the notion of canon is capable of being understood need not occupy too much of our attention. The discussion has tended, perhaps inevitably, towards discussion of the significance of the range and limits of the biblical canon, both in its Hebrew and Christian forms, and to the weight which should be placed upon ecclesiastical and synagogal authority for the final shape of the canon.

In endeavoring to single out those areas where a substantial basis of reference to the canon can be of greatest assistance to the biblical exegete, two features can be singled out. The first of these is that, over against the very extensive emphasis upon the defining and dating of "sources" within the biblical materials, it is important that the extant form of the biblical books should be fully understood and recognized. The final form of the text does not have to be the only form that concerns us, since it was undoubtedly the end product of a long process, but it is nonetheless the form that has survived for use within both church and synagogue. This undoubtedly meant that, understood from the point of view of a literary meaning of the text, passages of scripture, and, indeed, all the books of the Bible, were read as continuous wholes. A synchronic reading of the whole was, therefore, the way in which both Jews and Christians understood the text. As far as we can tell from the way in which single authorship came to be ascribed even to such immense literary constructions as the Pentateuch, which was undoubtedly the product of many centuries of scribal activity, this assumption of a synchronic unity gave rise to certain expectations of uniformity of interpretation. This is particularly important when we consider the complex literary composition that modern scholarship has adduced as the explanation for such a work as the prophecy of Isaiah. We can readily recognize, by the aid of the accumulated insights and research of many generations of critical scholars, that this complexity in respect to text finds its most satisfactory explanation in the assumption of multiple authorship over a long period of time. What is of importance for the modern biblical interpreter for understanding how and why the scholars of antiquity arrived at their interpretations of the text is that they did so from the perspective of very different assumptions. Rightly expecting to find integrity and consistency in the divinely given message, they resorted to subtle harmonizations and to the belief in multiple meanings in particular words and metaphors in a way which the modern reader finds confusing and disturbing. Yet such scribal techniques were in themselves important steps in the direction of establishing meaning in relation to texts that they had come to value very highly.

When we realize the impact of literacy upon the interpretation of prophecy we have found the most important key for understanding how the prophetic literature came to be drawn more and more fully into the new, and very distinct, dimension of apocalyptic. This is, indeed, "prophecy among the scribes"; but in order for the scribes to have had access to the prophecies, the original prophetic word had to be written down. This point is of considerable importance when we consider the question whether apocalyptic began with any coherent and systematized body of doctrines. It appears unlikely that this was the case. Rather, apocalyptic made certain basic assumptions about the divine purpose for Israel, as revealed through prophecy, but came only gradually to develop these assumptions further in the direction of establishing a coherent picture of what the future held in store for Israel and the world. At so many points we discover diversity and flexibility to be the watchwords of an apocalyptic understanding of history. Basic to its understanding was that it needed to identify what had been "decreed" (i.e., revealed through a prophet and preserved in writing for posterity). To this extent literacy was an indispensable tool of interpretation for the apocalyptists.

A further feature of what was implied by the injunction "Let the one who reads understand" also calls for consideration. It is fundamental to the contention set out here that this injunction was concerned to relate the eschatological message of Jesus to the Old Testament scriptures and in particular to the book of Daniel. The literate person would perceive the connections and links which the nonliterate person would be incapable of doing. It may then be argued that this points us to one of the most significant and valuable features of a canonical approach to the Bible. The collection of texts into a corpus and the elevation of this corpus to the status of forming a "canon" implies that one passage may, and indeed should, be read in conjunction with another. To this extent we can discern a very large gulf between the established historico-critical approach to the interpretation of the Bible and the older and more traditional method of "interpreting scripture by scripture." Where the "historical" method seeks to uncover the original circumstances, intentions, and ideas of the author, the "canonical" approach ignores this in favor of regarding the remainder of the canonical scriptures as forming the true spiritual context.[17]

It is not difficult to perceive that this latter approach can lead to distortions and false understandings, because very dissimilar passages can be brought into conjunction with each other. Purely superficial connections can be adduced through the chance occurrence of words; however, it must also be noted that the historical approach may also lead to difficulties precisely on account of the limitations endemic to the original historical setting. Often, of course, this may not even be known, as is true still today of a host of passages in the prophetic literature of the Old Testament. We can at most conjecture what the original setting was. However, even when the occasion of a prophecy is known, the extent to which the prophet's original situation can be seen to have historical analogies and counterparts in a later age is dependent entirely upon individual opinions. The rather heavy-handed way in which the prophets' denouncements of their contemporary social leadership has been adduced as applicable in the modern age is a case in point. It must be noted, therefore, that the attempts of the scribal apocalyptists to provide for prophecy a larger and more ongoing understanding of its meaning is of genuine interest and exegetical value. It would be wholly regrettable, therefore, if the ideas of interpretation in a canonical context were allowed to be set over against interpretation in a historical context of the kind that so much modern critical work on the Bible has sought to achieve. Each does in its own way express something of the dialogue between the text and its interpreters which is very important to the rich and extensive task of hearing the word of God.

Apocalyptic patterns of biblical interpretation are to be seen not simply narrowly confined to the biblical books of Daniel and Revelation, but quite extensively spread throughout the prophetic literature of the Old Testament, widely present in the biblical interpretations of Paul and, most centrally of all, present in the teaching of Jesus. It may then be hoped that the seeming vagaries and excesses of the biblical apocalyptists, which have so often in the history of the Christian church been the target of heavy criticism and even outright rejection by theologians, may be seen not to be so repulsive as they at first appear. They belong by a kind of theological necessity to the processes by which the word of God, originally proclaimed orally, came to be preserved and disseminated for the benefit of later generations. The tasks of preserving in written form, editing, reappropriating, and reinterpreting the word of God that had been given "once and for all" was in itself a compound process. The separate techniques and aims came to be fused together in the work of the scribe, who became at one and the same time the guardian of the tradition and also its interpreter.[18] That one scripture should be understood in the light of other passages of the same canonical corpus served both as a springboard for the possibilities of ever-new understandings of the word of God and, at the same time, a check and corrective, lest one part of its message should be stressed to the detriment of the whole.

Historically the function the Bible in Christian worship and its central importance for the formulation of Christian teaching and the development of Christian spirituality have meant that the Christian faith has provided a major stimulus towards literacy. Only the person who can read can explore the full riches of the Christian message and its biblical heritage. "Let the one who reads understand" has therefore served as a characteristically Christian injunction for the strengthening of faith and the deepening knowledge of God. Whatever the source of its entrance into Mark 13:14, it undoubtedly represents a very illuminating comment on the complexities of biblical apocalyptic and on the demands that its interpretation places upon the Christian scholar. It also indirectly reveals something of the divide that existed between the literate person and the nonliterate one in the life of the Christian church. In the modern world those distinctions still continue to apply, so that we are continually indebted to those scholars through whom we have learned to read the scriptures discerningly.

12   The Interpretation of Prophecy and the Origin of Apocalyptic

The question of the origins of biblical apocalyptic has remained a controversial subject of study and, although many questions have been clarified, no fully satisfactory solution has yet appeared. In his very important study *The Relevance of Apocalyptic*, H. H. Rowley[1] argued strongly that it emerged on the basis of a postexilic Jewish extension and reinterpretation of earlier prophecy. Gerhard von Rad's rejection of such a position[2] has largely led, in further investigations, to a reaffirmation of the rightness of Rowley's position, but not without a number of modifications to it.[3] This is also the conclusion advocated by David Russell,[4] and it may certainly be regarded as pointing in the right direction. At the same time, the import of von Rad's objections has been to draw fresh attention to the fact that there can have been no smooth transition from prophecy to apocalyptic and that the latter incorporates many features and assumptions originally alien to prophecy,[5] especially that consciousness of a broad historical determinism which allowed that the final outcome of human history had been decreed in advance by divine ordinance.

Much of the difficulty pertaining to the attempts to trace the origins of Jewish apocalyptic lies in the impossibility of establishing a widely agreed definition concerning what constitutes such a movement of thought and literature. As it progressed, apocalyptic came to take on a more clearly identifiable form, to promote the composition of separate and self-contained writings, and to make extensive use of certain easily recognised themes and techniques. Yet, in its early stages, it was certainly not essential that all of these features should be present for many of the central tendencies of apocalyptic to manifest themselves. Many scholars now recognise that a substantial layer of apocalyptic elaboration and reworking of earlier prophecy is to be found in the book of Isaiah,[6] that similar trends appear in the book of Ezekiel,[7] and that a substantial level of apocalyptic-type eschatology has been introduced into the Book of the Twelve Prophets.[8] Only the book of Jeremiah, with its more uniform style of Deuteronomistic editing and composition, appears largely to have escaped this apocalyptic reworking. Consequently, although it represents only a rather minimal definition, Lars

Hartman's characterisation of apocalyptic as "prophecy among the scribes" remains especially helpful.[9]

It emphasises the decisively literary character of apocalyptic, with its predilection for metaphors and unusual imagery, often applied in a coded fashion to situations far removed from those envisaged in its original context. The development of multiple meanings for specific words, images, and themes, such as those of "remnant" (cf. Isa. 10:20–22) or the "felling of a tree" (cf. Isa. 10:17–19, 33–34), becomes a frequently used technique. Such a literary device highlights the strange variety and open-endedness of much that is to be found in apocalyptic, where the sense of a predetermined end is often combined with an extraordinary sense of human choice and freedom as to the identity of victors and vanquished, faithful and rejected.

The present study is designed to draw attention to three short passages, all undoubtedly editorial comments, which are markedly apocalyptic in character and where a virtually identical phraseology appears. The passages concerned are Isa. 10:23; 28:22; and Dan. 9:27. Students of the New Testament will readily recognise the prominent significance of the Daniel passage, which is alluded to in Mark 13:14 in the eschatological discourse of Jesus. The phrase that provides a clue for the understanding of all three texts is the reference to "the full end that is decreed" (Heb. *kālāh wĕ neḥĕrāṣāh*), which is to be unleashed upon the whole earth. This is so striking that it must point to the recognition that all three passages are directly related to each other in some way. Precisely in what chronological sequence may be open to question, with the Danielic passage coming last, but with some uncertainty over the priority in regard to the two Isaianic instances. What is striking about all three references is that they employ an almost identical wording and presuppose as already well known a broad assertion about coming judgment upon the whole earth, regarded as already revealed and fixed, even though details and circumstances still remain open to different interpretations.

We consider all three passages in their biblical order. Isa. 10:23: "For the Lord Yahweh of Hosts is about to perform in the midst of all the earth the full end that is decreed." This comes as an apocalyptic editorial comment upon the preceding three verses (Isa. 10:20–22), where three separate and distinct interpretations are presented concerning the possibility and identity of a remnant of Israel, based on an interpretation of the meaning of the name Shear-jashub given to Isaiah's first child in Isa. 7:3. A feature in all three interpretations of this name, which introduces the idea of a "remnant," is they affirm that, in the time of salvation when the Assyrian oppressor is overthrown (Isa. 10:5–15), not all of Israel will be saved—"destruction has been decreed, overwhelming and righteous" (Isa. 10:22). The assumption is very clearly that, although salvation has undoubtedly been promised to Israel through the prophetic word of God, this does not invalidate the parallel warning that judgment must befall the entire land.

Isaiah 10:20–22 is a late editorial development added to the unit declaring Assyria's destruction, and based on a written collection of Isaiah's prophecies.[10] This is shown by the reinterpretation of the name Shear-jashub in a very different way from that originally envisaged in 7:3, where it forms part of an intended message of assurance to Ahaz. Further indications of the scribal character of the unit are provided by the allusion to the promise to Israel's patriarchal ancestors that their descendants will become as numerous as the sand of the sea (Gen. 22:17; 32:13; 41:49; Josh. 11:4; Judg. 7:12; 1 Sam. 13:15; 2 Sam. 17:11; 1 Kings 4:20; 5:9). There can be no doubt that, even though the simile may have been a popular one, the writer had before him the Deuteronomistic History containing these promises of Israel's greatness, and was concerned to modify them in the light of his knowledge of the threat of judgment upon the whole land.

But whence then has he taken this message that a fearful and righteous destruction has been decreed upon the entire earth? Here we encounter a feature that has been of great significance to the apocalyptic development of earlier prophecy that the Hebrew word for "earth, land" (Heb. *'eres*) is ambiguous as to whether it indicates a national, or even more local, area of land, or whether it refers to the whole earth. This worldwide significance would appear to be intended here. In any case the belief that such a massive destruction has been "decreed" by God can best be traced back to Isa. 6:11. This was clearly a central text for the tradition of Isaiah's prophecies in general, since it summarises the central message given to the prophet at the time of his call. It affirms in the strongest possible terms the warning that judgment is coming upon "the land."

All of this indicates that Isa. 10:20–22 is the work of an editorial scribe who has found himself wrestling with the seeming contradictions between the assurances of hope and greatness promised to Israel and warnings of judgment that must befall it (as Isa. 6:11).[11] This promise of greatness has been linked with words affirming the destruction of all Israel's enemies (cf. Isa. 14:26–27, which has been added to the more circumscribed promise of the defeat of Assyria in Isa. 14:25).[12] O. Kaiser very convincingly suggests, therefore, that the parallel assurance concerning the coming defeat of Assyria expressed in Isa. 10:24–25 had already been added to Isa. 10:5–15 before the whole attempt to wrestle with the idea of a judgment upon Israel, now set down in verses 20–23, was made.[13] The solution to these seeming contradictions has been found in the idea of a "remnant," an ever popular concept used by some Christians to reconcile a belief in divine election with awareness of their shortcomings and failings, which render them open to divine judgment.

Hartman's contention that apocalyptic took its origins when prophecy was placed in the hands of scribes is supported by all this. It is a self-evidently literary development, since it depended for its techniques upon the ability to reapply and reuse earlier words and images from prophecy.[14] Moreover, as is evident here, the scribes who were responsible for Isa. 10:20–23 had access, not simply to a written collection of Isaiah's words, but also to at least an edition of the Deuteronomistic History of Joshua–2 Kings. What motivates the apocalyptic mentality which created Isa. 10:23 is the conviction that the threat that a "full end" has been "decreed" (by God in the written word of prophecy) will be fulfilled in the end time, a period which the scribe clearly believed to be imminent in his own day. The notion that the apparent contrasts and contradictions of prophecy can be reconciled by recognising that different prophecies applied to quite different situations and circumstances has been set aside in the attempt to work out some knowledge of God's great "Plan" for the end time.

Kaiser suggests that the distinctive message and wording of Isa. 10:23 has been taken from the first intimation in the book of Isaiah that "a full end has been decreed upon the whole earth" in Isa. 28:22.[15] This may well be so, but certainty on the point would appear to be unlikely, since it is most probable that verse 22 has been added to the more original unit of Isa. 28:14–21. This is a short piece of prophetic invective warning the leaders of Jerusalem that God is indeed capable of performing a work of judgment against his own people. Their political strategy and agreements and their expectation of military support from Egypt, mockingly characterised as a treaty with death (v. 15), are declared to be no true refuge. It may be, as Kaiser argues, that some expansions of the original prophecy have been made. Nevertheless in general it should be recognised that the substance of verses 14–21 is an authentic record of the tradition of Isaiah's preaching in the period 705–701 B.C., when the prophet made strong denunciations of Hezekiah's formulation of a mutual defence treaty with Egypt, prior to the withdrawal of allegiance to Sennacherib. Verse 22 then follows on from this and reads:

> Now therefore do not mock,
> lest your bonds be made strong.
> For destruction is decreed upon the whole earth.

The concluding phrase, which may be translated either as "a full end is decreed," or "a full end and a decision," is identical to that found in Isa. 10:23. It would seem to be highly unlikely that this formed any part of the original content of the prophecy of verses 14–21. It has been added to it subsequently when a scribe found in the prophet's message warning against making "a covenant with death" precisely the kind of repudiation of self-assured hope and optimism which he felt to be most appropriate to bolster his own message of judgment concerning the time of the end. It therefore fits quite smoothly into the overall theological framework of the apocalyptic elaborations which have added a distinctive layer to the book. Any assumption on the part of the Jewish community that when the judgment came upon all the nations that threatened Israel (Isa. 14:25, 29:5–9), there would be no comparable punishment of sinners in Israel, is sharply rejected. Clearly the scribal author of Isa. 28:22 felt very strongly on this point: "Now therefore do not mock [as the leaders of Jerusalem mocked Isa. in 28:9–10]." There must be a remembrance that God has decreed judgment upon the whole earth—so the sinners of Judah will not escape unscathed! It is precisely the same message that has occasioned the introduction of the theme in Isa. 10:20–22 that only a remnant will ultimately be able to enjoy God's exaltation of Israel.

Thus it is very difficult to determine where the priority lies between Isa. 10:23 and 28:22 since both should be reckoned as glosses added to the short units preceding them. It could indeed be the case that the same scribe has been responsible for both, since the message that is expressed is virtually the same—when the time of judgment comes, as has assuredly been decreed for the whole earth, then this will overtake sinners and the lawless in Judah as well as the nations that threaten it.

We recognise two important features here which are very significant for the pressures and tendencies which encouraged the rise of the apocalyptic movement. The first is the distinctly sectarian spirit which motivated such additions to the written text of prophecy.[16] Whilst it appears to be regarded as an accepted truth that God had foreordained Israel to a position of ultimate greatness among the nations, all too readily this had led to a false complacency and to a cynical indifference to attempts to uphold a strict religious loyalty on the part of many Jews. They got on with their daily lives and left the larger questions of Israel's destiny to an unknown and uncertain future. In doing so they posed a challenge to the more zealously law-abiding and torah-conscious men and women of Judah. By affirming that only some in Judah would be saved at the end time, a determined effort was made to encourage a sincere, and self-denying, loyalty on the part of all members of the community. Such loyalty would really matter at the time of the end! The second feature is that, although the broad framework of God's plan for Israel and the nations is assumed to have been revealed through prophecy, an element of openness in such a message remains. Judgment had indeed been decreed, but when, for whom, and with what severity and purpose, had all to be worked out from a careful study of scripture. So the parameters of eschatology and of judgment had yet to be more fully unravelled by a careful searching of the scriptures.

The third of the passages where the mysterious message of "the full end that has been decreed" is given in Dan. 9:27, a very important verse for the interpretation of the book of Daniel as a whole, and many difficulties of translation and meaning have been recognised.[17] In what is presented as the revelation given to Daniel by the angel Gabriel (Dan. 9:24–27), the significance of Jeremiah's prophecy of a duration for the exile of seventy years is disclosed (Dan. 7:24; cf. Jer. 25:11ff., 29:10). This message is then interpreted in terms of an historical event which can only be a reference to the desecration of the sanctuary of Jerusalem by Antiochus Epiphanes: "And he shall make a firm covenant with many for one week; and for half of the week he shall cause sacrifice and offering to cease; and upon the wing of abominations shall come one who makes desolate, until the decreed end is poured out on the desolators." Whilst the passage has been extensively discussed by commentators and some details of the translation remain obscure,[18] what cannot be in doubt is the fact that the historical event that is alluded to is the suspension of the daily offering in the Jerusalem temple in the three-year period Chislev 15 or 25, 167 B.C., until Chislev 25, 164 B.C. Our immediate concern, however, is not with the historical reference as such but rather with the occurrence yet again of the phrase "the end that is decreed" (J. A. Montgomery would translate it "an end and determination"), the precise phrase found earlier in Isa. 10:23 and 28:22.[19]

What is more significant in this case is that the phrase, now found to be so distinctive of the development of apocalyptic out of written prophecy, is a structural part of the whole Gabrielic revelation in Dan. 9:24–27. It is taken for granted that "a full end" has indeed been decreed by God at the end time. This is assumed to be well known to those who had explored the message of prophecy. What has been left unclear and indeterminate is precisely when, and upon whom, such a judgment must fall. Here in this vision given to Daniel by the angel Gabriel, the time and circumstance of this long foreordained judgment is declared. When we look further ahead to the New Testament, we find that the Markan allusion back to this verse (Mark 13:14) is intended to convey exactly the same sense of a long-awaited fulfilment of a visionary warning given beforehand through prophecy.

The purpose of the present study of these three passages, all of which are linked together by this highly meaningful and distinctive phrase, is to demonstrate how apocalyptic has indeed arisen on the basis of prophecy. We can reassert the contention that all three passages are interrelated in that they share a literary dependence. Whether, as Kaiser thinks, Isa. 28:22 was the first to formulate the phrase "a full end that is decreed" cannot be affirmed with any certainty. What is certain, however, is that both Isaianic passages reflect a broadly similar intention of affirming that only some within Judah will be among those who escape judgment at the time of the end.

Both instances in the book of Isaiah must be credited to late postexilic scribes who were reinterpreting the prophecies of the book in an apocalyptic pattern of thought. Ancient prophecy was believed to contain knowledge concerning the mysteries of future judgment and salvation. The use of the same distinctive phrase in Dan. 9:27 must certainly be later still, but can be regarded as intrinsic to the structure and composition of the vision set out in Daniel 9:20–27. M. Fishbane comments, "The compiler of Daniel 9 thus produced a skilful exegetical ensemble."[20] The fact that all three passages are held together by their use of such a highly distinctive phrase is itself not without significance. It reflects the desire to piece together a comprehensive and final interpretation of the time of the end on the basis of biblical prophecy.

The ultimate point of reference of the phrase, however, must be traced back to the call of Isaiah and to the summary of his message given in Isa. 6:11, which was seen to provide a revelation of the purpose of God central to the message of prophecy as a whole. What we are faced with then is an example of what Fishbane has called "mantological exegesis," in which one passage has provided a kernel upon which a series of further prophetic revelations has been built up. Further to these points we can also draw attention to the way in which the terse formulation "a full end that is decreed," or "a full end and a determination (decreed destiny)," which has proved awkward for translators, sums up remarkably concisely a central tenet of apocalyptic. It points to the belief that a fearful and climactic judgment awaits all the inhabitants of the earth. When, and upon whom, remained a repeated challenge and incentive for those who observed "the signs of the times" to discover.

Part 6

THE CANON
OF THE PROPHETS

13   Patterns in the
                                      Prophetic Canon

In his book entitled *The Law and the Prophets*[1] Walther Zimmerli raised afresh the question of the mutual relationships of law and prophecy in the Old Testament in the light of modern critical research. Since the issue is of fundamental importance to the respective hermeneutical traditions of both Judaism and Christianity, it must undoubtedly continue to elicit the attention of scholars, and can bear a good deal of further inquiry. The extent to which the preaching of the prophets can be shown to be dependent on specific traditions of Israelite law, of a developed social and clan ethic, and of the older cultic election traditions of the people, is a significant part of this inquiry, which has received considerable attention. However, in its basic formulation and in the manner in which it has been most keenly felt in Jewish and Christian traditions of interpretation, the question of the relationship of law to prophecy is only a part of the wide issue concerning the Law and the Prophets. This is essentially a question about the canon of the Old Testament, and of the way in which its two basic parts are to be understood in their mutual interrelationships. What light does the Law shed upon the Prophets, and, conversely, what light is shed by the Prophets back upon the first section of the canon? Growing awareness of the hermeneutical significance of the interpretation of the first part of the canon as Torah[2] and of the complex history of the way in which this term was understood in its application to the Old Testament writings has highlighted the problem still further. If so basic a hermeneutical feature can be seen to be present in the categorization of the first part of the canon, what significance attaches to the canonical form and structure of the second part of the canon, the Prophets?

As soon as we formulate the issue in this way we encounter some striking features which have a considerable bearing on the understanding of prophecy in its written form. When we turn to the New Testament, for example, we find some valuable guidelines to the way in which prophecy was being interpreted in the first Christian century. In Peter's speech, as it is reported in Acts 3, we are presented with an illuminating picture of the way in which the prophetic corpus of the canon was conceived to present a unified and coherent message: "And all the prophets who have spoken, from Samuel and those who came afterwards, also proclaimed these days" (Acts 3:24; see also Acts 3:18; 1 Peter 1:10–12). Two things are immediately striking in this summary of Old Testament prophecy; the prophets are regarded as having proclaimed a unified message, and this message is regarded as one concerning the era of salvation which the New Testament writers now regard as having dawned. These two features—the unity of the prophetic message and its concern with the age of salvation—provide a basic pattern of interpretation for the New Testament understanding of prophecy. Yet it leads us immediately to face the fact that it is precisely these features which modern literary-critical scholarship has found most difficult to accept in its own study of the prophetic literature. The great preexilic prophets who stand at the fountainhead of the Israelite prophetic achievement have been primarily, although not entirely uniformly, regarded as *Unheilspropheten*—prophets of doom and destruction. Furthermore, far from regarding the prophets as having spoken with one voice, the interest of scholarship has been to identify the many voices which lie behind the prophetic writings and to relate these many voices, so far as is possible, to individual flesh-and-blood personalities. The result undoubtedly is that the early Christian regard for Jesus as the one whom all the prophets foretold stands at a considerable distance from the way in which modern critical scholarship has endeavored to show a development and continuity between the Old Testament prophets and Jesus' preaching of the kingdom of God. How are we to bridge this gap, and how are we to relate the extant prophetic writings of the Old Testament with the way in which the New Testament, and the main lines of Christian hermeneutical tradition afterward, have interpreted them? Nor is this solely a concern for Christian theological scholarship, since we find too that Jewish understanding of prophecy has been deeply affected in the same way.

The answer is to be found, at least in an important part, by devoting more attention than has usually been given to the literary structure and "patterns" of the written prophetic collections. It is this canonical form of prophecy which brings together the various sayings and messages of individual prophets and coordinates them into a unified "message." Likewise it is this same canonical form and structure which make prophecy as a whole a message of coming salvation. Even a prophet such as Amos, with his dire warnings of coming judgment and disaster, is, in the canonical form in which his prophecies have now been given, a prophet of coming salvation for Israel (Amos 9:11–15).[3] Our concern here is not to reopen the much-discussed question whether such a promise of salvation can be regarded as authentic to the original prophet or not, but simply to note that the form in which his prophecies have been remembered and reaffirmed in Jewish and Christian tradition is how he has been understood. From Ben Sira we obtain a further important clue to the way in which the written canonical form of prophecy has contributed to the establishing of this interpretation. In Sirach 49:10 we read: "May the bones of the twelve prophets revive from where they lie, for they comforted the people of Jacob, and delivered them with confident hope." Here we find the same essential element of concern with salvation— "confident hope"—as we have already noted to be present later in the interpretation of prophecy in the New Testament. Here, however, it is not all the prophetic writings, but simply the twelve, which are characterized in this way. Nevertheless, Ben Sira leaves little doubt that this is how he understood all the Old Testament prophets (cf. Sirach 48:17–25), and it becomes plain that it is the canonical written collection of prophecies which has helped to make this interpretation possible.

The tradition that prophecy is to be understood in this way can be traced back still further, for we find in the important *Prophetenaussage* of 2 Kings 17:13–15 that prophecy could be viewed as possessing some kind of uniform message, and one that held out hope for Israel. In this case the evidence is all the more noteworthy because it must refer to only a part of the canonical corpus of prophecy. "Yet the LORD warned Israel and Judah by every prophet and every seer, saying 'Turn from your evil ways and keep my commandments and my statutes in accordance with all the law which I commanded your fathers, and which I sent to you by my servants the prophets.'" I have already argued elsewhere that this statement has a significant bearing on the development of a conception of canonical prophecy.[4] There are therefore good reasons for recognizing that the basic features of the interpretation of Old Testament prophecy which are evident by New Testament times do not represent a hermeneutic imposed upon the prophetic writings entirely from outside, but rather must be seen as an extension of patterns of interpretation which are woven into the literary structure of the prophetic corpus. When we turn to look at the main features of the interpretation of prophecy to be found in the Qumran literature, most especially 1QHab, we find that this also falls within the categorization that we have outlined. We may conclude this brief outline of the way in which prophecy was being understood by the close of the Old Testament period by summarizing three of its salient features:

1. The prophets were interpreted in relation to their message, not the special experiences of God which they encountered. Hence it was the message that was regarded as inspired, and the inspiration of the prophet was inferred from this.
2. This message concerned the destruction and restoration of Israel, but special emphasis was attached to the latter. This was because this restoration was still looked for in the future, while the destruction was believed to have already taken place. The

prophets therefore were felt to have foretold the future, but in certain very broad categories.

3. This message of restoration allowed great flexibility of interpretation as regards time, circumstances, and the particular form which Israel would assume in the time of its salvation. The great variety of ways in which Jewish messianism has been expressed and understood is a consequence and expression of this.

That the problem of identifying and tracing the development of an eschatological hope in the prophets is a complex one is so self-evident as to need no separate explanation here.[5] Increasingly scholarship has sought to bring light to this problem by its examination of tradition-elements within the individual prophetic books. This concern with the traditions which lie behind the preaching of the prophets, however important they have been, has not been able to resolve the peculiar difficulties which attend the emergence of a prophetic eschatology. On the other hand, the attempts to regard the growth of a prophetic eschatology as a purely postexilic phenomenon have not been altogether successful in relating the pre- and postexilic elements of prophecy to each other.[6] We can at least see now that a part of the reason for this lies in the fact that it is the literary shaping of the prophetic material into a canon which has contributed to this difficulty, and that it was at this stage that sayings and utterances took on a significance which can properly be described as eschatological. As a result, sayings and prophecies which possessed a relatively straightforward historical interpretation in the situations in which they were originally given can be seen to have acquired further meanings in the extended context which the canonical collection provided. This is not to claim that we must make an artificial distinction between an "original" and a "canonical" meaning, but rather to argue that the original meaning took on a certain extension and development once it was allied to other prophecies in a written collection which held a proto-canonical status.

A single example of this may be sufficient for our immediate purpose, although examples could easily be multiplied. In Ezek. 7:1–4 we find a prophetic pronouncement given by Ezekiel upon the theme that "the end" is about to come upon Israel, which harks back to the prophecy of "the end" in Amos 8:2. Thus a prophecy which originally applied to the downfall of the Northern Kingdom of Israel has been carried forward into a later situation and made applicable to the threatened fall of the surviving kingdom of Judah more than a century later. By such a development the earlier prophecy of Amos is certainly affected, in its written form, since this too acquired new meaning in relation to the new context. The theme of the end and destruction of Israel, which is to be found extensively throughout the preexilic prophets in the very center of their preaching, becomes supremely related to the debacle of 587 B.C., with its fateful consequences for Israel-Judah. That a very extended sequence of disasters and political misfortunes led up to this tragic climax provides one clue to the way in which the various prophetic messages have been coordinated so that they point to a unified message. The message is the destruction of Israel, although the separate pronouncements and warnings given by the prophets refer more directly to specific situations and dangers in which first Israel and then Judah were threatened. In this way the individual threats became a part of a greater threat—the threat of all Israel's destruction. It is this larger threat which properly deserves the description eschatological, if that term is to be employed at all in relation to preexilic prophecy. Events which historically spanned a long period, from the mid–eighth century to the first quarter of the sixth century B.C., have been linked together and viewed connectedly as an expression of divine judgment upon Israel. In this process the formation of written collections of prophecies has contributed to such a connected pattern of interpretation.

If this process of connecting separate prophecies together and of viewing them collectively is evident in regard to the message of doom and destruction, even more prominent is its effect in regard to the message of hope and salvation. It is impossible to deny the fundamental soundness of scholars who have seen that it is only toward the end of the Babylonian exile, in the second half of the sixth century B.C., that a truly "eschatological" message of hope was delivered to Israel.[7] This sounded forth with the preaching of Deutero-Isaiah, who must be reckoned above all other prophets as the herald of salvation for Israel. Yet it is certainly wrong to regard his preaching as coming from an isolated voice, bereft of any antecedents and sounding an entirely new note of hope and comfort for a suffering nation. We cannot justifiably deny to Ezekiel his rightful place as "the watchman of Israel," assuring the Jews who had survived in Babylon that there was hope for them, and the promise of a restored nation. Similarly we must also accept as certain that Jeremiah was a true comforter of Israel by his proclamation of a message of hope and reassurance to Judah in its darkest hour.[8] Admittedly this original Jeremianic word of hope has been much elaborated and expanded at the hands of a Deuteronomistic preaching circle, but its roots in the authentic words and actions of Jeremiah remain secure. Furthermore, it is unlikely that this Deuteronomistic expansion of the Jeremianic prophecies stems from a period as late as that to which we must ascribe the beginning of Deutero-Isaiah's activity. The latter's preaching therefore does not mark the first emergence of a prophetic promise of restoration for Israel, even though it gives to it an immediacy and an attachment to political and historical realities which is of the utmost importance. The hope of Israel's restoration is therefore a message which was given over a wide period of time, through more than one prophetic voice, and clearly looked for the reversal of Israel's fortunes after the catastrophe of 587 B.C. As in the case of the message of judgment, so also with that of the hope of restoration, there is a broad thematic unity linking prophecies which display a great deal of variety and individual expression.

To view the question of the message of restoration in the prophetic literature of the Old Testament in this way, however, is to consider only a part of the difficulty which it has provided for the critical scholar. Were we to restrict the question of the authenticity and meaning of the message of hope to the post-587 situation there would be no great literary and theological problem for scholarship to unravel. This is not the case, however, for all of the prophets, even Amos, the earliest and most threatening of them, are presented in the extant prophetic books as heralds of salvation. How can this have been the case if the hope which they are reported to have foretold was only to be realized, or even capable of being realized, after 587 B.C., approximately two centuries after the earliest of these prophecies was given? As a consequence there has grown up the observation, familiar enough to commentators, that we are dealing here with postexilic additions. To some extent this is undoubtedly the case, and there can be little opposition to the claim that such passages as Amos 9:13–15 and Hos.14:4–9 derive from the sixth century or later.

What we must endeavor to understand is how such additions have come to be made. That it was purely for liturgical purposes, to alleviate an excessively somber note when the prophetic writings were read in worship, is quite inadequate.[9] It is rather precisely the element of connectedness between the prophets, and the conviction that they were all referring to a single theme of Israel's destruction and renewal, which has facilitated the ascription to each of them of the message of hope which some of their number had proclaimed after 587 B.C. In this way the collection of the various prophetic sayings into books, and of these books into collections, has been a process which was concerned to present the wholeness of the prophetic message, not an attempt to preserve separately the *ipsissima verba* of individual prophetic personalities. The canonical interest lies in the message, not in witness to the prophetic personalities as such, even though this cannot remain altogether hidden. The formation of a canonical corpus of prophetic literature therefore has not felt any element of impropriety in affirming the message of the hope of coming salvation in relation to all of the forewarnings of doom which individual prophets made. So far as the redactors and scribes were concerned, who must be postulated as the agents of this activity, they were simply expressing a feature which they regarded as authentic to the message, even though a modern critic would have to admit that it was not necessarily authentic to each particular prophet's lips.

In such fashion we can at least come to understand the value and meaning of the way in which distinctive patterns have been imposed upon the prophetic collections of the canon so that warnings of doom and disaster are always followed by promises of hope and restoration. By such means all the prophets have been presented, in the canonical testimony to their preaching, as prophets of salvation. They are *Heilspropheten*, as the concerted witness of early Jewish and Christian interpretation has understood them to be. They spoke with one voice of the salvation that was to come. Yet, just as in the case with the message of doom and judgment, so also that of coming salvation, a process of telescoping, and of the reinterpretation of prophecies to meet the exigencies of later situations, can be seen to have occurred. Already this is evident in the case of Amos, for, as it has been argued by Gerhard von Rad,[10] the hope of the restoration of Israel under a Davidic kingship expressed in Amos 9:11–12 is best understood as originally applicable to a situation in the eighth century. It is not necessarily therefore to be regarded as a postexilic addition, but may be understood as a part of the hope that Israel would once again become a single united nation under a Davidic ruler, a hope which is entirely credible and appropriate in this century. Particularly is this hope understandable after the fall of Samaria in 722 B.C., but there is no need to restrict its setting to such a time. Whether or not such a saying can then be ascribed to Amos personally remains a matter of doubt, but this is in any case not our present concern, and is scarcely capable of being resolved with any certainty. What concerns us here is that it provides an interesting example of how a prophecy which makes perfectly good sense if it is regarded as deriving from the eighth century B.C. would have taken on a much wider meaning in the sixth.[11]

As with the message of doom, the hope of national restoration after 587 B.C. gave to earlier prophets of hope an "eschatological" dimension, and greatly extended the range of meaning which was found in them. There is certainly no necessity therefore for restricting the emergence of a message of hope for Israel entirely to the post-587 situation, or for insisting that all the canonical prophets before this time were exclusively prophets of doom. On the contrary, the more carefully the actual expressions of hope ascribed to the preexilic prophets are examined, the more apparent does it become that many of them can be perfectly well understood in a preexilic context. This does not mean that all such prophecies are to be regarded in this way, but rather that the message of hope which emerged during the Babylonian exile had an important basis in prophetic tradition.

When we look at the various prophecies which make up the Old Testament collection of the prophets we find that three particular historical events provide basic points of reference. These are (1) the fall of the Northern Kingdom of Israel, epitomized in the fall of Samaria to the Assyrians in 722

B.C.; (2) the fall of Jerusalem and Judah, visibly attested in the collapse of Judean power after the siege and fall of Jerusalem in 587 B.C.; (3) the restoration of political and religious life in Jerusalem after the advent of Persian power in 538 B.C. Each of these events provided a point of focus for political changes and threats which extended over a lengthy period, so that the activities of prophets, and individual prophetic sayings, range over a wide span of time. Nevertheless, it was these events which provided a series of catalysts, relating prophecies firmly to political realities and giving to them a basis of "fulfillment."

So far as the emergence of a message of hope is concerned, there are good reasons for recognizing that the downfall of Israel and Samaria in 722 was followed by a period of hope centered upon Judah. The roles of Jerusalem as Yahweh's chosen sanctuary and of the Davidic dynasty in the divine purpose for Israel are firmly stressed in the Deuteronomic literature, especially the history from Joshua to 2 Kings.[12] The problem of the message of hope in the eighth-century prophets is well exemplified in the case of Hosea. The undoubted relevance of his warnings of judgment to the final collapse of the Northern Kingdom of Israel in 722 B.C. poses a major puzzle to understanding how any message of hope that he gave may have been expected to be realized. At the same time the importance of the element of hope in his preaching is so strong that few scholars have been willing to deny that it has an authentic place among Hosea's prophecies.[13] What is certain is that, whenever it may originally have been proclaimed, in the form in which it is now preserved it has meaning for the situation which came into being after the fall of Samaria in 722.[14] From this time the hope of Israel's restoration was closely linked with the political fortunes of Judah and of the reestablishment of a united Israel under a Davidic head. In this way the very foundations were laid for the essential features of the hope of restoration which took on a far wider significance after 587. Old prophecies, expressing a message of hope, could be reapplied to subsequent situations as the political possibilities underwent change.

When we turn to Isaiah, the greatest of the eighth-century prophets, we find something of the same dilemma regarding the presence in Isaiah 1—39 of very prominent expressions of hope for Israel's future salvation, linked especially with the Davidic kingship and the traditions regarding the role of Mount Zion. Very frequently scholars have relegated such hopes to an origin in the postexilic age, at times to a surprisingly late date. Yet they possess a perfectly credible setting in the eighth century in regard to the role of Judah after most of Israel had been lost to the ravages of Assyrian expansion in the west. While the Northern Kingdom disappeared, the inheritance of all Israel had not been lost. Yet, as we now know, such hopes proved abortive, in the form in which they had originally been nurtured, for eventually Judah also suffered a similar fate, and only an exiled community in Babylon remained as the main bearer of such a hope after 587. When this happened, it is once again clear that earlier prophecies expressing such hope came to be seen in an entirely new light. In the form in which the collections of the prophecies of such men as Hosea and Isaiah are now preserved, there are good grounds for recognizing that it is to the post-587 situation that their affirmations of hope are indeed to be referred, although this is not the situation to which they were originally addressed. New events have created the need for new interpretations of old prophecies, and this process had already been firmly established by the time an exilic, or postexilic, collection of such prophecies came to be assembled together, as is presupposed by 2 Kings 17:13–15. This is not in any way an attempt to argue that all the prophecies of hope to be found in the eighth-century prophets are authentic to them. Such is certainly not the case, but we may at least recognize some of them as quite correctly emanating from the period to which the editorial structure of the separate books now ascribes them.

What has happened is that quite disparate prophecies, expressing greater or lesser possibilities of hope for Israel's future, have acquired a relatively uniform pattern of interpretation in the light of the situation which arose after 587. The process of collecting and editing, leading to the canonization of prophecy, came to be invested with a number of basic guidelines as to its meaning, especially its spelling out of hope for the restoration and salvation of Israel. In this process we can see that the broad features which prophecy had drawn to itself by the end of the Old Testament era, namely, that it was a message, given with one voice concerning the future salvation of Israel, came to be firmly established.

That prophecy was regarded as a mysterious and enigmatic phenomenon, capable of bearing more than one meaning, is well attested from the way in which the prophetic writings of the Old Testament show the application of more than one interpretation to specific prophecies. An excellent illustration is provided by the three sign-names given to Hosea's three children (Hos. 1:4–5, 6, 9), where each is given two further, and radically different, interpretations (Hos. 2:2, 3, 24–25 [=RSV 1:11; 2:1, 22–23]). What we are concerned to argue in the present context is that this same process of reinterpreting prophecy has taken place in the stage of the formation of a canonical collection of prophecies. By such a process of hermeneutical development, a much more markedly "eschatological" character has been given to the whole, and the element of hope has been much more emphatically brought into the forefront. What has so often been dismissed as "secondary" material in the various prophetic writings must be recognized as contributing a vital stage, or series of stages, in fixing a pattern of how earlier prophecies are to be understood.[15]

No one has demonstrated this principle of exegesis more ably and convincingly than has Zimmerli in his masterly commentary on Ezekiel.[16] By conjoining words of hope to threats of doom, the original threats take on a more timeless significance and are set in a new perspective. As Zimmerli has argued, this process of developing a prophetic saying may, in a number of instances, go back to the original prophet himself. What we are concerned to argue here is that this process of development cannot be restricted to the separate prophetic books, so that each of them can be treated in relative isolation from the rest as a self-contained entity. Rather we must see that prophecy is a collection of collections, and that ultimately the final result in the prophetic corpus of the canon formed a recognizable unity not entirely dissimilar from that of the Pentateuch. As this was made up from various sources and collections, so also the Former and Latter Prophets, comprising the various preserved prophecies of a whole series of inspired individuals, acquired an overarching thematic unity. This centered on the death and rebirth of Israel, interpreted theologically as acts of divine judgment and salvation.

In such judgment and salvation the events of 587 B.C. marked a vital turning point, establishing the dividing line between them. However, as later Jewish and Christian interpretations of prophecy make abundantly clear, the salvation was not regarded as realized through the early returns from exile and the restoration of political and religious life in Jerusalem. This brings us to another feature concerning the way in which the overall pattern provided by the canonical collection served to heighten and intensify the eschatological element in prophecy. The saving events for which the exilic prophets Jeremiah, Ezekiel, and Deutero-Isaiah looked were primarily pointed in the direction of a return from Babylon and the rebuilding of the temple in Jerusalem. These were to be central aspects of the restoration of Israel to a full and independent national life. The actual restoration which was achieved under Persian domination fell far short of this expectation, and so we find the prophetic voices of this period pointing increasingly toward a more remote and transcendent salvation, ultimately bordering on the frontiers of apocalyptic vision. In this respect also we may discern an important consequence of the way in which the compilation of a canonical collection has affected the interpretation of its parts. Where we might easily have looked back upon the promise of salvation given by the exilic prophets as one that was realized under the years of Persian rule, we find that this was not how later ages of Jews regarded it. It was a promise that still awaited fulfillment, and this was in many ways regarded as the most central of all the features of prophecy. It was a message of the salvation that was to come.

This directs our attention to those prophets of the fifth and fourth centuries B.C. whose preaching provides for the interpreter a host of problems.

Where the background of such men as Haggai and Zechariah is firmly attested, so that their preaching can be readily related to historical events, that of Isaiah 56—66, of Malachi, and of Zechariah 9—14 are obscure in the extreme, to say nothing of the problems attendant upon understanding Isaiah 24—27 and Joel. The very character of prophecy has evidently undergone a change, so that it has become more concerned with themes, and religious institutions such as the temple and the priesthood, and less directly related to events. It has taken on a more explicitly eschatological and supra-historical character. Yet this is not simply true for these prophets only, as separate contributors to the prophetic corpus of the Old Testament, for it is their preaching which has established the guidelines by which the earlier prophets came to be understood. Their preaching also was invested with the same eschatological reference which colored the preaching of the prophets of the Persian era. Once again, as in the case of the proclamation of doom, the process of forming a canonical collection has carried with it a tendency toward establishing a uniformity of interpretation. In consequence, all the prophetic assurances about a future salvation have been affected by the predominantly eschatological character which the latest parts of the prophetic corpus attest.

If our contention is correct, that the formation of a canonical corpus of prophecy has served to encourage the development of a unifying frame of reference by which each of them has been affected, then we cannot leave this layer of interpretation out of account in understanding them. The way in which prophecy was understood in the Judaism of the first century B.C., and by the Jews and Christians of the ensuing century, does have a very significant basis in the patterns woven into the prophetic collections. It has naturally and rightly been the aim of critical scholarship to pay every possible attention to the elements of diversity within the prophetic collections, since these offer an invaluable guide toward rediscovering the origin and setting of each of its constituent parts. Yet we must also note that the ancient hermeneutical traditions of both Jews and Christians have rather contrarily stressed the unity of the message which they proclaimed. It is evident that a comprehensive exegesis of the Old Testament must pay attention to both, for only so can the wholeness of the divine words be properly grasped. Not only is this required by a truly "historical" exegesis, but it is of very special importance for the study of the prophetic books, if the literary-critical and theological aspects of the task are not to fall apart into two irreconcilable compartments of scholarship.

We have already pointed out that it is fundamental to the hermeneutical traditions of both Jews and Christians that the prophets spoke of a coming salvation for Israel. On the other hand, critical scholarship has consistently found the most challenging feature of prophecy to lie in its threats and denunciations, warning of the coming of judgment upon a godless people. The place where both aspects are brought together is to be found in the structure of the canonical collection of prophecy. The threat of doom is followed by the word of salvation, which does not evade the judgment but looks beyond it. By holding these two things together in this way, the prophetic part of the Old Testament canon witnesses to the wholeness of the Word of God.

14   Prophecy as Literature: A Reappraisal

The phenomenon of ancient Israelite prophecy is known to us today through the corpus of writings preserved in the second part of the Old Testament canon. This consists of the Former and Latter Prophets, but it is this second part, the Latter Prophets, which contains an amazingly rich collection of prophetic sayings and records of prophetic experiences originating over a period of more than three centuries. This body of prophetic writings is wholly unique, in its form as well as in its character, since nowhere else from antiquity has there been preserved such a literary collection. As features of a very widely occurring religious activity, prophecy and divination were essentially oral in their character and belonged within an oral spoken framework of communication. Even when it had become accepted for prophecies to be written down and oracular utterances and sign-words recorded in order to be read, this fundamental oral setting was only very partially modified. It is in accord with this that the most popular forms of oracular utterance and divination, or dream interpretation, were brief and closely related to the context in which they were initially given.[1] A prophetic literature, therefore, on the scale that the Old Testament has preserved for us, in which long series of prophetic sayings are brought together, remains a wholly unique product of ancient Israel's religious tradition.

It has been a consistent feature of the modern critical study of this prophetic literature since the beginning of the nineteenth century to endeavor to penetrate behind this literary form of prophecy in order to recreate its original historical context where its oral nature prevailed. The goal of critical interpretation ever since the work of J. G. Herder and J. G. Eichhorn has been to "hear" the word of prophecy as it was originally proclaimed.[2] To this extent the literary form of prophecy has been regarded as both a help and a hindrance. It is a help, since without it we should not know of the prophecy at all, but it has been looked upon also as a hindrance since it often obscures the proper authentic setting in which the saying was first given. However, it is abundantly clear, as a number of fresh critical studies have noted, that the literary form of prophecy in the Old Testament establishes not simply a medium of preservation, but also a medium of interpretation. Written prophecy is necessarily different from oral prophecy precisely because it is written and is thereby made subject to the gains and losses that written fixation entails. The purpose of this essay is, therefore, to explore some of the issues that are raised by the transition from oral to written prophecy and in particular to argue that these issues are far more central to the understanding of prophecy than has customarily been allowed.

Literary Aspects of the Prophetic Tradition

Attention to the written form of the prophetic literature has been stimulated during recent years by two main currents of biblical research. First of all, it almost goes without saying that the aims of canon criticism—to accept and interpret the biblical text in the form in which it now exists—have inevitably raised afresh the question of how we are to understand the complex structure of the four great prophetic books, Isaiah, Jeremiah, Ezekiel, and the Book of the Twelve.[3] For Judaism, as for the early Christian church, written prophecy existed primarily in this canonical form and this had inevitable consequences for the way in which it was interpreted. Prophecies could be drawn indiscriminately from any part of the established canon and assumed to proclaim a coherent message such as we see, for instance, at Qumran and in the way in which New Testament writers make use of prophetic sayings. Without wishing to raise questions here about the degree of authority which we should accord to the canonical from of prophecy, we may be content to note that this form is an indispensable prerequisite for understanding how prophecy came to be used and understood by Jews and Christians. The canonical form of the prophetic literature is also important for understanding how and why certain assumptions came to be made about its authorship.

Alongside canon criticism, however, we must also note the great importance of redaction criticism as a stimulus to questioning how and why prophecy exists as a literature. The processes of literary growth, from smaller to larger units, may appear at times to have been a random process, and even little more than an accident of transmission and preservation. Closer examination, however, shows that this was not often, or even normally, the case and that intricate structures were planned and imposed upon the smaller units of material. Even so complex a composition as the book of Isaiah, which evidently took centuries to reach its final form, shows evidence that, through its many stages of growth, intentional connections and interrelationships between the parts were planned. Such larger compositional units, with the possibilities which they present for pointing to significant theological aims, have only been rendered possible because of the written fixation of prophetic oracles.

It is noteworthy that a most recent avenue of research into the prophetic

texts has made use of rhetorical criticism to draw attention to structural connections and poetic artifices which embrace quite substantial literary blocks
of material.[4] So, for instance, M. Greenberg's "holistic" pattern of interpretation of Ezekiel 1—20 has recognized compositional unity where earlier
critics had noted more heavily the distinctions and separateness of units of
material.[5] Not least, however, it must be noted that the literary fixation of
prophecies has undoubtedly provided a fundamental datum for the formulation of new prophecies. So the New Song of the Vineyard in Isaiah 27:2–6
has been composed with conscious reference to the original Isaianic Song of
the Vineyard in Isaiah 5:1–7,[6] and this is merely one example of a whole
range of elements in the prophetic writings where later prophecies have
been built upon, and related to, earlier ones. Although, therefore, it is clear
that there is a great deal of material in each of the four major prophetic books
which can be described as "redactional" in the literary sense of having been
added by an editor to assist the reader, there is also much that must be regarded as genuinely new prophecy, even though it has been based upon an
earlier written one. Ultimately this was to give rise to a vast range of commentary material which sought to interpret old prophecies in relation to
much later events, a process that is in some measure still with us. Even so,
we must insist that there is no clear line of demarcation between the work
of an editor and the work of a prophet, since the former, too, can fulfil a truly
prophetic function in the way in which earlier prophecies are handled.

A number of recent studies from the perspectives of social anthropology
have concentrated attention upon the great impact that literacy has had
upon ancient society.[7] So far as the rise of epic narrative is concerned, it is
evident that written form made possible a vastly extended and enriched type
of literary composition. The short anecdotal narratives which could be recounted orally became interconnected into much lengthier compositions
with the opening of many new possibilities for the intrusion of plots and sub-
plots. At the same time, the greater length that became easily accommodated
into written narratives imposed new restraints and demands in the interests
of consistency and coherence. Undoubtedly other forms of enlightenment
and instruction which had their origins in oral tradition were compelled to
submit to the demands of a stricter measure of editorial control and shaping
once they were committed to writing. We can easily extend this list to indicate how literacy influenced and shaped all kinds of narrative and didactic
compositions, and thereby inevitably served to change the patterns and
disciplines of human thinking.[8] The possibility of constant reference back to
an original proposition or starting point and the opportunity provided by
written preservation for delayed reflection and examination both served
to impose new controls over thought and artistry. The wider implications
of this for the impact of literacy upon the powers and processes of human

reasoning, and for the gains and losses which it imposed upon artistic forms, are only just beginning to be extensively examined and range far beyond the scope of this essay. Nevertheless we may maintain that prophecy, too, as a widespread and popular feature of religious activity, was profoundly influenced and changed by its preservation in written form.

We may recognize that prophecy consisted, at an elementary level, in a pronouncement of a divine message by a recognized individual. The prophet served as a messenger of the gods, or of God. Such a message usually contained some disclosure of the divine attitude, or intention, most often backed up with a fuller explanation of the reason for this. It is then not difficult to see how, once a sequence of prophecies was brought together and preserved in writing, they could be examined and reflected upon as to their consistency and in regard to the possibility of extracting from them some fuller understanding of the divine nature and purpose. In a very real measure, therefore, a genuine prophetic theology only became possible once prophecy had acquired written fixation. It is in this respect that the significance of the differences between oral and written prophecy come most fully to the fore. On the one hand it is true that, when a prophet delivers a divine message, he presupposes some understanding of the divine nature. It is this aspect of prophecy, with its enquiry into the assumed implications concerning the divine purpose which the prophet's utterance presumes, which constituted the central theological feature of Old Testament prophecy for Bernhard Duhm.[9] There is undoubtedly an element of truth in this assumption, since how the prophet thought of God's nature inevitably served to shape his understanding of the divine intention. It is our contention, however, that it was not until a whole corpus of prophetic sayings came into being as a written record that it became possible and necessary to look for a larger degree of coherence and consistency in their implied disclosure of the divine nature and a genuine theology became possible.

It is precisely because the two essential preconditions for the constructing of such a theological understanding of God were present in ancient Israel that this process of "theologizing" on the basis of prophetic utterances became so important. These were that all the prophecies so brought together should be regarded as emanating from the same deity and that this deity should be regarded as possessing a completely consistent and unchanging nature. These conditions were undoubtedly present in Israel, with its strong monotheising tendency. We may argue, therefore, that prophecy was of the greatest importance for the rise of a genuine theology, not because each prophet presupposed a distinct cultic tradition, as Gerhard von Rad has so strongly stressed, nor because each prophet unconsciously reveals his own inner picture of God, as Duhm argued more than a century ago.[10] Rather it is that the bringing together of a variety of different prophetic sayings, some given from the same prophet at different times and others from a variety of prophets of different periods, raised fundamental issues about the integrity and consistency of the one divine Being who was understood to have brought Israel into existence and to have planned its destiny. To this extent we must insist that the true groundwork of theology, seen in a biblical context, is not simply a matter of drawing together a number of distinct divine attributes—justice, righteousness, holiness, mercy, and so on—which are commonplace in most ancient (and modern) religious traditions, but of showing how they can cohere in a single divine Being. It is this aspect which is so strikingly present in the Old Testament and so dramatically highlighted by the canonical corpus of prophecy. God is both just and merciful, as appears in most human religious traditions, but the more profound dimension of genuine theologizing only appears when a given range of human experiences are interpreted in the light of this justice and mercy. This calls for a more profound level of reasoning than simply to regard painful experiences as divine acts of judgment and pleasurable ones as acts of godly kindness and mercy.

A further feature may be raised in consideration of an earlier phase of scholarly research into the questions of oral and written preservation of the prophetic traditions of the Old Testament. This concerns the fact that such discussion centered largely upon questions of accuracy and fidelity of transmission of the sayings of particular prophets.[11] Once it came to be widely argued that, since prophecy was essentially a proclaimed medium of divine message-giving it was preserved orally before being committed to writing, matters of accuracy and authenticity in respect of oral tradition loomed large in scholarly discussion. Although interesting and illuminating comparisons can be made from the careful study of other religious traditions outside the Old Testament, no hard and fast general conclusions can be drawn. Oral transmission may, given certain conditions, be very accurate, but there is no necessity to suppose that it was always so in ancient communities. In this regard the debate that has now largely been exhausted about oral and literary aspects of the transmission of Old Testament prophecy offers few firm conclusions. Our present concern, however, is not directly with these questions of the accuracy and fidelity of oral transmission.

This earlier period of scholarly discussion served to bring firmly to the fore a picture of ancient prophetic activity that has had widespread repercussions for understanding the complex character of the prophetic books of the Old Testament. Ever since the work of critical scholarship in the late nineteenth century the need for distinguishing between "original" and "secondary" elements in the prophetic writings has proved one of the most prominent, as well as most controversial, features of their interpretation. The matter of authenticity has proved to be a very important, if often unanswerable, question, even, at times, of passages of central significance. The belief in a period of oral transmission has served to offer one possible avenue of explanation for this. On the assumption that the great prophetic individuals gave rise to small schools of disciples, whose existence continued long after the original prophet's death, it has been possible to argue that our major prophetic books, especially those of Isaiah and Ezekiel, are the products of prophetic schools.[12] Hence, the tradition of the original prophet's sayings was combined with further elaborations of them and their supplementation by new ones until the conglomerate of primary and secondary elements which our books now contain was reached. In this, reconstruction of the activity of prophetic schools in ancient Israel an explanation is offered for the agency of transmission of the original prophet's sayings, at first orally and then in writing, as well as their supplementation by a great deal of secondary material which may nevertheless be regarded as genuinely prophetic. Furthermore, in spite of the corporate origin of the extant book bearing the prophet's name, it may be regarded as deeply marked by his authoritative and authorial stamp. The wider implications of this reconstruction of how at least two of the prophetic books came into being need not detain us here, except to note that such a view presupposes that oral transmission and authorship traditions may serve to some extent to explain each other.

The Foundations of Prophetic Literature

We cannot ignore the fact that the processes by which the first written prophetic collections were made are not at all clear. Only in the case of one prophet, Jeremiah, do we have a detailed tradition concerning how a written collection of his prophecies came to be made (Jeremiah 36). Even here questions have been raised as to the reliability of the tradition concerning this account of how the written collection of these prophecies came to exist. In part the story is aetiological, serving to explain how the word of God was rejected by the king Jehoiachin and how the prophet responded to this by committing his prophecies to writing a second time.[13] The initial reason for Jeremiah's inability to deliver his divinely given message in person is not made wholly clear (Jer. 36:5), but is intelligible enough. Whatever explanatory purposes the story has now been adapted to serve, its authentic historical basis in events can be perfectly reasonably accepted. What is especially striking is that the date given for this action—the fourth year of Jehoiachin (605/4 B.C.)—is remarkably late in Jeremiah's career if his call to prophesy came in 627/6 B.C. (Jer. 1:2). However, there would appear to be good reason for accepting as reliable both the date of the prophet's call and the date of the first written collection of his prophecies, since there is no reason to suppose that from the beginning a prophet would naturally wish to have all his prophecies written down. In this case it would appear to have been the restraints imposed upon the prophet, and his anticipated expectation of the rejection of his words, which serve to offer a reason why the choice of establishing a written collection of his prophecies was made. To what extent we should regard Baruch as a deeply committed personal disciple of the prophet, or as a professional scribe, may be left aside.

Here we are called upon to raise the larger question of the extent to which literacy may be presupposed as a widely employed accomplishment in ancient Israel. Clearly Israel was a semiliterate society since writing had been known for centuries, and, where appropriate, written documents and written messages were commonplace. The discovery of the Lachish letters from the time of Jeremiah is sufficient evidence of this. Why, however, should some prophetic messages be written down and others not? Clearly it was not simply the contemporary reaction to their poetic and religious excellence which occasioned this, but rather the dire nature of the events which they foretold which occasioned such preservation. A.H.J. Gunneweg has suggested that prophets, being closely linked to the centres of cultic life, would have had ready access to literary skills and reason enough for attaining and developing them.[14] Yet it would appear that more than this was involved and that the official rejection of Jeremiah's message, and the restraints imposed on him as a prophet, were primary factors in forcing him to adopt a literary preservation of his prophetic words. A closely comparable situation to this appears to have existed from Isaiah at the time of the Syro-Ephraimite crisis and provides the most obvious explanation for the composition of Isaiah's "Memoir" of his prophecies from this time (cf. Isa. 8:16f.).[15] We can then note still further in respect of Amos that, although the event does not have any explicit connection with the writing down of prophecies from him, the rejection of his message and of his prophetic role in Bethel forms a central biographical event in his activity. There are powerful circumstantial features which indicate, therefore, that in the cases of Amos, Isaiah, and Jeremiah it was the experience of rejection, and a refusal on the part of governmental authority to heed the messages given, which compelled each of these men to resort to written recording of the pronouncements given.

These points are of very considerable significance when we come to consider the reasons for a transition from oral to written prophecy and the likely factors which must have operated in the manner and circumstances of such a change. It is almost too obvious to point out that, in a broad historical context, it was the impact of Assyrian and Babylonian imperial expansion upon Israel, with Israel's consequent loss of national freedom and national identity, which provided the primary stimulus for preserving prophecies dealing with these events. It is noteworthy, then, to consider that a prophecy preserved in writing must be regarded as significantly affected once events have taken place which can be regarded as fulfilling its forewarnings of doom. The prophecy has been "confirmed" by divine action, and has undoubtedly acquired new status and authority as a result of this.[16] At the same time, not only is the prophecy itself deeply affected, but the situation of those who read it in the wake of such events would have inevitably differed greatly from the circumstances of those who first heard the prophet declare it publicly. Nor should we suppose that the prophet himself would have felt satisfaction in being proved right. On the contrary, he had in a measure failed, since his hearers had not heeded the warnings that God had given to them. The situation of those who read the prophet's words in the light of events, even granting that they had been preserved exactly in the form in which he had given them, was no longer the same situation that had prevailed for those who had originally heard him. In a sense, the readers of the written collection may be regarded as the victims of the events which had taken place when the prophet's original hearers had rejected him and his message. This alone can assist us in understanding the very heavy interest in the theme of rejection of God's word which colors the prophecies of Jeremiah in particular, but others also to varying degrees. Nor is it altogether out of place to suggest that, if a sense of the prophet's having been rejected by his contemporaries but nevertheless having been proved right by events belongs to the essence of written prophecy, this will have influenced what was preserved. The concern would have been less to record accurately and precisely what the original prophet's words had been at the time when he gave them, and more carefully to show how they had fallen on deaf ears through human sinfulness and obstinacy. This is in no way to concede the kind of exaggerated and extreme claims that all prophecy must be understood as really a *post eventum* product of communities trying to understand their painful present. Rather the genuineness of the prophet's warnings and threats would appear to be unassailable. Nevertheless a measure of truth must be allowed to those recent critics who have drawn attention to the later editorial interests which colored the preserved prophetic texts.[17] The earlier prophecies are necessarily being remembered in the light of events which have subsequently taken place.

A further factor must also be taken into consideration. Although there was a measure of ad hoc particularism about what a prophet said in a specific situation, there was a necessary requirement of a prophet, if he were to retain credibility, that he should be consistent and that his message should presuppose a consistent picture of the divine nature and intentions. A prophet could not be constantly changing his message and its implications, even though his audiences and their situations would inevitably change. We have already remarked that this is one of the most marked ways in which sayings recorded in writing are affected by their written preservation. It becomes possible to reflect upon, and if practicable to harmonize, the implications of each separate saying. To this extent it became possible, in the formation of written prophetic collections, to conjoin ideas and themes which the prophet had given at different times in order to establish a more comprehensive whole. As all critical examination of the overall structure of the major prophetic collections has demonstrated, neither chronology nor thematic connectedness can provide a total and inclusive explanation for the way in which the separate prophecies have been brought together. At best they serve as only a partial basis for unravelling the reasons for the complex structure of the books.

All of this points us to recognize the serious limitations of a type of interpretation of prophecy which is concerned only to hear what the prophet said at the time when he originally said it. Certainly this should by no means be dismissed as an unimportant and unworthy goal, but it may often be beyond the powers of critical scholarship to do more than arrive at an approximation of this. Even more, it will undoubtedly fail to explain a great deal of other material which is to be found in the prophetic literature. To a not inconsiderable degree the situation of the readers for whom these sayings had been written down in a more or less permanent form was different from the situation of the first hearers. Furthermore, even the situation of the first readers would not have prevailed indefinitely but would have undergone progressive changes. As prophecies continued to be read in the light of contemporary events so all kinds of devices came to be employed to give them a more contemporary relevance. Included among such devices was a growing need to concentrate upon the more timeless aspects of religious life and spiritual duties. So such themes as unquestioning obedience and fidelity to Yahweh, adherence to the torah, often without specifying what form this torah took, rejection of idolatry, and waiting for God's ultimate vindication of his people, all combined to give to written prophecy a more "timeless" character. Overall we may claim that the tension between a historical particularism, dictated by the origin of prophecy in specific historical and politically defined situations, and a religious timelessness, determined by the need of succeeding generations to continue reading, and learning from, preserved prophecies marks the most prominent concern in its interpretation.

Prophetic Literature and Prophetic Theology

We may attempt to draw certain basic guidelines from these considerations for a useful modern goal of biblical interpretation. Not least here we must affirm at least a relative measure of endorsement to the principle of canon criticism. We may do this on two counts: first the canonical shaping of the four great collections of the Latter Prophets has undoubtedly arisen on the basis of deep and genuine concerns for the preservation and understanding of prophecy. No doubt this could be sufficiently taken care of in the province of redaction criticism, if the interpreter simply retains a concern to understand the form and structure of the extant text. Yet this leads us to consider the second point that needs to be made here. There are marked similarities and connections, at times amounting to explicit cross references, between the various prophetic books. It would appear to be a highly misleading model to suppose that each of the prophetic collections was formed independently of the others, and that each took shape without reference to the others. The degree of interconnectedness is such as to show that this was not the case.[18] It would appear to be necessary therefore, if the prophetic books are truly to be understood as a fundamental part of the literature of the Old Testament, that the social, political, and religious context which affected all of these books should be properly taken into account. So, for example, the reasons why prophecies threatening doom and judgment are so often brought to a conclusion by words of hope—a phenomenon that affects all of the collections to varying degrees—can scarcely be resolved by looking for independent explanations in each separate case. The fact that this recurs with sufficient frequency to manifest itself as a pattern suggests that it is the same basic needs that have prompted this redactional activity throughout the prophetic corpus. So also the shift towards a more apocalyptic type of prophecy, which is most evident in Isaiah and the Book of the Twelve, would point us in the same direction. The growth of a kind of corpus of authoritative prophetic literature would appear, therefore, to have been taking place alongside, and in conjunction with, the shaping of the individual prophetic books.

This raises the further question, of greatest interest to any quest for a prophetic theology, concerning the extent to which messages given by one prophet have been affected by messages given through other prophetic figures. Once the concern with the genius of each individual prophetic personality had become important to the modern interpretation of prophecy in the wake of the German Enlightenment, then clearly the concern with authenticity was a matter of very real and deep theological importance. Yet such was not the view of the ancients, if we may judge from the kind of literature which has been preserved for us. Since prophecy was a message, or series of messages, from God, then not only was it reasonable to look for some kind of consistency and coherence in the sayings of each individual prophet, but also across the whole spectrum of prophecy. The very natural assumption was undoubtedly present among those who preserved and interpreted prophecy to believe that God must be consistent with himself. This, of course, allowed fully for differences of emphasis in particular situations, but assumed that God's overall plan and intentions for his people, and for all nations, must be a consistent one. It would certainly appear to have been the case that some of the minor inconsistencies which manifest themselves in each prophetic book have really been occasioned by the desire to achieve this larger consistency in the presentation of God's plans, especially where these related directly to the future hope and expectations of Israel in Diaspora.

Nor can we leave this matter aside without noting its significance for the changing distinctions that emerged in the understanding of "true" and "false" prophecy. Initially a simple formula relating to the way in which a prophecy was, or was not, confirmed by events appeared sufficient to explain this (cf. Deut. 18:21f.).[19] Alongside this it became more and more important to extend these distinctions to take account of more factors than just this single historical one, as Deut. 13:1–5 shows. In the still larger perspective of the emergence of a substantial corpus of prophetic literature after the exile it would certainly have been essential to achieve, even if at times through rather strained literary devices, a consistent picture of what the prophetic hope entailed. This too, therefore, would have intruded itself as a major factor in helping to shape these documents into their final form and in compelling the abandonment of prophecies that could no longer be brought into such a scheme. False prophecy came to be understood in terms of a larger range of (proto-canonical) assumptions concerning the reasons for Israel's past failure and the contents of its future hope. At the same time, if we may judge from the complexities of the verbal imagery and interpreted metaphors to be found in apocalyptic, the pressure grew for maintaining considerable flexibility in the understanding of what the authoritative canonical tradition of prophecy foretold. The theological interpretation of prophecy, therefore, must undoubtedly be open to the way in which prophecy was affected by the canonical context in which it has now been preserved. This not only concerns the growth of the separate prophetic books in a redaction critical perspective but also the ways in which the shaping of the prophetic corpus as a whole has left its impress upon each of the separate collections.

There is, however, a further theological consideration of major importance for the understanding of ancient Israelite prophecy in its preserved form. This concerns the relationship between its pronouncements of doom and judgment, with the invective employed to sustain this, and the declarations of hope and coming salvation which appear within it at many levels. The earlier critical perspective, which viewed the fall of Jerusalem in 587 B.C. and the experience of the Babylonian exile as providing the dividing line between the message of doom and the message of hope, clearly possessed a kind of commonsense persuasiveness. That it represents an oversimplification and succeeds only in telescoping together a much more varied and fluctuating series of political and historical developments should now be conceded. Nevertheless, it does contain a substantial element of truth, since it was clearly in the wake of the catastrophe of 587 B.C. that Israel came to believe that the nadir of its fortunes had passed. The paradox is fully apparent, therefore, that, in spite of such extensive retention of pronouncements of coming doom, backed up by appropriate invective, the corpus of prophetic writings as a whole is profoundly and firmly hopeful in its message. The message of doom serves both to explain the past, in the manner of a theodicy, to warn and admonish the present, since Israel is seen to be living under the consequences of its past experiences of judgment, and to provide a groundwork of hope for the rich and glorious future. From the perspective of the editors of these prophetic collections it would have appeared more essential that the larger theological (prophetic) context should have been kept in the reader's attention than that each separate historical context should have been fully made clear. In consequence, the pattern of bringing even the most fearful of warnings and threats to a hopeful conclusion by words of reassurance and hope would appear to reflect the theological and literary needs of the prophetic redactors rather than a startling ambivalence in what an individual prophet proclaimed in the face of the various crises which his hearers confronted. This is not to seek to return to the older dogmatism which insisted that all prophecies of hope must be postexilic. Rather it is to try to understand the fact that, in preserving a collection of written prophecies, the scribes and editors who have done so were endeavoring to serve a wider range of concerns and religious purposes than simply to observe a kind of biographical exactitude which ensured that each literary unit matched precisely the occasion in the prophet's activity in which it had originated. So much confusion has arisen and strained interpretation has been encouraged as a result of this false assumption that the redactional aims of those who have given us the prophetic books of the Old Testament were primarily biographical.

It may not be out of place in this respect to suggest that the frequently adopted assumption that historical and literary questions must first be settled before useful theological insights can be gained may all too readily ignore the deep interconnectedness of all three. Nor can it be ignored that, as we begin more fully to explore the religious and editorial interests which have helped to shape our prophetic corpus of literature, we find that these editorial interests lead on directly to the more elaborate patterns of interpretation employed later by Jews and Christians and which gave rise to a distinctive type of secondary literature with a methodology and techniques of interpretation peculiar to itself. If we are seeking to recover a genuine awareness of the theological meaning of prophecy, then we must surely be wholly committed to a historical understanding of how prophecy was appropriated as "the word of God," rather than to create for ourselves a rather artificial outline of the main ideological assumptions of the prophetic preaching. The counter argument that could be raised that, in the ways in which they interpreted prophecy, Jews and Christians have been very artificial and arbitrary, no doubt contains some truth. It has proved a difficult and demanding task to follow through the intricate web of verbal and literary artistry by means of which Jews and Christians have sought to hear in prophecy the word of God. Yet such processes are neither wholly unrestrained, nor yet wholly fanciful, but genuinely represent an attempt to find in prophecy a consistent and coherent message.

Before concluding this examination of some of the theological implications of the production of a body of prophetic literature in ancient Israel we may note what is probably its most startling and enduring consequence. This is the belief that a prophecy could be delivered and await its fulfilment at an interval of several centuries after the time in which it had been given. So Matt. 1:22–23 could assert that the prophecy of the birth of the Immanuel child (Isa. 7:14) could take place more than seven centuries after Isaiah's day, and without any attempt to understand the prophecy in the context of the circumstances in which it had originally been declared. Christianity has become wholly familiar with such an understanding of prophecy, although its roots go far back in the text of the Old Testament (cf. 1 Kings 13:32 and 2 Kings 23:17).[20] This expectation of a very prolonged interval between the giving of a prophecy and the time of its fulfillment must itself surely have been profoundly influenced, even if not actually originated, by the preservation of prophecies in writing. It no longer required living memory to retain a consciousness of the prophetic word that God had given, but its written preservation could ensure this. Moreover, as we have sought to emphasize in this study, the loss of the original context in which a prophetic saying had been spoken was replaced, once it was written down, by a new context of a literary nature. One type of context gave way to another with important consequences for the way in which the message was then to be understood.[21] More strikingly still, prophecies could be regarded as held in suspense, so that the time of their fulfilment could be regarded as not finally determined, or they could be regarded as susceptible of more than one fulfilment. I have argued elsewhere that it was an important feature of the New Testament's claim that prophecy had been fulfilled (i.e., "filled full") with the coming of Jesus Christ in order to regard Old Testament prophecy as completed and thereby closed off.[22] In any case the beliefs that written prophecy did so much to encourage—that fulfilment could take place after a centuries-long interval of time, or that a particular prophecy might have a multiplicity of fulfilments—inevitably had repercussions upon those aspects of prophecy which were felt to have greatest significance. Inevitably metaphors and verbal imagery of many kinds came to be recast and reinterpreted away from their original contexts to convey many meanings. Instead of the plain declarations of prophetic utterance, rooted in known events and related to known personalities, greater interest came to be attached to themes and imagery that could readily be applied and adapted to a variety of contexts. It is in this world that so much of the later Jewish and Christian apocalyptic imagery established its origins so that the dividing line between prophecy and apocalyptic becomes an increasingly blurred and indistinct one. In some measure the transition from prophecy to apocalyptic has provided for the theologian some exceedingly difficult and uncomfortable questions. Where religious meaning was at one time clear and unequivocal it seems to have become indistinct and many-faceted.[23] Yet we must contend that this same process was one which inevitably had its contrasting side. *Torah* and apocalyptic grew up together, so that eventually Christianity and Judaism responded in different ways to the inherent complexities and tensions of Jewish apocalyptic.

We may conclude, then, by arguing that the transition from oral to written prophecy had very far-reaching repercussions for the rise of a genuine theological understanding of the nature and activity of God. The claim of prophecy to present a message from the divine world about human affairs inevitably raised questions about the providential goals implicit in the divine will towards humankind. Once prophecy had come to be written down it became possible to formulate more elaborate and wide-ranging pictures of the nature of this divine activity, demanding of necessity more clearly defined descriptions of the nature and character of God. On the one hand, this encouraged intensely nationalistic and otherworldly portrayals of God's ultimate purpose. Yet alongside these apocalyptic projections of the providential goal of history there was a need for a humane, relevant, and more immediate outline of what the God-humankind relationship demanded. This found expression in a written *torah*, claiming itself to be a divinely revealed compendium of truth given through Moses. In this, something of the prophetic model of divine revelation has undoubtedly been powerfully influential. We may claim therefore that, in their different ways, both *torah* and apocalyptic owed much to the earlier manifestations of prophecy in ancient Israel. A marked turning point in the change from the older, more open, religion in which prophecy had played a major part to the later religion of a book was occasioned by the writing down of prophecy. This necessitated a deeper questioning of the nature and character of the One who was looked upon as the ultimate source and inspiration of all prophecy.

The Prophet and His Editors

The study of the prophetic literature of the Old Testament has undergone many substantial shifts of emphasis since the work of J. G. Herder and J. G. Eichhorn heralded in a new era at the beginning of the nineteenth century.[1] In fact, such a shift had already begun to emerge with the work of J. C. Doederlein and Robert Lowth in the second half of the eighteenth century, since the newer literary insights of these earlier scholars had inevitably carried implications regarding the authorship and context of the prophetic writings. Doederlein rightly receives recognition for having argued for the full separation of Isaiah 40—66 as the work of a different prophet from that who gave us Isaiah 1—39.[2] It is true that even this was not a wholly new conclusion, having already been anticipated in medieval times by Ibn Ezra, but it undoubtedly marked a strikingly new recognition that our extant prophetic books cannot be assumed to represent the work of single authors. Rather we must be prepared, from a critical perspective, to find evidence of a more varied range of authors, compilers and editors at work in the formation of the preserved biblical collections. In Doederlein's view "Second Isaiah" could be regarded as a wholly independent prophet from "First Isaiah," but by the time of the publication of commentaries by Bernhard Duhm on Isaiah (1892) and Jeremiah (1901), the literary complexity of these two prophetic writings had become even more fully evident. A very significant amount of material in each of these books had come to be ascribed to "secondary" authors.

In turn, and perhaps understandably, a conservative reaction to such critical dissection of the prophetic writings emerged during the nineteenth century. This reaction sought to defend their traditional literary unity under the names of the authors to which they had traditionally been ascribed. The assumption concerning unity of authorship appeared to be a major factor in defending their inspiration and authenticity as prophetic writings. As a consequence a very wide range of convictions about the nature of the prophetic literature came to be adopted by both critical and conservative scholars regarding the nature and contents of the prophetic writings. At one time the classification of "authentic" and "inauthentic" sayings attributed to individual prophets rose to become a primary goal of serious criticism. It is also noteworthy that recent trends of scholarship have witnessed in some circles a strong reaction against the conclusions and methodology of such critical analysis. In this there is an a priori assumption that, until proven otherwise, the sayings contained within a particular prophetic writing should be assumed to emanate from the period of activity of the prophet to which the book as a whole is ascribed. Yet this is to impose upon the interpretation of such writings a very far-reaching assessment about their nature prior to an evaluation of their contents.

Admittedly there is no doubt that any attempt to analyze and locate the historical setting of a particular prophetic saying must be fraught with some measure of uncertainty. Over against this, however, to make the a priori assumption that the prophetic writings were composed as books in the modern manner, with the strict intention of preserving only those sayings which were known, or believed, to have been delivered by a single identifiable prophet, is to impose upon these complex ancient writings a purpose and literary intention which is itself a very questionable and doubtful assumption. The first requirement is therefore that some adequate critical evaluation should be made of the nature of such documents.

Consistently throughout the study of the prophetic literature, both ancient and modern, there has existed an awareness that prophets were primarily spokesmen and preachers. Written collections of prophecies therefore represent a secondary phase of development within prophecy which has resulted in the collection, preservation, and editing of messages that prophets originally gave orally.[3] The phenomenon of prophecy that was written from the outset marks a late development of Old Testament prophetic activity and appears to have had only a relatively minor impact upon the production of the major prophetic writings of the Old Testament. This is not to deny that such a prophet as Isaiah wrote down certain sayings, but to note that, as in the case of Jeremiah (chap. 36), these were messages that had first been given orally. Fundamentally, we encounter prophetic literature as a written record based on messages that prophets originally spoke to their contemporaries.

The question of orality and literacy has a significant bearing upon the present issue under investigation, which is that of the nature of the relationship which existed between the prophet and his editors. This itself then breaks down into further questions concerning the identity of such editors, their relationship to the prophet and to other religious groups, and their purpose in recording his prophecies for a larger posterity to study. Answers to these questions, if they can be found, will then raise further questions regarding the extent to which such editors themselves added material in order to form a coherent written document. They may, in certain cases, have drawn material from other prophets or they may themselves have fashioned material as a kind of primitive commentary in order to clarify what they understood to be the essential meaning of the prophet's message.

In a sense the conservative attempts to resolve such issues have inevitably tended to classify the contents of the prophetic books as predominantly of only one kind and either to regard the prophet as his own literary executor or at most to treat the prophet's editors as self-effacing literary traditionists who left little material of their own in the books they compiled. For the sake of simplicity and clarity we shall restrict the examples we are concerned with to the book of Jeremiah, where a relatively definable situation appears. At the same time we shall need to recognize that there are grounds for assuming that all four of the major collections which constitute the Latter Prophets were formed in precisely the same way.

Prophetic Editors as Preservationists

By the beginning of the twentieth century it had become clear that the primary mode of spoken prophetic address in ancient Israel was poetic in its nature and rhythmic in its structure. This further suggested that many prophetic sayings were originally quite short in their form as originally delivered. Hence Duhm's important commentary on Jeremiah published in 1901[4] made a sharp distinction between the primary prophetic sayings of Jeremiah which were in rhythmic poetry, the prose narratives in which Jeremiah's actions and experiences were recorded, and addresses in an elevated prose form which were markedly unlike the prophet's original poetic utterances. Duhm ascribed these "prose sermons" to a late (fourth–third centuries B.C.) nomistic editing of the book. These sermons were significantly distinct from the historical Jeremiah tradition and displayed a proto-Pharisaic concern with ideas of covenant and *torah*.

In many ways Duhm's insights into the different classes of literary material to be found in the book of Jeremiah took on a much deeper significance in the light of Sigmund Mowinckel's reaction to them. There can be little doubt that Duhm's work was the primary target that Mowinckel had in mind when he published his own assessment of the literary "sources" of the book of Jeremiah in 1914.[5] This placed greatest emphasis upon the different literary types of material that are evident and the different channels of preservation to which these bear testimony. So important has Mowinckel's classification of the sources A, B, C, and D in the book of Jeremiah become that any detailed summary of it would be superfluous here.[6] In particular Mowinckel's identification of a source C, consisting largely of the prose sermons that Duhm had characterized as marking the late nomistic editing of the book, has become a central feature of subsequent investigation.

Mowinckel argued, against Duhm, that these marked a distinct stream of prophetic material deriving from Jeremiah which had been handed down separately from the rhythmic poetic sayings.[7]

The point that is of primary concern here is the way in which Mowinckel framed the basic questions. In line with the aims of scholarship that had emerged at the period, these focused attention almost exclusively upon the closeness of the relationship between the original prophet and the written record of his prophesying. For Mowinckel, as for Duhm, this was a question about "authenticity," or "closeness," of the preserved written material attributed to the prophet and the prophet himself. An element of "distance" could be perceived which was evident in the fact that the different types of material in the book revealed the varied lines through which the message had been handed down until fixed in writing.

Mowinckel himself was later (1946) to define this relationship between the prophet's own activity and the book recording his prophecies and actions as one of "Prophecy and Tradition."[8] It remains essentially the problem with which we are concerned here, but scarcely still in the terms that Mowinckel envisaged it. For him the issue remained that of the authenticity of the preserved form of the prophet's sayings. More recent study has recognized that this does not exhaust the possibilities concerning the relationship between a prophet and his editors.

Following Mowinckel's original publication on the sources of the book of Jeremiah two features came increasingly to dominate the scholarly discussion of this question, especially in Scandinavia. The first of these was a concern to posit the existence of a small community of "disciples" who could be regarded as the preservers and transmitters of the original prophet's sayings.[9] Indeed Mowinckel's study of 1914 already pointed in this direction without saying as much. The very existence of the prophetic books could be regarded as proof that such circles of prophetic followers had been active in transmitting their master's sayings. How else could the prophetic writings have been produced?

The second feature of the study of the prophetic writings came to be inseparably linked to this, since it was to explore the possibilities inherent in the idea of oral transmission.[10] In this, not only was it recognized that the prophet had originally proclaimed his messages orally, but it appeared probable that the first stages in their preservation were also undertaken orally. Prophecy had originally been an oral literature which assumed a written form only after some interval of time had elapsed since its initial delivery. Differences in form and style in the material could then be explained as occurring during this stage of oral transmission, which the modern scholar could hardly be expected to retrace in detail.

It should certainly be noted that, although Mowinckel was staunch in his advocacy of such groups of "disciples" having acted as the transmitters of the original prophet's sayings, he was noticeably more cautious than other Scandinavian scholars in pressing the claims of oral, over against written, transmission. His study of 1946 paid special attention to the Jeremiah tradition and was particularly concerned to argue that oral and written transmission took place side by side.[11] Certainly no single consistent pattern of transmission and preservation should be presumed to have taken place. This contrasted with the quite dogmatic insistence that other scholars placed on the central role played by a relatively long period of oral transmission in giving rise to the extant prophetic books. Overall, however, in spite of many variations in emphasis and detail, the point that primarily concerns us in the present context is that the relationship between a prophet and his editors could be defined almost exclusively in terms of the accuracy and faithfulness with which the transmission had preserved the prophet's own words. The idea that the editors might have had some more creative and formative role to play in shaping the literary form and interpretation of the prophet's message was scarcely entertained at all. Rather, the contrary was assumed to be the case: the further the prophet's editors strayed from reporting his actual words the less satisfactory was their work assumed to be. In this both the more critical and the more conservative approaches to the prophetic literature shared many common assumptions, even where they differed considerably over their conclusions. Knowing only the prophet's actual words was taken to be all that really mattered in the study of a prophetic book.

Certainly it may be claimed that the study of the prophetic literature in the first half of the twentieth century, even where it brought many new insights, found itself largely dominated by assumptions and aims that had been formulated in the early part of the nineteenth century. The editors of the prophetic writings were simply regarded as the necessary mediators between the inspired preaching of the prophet and the preservation of this preaching within the biblical record. This accorded fully with the belief that the task of the scholar was essentially to recover a clear portrayal of the prophet's life and times. So the literary side of this task was conceived in terms of identifying, and where necessary eliminating, the distortions left by the prophet's editors.

The Prophetic Editors as Creative Originators of Tradition

It is not unfair to claim that, after half a century of studies of the book of Jeremiah in the wake of the work of Duhm and Mowinckel, scholarship found itself faced with as much of an impasse at the end of it as it had at the beginning. It appeared to be equally possible to arrive either at a very positive estimate of the degree to which Jeremiah's editors had preserved his actual words and pronouncements or at a rather negative one. The nature of the divergent types of material which were in question was what such divergencies implied. New approaches were certainly called for, and we may single out certain of them as indicating a significant shift in the line of scholarly questioning.

The first of these, by E. W. Nicholson,[12] was concerned primarily with the material which Mowinckel had identified as "source C," and which took the form of prose sermons scattered through Jeremiah 1—25. The very title of Nicholson's book, *Preaching to the Exiles*, indicates much of the argument regarding the content. The prose sermons were seen not to be from Jeremiah himself but rather to represent fresh creative addresses delivered to the small community of Judaean exiles in Babylon.[13] They used the name of Jeremiah because they addressed the situation of exile which his prophecies had served to interpret and foretell, but they bore little other effective relationship to Jeremiah himself. Their importance was to be found in the way in which they brought new messages to bear upon the situation which formed the aftermath of the events which had formed the background to Jeremiah's prophetic activity. In particular, the loss of confidence that had survived in Judah after 587 B.C. became a dominant feature of their message.

What was important regarding this fresh line of questioning was that, in spite of some attention still to the question of whether or not they represent part of the preserved Jeremiah tradition, these prose sermons were viewed as creative attempts to address a situation subsequent to that of Jeremiah's prophetic activity. They expanded further upon the meaning of the Babylonian exile which Jeremiah's own prophecies had addressed in an earlier, and still emergent, phase. In other words it was the situation which had arisen subsequent to Jeremiah's own preaching that had elicited the concern to elaborate and expand upon his own pronouncements. The prophet's editors had done more than simply strive to preserve his own words. They had added words of their own to make the prophet's sayings more meaningful! It is true that a living connection could still be traced between Jeremiah and the work of these exilic preachers but it was far too oblique for it to be classed simply as that of the transmission of a body of sayings.

Nicholson's work explored the connections and overlap between the style and content of the Jeremianic "prose sermons" and the vocabulary and theological interests of the Deuteronomistic literature. This connection formed the central focus of attention for the two volumes from W. Thiel[14] which sought to demonstrate the point that Jeremiah's literary editors can be seen, on the basis of literary and theological evidence, to have belonged to the circle of the Deuteronomistic "school." The importance of this observation, which had become part of the investigation into the literary makeup of the book of Jeremiah since the work of Duhm and Mowinckel, was only now beginning to be fully appreciated. What was abundantly clear was that Jeremiah's editors had assimilated his prophetic message into the framework of the aims and theological ideals of a dominant scribal group of the sixth century B.C.[15] Accordingly, it was not the relationship of the preserved literary tradition to Jeremiah the prophet that mattered, but rather the ideological circle into which the prophet's message had been incorporated.

With Thiel's work, combined with that of other scholars, the relationship between a prophet and his editors could be set in a fresh light which made the assumption of a group of prophetic "disciples" an increasingly irrelevant one. The tradition of Jeremiah's preaching had evidently been "adopted" into a major scribal and reforming circle of Judaean leaders at the time that Judah collapsed in its attempts to resist Babylonian imperial control. The same basic assumption, that the editors of Jeremiah's prophecies belonged, in significant measure, to the same scribal circle that had produced the law-book of Deuteronomy and the Deuteronomistic History, was fundamental also to P. Diepold's study of the concept of "The Land"[16] during this vitally important period of the collapse of the Judaean state. He could build upon the recognition that the editing of the prophecies of Jeremiah represented the third of the major literary productions of this Deuteronomistic "school."

A further major attempt to reevaluate the aims and methods of the editors who had been responsible for producing a book, or more accurately, a scroll, of Jeremiah's prophecies has been forthcoming from Robert Carroll.[17] We should note however that, even before the appearance of Carroll's studies, P. R. Ackroyd had addressed very directly the question of how we should understand the nature of the preserved Jeremiah tradition.[18] In particular he focused attention upon the recognition that written prophecy, based upon a preserved collection of a prophet's spoken words, could be used to legitimate changes in cultic and political institutions. Such a written prophetic testimony could appeal to the prophet's words as divine authorization for political changes which had been made inevitable by events, or to bolster the claims of particular religious groups over against those of rival groups. Written prophecy could become a literature of legitimization affecting the political and religious shape of a community in a very different way from that in which the original spoken words of the prophet had done.

In a number of respects Carroll's work has developed very extensively the contention that written prophecy, in his judgment often only very tenuously related to the work of the prophet to which it was ascribed, served to legitimate developments within a community.[19] By claiming divine foreknowledge in advance of events, the prophetic tradition sought to affirm that a divine purpose had shaped those events. The starting point of Carroll's study *When Prophecy Failed* is to be found in Leo Festinger's analysis of the responses shown by millennial prophetic movements to the experience of disappointed hopes.[20] Hence rather extreme forms of disappointed hope provide a norm of comparison for community responses to prophecy more generally. At the same time a psychological concern with the phenomenon of cognitive dissonance, where reality stands at some distance from prior expectations, occupies the central field of attention. Written prophecy is then seen by Carroll as one way by which the ancient Israelite community learned to cope with the frustration and disappointment of its expectations.

It is not surprising that, in the light of this broad social setting for prophetic activity, Carroll adopts a rather dogmatic scepticism over many aspects of the Jeremiah tradition in his study *From Chaos to Covenant*. He remains doubtful whether we may at all know if the material ascribed to Jeremiah derived in any recognizable sense from his actual sayings. Rather, all attention is devoted to the question of how a community responded to the catastrophic events which took place during Jeremiah's lifetime and how they used the figure of Jeremiah as a prophet to interpret their own confusion and despair. To this extent, with Carroll's work, the question of whether or not Jeremiah's editors had faithfully preserved and recorded the tradition of his sayings has largely become an irrelevance. Their concern is assumed to have been throughout one of understanding and interpreting the disasters and despair which followed the prophet's period of activity. Prior hopeful expectation and painful historical reality had given rise to a situation of cognitive dissonance which only a prophetic hermeneutic could dispel.

We can certainly recognize that Carroll's studies provide an important corrective to the earlier work which took it for granted that all that mattered in examining the relationship between a prophet and his editors was whether or not they had painted his theological and spiritual portrait faithfully. This was never their intention, and in most respects the very nature of prophecy indicates that its concerns were far too urgent and existential for such a careful literary proceeding to have been their aim. Nevertheless to explain the origin of a major part of the book of Jeremiah on the basis of a need for a hermeneutic arising out of the experience of cognitive dissonance is to lose sight of the uniqueness and inspired charisma which lent a very distinctive divine authority to the prophet's words in the first place. Carroll's picture of Jeremiah is one of a figure so lacking in definition that he appears virtually lost altogether behind the tradition that has made use of his name.

Clearly there is a need for recognizing that the relationship which existed between the prophet and his editors, and which led to determined efforts to record a prophet's actual words, was a more genuinely reciprocal one than this. The prophet did stand apart from other men, and he was believed to possess an inspiration accorded to only a very few individuals which made his actual words memorable and vital. At the same time there was evidently a need, as the complex literary structure of all the biblical prophetic collections reveals, to edit, record, and interpret those words with the help of some additional material and supplementation. If an emphasis upon the prophetic editors as preservationists erred in one direction, the attempt to present them as freelance writers who used the prophet's name simply for their own convenience erred in another.

The Prophetic Editors as Interpreters

If we are to look for some guidance as to the overall role which the editors of the prophetic literature adopted for themselves then we find some helpful guidelines in Max Weber's basic studies of prophetic tradition.[21] In this he placed strong emphasis upon the role of the prophet as an inspired individual. The prophet's charisma was personal to himself and lent him a unique divine authority, not transferable to others. Yet against this his messages, often brief and some times cryptic, needed to be interpreted to make them more effective and meaningful for the life of the ongoing religious community to which he belonged. Accordingly, what the prophet's words meant for the future of established religious leaders and institutions needed to be spelled out. Weber described this process as one of "routinization" in which the implications of what the prophet had said were adapted and interpreted in more precise and concrete terms and in relation to organized religious life. The prophet's message was perceived to lend direction and support to some groups, while he brought reproof, and sometimes outright rejection, to others.

So far as the theory of cognitive dissonance is concerned, it is noteworthy that Weber discerned an element of tension between the religious meaning of what a prophet declared and the empirical experience of what actually happened to the groups the prophet addressed. However, this is peripheral to the more substantive feature that the "routinization" of prophecy marked its integration into the life of a community. Its meaning was spelled out in terms of priestly administration, pastoral care, and the spiritual development of the individual's life. Revealed truth became embodied in the institutional life of a larger group and spelled out in ethical rules and support for specific forms of administrative authority.

Our argument is that this process of "routinization" is the most appropriate one to describe the nature of the relationship between a prophet and his editors. Especially does it highlight the difference in status and perceived authority between the individual persona of the prophet and that of the editors and interpreters who transmitted his sayings. It explains the aims and characteristics of the editorial supplementation which shaped and adapted the prophet's words in order to give them a more permanent and practical meaning. Most especially such a process serves to show why it was important to retain some recognizable portrait of the prophet himself, together with a record of his actual words so far as this was possible and to relate these words to the events which formed the sequel of the situation to which the prophet had originally spoken. In such a context the uniqueness and individuality of the prophet was of the very essence of his charismatic authority to which his editors needed to appeal. At the same time it was clear to these editors that the actual import of the prophet's words would be lost if their implications were not spelled out with great clarity to those who held the prophet in high regard as the spokesman of God.

We may contend therefore that this process of "routinization" best describes the relationship between the prophet and his editors. Certainly this is so in the case of both Jeremiah and Ezekiel, where the connections between the editorial word and more central circles of Jewish life have long been recognized.[22] In regard to the complex literary histories of the books of Isaiah and of the Twelve Prophets the situation is not so obviously clear, although in these also many facets of the routinization process are evident. In the case of Jeremiah this routinization has taken place in very direct application to central concerns of what we have broadly come to identify as a Deuteronomistic party, or group. These concerns show themselves in regard to three major features of Judah's national life: temple, kingship, and national sovereignty.

So we find that the meaning of Jeremiah's prophecies has been spelled out very forcefully in respect of the temple as the primary religious institution of the nation, the Davidic kingship as its foremost political pillar, and the future of the remnants of the nation, in Judah and in Babylon, under a prolonged period of Babylonian political control.

It is not difficult to see how the fact of the destruction of the temple in Jerusalem has exercised a formative effect upon the literary shaping of the Jeremiah tradition. A conditional warning of the destruction of the building is set out in Jer. 7:1–15 in a unit which has long been recognized as showing traces of editorial reworking. It heads a substantial section dealing with false worship extending down to Jer. 10:25. Furthermore a repetition of this warning of the temple's destruction commences the narrative section in Jer. 26:1–15, where it is highlighted as a major cause of conflict between Jeremiah and the Jerusalem authorities. It is then noteworthy that this threat of the destruction of the temple is coupled with threats concerning the fall of the city of Jerusalem (cf. Jer. 7:34; 8:1–3; 9:12; 25:29; 38:3, 23). This is given such emphasis as to suggest that the presence of the temple there had provided the basis for the belief that the city as a whole would be spared for the temple's sake.

Since the book of Jeremiah, unlike the comparable books of Isaiah, Ezekiel, and the Twelve, contains no explicit promise regarding the temple's restoration, the way in which the prophet himself envisaged the future of the cultus is never made wholly clear. It is often assumed that he advocated a very inward and spiritual form of worship which needed no formal cultus.[23] Nevertheless it has to be kept in mind that this is not made formally explicit. Rather the staunch advocacy, undoubtedly by the scroll's editors, of a necessary role for the levitical priests in the future (Jer. 33:18, 21–24) suggests that a restored temple was certainly not precluded.

Significantly too the ambiguity of this situation is left even more marked by the inclusion of an assurance that the loss of the ark would not inhibit the divine blessing of all Jerusalem in future years (Jer. 3:15–17). This loss, and the fact that it would not be replaced, appear at a point where we should readily have expected the temple itself to have been mentioned. Nor can we leave out of reckoning the very surprising fact that the return of the temple vessels to Jerusalem, with the implication that they embodied much of the holiness of the temple itself, is introduced in Jer. 27:16–22, once again by the prophet's editors, as a major point.[24] Obviously such a concern for the temple vessels could only have meaning on the assumption that the temple itself would eventually be restored.

Overall the question of what Jeremiah's prophecies implied about the future of the temple was evidently a major point of concern for his editors. The end result is more than a little ambiguous as to what it discloses both about the attitude of Jeremiah to the matter and about the role a restored temple might have for a renewed and reunited Israel. Clearly a strong concern was felt to show why the temple had to be destroyed, and how Jeremiah had declared as much. At the same time this had to be set out in such a way as not to preclude the expectation that, in future, Jerusalem would once again become the spiritual centre of Israel's life. The absence of any prophecy concerning the rebuilding of the temple suggests that this had still not been raised as a major issue by the time the editing of the prophetic scroll was completed. At the same time such a rebuilding is clearly not ruled out.

The future of the kingship also becomes an issue where a significant level of tension exists between what appears to have been Jeremiah's own attitude and the expectations that were nursed by his editors. The finality with which Jeremiah ruled out any possible return to the throne of Jehoiachin, or his descendants (Jer. 22:24–27, 28–30) contrasts strikingly with the forthright assurance about the future of the Davidic dynasty set out in Jer. 33:14–26. The latter must certainly be the work of the editors, and this must also be true of the even more enigmatic prophecy of Jer. 23:5–6, with its play on the name of Zedekiah. Uncertainty about Jeremiah's hope for Zedekiah is shown up by 38:17–23, with its muted words of hope which events evidently refuted. Because the kingship was the central political institution of Israel's life, and because the return to the throne of Jerusalem of an heir of David's line became so important an aspect of the exilic hope (cf. Isa. 11:1–5; Ezek. 37:24–28), editorial work on Jeremiah's prophecies has endeavoured to give room to it.

It seems unlikely that Jeremiah personally attached much importance to the issue of restoring the Davidic monarchy after Zedekiah's removal from his throne. Since such a restoration in any case did not eventually take place, in spite of evident hopes that the survival of Jehoiachin's family in Babylonian exile would make it possible (as is suggested by 2 Kings 25:27–30), it is striking that it is the editorial work which has generated an element of dissonance. It is Jeremiah's editors who, in upholding his condemnation of Judah's last kings, have nevertheless sought to show that the Davidic monarchy would play an important role in the future of a renewed Israel, even though actual events turned out contrary to this.

The third point that has deeply affected the editorial shaping of the Jeremiah scroll was evidently that of Judah's national sovereignty under the suzerainty of Babylon. This comes most startlingly into the forefront in the narratives of Jeremiah 40—43, which contain so much valuable and detailed information about the events in Judah under Gedaliah's brief governorship. What stands out is the repeated emphasis upon the necessity for continued submission to Babylon for the time being (Jer. 40:5, 7; 41:2, 18). This is spelled out so affirmatively as to insist that there was nothing to fear under such Babylonian jurisdiction:

> Gedaliah the son of Ahikam, son of Shaphan, swore to them and their men, saying, "Do not be afraid to serve the Chaldeans. Dwell in the land, and serve the king of Babylon, and it shall be well with you." (Jer. 40:9)

Similarly Jeremiah could be represented as affirming as God's word:

> Do not fear the king of Babylon, of whom you are afraid; do not fear him, says the LORD, for I am with you, to save you and to deliver you from his hand. I will grant you mercy, that he may have mercy on you and let you remain in your own land. (42:11–12)

Clearly the Jeremiah scroll has been the subject of an editorial shaping which has made a very major issue of the necessity for the remnant in Judah to remain subservient, for an indefinite period, to the rule of the king of Babylon (cf. Jer. 25:11–14, 17, 26; 27:1–7; 29:10; 38:2). This has been felt to stand wholly in line with Jeremiah's personal advocacy of surrender to the Babylonian forces at the time of the siege of Jerusalem in 587 B.C. (Jer. 38:2, 17–23). It clearly also had much to do with the condemnation of those prophets who declared the fall of Babylon and the return of the exiles to be imminent.

K. F. Pohlmann's tracing of this "pro-Babylonian" editing in Jeremiah places it very late,[25] whereas all the indications are that it arose as an urgent issue affecting the survival of Judaean exiles very much closer to the time consequent upon Gedaliah's murder.[26] There seems little reason for dating it much later than the middle of the sixth century B.C. However, our primary concern is to note how it was the emergence of such a basic political issue, and its evident relationship to a position which Jeremiah himself had adopted, which has elicited extensive treatment by Jeremiah's editors. It falls fully within the process which we can identify as that of the routinization of prophecy. This necessitated the elaboration and clarification of an inspired prophet's message in relation to concrete political and religious issues. The message itself was sensed to lack the specificity which was needed if its import was to be fully heeded by the community which looked back with genuine trust and confidence to the prophet who was the interpreter of their times. Hence we can claim that a genuine and positive relationship existed between the prophet and his editors. In no way were these latter trying to compensate for the limitations, or even errors, of the prophet whose heirs they felt themselves to be. Rather their profound respect for him made them eager and anxious interpreters of his words, spelling out in detail how they could be applied to the situation which his warnings and reproof had forewarned them of.

Abbreviations

AnBib	Analecta biblica
AncB	Anchor Bible
AOAT	Alter Orient und Altes Testament
ASTI	*Annual of the Swedish Theological Institute*
ATANT	Abhandlungen zur Theologie des Alten und Neuen Testaments
ATD	Das Alte Testament Deutsch
AthD	*Acta Theologica Danica*
BBB	Bonner biblische Beiträge
BETL	Bibliotheca ephemeridum theologicarum lovaniensium
BEvT	Beiträge zur evangelischen Theologie
BFCT	Beiträge zur Förderung christlicher Theologie
BHS	*Biblia hebraica stuttgartensia*
BHTh	Beiträge zur historischen Theologie
BKAT	Biblischer Kommentar: Altes Testament
BN	*Biblische Notizen*
BSt	Biblische Studien
BWANT	Beiträge zur Wissenschaft vom Alten und Neuen Testament
BZ	*Biblische Zeitschrift*
BZAW	Beihefte zur *ZAW*
CB.OT	Coniectanea biblica, Old Testament
CBQ	*Catholic Biblical Quarterly*
EBib	Etudes bibliques
E.T.	English translation
EvTh	*Evangelische Theologie*
ExpTim	*Expository Times*
FRLANT	Forschungen zur Religion und Literatur des Alten und Neuen Testaments
FS	Festschrift
HAT	Handbuch zum Alten Testament
HK	Handkommentar
HKAT	Handkommentar zum Alten Testament

ICC	International Critical Commentary
JBL	*Journal of Biblical Literature*
JQR	*Jewish Quarterly Review*
JSOT	*Journal for the Study of the Old Testament*
JSOTSup	*JSOT* Supplement Series
KAT	Kommentar zum Alten Testament
KS	*Kleine Schriften*
LD	Lectio divina
NF	Neue Folge (new series)
OBO	Orbis biblicus et orientalis
OTL	Old Testament Library
OTS	*Oudtestamentische Studien*
RevExp	*Review and Expositor*
RHPR	*Revue d'histoire et de philosophie religieuses*
SAT	Die Schriften des Alten Testament
SBLDS	Society of Biblical Literature Dissertation Series
SBT	Studies in Biblical Theology
SEÅ	*Svensk exegetisk Årsbok*
StTh	*Studia Theologica*
TBü	Theologische Bücherei
ThWAT	*Theologisches Wörterbuch zum Alten Testament*
ThZ	*Theologische Zeitschrift*
VT	*Vetus Testamentum*
VTSup	Vetus Testamentum, Supplements
WMANT	Wissenschaftliche Monographien zum Alten und Neuen Testament
ZAW	*Zeitschrift für die alttestamentliche Wissenschaft*
ZDMGSup	Zeitschrift der deutschen morgenländischen Gesellschaft, Supplements
ZThK	*Zeitschrift für Theologie und Kirche*

Notes

Introduction: The Interpretation of Old Testament Prophecy

1. P.H.A. Neumann, *Das Prophetenverständnis in der Deutschsprachigen Forschung seit Heinrich Ewald*, Wege der Forschung (Darmstadt: Wissenschaftliche Buchgesellschaft, 1979).
2. See the survey in my study *A Century of Old Testament Study*, rev. ed. (Guildford: Lutterworth Press, 1983), 61–94.
3. R. E. Clements, *Prophecy and Covenant*, SBT First Series 43 (London: SCM Press, 1965).
4. C. Westermann, *Basic Forms of Prophetic Speech* (London: Lutterworth Press, 1967); from the German *Grundformen prophetische Rede* (Munich: Chr. Kaiser Verlag, 1960). Cf. now also the same author's *Prophetic Oracles of Salvation in the Old Testament* (Louisville, Ky.: Westminster/John Knox Press, 1991); from the German *Prophetische Heilsworte im Alten Testament* (Göttingen: Vandenhoeck & Ruprecht, 1987). H. Gunkel's pioneering studies had been published as "Einleitungen zu 'Die grossen Propheten,'" in *Die Schriften des Alten Testaments* II/2, 2d ed., 1923.
5. This was published in a slightly revised form as *God and Temple: The Idea of the Divine Presence in Ancient Israel* (Oxford: Basil Blackwell Publisher, 1965).
6. See Clements, *A Century of Old Testament Study*, 113–18. See also W. Bellinger, Jr., *Psalmody and Prophecy*, JSOTSup 27 (Sheffield: JSOT Press, 1984).
7. J. Begrich, *Studien zu Deuterojesaja*, BWANT 4 Folge Heft 25 (77) (Stuttgart: W. Kohlhammer, 1938), reprint ed. W. Zimmerli, as TBü 20 (Munich: Chr. Kaiser Verlag, 1963).
8. James Muilenburg, "Introduction and Exegesis to Isaiah, Chapters 40—66," *The Interpreter's Bible*, vol. 5, ed. G. A. Buttrick (Nashville: Abingdon-Cokesbury Press, 1956), 381–773.
9. G. von Rad, *Old Testament Theology, vol. 2: The Theology of Israel's Prophetic Traditions* (Edinburgh: Oliver & Boyd, 1965); from *Theologie*

des Alten Testaments: Bd. II, Die Theologie der prophetischen Überlieferungen Israels (Munich: Chr. Kaiser Verlag, 1960).

10. R. E. Clements, *Prophecy and Tradition* (Oxford: Basil Blackwell Publisher, 1975).

11. Cf. D. J. McCarthy, *Old Testament Covenant: A Survey of Current Opinions* (Oxford: Basil Blackwell Publisher, 1972); E.W. Nicholson, *God and His People: Covenant and Theology in the Old Testament* (Oxford: Oxford University Press, 1986).

12. A balancing corrective began to emerge with the detailed studies by L. Perlitt, *Bundestheologie im Alten Testament*, WMANT 36 (Neukirchen-Vluyn: Neukirchener Verlag, 1969); E. Kutsch, *Verheissung und Gesetz: Untersuchungen zum sogenannten "Bund" im Alten Testament*, BZAW 131 (Berlin/New York: Walter de Gruyter, 1972).

13. N. K. Gottwald, *All the Kingdoms of the Earth* (New York: Harper & Row, 1964).

14. My first essay to investigate some of these problems appeared as "Patterns in the Prophetic Canon," in *Canon and Authority: Essays in Old Testament Religion and Theology*, ed. G. W. Coats and B. O. Long (Philadelphia: Fortress Press, 1977), 42–55.

15. The background to, and rise of, this new critical approach is well studied in Jean M. Vincent's *Studien zur literarischen Eigenart und zur geistigen Heimat von Jesaja, Kap. 40–55*, Beihefte zur Evangelische Theologie 5 (Frankfurt: Peter Lang, 1977). Cf. also U. Simon, "Ibn Ezra between Medievalism and Modernism: The Case of Isaiah, 40—66," *Congress Volume: Salamanca 1983*, ed. J. A. Emerton, VTSup 36 (Leiden: E. J. Brill, 1985), 257–71.

16. R. E. Clements, *Isaiah 1—39*, New Century Bible Commentary (Grand Rapids: Wm. B. Eerdmans Publishing Co., 1980).

17. George Adam Smith, *The Book of Isaiah*, 2 vols., Expositor's Bible (New York: Harper & Brothers, 1927).

18. O. C. Whitehouse, *The Book of Isaiah*, Century Bible, 2 vols. (London: T. & C. Jack, 1905–1909).

19. J. Skinner, *Isaiah*, 2 vols, CBSC (Cambridge: Cambridge University Press, 1910, 1915).

20. Cf. von Rad, *Old Testament Theology*, vol. 2, 147ff.

21. Cf. especially B. S. Childs, *Isaiah and the Assyrian Crisis*, SBT Second Series 3 (London: SCM Press, 1967), and my own study *Isaiah and the Deliverance of Jerusalem*, JSOTSup 13 (Sheffield: JSOT Press, 1980).

22. H. Wildberger, *Jesaja 1—39*, BKAT, 3 vols. (Neukirchen-Vluyn: Neukirchener Verlag, 1975–82); E.T. of vol. 1 as *Isaiah 1—12* (Minneapolis: Fortress Press, 1991). Cf. also the same author's summaris-

ing work *Königsherrschaft Gottes: Jesaja 1—39*, 2 vols. (Neukirchen-Vluyn: Neukirchener Verlag, 1984).

23. Cf. the various essays in O. H. Steck, *Wahrnehmungen Gottes im Alten Testament: Gesammelte Studien*, TBü 70 (Munich: Chr. Kaiser Verlag, 1982), and *Gottesknecht und Zion: Gesammelte Aufsätze zu Deuterojesaja.* Forschungen zum Alten Testament 4 (Tübingen: J.C.B. Mohr, 1992).

24. H. Barth, *Die Jesaja-Worte in der Josiazeit*, WMANT 48 (Neukirchen-Vlyun: Neukirchener Verlag, 1977).

25. Clements, *Isaiah 1—39*.

26. M. Noth, *Überlieferungsgeschichtliche Studien I, Die sammelnden und bearbeitenden Geschichtswerke im Alten Testament* (Halle: Max Niemeyer Verlag, 1943; E.T. of pp. 1–110 as *The Deuteronomistic History*, JSOTSup 15 (Sheffield: JSOT Press, 1981).

27. Cf. R. E. Clements, "Isaiah 14:22–27: A Central Passage Reconsidered," in *The Book of Isaiah, Les Oracles et leur Relectures: Unité et complexité de l'ouvrage*, ed. J. Vermeylen, BETL 81 (Leuven, 1989), 253—62; idem, "The Prophecies of Isaiah to Hezekiel concerning Sennacherib: 2 Kings 19:21–34//Isa. 37:22–35," in *Prophetie und geschichtliche Wirklichkeit im Alten Israel: FS S. Herrmann zum 65. Geburtstag*, ed. R. Liwak and S. Wagner (Stuttgart-Köln: W. Kohlhammer, 1991), 65–78; idem, "The Politics of Blasphemy: Zion's God and the Threat of Imperialism," in *"Wer ist wie du, HERR, unter den Göttern?" Studien zur Theologie und Religionsgeschichte Israel für Otto Kaiser zum 70. Geburtstag*, ed. I. Kottsieper, J. van Oorschot, D. Römheld, and H. M. Wahl (Göttingen: Vandenhoeck & Ruprecht, 1994), 231–46.

28. R. E. Clements, "The Prophecies of Isaiah and the Fall of Jerusalem in 587 B.C.," *VT* 30 (1980): 421–36.

29. Besides those included in n. 28 may be mentioned "The Unity of the Book of Isaiah," *Interpretation* 36 (1982): 117–29, and the introduction to Isaiah included in *The Books of the Bible*, ed. B. W. Anderson (New York: Charles Scribner's Sons, 1989), 1:247–80.

30. J. Vermeylen, *Du prophète Isaïe à l'apocalyptique: Isaïe, i–xxxv, miroir d'un demi-millénaire d'expérience religieuse en Israël*, 2 vols., EBib (Paris: J. Gabalda, 1977).

31. C. R. Seitz, *Zion's Final Destiny: The Development of the Book of Isaiah, A Reassessment of Isaiah 36—39* (Minneapolis: Fortress Press, 1991).

32. H.G.M. Williamson, *The Book Called Isaiah: Deutero-Isaiah's Role in Composition and Redaction* (Oxford: Oxford University Press, 1994).

33. See n. 22.

34. O. Kaiser, *Isaiah 1—12* (London: SCM Press, 1983, 2d ed., E.T. from

the fifth German ed. of 1981); *Isaiah 13—39* (London: SCM Press, 1974, from the German first ed. of 1973).

35. W.A.M. Beuken, *Jesaja*, 4 vols. (Nijkerk: G. F. Callenbach, 1983–89).
36. Cf. A. Motyer, *The Prophecy of Isaiah* (Leicester: Inter-Varsity Press, 1993).
37. The interested reader may note the list set out in H. Wildberger, *Jesaja*, Bd. II, 13–27, pp. 910f.; see also M. A. Sweeney, "Textual Citations in Isaiah 24—27: Toward an Understanding of the Redactional Function of Chapters 24—27 in the Book of Isaiah," *JBL* 107 (1988): 39–52.
38. The splendid study by Michael Fishbane, *Biblical Interpretation in Ancient Isaiah* (Oxford: Oxford University Press, 1985), contains much excellent and relevant material but is very brief in its survey of the prophetic literature (pp. 443ff.).
39. Cf. especially, K. Nielsen, *There Is Hope for a Tree: The Tree as Metaphor in Isaiah*, JSOTSup 65 (Sheffield: JSOT Press, 1985); E. W. Conrad, *Reading Isaiah* (Minneapolis: Fortress Press, 1991); Katheryn Pfisterer Darr, *Isaiah's Vision and the Family of God* (Louisville, Ky.: Westminster/John Knox Press, 1994).
40. R. Rendtorff, *The Old Testament: An Introduction* (Philadelphia: Fortress Press, 1986), E.T. from the German ed. of 1983; idem, "The Composition of the Book of Isaiah," in *Canon and Theology: Overtures to an Old Testament Theology* (Edinburgh: T. & T. Clark, 1983), 146–69; idem, "Isaiah 6 in the Framework of the "Composition of the Book," in *Canon and Theology*, 170–80.
41. Conrad, *Reading Isaiah*, 21ff.
42. Cf. my remarks in "Prophecy as Literature: A Re-appraisal," in *The Hermeneutical Quest: Essays in Honor of James Luther Mays on his Sixty-Fifth Birthday*, Princeton Theological Monographs 4, ed. D. G. Miller, 56–76 (Allison Park, Pa.: Pickwick Publications, 1986), and "The Prophet and His Editors," in *The Bible in Three Dimensions: Essays in Celebration of Forty Years of Biblical Studies in the University of Sheffield*, JSOTSup 87 (Sheffield: Sheffield Academic Press, 1990), 202–30.
43. Cf. my essay "Prophecy and Fulfilment," in *Epworth Review* 10/3 (1983): 72–82.
44. Cf. my observations in "Beyond Tradition-History: Deutero-Isaianic Development of First Isaiah's Themes," *JSOT* 31 (1985): 95–113.
45. M. Weber, *Ancient Judaism* (New York: Free Press, 1952). E.T. from *Das antike Judentum*, vol. 3 of *Gesammelte Aufsätze zur Religionssoziologie* (Tübingen: J.C.B. Mohr, 1921).
46. Max Weber, "Charisma and Old Testament Prophecy," forthcoming in the journal *Semeia*.

47. For Weber's studies on this theme cf. Max Weber, *On Charisma and Institution Building*, Selected Papers, edited and with an introduction by S. N. Eisenstadt (Chicago: University of Chicago Press, 1968).
48. Cf. R. E. Clements, "Jeremiah 1—25 and the Deuteronomistic History," in *Understanding Poets and Prophets: Essays in Honour of George Wishart Anderson*, ed. A. Graeme Auld, JSOTSup 152 (Sheffield: Sheffield Academic Press, 1993), 93–113.
49. Cf. my essay "The Prophet and His Editors," cited in n. 42.
50. R. E. Clements, "The Ezekiel Tradition: Prophecy in a Time of Crisis," in *Israel's Prophetic Tradition: Essays in Honour of P. R. Ackroyd*, ed. R. J. Coggins, A. C. J. Phillips, and M. A. Knibb (Cambridge: Cambridge University Press, 1982), 119–36.
51. R. E. Clements, "The Chronology of Redaction in Ezekiel 1—24," in *Ezekiel and His Book*, ed. J. Lust, BETL 74 (Leuven: J. Peeters, 1986), 283–94.
52. W. Zimmerli, *Ezekiel*, 2 vols., Hermeneia (Philadelphia: Fortress Press, 1979/1983), E.T. from the German *Ezechiel*, BKAT (Neukirchen-Vluyn: Neukirchener Verlag, 1969).
53. Cf. my essay "The Study of the Old Testament," vol. 3: *Nineteenth-Century Religious Thought in the West*, ed. N. Smart, J. Clayton, S. Katz, and P. Sherry (Cambridge: Cambridge University Press, 1985), 109–41.
54. Cf. R. E. Clements, "The Immanuel Prophecy of Isa. 7:10–17 and Its Messianic Interpretation," in *Die Hebräische Bibel und ihre zweifache Nachgeschichte: FS R. Rendtorff 65. Geburtstag*, ed. E. Blum, Chr. Macholz, and E. W. Stegemann (Neukirchen-Vluyn: Neukirchener Verlag, 1990) 225–40; idem, "Messianic Prophecy or Messianic History," *Horizons in Biblical Theology* 1 (1979): 87–104; idem, "The Messianic Hope in the Old Testament," *JSOT* 43 (1989): 3–19.
55. Cf. R. E. Clements, "George Stanley Faber (1773–1854) as Biblical Interpreter," in *Altes Testament: Forschung und Wirkung, FS für Henning Graf Reventlow*, ed. P. Mommer and W. Thiel (Frankfürtam Main: Peter Lang, 1940), 247–68. The wider issues are covered in G. M. Marsden's *Fundamentalism and American Culture: The Shaping of Twentieth-Century Evangelicalism, 1870–1925* (New York: Oxford University Press, 1980).

Chapter 1. Amos and the Politics of Israel

1. Cf. R. Smend, "Das Nein des Amos," *EvTh* 23 (1963): 404–23.
2. Cf. K. Koch, *The Prophets*, vol. 1: *The Assyrian Period*, trans. M. Kohl

(London: SCM Press, 1982), 68: "According to things as they were, he can only have meant the Assyrians."

3. The sole reference to Assyria in the book in 3:9 is usually emended to read "Ashdod," but complete certainty over the propriety of following this proposal is lacking. It is followed by W. Rudolph, *Joel, Amos, Obadja, Jona*, KAT 13/2 (Gütersloh: Gerd Mohn, 1971), 158f; H.W. Wolff, *Joel and Amos*, trans. W. Janzen et al. (Philadelphia: Fortress Press, 1977), 189. Wolff compares the comparable parallel references in Hosea to Assyria and Egypt.

4. Constructively fresh treatments are presented by G. M. Tucker, "Prophetic Authenticity: A Form-Critical Study of Amos 7:10–17," *Interpretation* 27 (1973): 423–34; P. R. Ackroyd, "A Judgment Narrative between Kings and Chronicles? An Approach to Amos 7:9–17," in *Studies in the Religious Tradition of the Old Testament* (London: SCM Press, 1987), 195–208 (= *Canon and Authority: Essays in Old Testament Religion and Theology*, ed. G. W. Coats and B.O. Long [Philadelphia: Fortress Press, 1977], 71–87).

5. G. Brunet, "La Vision de l'étain: Réinterprétation d'Amos 7:7–9," *VT* 16 (1966): 387–95.

6. W. Beyerlin, *Bleilot: Brecheisen oder was sonst? Revision einer Amos-vision*, OBO 81 (Göttingen: Vandenhoeck & Rupprecht, 1988).

7. Rudolph, *Joel, Amos, Obadja, Jona*, 234f.

8. Cf. H. J. Zobel, *ThWAT*, 111, *Yisra'el*, 1006; G. W. Ahlström, *Who Were the Israelites?* (Winona Lake: Eisenbrauns, 1986), 102.

9. So especially Amos 1:2; 3:1; 6:1; 9:7.

10. Ackroyd, *A Judgment Narrative*, 196.

11. Cf. M. Cogan, *Imperialism and Religion: Assyria, Judah, and Israel in the Eighth and Seventh Centuries B.C.E.*, SBLDS 19 (Missoula: Scholars Press, 1974).

12. So Wolff, *Joel and Amos*, 295, 301, following V. Maag, *Text, Wortschatz und Begriffswelt des Buches Amos* (Leiden: E. J. Brill, 1951), 47f.

13. Cf. B. Oded, "The Historical Background of the Syro-Ephraimite War Reconsidered," *CBQ* 34 (1972): 153–65.

14. This conclusion is supported by the observations of A. G. Auld, *Amos*, Old Testament Guides (Sheffield: JSOT Press, 1986), 28.

15. Like many earlier interpreters, K. Koch begins his study of the classical prophets of the Assyrian period with an interpretation of the narrative of Amos 7:10–17 and presents this as a central platform from which Amos's prophesying is to be understood. Such a proceeding can no doubt still be justified, but it needs to be viewed in a far more critical light than has customarily been done. Cf. Koch, *The Prophets*, 36ff.

16. Ackroyd, *A Judgment Narrative*, 200–203.

17. Ibid., 203. Ackroyd claims that the narrative is "independent of the other material in the book."

Chapter 2. The Prophecies of Isaiah to Hezekiah concerning Sennacherib

1. R. E. Clements, "Isaiah and the Deliverance of Jerusalem," JSOTSup 13 (1980): 52–71; see also my commentary to *Isaiah 1—39*, New Century Bible Commentary (London: Marshall, Morgan & Scott, 1980), 280–96.
2. Cf. P. R. Ackroyd, "Isaiah 36—39: Structure and Function," in *Von Kanaan bis Kerala: FS van der Ploeg*, ed. W. C. Delsman et al., AOAT 211 (1982): 3–21 (= *Studies in the Religious Tradition of the Old Testament* [London, SCM Press, 1987], 105–120).
3. B. Stade, "Miscellen," *ZAW* 4 (1884): 250–77.
4. Several major studies have appeared endeavouring to use the evidence of the Isaiah-Hezekiah narrative to clarify the picture of the events of 701 B.C. Cf. most recently, E. Vogt, *Der Aufstand Hiskias und die Belagerung Jerusalems 701 v.Chr.*, AnBib 106 (1986); F. J. Gonçalves, *L'Expédition de Sennacherib en Palestine dans la Littérature Hebraique Ancienne*, EBib, n.s. 7 (1986); C. Hardmeier, *Prophetie im Streit vor dem Untergang Judas*, BZAW 187 (1990).
5. For the speeches of the Rabshakeh, cf. now Ehud Ben Zvi, "Who Wrote the Speech of the Rabshakeh and When?" *JBL* 109 (1990): 79–92.
6. Clements, "Isaiah and the Deliverance of Jerusalem," 58f.
7. Cf. especially K.A.D. Smelik, "Distortion of Old Testament Prophecy: The Purpose of Isaiah 36 and 37," in *Crises and Perspectives*, OTS 24 (1986): 70–93, especially 71–74.
8. See for this redactional material my essay "Isaiah 14:22–27: A Central Passage Reconsidered," in *The Book of Isaiah*, ed. J. Vermeylen, BETL 81 (1989): 253–62.
9. See most recently the extensive study by C. Hardmeier, *Prophetie im Streit*.
10. The Deuteronomistic connections are particularly noted in M. Cogan and H. Tadmor, *Second Kings*, AncB 11 (1988): 223ff.
11. See especially Isa. 7:9; 30:15; 31:1–3.
12. A critique of the arguments of Gesenius and Stade is noted in Smelik, "Distortion of Old Testament Prophecy," 71ff.
13. Cf. R. Smend, "Das Gesetz und die Völker: Ein Beitrag zur deuteronomistischen Redaktionsgeschichte," in *Probleme Biblischer Theologie, FS G. von Rad*, ed. H.W. Wolff (München, 1971), 494–509.

14. Cf. most recently Ben Zvi, "Who Wrote the Speech of the Rab-shakeh," 92: "they are later than 701 BCE and therefore not contemporary with the events . . . and even certain times in post-monarchic Judah cannot be ruled out."
15. Clements, "Isaiah and the Deliverance of Jerusalem," 93ff.
16. R. E. Clements, "The Isaiah Narrative of 2 Kings 20:12–19 and the Date of the Deuteronomic History," *Isaac Leo Seeligmann Volume*, vol. 3, ed. A. Rofé and Y. Zakovitch (Jerusalem, 1983), 209–20, Non-Hebrew Section.
17. Clements, "Isaiah 14:22–27."
18. Cf. especially C. R. Seitz, "The Crisis of Interpretation over the Meaning and Purpose of the Exile," *VT* 35 (1985): 78–97; idem, "Theology in Conflict: Reactions to the Exile in the Book of Jeremiah," BZAW 176 (1989): 236ff.

Chapter 3. The Messianic Hope in the Old Testament

1. As, for example, in H. Graf Reventlow, *Problems of Biblical Theology in the Twentieth Century*, E.T. by J. S. Bowden (London: SCM Press, 1986), 47–50.
2. Something of an exception is B. S. Childs, *Old Testament Theology in a Canonical Context* (London: SCM Press, 1985), 119–21. See also W. H. Schmidt, *The Faith of the Old Testament* (Oxford: Basil Blackwell Publisher, 1983), 198–206.
3. A. F. Kirkpatrick, *The Doctrine of the Prophets*, 3d ed. (London: Macmillan Publishers, 1901).
4. The course of the debate was especially centred on the writings of J. Locke's disciple Anthony Collins (1676–1729) and the mathematician William Whiston (1667–1752). The issues are discussed in J. O'Higgins, *Anthony Collins, The Man and His Works*, International Archives of the History of Ideas (The Hague: Nijhoff, 1970), 35. See also my essay "Messianic Prophecy or Messianic History?" in *Horizons in Biblical Theology* 1 (Pittsburgh: Pickwick Press, 1979), 87–104.
5. F.D.E. Schleiermacher, *The Christian Faith*, trans. H. R. Mackintosh and J. S. Stewart (Edinburgh: T.&T. Clark, 1928), 60–62, 115f.
6. An English translation by R. Keith was published at Alexandria, 1836–39, and reprinted at Grand Rapids, 1956. The issue with Schleiermacher is especially taken up in vol. 4, Appendix 1, pp. 259–71 (from the 2d ed.; trans. J. Martin; Edinburgh: T.&T. Clark). However, von Hengstenberg's entire work is built upon the contention that messianic expectations, in various forms and with varying degrees of emphasis, are to be found throughout the entire Old Testament.

7. See Clements, "Messianic Prophecy."
8. E. Schürer, *Lehrbuch der neutestamentlichen Zeitgeschichte* (Leipzig: Hinrichs, 1874, from its 2d ed. [1886–1887] retitled *Geschichte des jüdischen Volkes im Zeitalter Jesu Christi*, (A History of the Jewish People in the Time of Jesus Christ), 5 vols. [Edinburgh: T. & T. Clark, 1885–1891]).
9. The messianic hope is dealt with by Schürer in, *Geschichte*, vol. 2 (3d German ed. 1901), 496–556.
10. For H. Gunkel, see W. Klatt, *Hermann Gunkel: Zu seiner Theologie der Religionsgeschichte und zur Entstehung der formgeschichtlichen Methode*, FRLANT 100 (Göttingen: Vandenhoeck & Ruprecht, 1969). For Wilhelm Bousset, see A. F. Verheule, *W. Bousset: Leben und Werk, Ein theologiegeschichtlicher Versuch* (Amsterdam: Bolland, 1973). For E. Troeltsch, see J. P. Clayton, *Ernst Troeltsch and the Future of Theology* (Cambridge: Cambridge University Press, 1976).
11. W.O.E. Oesterley, *The Evolution of the Messianic Idea: A Study in Comparative Religion* (London: Pitman, 1908).
12. H. Gressmann, *Der Messias*, FRLANT 43: (Göttingen: Vandenhoeck & Ruprecht, 1929).
13. A. Bentzen, *Messias-Moses Redivivus-Menschensohn*, ATANT 17 (Zürich: Zwingli, 1948); E.T. (by the author): *King and Messiah* (London: Lutterworth Press, 1955); 2d. ed. revised by G. W. Anderson (Oxford: Basil Blackwell Publisher, 1970).
14. S. Mowinckel, *Han Som Kommer* (Copenhagen: Gad, 1951). E.T. by G. W. Anderson: *He That Cometh* (Oxford: Basil Blackwell Publisher, 1954).
15. A major survey in English of the debate is presented by A. R. Johnson, *Sacral Kingship in Ancient Israel* (Cardiff: University of Wales Press, 1955; 2d. ed., 1967).
16. I. Engnell, *Studies in Divine Kingship in the Ancient Near East* (Lund, 1943; 2d ed., Oxford: Basil Blackwell Publisher, 1967).
17. J. Becker, *Messias-Erwartung im Alten Testament* (Stuttgart: Katholisches Bibelwerk, 1977); E.T. by D. E. Green: *Messianic Expectation in the Old Testament* (Edinburgh: T. & T. Clark, 1980).
18. Cf. Mowinckel, *Han Som Kommer*, 97ff.; P. Kyle McCarter, Jr., *II Samuel*, AncB 9 (Garden City, N.Y.: Doubleday, 1984), 190–231, especially 217–20.
19. D. J. McCarthy, "II Samuel 7 and the Structure of the Deuteronomistic History," *JBL* 84 (1965): 131–38 (= *Institution and Narrative: Collected Essays* (Rome: Biblical Institute Press, 1985), 127–38.
20. J. Vermeylen, *Du prophète Isaïe à l'apocalyptique: Isaïe, 1—35, miroir d'un demi-millénaire d'expérience religieuse en Israël*, EBib (Paris: J. Gabalda, 1977), 1:187–224.

21. J. Vermeylen, *Le Dieu de la Promesse et le Dieu de l'Alliance: Le dialogue des grandes intuitions théologiques de l'Ancien Testament*, LD 126 (Paris: Les Editions du Cerf, 1986), 263ff.
22. B. S. Childs, *Introduction to the Old Testament as Scripture* (London: SCM Press, 1979), 515–17. Cf. especially p. 517: "the royal psalms . . . were treasured . . . as a witness to the messianic hope which looked for the consummation of God's kingship through his Anointed One."
23. The main points of this literary proceeding are that a surprising similarity is evident in the major themes of all the prophetic collections and that the editions of all of them have, at many points, been demonstrably influenced by passages from other of the sacred writings. Cf. my essay, "Patterns in the Prophetic Canon," in *Canon and Authority*, ed. G. W. Coats and B. O. Long (Philadelphia: Fortress Press, 1977), 42–55.
24. Cf. the list of passages indicated by H. Wildberger which have influenced the text of Isaiah 24—27. H. Wildberger, *Jesaja 13—27*, BKAT 10 (Neukirchen-Vluyn: Neukirchener Verlag, 1978), 910.
25. The subject is treated by M. Fishbane, *Biblical Interpretation in Ancient Israel* (Oxford: Clarendon Press, 1985), 443ff.
26. H. Gese, "Erwägungen zur Einheit der biblischen Theologie," *ZThK* 67 (1970), 417–36 (= *Vom Sinai zum Zion: Alttestamentliche Beiträge zur biblischen Theologie*, BEvT 64 [Munich: Kaiser], 11–30). A valuable survey and critique of recent attempts to evaluate the role and method of such a theology is presented by M. Oemig, *Gesamt biblische Theologien der Gegenwart* (Stuttgart: W. Kohlhammer, 1985; 2d. ed, 1987). Cf. especially pp. 104ff. for a critique of Gese's suggestions.
27. H. Graf Reventlow, *Problems of Biblical Theology in the Twentieth Century*.

Chapter 4. The Immanuel Prophecy of Isaiah 7:10–17 and Its Messianic Interpretation

1. See especially A. Laato, *Who Is Immanuel? The Rise and Foundering of Isaiah's Messianic Expectations* (1988); "Immanuel—Who Is With Us?—Hezekiah or Messiah?" in *Wünschet Jerusalem Frieden: Collected Communications to the XIIth Congress of the IOSOT*, Jerusalem 1986 (1988), 313–22. See also J. Høgenhaven, "Gott und Volk bei Jesaja: Eine Untersuchung zur biblischen Theologie," *AThD* 24 (1988).
2. This point remains disputed, but a significant line of interpretation has been able to find in the Immanuel prophecy of Isa. 7:10–17 a reference to a child shortly expected to be born to the prophet's wife. The accession oracle of Isa. 9:1–6, with its introduction in 8:23, could then be located in Isaiah's ministry, at the time of, or shortly before, Heze-

kiah's accession to the throne of Judah. See my commentary to *Isaiah 1—39*, New Century Bible Commentary (Grand Rapids: Wm. B. Eerdmans Publishing Co., 1980).

3. K. Budde, *Jesajas Erleben: Eine gemeinverständliche Auslegung der Denkschrift des Propheten (Kap. 6,1–9,6)* (1928); idem, "Das Immanuelzeichen und die Ahaz-Begegnung Jesaja 7," *JBL* 52 (1933):46–51.

4. H. Graf Reventlow, "Das Ende der sog. 'Denkschrift' Jesajas," *BN* 38/39 (1987): 62f.

5. B. Duhm, *Das Buch Jesaja*, HKAT III/1 (1892).

6. Cf. Budde, *Jesajas Erleben*.

7. Cf. O. Kaiser, *Jesaja 1—12*, ATD 17 (1981): 117–20.

8. Cf. Reventlow, "Das Ende der sog. 'Denkschrift' Jesajas."

9. O. H. Steck, "Bemerkungen zu Jesaja 6," *BZ* NF 16 (1972): 188–206 (= *Wahrnehmungen Gottes im Alten Testament: Gesammelte Studien*, TBü 60 [Munich: Chr. Kaiser Verlag, 1982], 149–70); idem, "Rettung und Verstockung: Exegetische Bemerkungen zu Jesaja 7:3–9," *EvTh* 33 (1973): 77–90 (=*Wahrnehmungen*, 171–86); idem, "Beiträge zum Verständnis von Jesaja 7:10–17 und 8:1–4," *ThZ* 29 (1973): 161–78 (=*Wahrnehmungen*, 187–203).

10. K. Nielsen, "Is 6:1–8:18* as Dramatic Writing," *StTh* 40 (1986): 1–16.

11. Høgenhaven, "Gott und Volk bei Jesaja," 77ff.

12. H. Gese, "Natus ex virgine," in *Probleme Biblischer Theologie, FS G. von Rad*, ed. H. W. Wolff (München, 1971), 73–89, 85.

13. See R.E. Clements, *Isaiah 1—39*, New Century Bible Commentary (Grand Rapids: Wm. B. Eerdmans Publishing Co., 1980).

14. Laato, *Who is Immanuel?* 136ff.

15. Steck, "Beiträge," 161ff. (= *Wahrnehmungen*, 187ff.).

16. Both Steck and Nielsen argue that the central feature of the memoir, the series of three children's sign-names, are to be interpreted in parallel. However, this perspective does not take adequately into its reckoning the sequential buildup and the narrowing of the time scale that was present as the various names are unfolded. This aspect of a sequential development is significant in regard to the claim that all three of the children were born to the prophet's wife. Undoubtedly this implied a protracted time scale over two to three years.

17. See, besides the writings of Steck and Nielsen, Th. Lescow, "Jesajas Denkschrift aus der Zeit des syrisch-ephraimitischen Krieges," *ZAW* 85 (1973): 315–31; W. Werner, "Vom Prophetenwort zur Prophetentheologie: Ein redaktionskritischer Versuch zu Jes 6,1–8,18," *BZ* NF 29 (1985): 1–30; H.-P. Müller, "Glauben und Bleiben: Zur Denkschrift Jesajas Kapitel 6:6–8:18," *VTSup* 26 (1974): 25–54.

18. Steck delineates the memoir as consisting of Isa. 6:1–11; 7:1–9, 10–17; 8:1–8a, 11–15, 16–18, and this is followed by Nielsen. Lescow would find the memoir only in 7:1–8:18.
19. See Clements, *Isaiah 1—39.*
20. Laato, *Who Is Immanuel?* 158ff.
21. J. J. Stamm, "La prophétie d'Emmanuel," *RHPR* 23 (1943): 1–26; idem, "Die Immanuel-Weissagung und die Eschatologie des Jesaja," *ThZ* 16 (1960): 439–55; idem, "Die Immanuel-Weissagung: Ein Gespräch mit E. Hammershaimb," *VT* 4 (1954): 20–33; idem, "Neuere Arbeiten zum Immanuelproblem," *ZAW* 68 (1956): 46–54; idem, "Die Immanuel-Perikope im Lichte neuerer Veröffentlichungen," ZDMGSup 1 (1969): 281–90; idem, "Die Immanuel-Perikope: Eine Nachlese," *ThZ* 30 (1974): 11–22.
22. Cf. Clements, *Isaiah 1—39.*
23. A. Alt, "Jesaja 8:23–9:6: Befreiungsnacht und Krönungstag," *KS* II (1953): 206–25.
24. Cf. T.N.D. Mettinger, "King and Messiah: The Civil and Sacral Legitimation of the Israelite Kings," CB.OT 8 (1976): 261f., 286 for Ps. 2:7 as a formula expressing divine adoption.
25. G. von Rad, *Old Testament Theology,* vol. 2, trans. D.M.G. Stalker (Edinburgh: Oliver & Boyd, 1965), 159.
26. This is a point that was noted in the discussion of the Immanuel prophecy by E. Hammershaimb, "The Immanuel Sign," *StTh* 3 (1949): 124–42.
27. R. E. Clements, *Isaiah and the Deliverance of Jerusalem,* JSOTSup 13 (Sheffield: JSOT Press, 1980).
28. Høgenhaven, "Gott und Volk bei Jesaja," 88ff., regards the very title העלמה as pointing to the person of the queen, and this follows directly his claim that a mythological background underlies it.
29. Laato, *Who Is Immanuel?* 159, 314ff.
30. H. Barth, *Die Jesaja-Worte in der Josiazeit: Israel und Assur als Thema einer produktiven Neuinterpretation der Jesajaüberlieferung,* WMANT 48 (Neukirchen-Vluyn: Neukirchener Verlag, 1977).
31. H. W. Wolff, *Dodekapropheton* 4: *Micha,* BKAT 14/4 (1982): 108.

Chapter 5. Beyond Tradition-History

1. For J. C. Doederlein's work on Isaiah a critical assessment is made by J. M. Vincent, *Studien zur literarischen Eigenart und zur geistigen Heimat von Jesaja, Kap. 40—55* (Beiträge zur biblischen Exegese und Theologie, 5; Frankfurt am Main, Bern, Las Vegas, 1977), 17ff. Doederlein's hypothesis was advocated in a review of the commentary by G. Hensler,

Jesaia neu übersetzt mit Anmerkungen (Hamburg und Kiel, 1788), published in *Auserlesenen theologischen Bibliothek*, Bd. 4/8 (Lepzig, 1788), 554–79.

2. Cf. F. Maass, "Tritojesaja?," in *Das ferne und nahe Wort: Festshcrift L. Rost*, ed. F. Maass, BZAW 105 (1967), 156–63.

3. So especially C. R. North, *The Second Isaiah* (Oxford, 1964).

4. O. T. Allis, *The Unity of Isaiah: A Study in Prophecy* (Philadelphia: Presbyterian and Reformed Publishing Co., 1950).

5. E. J. Young, *Studies in Isaiah* (London, 1954).

6. Cf. M. Luther, *Lectures on Isaiah Chapters 1—39*, ed. J. Pelikan and H. C. Oswald (St. Louis, 1969); *Chapters 40—66* (1972). Luther strongly stressed the importance of an historical knowledge of the prophet's background for the interpretation of his message (see preface to chaps. 1—39, p. 3) and noted that "we rightly divide Isaiah into two books" (*Chapters 40—66*, p. 3). The references to Cyrus, king of Persia in the sixth century, however, were interpreted by Luther as prophecies concerning him. In this way the later historical background is fully recognized as important, but it is explained in a distinctively prophetic manner.

7. Cf. D. R. Jones, "The Traditio of the Oracles of Isaiah of Jerusalem," *ZAW* 67 (1955): 226–46. Further suggestions along this line are made by J. H. Eaton, "The Origin of the Book of Isaiah," *VT* 9 (1959): 138–57.

8. B. S. Childs, *Introduction to the Old Testament as Scripture* (London: SCM Press, 1979), 311–38.

9. Ibid., 328.

10. This appears to me to represent an important misdirection in the work of Childs, with which in many of its aspects I am in agreement. So far as a book such as Isaiah is concerned, with its unique historical and literary problems, it appears to be methodologically wrong to attempt to resolve these problems by an all-embracing hermeneutical appeal to the perspective of the canon. The book of Isaiah had acquired its present shape by the time the limits of the canon were determined. No doubt the understanding of prophecy inherent in the way in which the book was given shape bore some relationship to the interests of those who finally endorsed the canon. Yet the redactional shaping of the book took place first, and it would appear to be an entirely proper and valuable field of enquiry to examine this, quite apart from an hermeneutical interest in the "canon" in its larger compass. Furthermore the varied interests which contributed to the shape of the book may then, incidentally, provide a better insight into the reasons why the whole corpus of the Former and Latter Prophets acquired the shape it did in the canon of the Old Testament.

11. H. Graetz, "Isaiah 34 and 35, *JQR* 4 (1891): 1–8.
12. C. C. Torrey, *The Second Isaiah* (Edinburgh, 1928), 279ff.
13. Cf. my study *Isaiah and the Deliverance of Jerusalem: A Study of the Interpretation of Prophecy in the Old Testament*, JSOTSup 13 (Sheffield: JSOT Press, 1980), 90ff.; also "The Unity of the Book of Isaiah," *Interpretation* 36 (1982): 117–29.
14. The conception of a prophetic "fulfilment" would appear to have been central to the understanding of the concerns which motivated the various editors of the book of Isaiah. Cf. Childs, *Introduction to the Old Testament*, 336ff. Yet Childs argues from this that, in shaping the material in the book, the tradents have consistently divorced it from its original "historical" setting and given to it another "thematic" or "theological" setting. This can only be conceded with considerable modification, since, so far as Isaiah 40—55 is concerned, it is quite clearly the historical Babylon of the mid-sixth century B.C. that is envisaged as Israel's oppressor and the historical Cyrus of Persia who appears as its deliverer. Only later was such a historical background veiled by the superimposing of a more complex set of interpretative guidelines, such as we find in the *pesher* techniques of Qumran.
15. Childs (ibid., 328ff.) points out the central position occupied by the question of the nature of the connections with the contents of the prophecies of the eighth-century Isaiah. This still leaves unresolved, however, the extent to which such connections may be thought to have been present at the compositional stage of Isaiah 40—55, or whether they were simply perceived by the redactors of the book. To a considerable extent the lack of clarity on this point stems directly from the prior assumption that such connections are essentially a feature of the "canonical" shape of the book. Against this we must insist that it was not the "canon" which established the connections within the material; these occurred at a very much earlier period in the process of forming the book of Isaiah. It then requires to be asked whether such connections existed in the material at the primary compositional stage of Isaiah 40—55.
16. This omits "which they have not known" as dittography. Cf. *BHS*.
17. Cf. Th. C. Vriezen, *Jahwes Eigentumsvolk*, ATANT 37 (Zürich-Stuttgart, 1960), 109ff.; H. Wildberger, *ThWAT* I, cols. 290f.
18. H. Barth, *Die Jesaja-Worte in der Josiazeit*, WMANT 48 (Neukirchen-Vluyn, 1977).
19. Childs, 328.
20. J. Begrich, *Studien zu Deuterojesaja*, BWANT 4/25 (Stuttgart: W. Kohlhammer, 1938; reprint ed. W. Zimmerli, as TBü 20 (Munich: Chr. Kaiser Verlag, 1963).

21. Cf. G. Fohrer, "Zion-Jerusalem im Alten Testament," in *Studien zur alttestamentlichen Theologie und Geschichte (1949–1966)*, BZAW 115 (Berlin, 1969), 195–241, especially 221f.

22. The issue here appears to me to be a deeper one than simply whether the so-called Deutero-Isaiah was familiar with, and alluded to, sayings of Isaiah of Jerusalem. Rather it raises the question whether the existence of the earlier Isaianic prophecies has not provided the primary stimulus in the shaping of much of the contents of chaps. 40—55. On this point also the attempt of S. Mowinckel and others to explain the presence of an "Isaianic connection" in chaps. 40ff. on the basis of an "Isaianic School" must be regarded as weak. Instead of serving to explain the meaning and intention of the material, it explains only the author's connections with the tradents of Isaiah's prophecies.

23. G. von Rad, *Old Testament Theology*, vol. 2, trans. D.M.G. Stalker (Edinburgh: Oliver & Boyd, London, 1965), 239f.

24. Vincent, *Studien zur literarischen Eigenart*, 256ff.

Chapter 6. The Unity of the Book of Isaiah

1. Georg Fohrer, "Jesaja 1 als Zusammenfassung der Verkündigung Jesajas," *ZAW* 74 (1962): 251–80; see *Studien zur alttestamentlichen Prophetie*, BZAW 99 (Berlin: A. Töpelmann, 1967):148–66.

2. Cf. O. T. Allis, *The Unity of Isaiah: A Study in Prophecy* (Philadelphia: Presbyterian and Reformed Publishing Co., 1950). Reprinted in 1972, distributed by Baker Book House, Grand Rapids.

3. Bernhard Duhm, *Das Buch Jesaja*, HKAT 3/1 (Göttingen: Vandenhoeck & Ruprecht, 1892, 1902, 1968).

4. Cf. James D. Smart, *History and Theology in Second Isaiah: A Commentary on Isaiah 35:40–66* (London, 1967; Philadelphia: Westminster Press, 1965). J. L. McKenzie, *Second Isaiah: Introduction, Translation, and Notes*, Anchor Bible (Garden City, N. Y.: Doubleday, 1968).

5. Sigmund Mowinckel, *Jesaja-disiplene: Profeten fra Jesaja til Jeremia* (Oslo: Forlagt AV. H. Aschhoug & Co. [W. Nygaard], 1925).

6. Cf. D. R. Jones, "The Tradition of the Oracles of Isaiah of Jerusalem," ZAW 67 (1955): 226–46.

7. For more detailed exegesis of the contents of these chapters reference may be made to my commentary to *Isaiah 1—39*, New Century Bible (Grand Rapids: Wm. B. Eerdmans Publishing Co., 1980).

8. Cf. my exegesis of these narratives in *Isaiah and the Deliverance of Jerusalem: A Study of the Interpretation of Prophecy in the Old Testament*, JSOTSup 13 (Sheffield: JSOT Press, 1980), 52ff.

9. This point was made by Heinrich H. Graetz, "Isaiah 34 and 35," *JQR*

4 (1891): 1–8; cf. also M. Pope, "Isaiah 34 in Relation to Isaiah 35:40–66," *JBL* 71 (1952): 235–43.

10. The distinctive role of these chapters in relation to Deutero-Isaiah and the development of apocalyptic is examined in Paul D. Hanson, *The Dawn of Apocalyptic* (Philadelphia: Fortress Press, 1975), 32ff. Cf. also J. Vermeylen, *Du prophète Isaïe à l'apocalyptique: Isaïe, 1—35, miroir d'un demi-millénaire d'expérience religieuse en Israël* (Paris: J. Gabalda, 1977), 2:449–517.

11. Cf. Otto Plöger, *Theocracy and Eschatology*, trans. S. Rudman (Oxford, 1968), 53–78.

12. Cf. Hans Wildberger, *Jesaja*, BKAT 10, 2 (Neukirchen-Vluyn: Neukirchener Verlag des Erziehungsvereins, 1965–72), 2:910.

13. Cf. Edmond Jacob, "Du premier au deuxieme chant de la vigne du prophète Esaïe: Reflexions sur Esaïe 27, 2–5," in *Wort—Gebot—Glaube, Festschrift W. Eichrodt zum 80 Geburtstag*, ATANT 59:325–30 (Zürich, 1970).

14. Cf. Hermann Barth, *Die Jesaja-Worte in der Josiazeit*, WMANT 48 (Neukirchen-Vluyn: Neukirchener Verlag, 1977); also Vermeylen's study, *Du prophète Isaïe à l'apocalyptique*.

15. Cf. my *Isaiah and the Deliverance of Jerusalem*, 41ff.

16. Cf. Barth, *Die Jesaja-Worte*.

17. J.F.A. Sawyer, *From Moses to Patmos: New Perspectives in Old Testament Study* (London, 1977), 113ff.

18. Brevard S. Childs said, "The 'former things' can now only refer to the prophecies of First Isaiah. The point of Second Isaiah's message is that this prophetic word has been confirmed" (*Introduction to the Old Testament as Scripture* [London, 1979; first American ed., Philadelphia: Fortress Press, 1979], 329).

19. Cf. my essay "The Prophecies of Isaiah and the Fall of Jerusalem in 587 B.C.," *VT* 30(1980): 421–36.

20. Ibid., 425ff.

21. Cf. Gerhard von Rad, *Old Testament Theology*, trans. D.M.G. Stalker (Edinburgh: Oliver & Boyd, 1962–65), 2:279ff. For a more detailed examination of the language, reference should also be made to Walther Zimmerli, "Zur Sprache Tritojesajas," in *Festschrift L. Köhler* (Bern, 1950), 62–74; see *Gottes Offenbarung: Gesammelte Aufsätze*, TBü (Munich: Chr. Kaiser Verlag, 1963), 19:217–33.

Chapter 7. Jeremiah 1—25 and the Deuteronomistic History

1. S. Mowinckel, *Zur Komposition des Buches Jeremia* (Kristiania: J. Dybwad, 1914). See also T. R. Hobbs, "Some Remarks on the Composition

and Structure of the Book of Jeremiah," *CBQ* 34: 257–75 (reprinted in *A Prophet to the Nations: Essays in Jeremiah Studies*, ed. L. G. Perdue and B. W. Kovacs (Winona Lake, Ind.: Eisenbrauns, 1984), 175–92.

2. S. Mowinckel, *Prophecy and Tradition: The Prophetic Books in the Light of the Study of the Growth and History of the Tradition* (Oslo: J. Dybwad, 1946), 61ff.

3. M. Noth, *The Deuteronomistic History*, trans. J. Doull et al., JSOTSup 15 (Sheffield: JSOT Press, 1981), 6.

4. E.g., E. W. Nicholson, *Preaching to the Exiles: A Study of the Prose Tradition in the Book of Jeremiah* (Oxford: Basil Blackwell Publisher, 1970), 38ff.; W. Thiel, *Die deuteronomistische Redaktion von Jeremia 1—25*, WMANT 41 (Neukirchen-Vluyn: Neukirchener Verlag, 1973), Verlag, 1973; L. Stulman, *The Prose Sermons of the Book of Jeremiah: A Redescription of the Correspondences with the Deuteronomistic Literature in the Light of Recent Text-Critical Research*, SBLDS 83 (Atlanta: Scholars Press, 1986), 49ff.

5. See T. W. Overholt, "King Nebuchadrezzar in the Jeremiah Tradition," *CBQ* 30 (1968): 39–48.

6. Thiel, *Die deuteronomistische Redaktion von Jeremia 1—25*, 83ff.; Stulman, *Prose Sermons of the Book of Jeremia*, 56ff.

7. See C. Hardmeier, *Prophetie im Streit vor dem Untergang Judas*, BZAW 187 (Berlin: Walter de Gruyter, 1990), 161ff.

8. Thiel, *Die Deuteronomistische Redaktion von Jeremia 1—25*, 103ff.; Stulman, *Prose Sermons of the Book of Jeremiah*, 58ff.

9. E.g., Thiel, *Die deuteronomistische Redaktion von Jeremia 1—25*, 139ff.; Stulman, *Prose Sermons of the Book of Jeremiah*, 63ff.

10. Thiel, *Die deuteronomistische Redaktion von Jeremia 1—25*, 178ff.

11. F. M. Cross, Jr., *Canaanite Myth and Hebrew Epic* (Cambridge, Mass.: Harvard University Press, 1973), 285–86; cf. R. D. Nelson, *First and Second Kings*, Interpretation (Atlanta: John Knox Press, 1987), 247ff.

12. C. R. Seitz, "The Prophet Moses and the Canonical Shape of Jeremiah," *ZAW* 101 (1989): 7.

13. Ibid., 7.

14. O. H. Steck, *Israel und das gewaltsame Geschick der Propheten: Untersuchungen zur Überlieferung des deuteronomistischen Geschichtsbildes im Alten Testament, Spätjudentum und Urchristentum*, WMANT 23 (Neukirchen-Vluyn: Neukirchener Verlag, 1967), 199f.

15. R. E. Clements, *Prophecy and Tradition*, Growing Points in Theology (Oxford: Basil Blackwell Publisher, 1975), 41ff.

16. Ibid.; Seitz, "The Prophet Moses," 3ff.

17. K. O'Connor, *The Confessions of Jeremiah: Their Interpretation and Role in Chapters 1—25*, SBLDS 94 (Atlanta: Scholars Press, 1988), 155; see

A. R. Diamond, *Jeremiah's Confessions in Context: Scenes of Prophetic Drama*, JSOTSup 25 (Sheffield: JSOT Press, 1987), 149ff.

18. Erik Aurelius, *Der Fürbitter Israels. Eine Studie zum Mosebild im Alten Testament*, Coniectanea Biblica, Old Testament Series 27 (Stockholm: Almqvist & Wiksell International, 1988), 18ff., 88ff.

19. O'Connor, *Confessions of Jeremiah*, 113, cf. Diamond, *Jeremiah's Confessions*, 182.

20. W. I. Holladay, *Jeremiah 1—25*, Hermeneia (Philadelphia: Fortress Press), 583.

21. Thiel, *Die deuteronomistische Redaktion von Jeremia 1—25*, 230ff; Stulman, *Prose Sermons of the Book of Jeremiah*, 81–82.

22. Holladay, *Jeremiah 1—25*, 580–81.

23. J. Unterman, *From Repentance to Redemption: Jeremiah's Thought in Transition*, JSOTSup 54 (Sheffield: JSOT Press, 1987), 56; see also Holladay, *Jeremiah 1—25*, 656–57.

24. Thiel, *Die deuteronomistische Redaktion von Jeremia 1—25*, 253ff.

25. R. E. Clements, "Prophecy as Literature: A Re-appraisal," in *The Hermeneutical Quest: Essays in Honor of James Luther Mays on His Sixty-Fifth Birthday*, ed. D. G. Miller, 56–76 (Allison Park, Pa.: Pickwick Publications).

26. M. Weinfeld, *Deuteronomy and the Deuteronomic School* (Oxford: Clarendon Press, 1972), 158ff.

27. C. Rietzschel, *Das Problem der Urrolle: Ein Beitrag zur Redaktionsgeschichte des Jeremiabuches* (Gütersloh: Gerd Mohn, 1966), 91ff.

28. G. von Rad, *Old Testament Theology*, vol. 2: *The Theology of Israel's Prophetic Traditions*, trans. D.M.G. Stalker (Edinburgh: Oliver & Boyd, 1962), 342ff.

29. H. W. Wolff, "The Kerygma of the Deuteronomistic Historical Work," in W. Brueggemann and H. W. Wolff, *The Vitality of Old Testament Traditions*, 2d ed. (Atlanta: John Knox Press, 1982), 99.

30. P. Diepold, *Israel's Land*, BWANT 95 (Stuttgart: W. Kohlhammer, 1972), 193ff.

Chapter 8. Jeremiah: Prophet of Hope

1. The most widely accepted classification of the different source materials in the book of Jeremiah is that advocated by S. Mowinckel, *Zur Komposition des Buches Jeremia* (Kristiania: J. Dybwad, 1914). A brief, but useful, survey of Mowinckel's position is set out in N. K. Gottwald, *A Light to the Nations* (New York: Harper & Row, 1959), 356ff. The main collection of poetic prophecies in chaps. 1—25 is ascribed by

Mowinckel to Source A, but on Mowinckel's own reckoning the poetic prophecies of chaps. 30—31 cannot be included in this; Mowinckel, *Zur Komposition*, 45ff., especially p. 55.

2. This narrative material was classified by Mowinckel as Source B; Mowinckel, *Zur Komposition*, 24ff.

3. This was classified by Mowinckel as Source C (ibid., 31ff.), and the materials it contains have provided the major literary-critical clues relating to the interpretation of the book of Jeremiah.

4. The narrative material (Source B) obviously focuses quite sharply upon the events of 588–87 and the fate of Jerusalem at that time.

5. Cf. J. Bright, *Jeremiah*, Anchor Bible (New York: Doubleday & Co., 1965), LXVIIff.

6. Cf. J. Bright, "The Date of the Prose Sermons of Jeremiah," *JBL* 70 (1951): 15–35.

7. Cf. J. P. Hyatt, "Jeremiah," in *The Interpreter's Bible* (Nashville: Abingdon Press, 1956), 5:777–1142. Concerning this "Deuteronomic edition" of Jeremiah's prophecies Hyatt states: "D sometimes preserves genuine prophecies of Jeremiah in the prophet's words; sometimes he gives the gist of Jeremiah's prophecies in his own words; and sometimes he composes freely and departs from Jeremiah's thought" (p. 789). See also the same author's *Jeremiah, Prophet of Courage and Hope* (Nashville: Abingdon Press, 1958), 38ff.

8. Cf. especially W. L. Holladay, "Prototype and Copies: A New Approach to the Poetry-Prose Problem in the Book of Jeremiah," *JBL* 79 (1960): 351–67.

9. J. Skinner, *Prophecy and Religion: Studies in the Life of Jeremiah* (Cambridge: Cambridge University Press, 1922), 108ff.

10. H. H. Rowley, "The Early Prophecies of Jeremiah in Their Setting," *Bulletin of the John Rylands Library*, 45 (1962–63): 198–234 (= *Men of God: Studies in Old Testament History and Prophecy* [London and Edinburgh: Thomas Nelson & Sons, 1963], 133–68).

11. Hyatt, "Jeremiah," *The Interpreter's Bible*, 5: 798; idem, *Jeremiah*, 31ff.

12. N. K. Gottwald, *All the Kingdoms of the Earth* (New York: Harper & Row, 1964), 239ff.

13. P. Volz, *Der Prophet Jeremia* (Leipzig: A. Deichert, 1922), 42ff., 274ff.

14. W. Rudolph, *Das Buch Jeremia*, 3d ed. (Tübingen: J.C.B. Mohr, 1968), 188ff.

15. Ibid., 25ff.

16. Ibid., 188ff.

17. Skinner, *Prophecy and Religion*, 311ff.

18. Besides the cautious conclusion ventured by Skinner noted above, see S. Herrmann, *Die prophetische Heilserwartung im Alten Testament: Ur-*

sprung und Gestaltwandel, BWANT 85 (Stuttgart: W. Kohlhammer, 1965), 210ff.

19. Bright, *Jeremiah*, 238.
20. Cf. ibid., 284ff., and nn. 12 and 13 above; Skinner, *Prophecy and Religion*, 298ff.
21. Cf. Hyatt, "Jeremiah," *Interpreter's Bible*, 5:1028; idem, *Jeremiah*, 103.
22. Cf. R. R. Wilson, *Prophecy and Society in Ancient Israel* (Philadelphia: Fortress Press, 1980), 231ff.
23. Bright, *Jeremiah*, 286.
24. Ibid., 285.
25. Cf. P. R. Ackroyd, *Exile and Restoration* (London: SCM Press, 1968), 57ff.

Chapter 9. The Ezekiel Tradition

1. P. R. Ackroyd, "The Vitality of the Word of God in the Old Testament," *ASTI* 1 (1962): 7–23.
2. H. Barth, *Die Jesaja-Worte in der Josiazeit: Israel und Assur als Thema einer produktiven Neuinterpretation der Jesajaüberlieferung*, WMANT 48 (Neurkirchen-Vluyn: Neukirchener Verlag, 1977).
3. J. Vermeylen, *Du prophète Isaïe à l'apocalyptique: Isaïe, 1—35, miroir d'un demi-millénaire d'expérience religieuse en Isräel*, EBib (Paris: J. Gabalda, 1977); see O. Plöger, *Theocracy and Eschatology* (Oxford, 1968), E.T. of *Theokratie und Eschatologie*, WMANT 2, 2d ed. (Neukirchen Kreis Moers, 1962); P. D. Hanson, *The Dawn of Apocalyptic* (Philadelphia: Fortress Press, 1975).
4. See J.F.A. Sawyer, *From Moses to Patmos: New Perspectives in Old Testament Study* (London, 1977), 103ff.
5. I. Engnell, "Prophets and Prophetism in the Old Testament," in *Critical Essays on the Old Testament* (London: SPCK, 1970), 163ff.
6. Ackroyd, "The Vitality of the Word of God," 15.
7. B. Duhm (*Das Buch Jeremia*, HKAT 3/1 [Tübingen and Leipzig, 1901], 16ff.) ascribes this "nomistic redaction" to the fourth to third centuries B.C. Cf. S. Mowinckel, *Zur Komposition des Buches Jeremia* (Kristiania: J. Dybwad, 1914), 31ff. The attempt of H. Weippert (*Die Prosareden des Jeremiabuches*, BZAW 132 [Berlin, 1974]) to ascribe this Deuteronomistic redaction to Jeremiah himself, and to deny its specifically Deuteronomistic character, must be regarded as unsatisfactory.
8. Mowinckel, *Zur Komposition des Buches Jeremia*.
9. R. E. Clements, *Isaiah and the Deliverance of Jerusalem*, JSOTSup, Series 13 (Sheffield: JSOT Press, 1980).

10. P. Diepold, *Israel's Land*, BWANT 95 (Stuttgart: W. Kohlhammer, 1972).

11. See L. Perlitt, *Bundestheologie im Alten Testament*, WMANT 36 (Neukirchen-Vluyn: Neukirchener Verlag, 1969), 15ff.

12. See ibid., 7ff.

13. Duhm, *Das Buch Jeremia*.

14. G. Hölscher, *Hesekiel, der Dichter und das Buch: Eine literarkritische Untersuchung*, BZAW 39 (Giessen, 1924).

15. V. Herntrich, *Ezechielprobleme*, BZAW 61 (Giessen, 1933).

16. A. Bertholet and K. Galling, *Hesekiel*, HAT (Tübingen, 1936); H. W. Robinson, *Two Hebrew Prophets: Studies in Hosea and Ezekiel* (London, 1948).

17. See G. Fohrer, *Die Hauptprobleme des Buches Ezechiel*, BZAW 72 (Berlin, 1952).

18. W. Zimmerli, *Ezechiel: Gestalt und Botschaft*, BSt 62 (Neurkirchen-Vluyn, 1972).

19. J. Garscha, *Studien zum Ezechielbuch: Eine redaktionskritische Untersuchung von Ez. 1—39*, Europäische Hochschul-schriften 23 (Berne and Frankfurt, 1974).

20. G. von Rad, *Old Testament Theology*, vol. 2 (Edinburgh and London, 1965), E.T. of *Theologie des Alten Testaments*, vol. 2: *Die Theologie der prophetischen Überlieferungen Israels* (Munich, 1960).

21. W. Zimmerli, *Ezechiel*, vol. 1 (Philadelphia: Fortress Press, 1979), 16f., E.T. of *Ezechiel*, vol. 1, BKAT 13, 1 (Neukirchen-Vluyn: Neukirchener Verlag, 1969).

22. H. Gese, *Der Verfassungsentwurf des Ezechiel* (Kap. 40–48) *traditionsgeschichtlich untersucht*, BHTh 25 (Tübingen, 1957).

23. See M. Noth, *Leviticus: A Commentary* (London, 1965), 16, 128, E.T. of *Das dritte Buch Mose, Leviticus*, ATD 6 (Göttingen, 1962); idem, *A History of Pentateuchal Traditions* (Englewood Cliffs, N.J.: Prentice Hall, 1972), 9, E.T. of *Überlieferungsgeschichte des Pentateuch* (Stuttgart, 1948); K. Elliger, *Leviticus*, HAT (Tübingen, 1966), 16ff.

24. J. Wellhausen, *Prolegomena to the History of Ancient Israel* (New York, 1957), 278f., 404, E.T. of *Prolegomena zur Geschichte Israels* (Berlin, 1883); cf. A Klostermann, "Ezechiel und das Heiligkeitsgesetz," in *Der Pentateuch* (Leipzig, 1893), 368–418.

25. Zimmerli, *Ezechiel*.

26. Ibid., 52; Fohrer, *Die Hauptprobleme des Buches Ezechiel*, 144f.

27. Gese, *Der Verfassungsentwurf des Ezechiel*, 122; A. Cody, *A History of Old Testament Priesthood*, AnBib 35 (Rome, 1969), 156ff; M. Haran, *Temples and Temple-Service in Ancient Israel* (Oxford, 1980), 103ff.

28. See G. Bettenzoli, *Geist der Heiligkeit: Traditionsgeschichtliche Unter-suchung des QDS—Begriffes im Buch Ezechiel*, Quaderni de Semitistica 8 (Florence, 1979), especially 105ff.
29. Zimmerli, *Ezekiel*, 52.
30. See R. Kilian, *Literarkritische und Formegeschichtliche Untersuchung des Heiligkeitgesetzes*, BBB 19 (Bonn, 1963), especially 180ff.
31. A. Cholewinski, *Heiligkeitgesetz und Deuteronomium: Eine vergleichende Studie*, AnBib 66 (Rome, 1976).
32. Barth, *Die Jesaja-Worte in der Josiazeit*.
33. See P. R. Ackroyd's "Continuity and Discontinuity: Rehabilitation and Authentication," in *Tradition and Theology in the Old Testament*, ed. D. A. Knight (London, 1977), 215–34, in which he points out that one of the functions of preserved written prophecy was to serve as authentication for particular developments within Israel's religion. In this case the specific application of the Ezekiel prophetic tradition has been to establish the divine authenticity of the renewal of the Jerusalem temple cultus after the exile.

Chapter 10. The Chronology of Redaction in Ezekiel 1—24

1. M. Greenberg, *Ezekiel 1—20*, The Anchor Bible, 22, (Garden City, N.Y.: Doubleday, 1983).
2. G. Fohrer, *Die Hauptprobleme des Buches Ezechiel*, BZAW 72 (Berlin, 1952).
3. W. Zimmerli, *Ezechiel*, 2 vols., BKAT (Neukirchen, 1969, 2d ed. 1979).
4. Cf. W. Zimmerli, "Das Phänomen der 'Fortschreibung' im Buche Ezechiel," in *Prophecy: FS G. Fohrer*, BZAW 150 (Berlin, New York: 1980), 174–91.
5. Cf. especially F. L. Hossfeld, *Untersuchungen zu Komposition und Theologie des Ezechielbuches* (Würzburg, 1977): The general assumptions regarding the formation of bands of prophets are to be found in A. Haldar, *Associations of Cult Prophets among the Ancient Semites* (Uppsala, 1945). Cf. further A. S. Kapelrud, "The Traditio-historical Study of the Prophets," in *The Productions of Time: Tradition History in Old Testament Scholarship*, ed. K. Jeppesen and B. Otzen (Sheffield, 1984), 53–66.
6. Cf. J. D. Levenson, *Theology of the Program of Restoration of Ezekiel 40—48* (Missoula, 1976).
7. R. E. Clements, "The Ezekiel Tradition: Prophecy in a Time of Crisis," in *Israel's Prophetic Tradition: Essays in Honour of P. R. Ackroyd*, ed. R. J. Coggins, A. C. J. Phillips, and M. A. Knibb (Cambridge: Cambridge University Press, 1982), 119–36.

8. Cf. especially W. Thiel, *Die deuteronomistische Redaktion von Jeremia 1—25*, WMANT 41 (Neukirchen, 1973); idem, *Die deuteronomistische Redaktion von Jeremia 26–45, mit einer Gesamtbeurteilung der deuteronomistischen Redaktion des Buches Jeremia*, WMANT 52 (Neukirchen, 1980).

9. J. W. Miller, *Das Verhältnis Jeremias und Hesekiels sprachlich und theologisch untersucht mit besonderer Berücksichtigung der Prosareden Jeremias* (Assen, 1955).

10. S. Herrmann, *Die prophetischen Heilserwartungen im Alten Testament: Ursprung und Gestaltwandel*, BWANT 85 (Stuttgart, 1965), 241ff.

11. Cf. my essay, "Patterns in the Prophetic Canon," in *Canon and Authority*, ed. G. W. Coats and B. O. Long (Philadelphia: Fortress Press, 1977), 42—55.

12. Cf. especially H. Gunkel, *Die Propheten als Schriftsteller und Dichter*, SAT 11/2 (Göttingen, 1915, 1923).

13. C. Westermann, *Basic Forms of Prophetic Speech*, trans. H. C. White (London: Lutterworth Press, 1967), 129ff.

14. Cf. W. J. Ong, *Orality and Literary: The Technologizing of the Word* (London and New York: Methuen, 1982), 78ff.: "Writing Restructures Consciousness."

15. Greenberg, *Ezekiel 1—20*, especially the introduction, 18ff.

16. Zimmerli, *Ezechiel*, 1:342 (E.T. p. 334).

17. S. Herrmann, "Die konstruktive Restauration: Das Deuteronomium als Mitte biblischer Theologie," in *Probleme biblischer Theologie: FS G. von Rad* (Munich, 1971), 155–70.

Chapter 11. Apocalyptic, Literacy, and the Canonical Tradition

1. G. R. Beasley-Murray, *Jesus and the Future* (London: Macmillan, 1956). Cf. also idem, *A Commentary on Mark 13* (London: Macmillan, 1957). The purpose of drawing attention back to these much-discussed words at this time is especially a mark of this writer's own deep indebtedness to George Beasley-Murray for the stimulus he has given to us over the years to maintain a deep and lasting love of the Bible. Not least has been his modeling a deep respect of the value and importance of scholarly research as a true expression of that love.

2. Cf. V. Taylor, *The Gospel According to St. Mark* (London: Macmillan, 1952), 511f. Taylor comments: "Alternatively, and perhaps more probably, it is interpreted as a pointed allusion to the Book of Daniel made explicit in Mt. xxiv:15" (p. 511). He goes on to suggest that more than this was intended and that the allusion is made in this cryptic

fashion because anything more precise would have been politically dangerous.

3. Beasley-Murray, *Commentary on Mark 13*, 57.

4. Beasley-Murray, *Jesus and the Future*, 18.

5. Cf. R. Bultmann, *The History of the Synoptic Tradition*, trans. J. Marsh (Oxford: Basil Blackwell Publisher, 1963).

6. This issue was raised especially by H. Riesenfeld, *The Gospel Tradition and Its Beginnings: A Study in the Limits of "Formgeschichte"* (London: A. R. Mowbray, 1957).

7. W. J. Ong, *Orality and Literacy: The Technologizing of the Word* (London and New York: Methuen, 1982), 78ff.

8. Cf. esp. J. Goody, *The Domestication of the Savage Mind* (Cambridge: Cambridge University Press, 1977).

9. This, of course, leaves open the possibility of whether or not there existed an earlier written record of an eschatological discourse from Jesus, as argued most recently by D. Wenham, *The Rediscovery of Jesus' Eschatological Discourse*, Gospel Perspectives 4 (Sheffield: JSOT Press, 1984), especially 217ff.

10. A. Schlatter, *Das Alte Testament in der johanneischen Apokalypse*, BFCT (Gütersloh, 1912), 16:6.

11. L. Hartman, *Prophecy Interpreted: The Formation of Some Jewish Apocalyptic Texts and of the Eschatological Discourse of Mark 13 Par.* (Lund: Gleerup, 1966).

12. R. E. Clements, "Prophecy as Literature: A Re-appraisal," in *The Hermeneutical Quest: Essays in Honor of James Luther Mays on His Sixty-Fifth Birthday*, ed. D. G. Miller (Allison Park, Pa.: Pickwick Publications, 1986).

13. Cf. O. Kaiser, *Isaiah 1—12*, OTL, trans. J. Bowden (Philadelphia: Westminster Press, 1983), 244: "Assyria has become a code name for the world power."

14. K. Koch, *The Prophets*, vol. 2: *The Babylonian and Persian Periods*, trans. M. Kohl (Philadelphia: Fortress Press, 1983), 202f. Cf. also his earlier study, *The Rediscovery of Apocalyptic*, SBT Second Series 22, trans. M. Kohl (London: SCM Press, 1972).

15. Hartman, *Prophecy Interpreted*, 111. Cf. J. Z. Smith, "Wisdom and Apocalyptic," in *Visionaries and their Apocalypses*, Issues in Religion and Theology 2, ed. P. D. Hanson (London: SPCK, 1983), 101–20.

16. Cf. especially B. S. Childs, *Introduction to the Old Testament as Scripture* (Philadelphia: Fortress Press, 1979); idem, *The New Testament as Canon: An Introduction* (Philadelphia: Fortress Press, 1985).

17. The different assumptions and their significance are well discussed in the review of the debate between James Barr and B. S. Childs by Frank

Kermode in "Canons," in *London Reviews*, ed. N. Spice (London: Chatto & Windus, 1985), 149–56.

18. The importance of the development of these patterns of scribal interpretation and their presence in the formation of the Old Testament literature as a form of inner-biblical exegesis is discussed by M. Fishbane, *Biblical Interpretation in Ancient Israel* (Oxford: Oxford University Press, 1985). The interpretation of prophetic materials is dealt with on pp. 443ff.

Chapter 12. The Interpretation of Prophecy and the Origin of Apocalyptic

1. H. H. Rowley, *The Relevance of Apocalyptic: A Study of Jewish Apocalypses from Daniel to the Revelation*, 3d ed. (New York: Association Press, 1964).

2. G. von Rad, *Wisdom in Israel* (Nashville, Abingdon Press, 1972), 263–83.

3. E. W. Nicholson, "Apocalyptic," *Tradition and Interpretation: Essays by Members of the Society for Old Testament Study*, ed. G.W. Anderson (Oxford: Clarendon Press, 1979), 189–213.

4. D. S. Russell. *The Method and Message of Jewish Apocalyptic, 200 B.C.–A.D. 100* (Westminster Press, 1964), 73ff, 189ff.

5. Cf. M. A. Knibb, "Prophecy and the Emergence of the Jewish Apocalypses," in *Israel's Prophetic Tradition: Essays in Honor of Peter R. Ackroyd*, ed. R. J. Coggins, A. Phillips, and M. A. Knibb (Cambridge: Cambridge University Press, 1982), 155–80.

6. O. Kaiser, *Isaiah 1—12*, OTL, trans. J. Bowden (London: SCM Press, 1983), 240–42. P. D. Hanson, *The Dawn of Apocalyptic* (Philadelphia: Fortress Press, 1975), 32ff.

7. This especially applies to Ezekiel 38—39. Cf. W. Zimmerli, *Ezekiel*, vol. 2, trans. J. D. Martin, Hermeneia (Philadelphia: Fortress Press, 1983), 281ff.

8. Cf. Hanson, *Dawn of Apocalyptic*, 280ff.

9. L. Hartman, *Prophecy Interpreted: The Formation of Some Jewish Apocalyptic Texts and of the Eschatological Discourse of Mark 13 Par*, Coniectanea Biblica, N.T. Series 1 (Lund: Gleerup, 1966).

10. Cf. my study, "A Remnant Chosen by Grace (Romans 11:5)," in *Pauline Studies: Essays in Honour of F. F. Bruce on His Seventieth Birthday*, ed. D. A. Hagner and M. J. Harris (Exeter: Paternoster Press, 1980), 106–21.

11. Kaiser, *Isaiah 1—12*, 242.

12. This pattern of enlarging the scope of an assurance concerning the de-

feat of Assyria into one concerning all the nations that threaten Zion is repeated in Isa. 29:5–9. I have dealt with such a feature in my study "Isaiah 14:22–27: A Central Passage Reconsidered," *The Book of Isaiah, Les Oracles et leur Relectures: Unité et complexité de l'ouvrage*, BETL 81 (Leuven, 1989), 253–62.

13. Kaiser, *Isaiah 1—12*, 242.
14. Compare my essay "Prophecy as Literature: A Re-appraisal," in *The Hermeneutical Quest: Essays in Honor of James Luther Mays on His Sixty-Fifth Birthday*, ed. D. G. Miller (Allison Park, Pa.: Pickwick Publications, 1986), 59–76.
15. Kaiser, *Isaiah 1—12*, 242.
16. Cf. P. D. Hanson, "Old Testament Apocalyptic Reexamined," in *Visionaries and Their Apocalypses: Issues in Religion and Theology*, Issues in Religion and Theology 2, ed. P. D. Hanson (London: SPCK, 1983), 54.
17. N. W. Porteous, *Daniel: A Commentary*, OTL (London, SCM Press, 1965), 143.
18. Cf. J. A. Montgomery, *The Book of Daniel*, ICC (Edinburgh: T.&T. Clark, 1927), 385f.
19. Cf. Montgomery, *Book of Daniel*, 386f; also M. Fishbane, *Biblical Interpretation in Ancient Israel* (Oxford: Oxford University Press, 1985), 485ff.
20. Fishbane, *Biblical Interpretation*, 489.

Chapter 13. Patterns in the Prophetic Canon

1. W. Zimmerli, *The Law and the Prophets: A Study of the Meaning of the Old Testament* (New York: Harper & Row, 1965).
2. J. A. Sanders, *Torah and Canon* (Philadelphia: Fortress Press, 1972).
3. See the interpretation of Amos 9:11–12 in Acts 15:16–18.
4. See my *Prophecy and Tradition* (Oxford: Basil Blackwell Publisher, 1975), 41–57.
5. See my *Prophecy and Covenant*, SBT 43 (London: SCM Press, 1965), 103–18. See also H. P. Müller, *Ursprünge und Strukturen alttestamentlicher Eschatologie*, BZAW 109 (Berlin: Walter de Gruyter, 1969).
6. This seems to me an important weakness in the otherwise fresh and valuable treatment by G. Fohrer, *History of Israelite Religion* (New York and Nashville: Abingdon Press, 1973), 316–29. Cf. also his "Die Struktur der alttestamentlichen Eschatologie," in *Studien zur alttestamentlichen Prophetie*, BZAW 99 (Berlin: Walter de Gruyter, 1967), 32–58.
7. Besides the work of G. Fohrer referred to above, see S. Mowinckel, *He That Cometh* (Nashville: Abingdon Press, 1956), 125–86.
8. See especially Jer. 32:6–15, which bears all the circumstantial marks of

its authenticity in itself, but which has been further expanded by a Deuteronomistic circle. See P. Diepold, *Israel's Land*, BWANT 5/15 (Stuttgart: W. Kohlhammer, 1972), 129ff.

9. Such a view has most recently been put forward by O. Kaiser, *Introduction to the Old Testament: A Presentation of Its Results and Problems* (Minneapolis: Augsburg, 1975), 224.

10. G. von Rad, *Old Testament Theology* (New York: Harper & Row, 1962–65), 2:138.

11. We should then add that such a meaning has been still further enlarged by the first century A.D., as shown in Acts 15:16–18, noted above.

12. Cf. Diepold, *Israel's Land*, 140ff.

13. That Hosea was exclusively a prophet of doom is argued by W. F. Stinespring, "A Problem of Theological Ethics in Hosea," in *Essays in Old Testament Ethics (J. Philip Hyatt in Memoriam)*, ed. J. L. Crenshaw and J. T. Willis, 133–44 (New York: KTAV Publishing House, 1974). The question is dealt with further in my essay "Understanding the Book of Hosea," *RevExp* 72 (1975): 405–23.

14. The strongest point of anchorage for such a message of hope in Hosea is to be found in Hos. 11:8–9. See W. Rudolph, *Hosea*, KAT 13/1 (Gütersloh: Gerd Mohn, 1966), 217–18.

15. Much useful material in this regard is to be found in I. Willi-Plein, *Vorformen der Schriftexegese innerhalb des Alten Testaments*, BZAW 123 (Berlin: Walter de Gruyter, 1971). Her treatment, however, appears to me to be defective precisely because she has dealt with secondary material as made up of independent units and not as a supplement to extant material, with which it must be read. The addition gives further direction to that which is there, and cannot be properly understood independently of this.

16. Cf. W. Zimmerli, *Ezechiel*, BKAT 13 (Neukirchen: Neukirchener Verlag, 1956–69), 367–71, 388–90, and 450–52.

Chapter 14. Prophecy as Literature: A Reappraisal

1. This may be regarded as essentially the case at Mari, where we possess letters referring to dream interpretations and prophetic revelations, but where no attempt was made to provide any comprehensive corpus of prophetic literature, or to provide a basis for comparing prophecies with each other. Cf. F. Ellemeier, *Prophetie in Mari und Israel* (Herzberg, 1968).

2. This becomes clear from the useful selection of viewpoints brought together by P.H.A. Neumann, *Das Prophetenverständnis in der Deutschsprachigen Forschung seit Heinrich Ewald* (Darmstadt: Wissenschaftliche

Buchgesellschaft, 1979). A fuller picture of Eichhorn's and Herder's work is to be found in E. Sehmsdorf, *Die Prophetenauslegung bei J. G. Eichhorn* (Göttingen: Vandenhoeck & Ruprecht, 1971).

3. So especially B. S. Childs, *Introduction to the Old Testament as Scripture* (London: SCM Press, 1979), 305ff. Cf. also J. Blenkinsopp, *Prophecy and Canon: A Contribution to the Study of Jewish Origins* (Notre Dame, 1977), 96ff.

4. Cf. J. J. Jackson, ed., *Rhetorical Criticism: Essays in Honor of James Muilenburg*, Pittsburgh Theological Monograph Series 1 (Pittsburgh, 1974), particularly the introduction by B. W. Anderson.

5. M. Greenberg, *Ezekiel 1—20*, Anchor Bible 22 (Garden City, N.Y.: Doubleday & Co., 1983), 18ff.

6. It is noteworthy that J. Vermeylen has argued that even the original Song of the Vineyard of Isa. 5:1–7 should be regarded as a Deuteronomistic redactional composition. Cf. *Du prophète Isaïe à l'apocalyptique: Isaïe 1—35, miroir d'un demi-millénaire d'expérience religieuse en Israël*, EBib (Paris: J. Gabalda, 1977), 1:159ff. The majority of commentators have not taken such a view, but it nevertheless highlights the need to consider more fully the distinctions between oral and literary aspects of the prophetic tradition.

7. Cf. especially J. Goody, *The Domestication of the Savage Mind* (Cambridge, 1977), 36ff. A more literary perspective on the issues is discussed in W. J. Ong, *Orality and Literacy: The Technologizing of the Word* (London and New York: Methuen, 1982).

8. W. J. Ong, "Writing Restructures Consciousness," in *Orality and Literacy* (see n. 7 above), 78ff.

9. Cf. especially B. Duhm, *Die Theologie der Propheten* (Bonn, 1875), and the somewhat modified position in his later work *Israels Propheten* (Tübingen, 1916; 2d ed., 1922).

10. G. von Rad, *Old Testament Theology*, vol. 2, trans. D.M.G. Stalker (Edinburgh: Oliver & Boyd, 1965).

11. Cf. especially S. Mowinckel, *Prophecy and Tradition: The Prophetic Books in the Light of the Growth and History of the Tradition* (Oslo: J. Dybwad, 1946); E. Nielsen, *Oral Tradition*, SBT 11 (London, 1954), 39ff. *Orality and Literacy*, 173f.: "biblical studies, like other textual studies, are inclined unwittingly to model the noetic and verbal economy of oral cultures on literacy, projecting oral memory as a variant of verbatim literate memory and thinking of what is preserved in oral tradition as a kind of text that is only waiting to be set down in writing."

12. Cf. S. Mowinckel, *Jesajas disiplene* (Oslo, 1926); J. Eaton, "The Origin of the Book of Isaiah," *VT* 9 (1959): 138–57; D. R. Jones, "The Tradition of the Oracles of Isaiah of Jerusalem," *ZAW* 67 (1955): 226–46.

For Ezekiel reference must especially be made to W. Zimmerli, *Ezekiel*, 2 vols., Hermeneia (Philadelphia: Fortress Press, 1979, 1983); also idem, "Das Phänomen der 'Fortschreibung' im Buche Ezechiel," in *Prophecy: FS G. Fohrer*, BZAW 150 (Berlin and New York, 1980), 174–91.

13. This aspect of the material is strongly emphasised by R. P. Carroll, *From Chaos to Covenant: Uses of Prophecy in the Book of Jeremiah* (London, 1981), 151ff.

14. A.H.J. Gunneweg, *Mündliche und schriftliche Tradition der vorexilischen Prophetbücher als Problem neueren Prophetenforschung*, FRLANT 73 (Göttingen, 1979).

15. This may be maintained despite the important criticisms of the thesis concerning the Isaiah "Memoir" by O. Kaiser, *Isaiah 1—12*, 2d ed., trans. J. Bowden (London, 1983), 114ff.

16. The necessity for giving more scope in the interpretation of prophecy to the idea of fulfillment is argued in my essay "Prophecy and Fulfilment," *Epworth Review* 10 (1983): 72–82.

17. I am thinking here especially of the work by R. P. Carroll, *When Prophecy Failed: Reactions and Response to Failure in the Old Testament Prophetic Traditions* (London: SCM Press, 1979).

18. Cf. my essay, "Patterns in the Prophetic Canon," in *Canon and Authority*, ed. G. W. Coats and B. O. Long (Philadelphia: Fortress Press, 1977), 42–55.

19. The complexity of this subject is highlighted by E. Osswald, *Falsche Prophetie im Alten Testament* (Tübingen, 1962); J. A. Sanders, "Hermeneutics in True and False Prophecy," in *Canon and Authority*, ed. G. W. Coats and B. O. Long, 21–41. Cf. also my treatment of the theme in *Prophecy and Tradition* (Oxford: Basil Blackwell Publisher, 1975), 41–57.

20. This point is brought out well by G. von Rad, *Studies in Deuteronomy*, SBT 9 (London, 1947), 78–83.

21. Cf. M. Fishbane, *Biblical Interpretation in Ancient Israel* (Oxford: Oxford University Press, 1985), 458ff.

22. Cf. my essay, "Prophecy and Fulfilment," 72–82.

23. This point is noted, rather inconclusively, by K. Koch in *The Prophets*, vol. 2: *The Babylonian and Persian Periods*, trans. M. Kohl (London, 1983), 188f.

Chapter 15. The Prophet and His Editors

1. Cf. especially E. Sehmsdorf, *Die Prophetenauslegung bei J. G. Eichhorn* (Göttingen: Vandenhoeck & Ruprecht, 1971). The development of

the study of the prophetic literature since H. Ewald is outlined in P.H.A. Neumann, *Das Prophetenverständnis in der deutschsprachigen Forschung seit Heinrich Ewald,* Wege der Forschung, 307 (Darmstadt: Wissenschaftliche Buchgesellschaft).

2. For the work of Doederlein see especially J. M. Vincent, *Studien zur literarischen Eigenart und zur geistigen Heimat von Jesaja: Kap. 40—55,* Beiträge zur biblischen Exegese und Theologie 5 (Frankfurt am Main, Bern, Las Vegas: Peter Lang, 1977).

3. Cf. my essay "Prophecy as Literature: A Re-appraisal," in *The Hermeneutical Quest: Essays in Honor of James Luther Mays on His Sixty-Fifth Birthday,* ed. D. G. Miller, Princeton Theological Monographs 4 (Allison Park, Pickwick Publications, 1986), 56–76.

4. B. Duhm, *Das Buch Jeremia,* HKAT (Göttingen: Vandenhoeck & Ruprecht, 1901).

5. S. Mowinckel, *Zur Komposition des Buches Jeremia* (Kristiania: J. Dybwad, 1914).

6. Cf. the essay by W. L. Holladay, "A Fresh Look at 'Source B' and 'Source C' in Jeremiah," *VT* 25 (1975): 394–412, reprinted in *A Prophet to the Nations: Essays in Jeremiah Studies,* ed. L. G. Perdue and B. W. Kovacs (Winona Lake: Eisenbrauns, 1984), 213—88.

7. A very positivist evaluation along these lines is presented by J. Bright, "The Date of the Prose Sermons of Jeremiah," *JBL* 70 (1951): 15–35 (= *A Prophet to the Nations,* 193–212).

8. S. Mowinckel, *Prophecy and Tradition: The Prophetic Books in the Light of the Study of the Growth and History of the Tradition,* ANVAO (Oslo: J. Dybwad, 1946).

9. Cf. the study by A. S. Kapelrud, "The Traditio-historical Study of the Prophets," in *The Productions of Time: Tradition History in Old Testament Scholarship,* ed. K. Jeppesen and B. Otzen (Sheffield: Almond, 1984), 53–66.

10. Cf. especially E. Nielsen, *Oral Tradtion,* SBT 1/11 (London: SCM Press, 1951). A strong statement of the contention that prophecy was given and preserved orally through groups of disciples is presented by I. Engnell, "Prophets and Prophetism in the Old Testament," in *Critical Essays on the Old Testament,* trans. J. T. Willis (London: SPCK, 1970), 123–79.

11. Cf. also C. R. North, "The Place of Oral Tradition in the Growth of the Old Testament," *ExpTim* 61 (1949–50): 292–96.

12. E. W. Nicholson, *Preaching to the Exiles: A Study of the Prose Tradition in the Book of Jeremiah* (Oxford: Basil Blackwell Publisher, 1970).

13. Nicholson, *Preaching to the Exiles,* 116ff.

14. W. Thiel, *Die deuteronomistische Redaktion von Jeremia 1—25*, WMANT 41 (Neukirchen-Vluyn: Neukirchener Verlag, 1973); idem *Die deuteronomistische Redaktion von Jeremia 26—45*, WMANT 52 (Neukirchen-Vluyn: Neukirchener Verlag, 1981).

15. Cf. also J. P. Hyatt, "The Deuteronomic Edition of Jeremiah," in *Vanderbilt Studies in the Humanities*, ed. R. C. Beatty, J. P. Hyatt, and M. K. Spears (Nashville: Vanderbilt University Press, 1951), 71–95 (= *A Prophet to the Nations*, 247–67).

16. P. Diepold, *Israel's Land*, BWANT 15 (Stuttgart: W. Kohlhammer, 1972).

17. R. P. Carroll, *When Prophecy Failed: Reactions and Responses to Failure in the Old Testament Prophetic Traditions* (London: SCM Press, 1979).

18. P. R. Ackroyd, "Historians and Prophets," *SEÅ* 33 (1968): 18–34 (= his *Studies in the Religious Tradition of the Old Testament* [London: SCM Press, 1987], 121–51).

19. Carroll, *From Chaos to Covenant*, 249ff.

20. L. Festinger, H. W. Riecker, and S. Schachter, *When Prophecy Fails* (Minneapolis, 1956).

21. M. Weber, *The Sociology of Religion*, trans. Ephraim Fischoff (Boston: Beacon Press, 1963), 60–79; cf. especially 60—61: "Primarily, a religious community arises in connection with a prophetic movement as a result of routinization (Ger. *Veralltäglichung*), i.e., as a result of the process whereby either the prophet himself or his disciples secure the permanence of his preaching and the congregation's distribution of grace, hence insuring the economic existence of the enterprise and those who man it, and thereby monopolizing as well the privileges reserved for those charged with religious functions." Cf. also "The Sociology of Charismatic Authority," in *From Max Weber: Essays in Sociology*, ed. H. H. Gerth and C. Wright Mills (London: Routledge & Kegan Paul, 1947), 245–52.

22. Some initial observations along these lines were presented in my essay "The Ezekiel Tradition: Prophecy in a Time of Crisis," in *Israel's Prophetic Tradition: Essays in Honour of P. R. Ackroyd*, ed. R. J. Coggins, A.C.J. Phillips, and M. A. Knibb (Cambridge: Cambridge University Press, 1982), 119–36.

23. Cf. the classic exposition in J. Skinner, *Prophecy and Religion* (Cambridge: Cambridge University Press, 1922), 165–84.

24. Cf. P. R. Ackroyd, "The Temple Vessels: A Continuity Theme," in *Studies in the Religion of Ancient Israel*, VTSup 23 (1972): 166–81 (= his *Studies in the Religious Tradition of the Old Testament*, 46–60).

25. K. F. Pohlmann, *Studien zum Jeremiabuch: Ein Beitrag zur Frage nach*

der Entstehung des Jeremiabuches, FRLANT 118 (Göttingen: Vandenhoeck & Ruprecht, 1978).

26. Cf. C. R. Seitz, "The Crisis of Interpretation over the Meaning and Purpose of the Exile: A Redactional Study of Jer. 21–43," *VT* 35 (1985): 78–97.

Selected Works
by Ronald E. Clements

BOOKS

Prophecy and Covenant, SBT 43 (London: SCM Press, 1965).

God and Temple: The Idea of the Divine Presence in Ancient Israel (Oxford: Basil Blackwell Publisher, 1965). Japanese translation, 1983.

The Conscience of the Nation: A Study of Early Israelite Prophecy (Oxford: Oxford University Press, 1967). Japanese translation, 1971.

Abraham and David: Genesis 15 and Its Meaning for Israelite Tradition, SBT, Second Series 5 (London: SCM Press, 1967).

God's Chosen People: A Theological Interpretation of the Book of Deuteronomy (London: SCM Press, 1968). Italian translation by M. Corsani, Torino, 1976.

Exodus, The Cambridge Bible Commentary on the NEB (Cambridge: Cambridge University Press, 1972). Japanese translation by M. Tokita, 1981.

Prophecy and Tradition, Growing Points in Theology (Oxford: Basil Blackwell Publisher, 1975).

A Century of Old Testament Study (Guildford: Lutterworth Press, 1976); rev. ed., 1983: *A Hundred Years of Old Testament Study* (Philadelphia: Westminster Press, 1976). Japanese translation, Tokyo, 1978.

Old Testament Theology: A Fresh Approach, Marshall's Theological Library (London: Marshall, Morgan & Scott, 1978).

Isaiah and the Deliverance of Jerusalem: A Study of the Interpretation of Prophecy in the Old Testament, JSOTSup 13 (Sheffield, JSOT Press, 1980).

Isaiah 1—39, New Century Bible Commentary (Grand Rapids: Wm. B. Eerdmans Publishing Co., 1980).

In Spirit and in Truth: Insights from Biblical Prayers (Atlanta: John Knox Press, 1985). Published as *The Prayers of the Bible* (London: SCM Press, 1986).

Jeremiah, Interpretation: A Bible Commentary for Teaching and Preaching (Atlanta: John Knox Press, 1988).

Deuteronomy, Old Testament Guides (Sheffield: JSOT Press, 1989).

Wisdom for a Changing World: Wisdom in Old Testament Theology, Berkeley Lectures 2 (Berkeley, Calif.: Bibal Press, 1990).

Wisdom in Theology, The Didsbury Lectures, 1989 (Grand Rapids: Wm. B. Eerdmans Publishing Co., 1992).

BOOKS EDITED

The World of Ancient Israel: Sociological, Anthropological, and Political Perspectives (Cambridge: Cambridge University Press, 1989).

TRANSLATIONS

W. Zimmerli, *The Law and The Prophets* (Oxford: Basil Blackwell Publisher, 1965).

W. Zimmerli, *Ezekiel*, vol. 1, Hermeneia (Philadelphia: Fortress Press, 1979).

DICTIONARY ARTICLES

Interpreter's Dictionary of the Bible, Supplementary Volume, ed. K. R. Crim (Nashville: Abingdon Press, 1976), Article: Exodus (Book of), cols. 310b–312b.

A New Dictionary of Christian Theology, ed. A. Richardson and J. Bowden (London: SCM Press, 1983). Articles: Covenant, Henotheism, Monotheism, Old Testament Theology (with N. W. Porteous).

Theologisches Wörterbuch zum Alten Testament, ed. H. Ringgren, G. J. Botterweck, and H.-J. Fabry (Stuttgart: W. Kohlhammer).

Articles: Bd I Abraham, cols. 52–62 (1973)
       Bd I *goy* (with G. J. Botterweck) cols. 238–43 (1973)
       Bd II *zakar* cols. 593–99 (1975)
       Bd IV *kokab* cols. 79–91 (1982)
       Bd IV *mayim* (with H.-J. Fabry) cols. 843–66 (1983)
       Bd VII *ramas* cols. 535–38 (1990)
       Bd VII *ša'ar* cols. 933–50 (1992)
       Bd VII *šaḥat* cols. 1214–18 (1993)

"Isaiah," *The Books of The Bible*, vol. 1, ed. B. W. Anderson (New York: Charles Scribner's Sons, 1989), 247–79.

A Dictionary of Biblical Interpretation, ed. Leslie Houlden and R. J. Coggins (London: SCM Press, 1990). Articles: Abraham, Isaiah, Messiah, Pentateuch.

The Oxford Companion to the Bible, ed. Bruce M. Metzger and Michael D. Coogan (New York: Oxford University Press, 1994). Article: Deuteronomy, cols. 164b–68a.

ARTICLES

"Temple and Land: A Significant Aspect of Israel's Worship," *Transactions of the Glasgow University Oriental Society* 19 (1963): 16–28.

"Deuteronomy and the Jerusalem Cult Tradition," *VT* 15 (1965): 300–12.

"The Problem of Old Testament Theology," *The London Quarterly and Holborn Review* (1965): 11–17.

"The Relation of Children to the People of God in the Old Testament," *The Baptist Quarterly* 21 (1966): 195–205 (= *Foundations* 9 [1966]: 133–44).

"The Meaning of Ritual Acts in Israelite Religion," in *Eucharistic Theology Then and Now*, SPCK Theological Collections 9, ed. G.W.H. Lampe (London: SPCK, 1968), 1–14.

"Baal-Berith of Shechem," Essays in Honour of D. Winton Thomas, *Journal of Semitic Studies* 13 (1968): 21–32.

"Theodorus C. Vriezen: An Outline of Old Testament Theology," in *Contemporary Old Testament Theologians*, ed. R. B. Laurin, 121–40 (Valley Forge: Judson Press, 1970.

"The Deuteronomistic Interpretation of the Founding of the Monarchy in 1 Sam. 8," *VT* 24 (1974): 398–410.

"Understanding the Book of Hosea," *RevExp* 72 (1975): 405–23.

"The Purpose of the Book of Jonah," *Edinburgh Congress Volume*, VTSup 26 (1975): 16–28.

"Covenant and Canon in the Old Testament," in *Creation, Christ, and Culture: Studies in Honour of T. F. Torrance*, ed. R.W.A. McKinney, 1–12 (Edinburgh: T.&T. Clark, 1976).

"Patterns in the Prophetic Canon," in *Canon and Authority: Essays in Old Testament Religion and Theology*, ed. G. W. Coats and B. O. Long, 42–55 (Philadelphia: Fortress Press, 1977).

"Prophecy and Revelation," in *Science, Faith, and Revelation, an Approach to Christian Philosophy: Essays in Honor of E. C. Rust*, ed. Bob E. Patterson, 283–300 (Nashville: Broadman Press, 1979).

"A Remnant Chosen by Grace (Romans 11:5)," in *Pauline Studies: Essays in Honour of F. F. Bruce on His Seventieth Birthday*, ed. D. A. Hagner and M. J. Harris, 106–21 (Exeter: Paternoster Press, 1980).

"The Prophecies of Isaiah and the Fall of Jerusalem in 587 B.C.," *VT* 30 (1980): 421–36.

"Jeremiah: Prophet of Hope," *RevExp* 78 (1981): 345–63.

"Heinrich Graetz as Biblical Historian and Religious Apologist," in *Interpreting the Hebrew Bible: Essays in Honour of E.I.J Rosenthal*, ed. J. A. Emerton and S. C. Reif, 35–55 (Cambridge: Cambridge University Press, 1982).

"The Unity of the Book of Isaiah," *Interpretation* 36 (1982): 117–29.

"The Form and Character of Prophetic Woe Oracles," *Semitics* (UNISA Miscellanea), Pretoria, S.A. (1982): 17–29.

"History and Theology in Biblical Narrative," *Horizons in Biblical Theology* 4 (1982), 45–60.

"The Ezekiel Tradition: Prophecy in a Time of Crisis," in *Israel's Prophetic Tradition: Essays in Honour of P. R. Ackroyd*, ed. R. J. Coggins, A.C.J. Phillips, and M. A. Knibb, 119–36 (Cambridge: Cambridge University Press, 1982).

"The Isaiah Narrative of 2 Kings 20:12–19 and the Date of the Deuteronomic History," in *Isaac Leo Seeligmann Volume*, ed. A. Rofé, 209–20 (Jerusalem: E. Rubinstein, 1983).

"Prophecy and Fulfilment," *Epworth Review* 10/3 (1983): 72–82.

"Preaching from the Wisdom Literature," in *Biblical Preaching: An Expositor's Treasury*, ed. J. W. Cox, 84–101 (Philadelphia: Westminster Press, 1983).

"Distinctive Ideas Revisited," *Expository Times* 95 (1984): 273–76.

"Christian Ethics and the Old Testament," *The Modern Churchman* 26 (1984): 13–26.

"Monotheism and the Canonical Process," *Theology* 87 (1984): 336–44.

"Beyond Tradition-History: Deutero-Isaianic Development of First Isaiah's Themes," *JSOT* 31 (1985): 95–113.

"The Use of the Old Testament in the Epistle to the Hebrews," *Southwestern Journal of Theology* 28 (1985): 36–45.

"Whither Old Testament Theology," *King's Theological Review* 8 (1985): 33–37.

"Expository Article, Isaiah 45:20–25: The Goal of Faith," *Interpretation* 40 (1986): 392–97.

"The Chronology of Redaction in Ezekiel 1—24," in *Ezekiel and His Book*, ed. J. Lust, 283–94, BETL 74 (Leuven: J. Peeters, 1986).

"Prophecy as Literature: A Re-appraisal," in *The Hermeneutical Quest: Essays in Honor of James Luther Mays on His Sixty-Fifth Birthday*, ed. D. G. Miller, 56–76 (Allison Park, Pa.: Pickwick Publications, 1986).

"Solomon and the Origins of Wisdom in Israel," *Perspectives in Religious Studies* 15 (1988): 23–35.

"Wisdom," in *It Is Written: Scripture Citing Scripture, Essays in Honour of Barnabas Lindars*, ed. D. A. Carson and H.G.M. Williamson, 67–83 (Cambridge: Cambridge University Press, 1988).

"Apocalyptic, Literacy, and the Canonical Tradition," in *Eschatology and the New Testament*, ed. W. Hulitt Gloer, 15–27 (Peabody, Mass.: Hendrickson, 1988).

"Patterns in the Prophetic Canon: Healing the Blind and the Lame," in *Canon, Theology, and Old Testament Interpretation: FS Brevard S. Childs*, ed. G. M. Tucker, D. L. Petersen, R. R. Wilson 189–200 (Philadelphia: Fortress Press, 1988).

"Isaiah 14:22–27: A Central Passage Reconsidered," in *The Book of Isaiah, Les Oracles et leur Relectures: Unité et complexité de l'ouvrage*, BETL 81, (Leuven, 1989), 253–62.

"The Messianic Hope in the Old Testament," *JSOT* 43 (1989): 3–19.

"The Interpretation of Prophecy and the Origin of Apocalyptic," in *Bible, Church, and World: Essays in Honour of D. S. Russell*, 28–35 (London: The Baptist Historical Society, 1989).

"Claus Westermann on Creation in Genesis," *Southwestern Journal of Theology* 22 (1990): 18–26.36.

"The Immanuel Prophecy of Isa. 7:10–17 and Its Messianic Interpretation," in *Die Hebräische Bibel und ihre zweifache Nachgeschichte: FS R. Rendtorff zum 65. Geburtstag*, ed. E. Blum, Chr. Macholz, and E. W. Stegemann, 225–40 (Neukirchen: Neukirchener Verlag, 1990).

"The Prophet and His Editors," in *The Bible in Three Dimensions: Essays in Celebration of Forty Years of Biblical Studies in the University of Sheffield*, JSOTSup 87 (Sheffield: Sheffield Academic Press, 1990), 202–30.

"The Old Testament Background of Acts 10:34–35," in *With Steadfast Purpose: Essays on Acts in Honor of Henry Jackson Flanders, Jr.*, ed. N. H. Keathley (Waco, Tex.: Baylor University, 1990), 203–16.

"Amos and the Politics of Israel," in *Storia e Tradizioni di Israele: Scritti in Onore di J. Alberto Soggin*, ed. D. Garrone and F. Israel, 49–64 (Brescia: Paideia Editrice, 1991).

"The Prophecies of Isaiah to Hezekiah concerning Sennacherib: 2 Kings 19:21–34 //Isa. 37:22–35," in *Prophetie und geschichtliche Wirklichkeit im Alten Israel: FS S. Herrmann zum 65. Geburtstag*, ed. R. Liwak and S. Wagner, 65–78 (Stuttgart-Köln: W. Kohlhammer, 1991).

"Jeremiah 1—25 and the Deuteronomistic History," in *Understanding Poets and Prophets: Essays in Honour of George Wishart Anderson*, ed. A. Graeme Auld, 93–113, JSOTSup 152 (Sheffield: Sheffield Academic Press, 1993).

"The Good Neighbour in the Book of Proverbs," in *Of Prophets' Visions and the Wisdom of the Sages: Essays in Honour of R. Norman Whybray on His Seventieth Birthday*, ed. H. A. McKay and D.J.A. Clines, 209–228, JSOTSup 162 (Sheffield: Sheffield Academic Press, 1993).

"Archaeology and Biblical Illustration: Visual Transformations of Biblical Interpretation in the Nineteenth Century," in *Text and Theology: Studies in Honour of Prof. Dr. Theol. Magne Saebø*, ed. A. Tångberg, 95–111 (Oslo: Verbum, 1994).

"George Stanley Faber (1773–1854) as Biblical Interpreter," in *Altes Testament, Forschung und Wirkung: Festschrift für Henning Graf Reventlow*, ed. P. Mommer and W. Thiel, 247–68 (Frankfurt am Main: Peter Lang, 1994).

"Social Justice in the Eighth-Century Prophets," *Dialogue: A Journal for Sixth Form Religious Studies*, Issue 2 (April 1994): 33–36.

Acknowledgments

All chapters in *Old Testatment Prophecy* first appeared in the following publications and are reprinted with permission.

Chapter 1. "Amos and the Politics of Israel," in *Storia e Tradizioni di Israele: Scritti in Onore J. Alberto Soggin*, ed. Daniele Garrone and Felice Israel (Brescia: Paideia Editrice, 1991), 49–64.

Chapter 2. "The Prophecies of Isaiah to Hezekiah Concerning Sennacherib: 2 Kings 19:21 // Isaiah 37:22–35," in *Prophetie und geschichtliche Wirklichkeit im Alten Israel: Festschrift S. Hermann zum 65. Geburtstag*, ed. R. Liwak and S. Wagner (Stuttgart: W. Kohlhammer, 1991), 65–78.

Chapter 3. "The Messianic Hope in the Old Testament." by R. E. Clements, from *Journal for the Study of the Old Testament*, Issue 43. Copyright © 1989. Reprinted by permission of Sheffield Academic Press Limited.

Chapter 4. "The Immanuel Prophecy of Isaiah 7:10–17 and Its Messianic Interpretation," in *Die Hebräische Bibel und ihre zweifache Nachgeschichte: Festschrift R. Rendtorff zum 65. Geburtstag*, ed. E. Blum, Chr. Macholz, and E. W. Stegemann (Neukirchen: Neukirchener Verlag, 1990), 225–40.

Chapter 5. "Beyond Tradition History: Deutero-Isaianic Development of First Isaiah's Themes," by R. E. Clements, from *Journal for the Study of the Old Testatment*, Issue 31. Copyright © 1985. Reprinted by permission of Sheffield Academic Press Limited.

Chapter 6. "The Unity of the Book of Isaiah," *Interpretation* 36 (1982): 117–29.

Chapter 7. "Jeremiah 1—25 and the Deuteronomistic History," by R. E. Clements, from *Journal for the Study of the Old Testament Supplements*,

Number 152. Copyright © 1993. Reprinted by permission of Sheffield Academic Press Limited.

Chapter 8. "Jeremiah: Prophet of Hope," *Review and Expositor* 78 (1981): 345–63.

Chapter 9. "The Ezekiel Tradition: Prophecy in a Time of Crisis," in *Israel's Prophetic Tradition: Essays in Honour of P. R. Ackroyd*, ed. R. J. Coggins, A.C.J. Phillips, and M. A. Knibb (Cambridge: Cambridge University Press, 1982), 119–36.

Chapter 10. "The Chronology of Redaction in Ezekiel 1—24," in *Ezekiel and His Book*, ed. J. Lust, BETL 74 (1986): 283–94, by permission of Peeters Publishers, Leuven.

Chapter 11. "Apocalyptic, Literacy, and the Canonical Tradition" is reprinted from *Eschatology and the New Testatment: Essays in Honor of George Raymond Beasley-Murray*, 15–27, ed. W. Hulitt Gloer, © 1988 Hendrickson Publishers, Inc., and is used by permission.

Chapter 12. "The Interpretation of Prophecy and the Origin of Apocalyptic," in *Bible, Church, and World: Essays in Honour of D. S. Russell* (London: Baptist Historical Society, 1989), 28–35.

Chapter 13. Reprinted from *Canon and Authority*, by George W. Coats and Burke O. Long, copyright © 1977 Fortress Press. Used by permission of Augsburg Fortress.

Chapter 14. "Prophecy as Literature: A Re-appraisal," in *The Hermeneutical Quest: Essays in Honor of J. L. Mays for His Sixty-Fifth Birthday*, ed. D. G. Miller (Allison Park, Pa.: Pickwick Publications, 1986), 56–76.

Chapter 15. "The Prophet and His Editors," by R. E. Clements, from *Journal for the Study of the Old Testament Supplements*, Number 87. Copyright © 1990. Reprinted by permission of Sheffield Academic Press Limited.

Index of Names

Ackroyd, P. R., 25, 30f., 145, 147, 223, 238f., 252, 254, 263
Ahlström, G. W., 238
Albright, W. F., 23
Allis, O. T., 79, 245, 247
Alt, A., 71, 244
Anderson, B. W., 235, 260
Anderson, G. W., 241
Auld, A. G., 238
Aurelius, E., 250

Barr, J., 256
Barth, Hermann, 8f., 75, 87, 99, 157, 235, 244, 248, 252, 254
Beasley-Murray, G. R., 173, 175, 255f.
Beatty, R. C., 263
Becker, J., 55f., 241
Begrich, J., 2, 91, 233, 246
Bellinger, W., 233
Bentzen, A., 55, 241
Ben Zvi, Ehud, 239f.
Bertholet, A., 151, 253
Bettenzoli, G., 254
Beuken, W.A.M., 10, 236
Beyerlin, W., 24, 238
Blenkinsopp, J., 260f.
Blum, E., 237
Bousset, W., 54
Bowden, J., 240, 261
Bright, J., 124, 128, 130, 132, 135, 250ff., 262
Brueggemann, W., 250
Brunet, G., 24, 238
Budde, K., 66f., 243
Bultmann, R., 256

Carroll, R. P., 223f., 261, 263
Childs, B. S., 57f., 79, 82, 234, 240, 242, 245f., 248, 256
Cholewenski, A., 156, 254
Clayton, J. P., 237, 241
Clements, R. E., 1, 2, 4, 9, 13, 15f., 233ff., 252, 254, 256ff.
Coats, G. W., 234, 238, 242, 255, 261
Cody, A., 253
Cogan, M., 238
Coggins, R. J., 237, 254, 257, 263

Colani, T., 173
Coleridge, S. T., 17
Conrad, E. W., 11, 236
Crenshaw, J. L., 259
Cross, F. M., 113, 249

Darr, K. P., 236
Delsman, W. C., 239
Diamond, A. R., 250
Diepold, P., 149, 223, 250, 253, 259, 263
Doederlein, J. C., 78, 81, 217, 244
Doull, J., 249
Duhm, B., 1, 16, 66, 78, 82, 94, 150, 206, 217, 219ff., 223, 243, 247, 252f., 260, 262

Eaton, J. H., 245, 260
Eichhorn, J. G., 13, 17, 203, 217
Eisenstadt, S. N., 237
Ellemeier, F., 259
Elliger, K., 253
Emerton, J. A., 234
Engnell, I., 55, 146f., 241, 252, 262
Ewald, H., 1, 17

Festinger, L., 224, 263
Fischoff, E., 263
Fishbane, M., 188, 236, 242, 257f., 261
Fohrer, G., 93, 151, 159, 247, 253f., 258

Galling, K., 253
Garscha, J., 152, 253
Gerth, H. H., 263
Gese, H., 60, 67, 154, 242f., 253
Gesenius, W., 39
Gonçalves, F. J., 44f., 239
Goody, J., 256, 260
Gottwald, N. K., 5, 126, 234, 250f.
Graetz, H., 80, 246f.
Green, D. E., 241
Greenberg, M., 159, 163f., 166, 168f., 205, 254f., 260
Gressmann, H., 54, 241

Gunkel, H., 1f., 54, 162, 233, 255
Gunneweg, A.H.J., 209, 61

Hagner, D. A., 257
Haldar, A., 254
Hammershaimb, E., 244
Handel, G. F., 49
Hanson, P. D., 248, 252, 256ff.
Haran, M., 253
Hardmeier, C., 44, 39, 249
Harris, M. J., 257
Hartman, Lars, 175, 178, 182f., 185, 256f.
von Hengstenberg, E. W., 50, 52
Hensler, G., 244f.
Herder, J. G., 13, 17, 203, 217
Herntrich, V., 151, 253
Herrmann, S., 161, 167, 251f., 255
Hobbs, T. R., 248f.
Høgenhaven, J., 67, 70, 242ff.
Holladay, W. L., 118, 250f.
Hölscher, G., 151f., 253
Hossfeld, F. L., 160, 254
Hyatt, J. P., 124, 250ff., 263

Ibn Ezra, 6, 78, 217

Jackson, J. J., 260
Jacob, E., 248
Janzen, W., 238
Jeppesen, K., 254, 262
Johnson, A. R., 241
Jones, D. R., 245, 247, 260

Kaiser, O., 10, 67, 184f., 187, 235, 243, 256ff., 261
Kapelrud, A. S., 254, 262
Katz, S., 237
Keith, R., 240
Kermode, F., 256f.
Kilian, R., 254
Kirkpatrick, A. F., 17, 51, 240
Klatt, W., 241
Klostermann, A., 253
Knibb, M. A., 237, 254, 257, 263
Koch, K., 177, 237, 256, 261
Kohl, M., 256, 261

Index of Names

Kottsieper, I., 235
Kovacs, B. W., 249, 262
Kutsch, E., 234

Laato, A., 67, 70, 75
Lescow, T., 243
Levenson, J. D., 254
Liwak, R., 235
Locke, J., 18, 51, 60
Long, B. O., 234, 238, 242, 255, 261
Lowth, R., 13, 17, 217
Luther, M., 79, 45

Maag, V., 238
Maass, F., 245
McCarter, P. Kyle, 241
McCarthy, D. J., 56, 234, 241
McKenzie, J. L., 247
Mackintosh, H. R., 240
Marsden, G. M., 237
Marsh, J., 256
Martin, J., 240, 257
Mettinger, T.N.D., 244
Miller, D. G., 236, 250, 256, 262
Miller, J. W., 161, 255
Mills, C. W., 263
Mommer, P., 237
Montgomery, J. A., 258
Motyer, A., 236
Mowinckel, S., 2, 16, 55, 94f., 107, 109, 121, 148, 219ff., 241, 247ff., 258, 260, 262
Muilenburg, J., 2, 233
Müller, H. P., 243

Nelson, R. D., 249
Neumann, P.H.A., 1, 233, 259, 262
Nicholson, E. W., 222, 234, 249, 262
Nielsen, E., 260, 262
Nielsen, K., 67, 236, 243f.
North, C. R., 245, 262
Noth, M., 9, 108, 121, 135, 249, 253

O'Connor, K., 249f.
Oded, B., 238
Oeming, M., 242
Oesterley, W.O.E., 54, 241
O'Higgins, J., 240
Ong, W. J., 175, 255f., 260
van Oorschot, J., 235
Osswald, E., 261

Oswald, H. C., 245
Otzen, B., 254, 262
Overholt, T. W., 249

Pelikan, J., 245
Perdue, L. G., 249, 262
Perlitt, L. 234, 253
Phillips, A., 237, 254, 257, 263
Plöger, O., 248, 252
Pohlmann, K. F., 229, 263
Pope, M. H., 248
Porteous, N. W., 258

Rendtorff, R., 11, 36, 77
Reventlow, H. Graf, 60, 66f., 240, 242f.
Riecker, H. W., 263
Riesenfeld, H., 256
Rietzschel, C., 250
Robinson, H. W., 151
Rofé, A., 240
Römheld, D., 235
Rowley, H. H., 126, 182, 251, 257
Rudman, S., 248
Rudolph, W., 24, 126, 130, 238, 251, 259
Russell, D. S., 182, 257

Sanders, J. A., 258, 261
Sawyer, J.F.A., 99, 248, 252
Schachter, S., 263
Schlatter, A., 175, 256
Schleiermacher, F.D.E., 19, 50, 52, 240
Schmidt, W. H., 240
Schürer, E., 53, 241
Sehmsdorf, E., 260f.
Seitz, C. R., 10, 235, 240, 249, 264
Sherlock, T., 59
Sherry, P., 237
Simon, U., 234
Skinner, J., 7, 51f., 126f., 234, 263
Smart, J. D., 247
Smart, N., 237
Smelik, K.A.D., 44f., 239
Smend, R., 237, 239
Smith, G. A., 7, 234
Smith, J. Z., 256
Smith, W. R., 17
Spears, M. K., 263
Spice, N., 257
Spinoza, B., 78
Stade, B., 35, 37, 39, 239

Stalker, D.M.G., 248
Stamm, J. J., 70f., 244
Steck, O. H., 8, 67f., 235, 243f., 49
Stewart, J. S., 240
Stinespring, W. F., 259
Stulman, L., 249f.
Sweeney, M. A., 236

Tadmor, H., 239
Taylor, V., 255
Thiel, W., 222f., 237, 249, 250, 255, 263
Torrey, C. C., 80, 246
Troeltsch, E., 54
Tucker, G. M., 238

Unterman. J., 118, 250

Verheule, A. F., 241
Vermeylen, J., 10, 56, 59, 235, 239, 241f., 248, 252, 260
Vincent, J. M., 92, 234, 244, 247, 262
Vogt, E., 239
Volz, P., 126, 130, 251
Vriezen, Th. C., 246

Wagner, S., 235
Wahl, H. M., 235
Weinfeld, M., 120, 250
Weippert, H., 252
Wellhausen, J., 154, 253
Wenham, D., 256
Werner, W., 243
Westermann, C., 1, 162, 233, 255
de Wette, W.M.L., 50
White, H. C., 255
Whitehouse, O. C., 7, 234
Wildberger, H., 7, 10, 234, 236, 242, 242, 248
Williamson, H.G.M., 10, 235
Willi-Plein, I., 259
Willis, J. T., 259, 262
Wolff, H. W., 238f., 243f., 250

Young, E. J., 79, 245

Zakovitch, Y., 240
Zimmerli, W., 16, 152, 154ff, 159f., 162f., 165, 168, 191, 200, 237, 246, 248, 253f., 257, 259, 261
Zobel, H. J., 238